8.95
cat.

END OF AN ILLUSION

END OF AN ILLUSION

BY
JAMES AVERY JOYCE

THE BOBBS-MERRILL COMPANY
INDIANAPOLIS   NEW YORK

The Bobbs-Merrill Company, Inc.
A Subsidiary of Howard W. Sams & Co., Inc., Publishers
Indianapolis · Kansas City · New York

To my friends
QUINCY WRIGHT and CARL SOULE
who have ennobled America as citizens of the world

Acknowledgments are made to
The British Weekly and *The Contemporary Review* (London)
and to *The Christian Century* (Chicago)
for permission to reproduce certain material published
therein by the author.

TABLE OF CONTENTS

INTRODUCTION

The Cold War alliances are falling apart, as anyone can see. This book explains how we got into the North Atlantic Treaty Organization (NATO) and the other alliances—thus helping to create their Communist counterparts—and what is happening to them all today.

The essence of every military alliance is that it aligns one set of countries against another set, and is called "collective defense." There have been thousands of such alliances in the history of nations. They have nearly always finished up in the conquest or destruction of one side or the other—sometimes both sides.

Today, however, there are some big differences. Foremost among these is that, if present-day alliances were actually to "work" and did in real life what they were all supposed on paper to do, the whole planet—or most of it—would disappear in radioactive dust.

Nuclear weapons have made nonsense of the whole alliance business. More and more ordinary folk are beginning to grasp this fact, even while the military people are frantically thinking up vaster schemes of planetary death to replace the out-of-date ones.

But the military people themselves have shifted their ground to meet this growing sense of futility. They now talk most about "deterrence." This means that the weapons themselves have become so devastating that no one dare use them and still hope to survive. So the *threat* to use them has to take the place of the real thing. That is one of the basic differences between yesterday's and today's alliances. Today's alliances can't work.

The biggest of them all—NATO—was for all intents and purposes moribund long before General de Gaulle publicized the fact so tactlessly at the beginning of 1966. Yet no one in top political authority has been willing to admit this. Nevertheless, a critical ground-swell against NATO has been growing apace for some years. The current search for a nostrum to reactivate its corpse has only hurried the pocess of disintegration.

★   ★   ★   ★

In delving beneath the surface of the contemporary debate, therefore, we shall have to look afresh at the national "defense" policies which all these alliances are supposed to be about. For example, the Southeast Asia Treaty Organization (SEATO) is credited with defending the people of Vietnam. Since it started to do this, however, at least two million Vietnamese have died terrible deaths or lost everything they had.

In the long run—and generally in the short run too—only at the U.N. can all sides save their skins, as well as their faces. When the Arab-Israeli War broke out in June 1967, the influence of the Central Treaty Organization (CENTO)—set up to safeguard the Middle East—was precisely nil. Similarly, "the Atlantic Alliance is not directly and formally concerned with the Israel-Arab conflict," said the Chairman of NATO's Political Committee at the Brussels meeting in November 1967; and he added sadly: "However . . . if we ever were meant to be an auxiliary fire brigade to help put down any explosive situation, we certainly in June disappeared, as one member of our Committee said, in a cloud of dust." Sensible people turned instinctively to the U.N. to get them out of the mess and NATO out of its cloud of dust. When the two NATO allies Greece and Turkey nearly went to war over Cyprus in December 1967, it was again the U.N. that stood between them.

Not the least, when suddenly in August 1968 Czechoslovakia suffered the "evil invasion" (to use Lord Caradon's phrase) of Warsaw Pact troops, it was the U.N. Security Council that met within hours and mobilized the indignation of the world behind the victims. But nobody informed NATO to rescue the Czechs from their erstwhile allies, although there were 800,000 NATO troops deployed at that moment in Europe.

So, in addition to asking what goes on in the minds of statesmen who are sanguinely gathered around NATO's death-bed or who are trying to pump new lifeblood into SEATO or CENTO, we have also to ask a more important question: Why not drop the alliances altogether and switch to the system of world security which was laid down in the U.N. Charter?

Even those national leaders who know perfectly well that the Cold War alliances are crumbling beyond repair do not seem, alas, to have acquired the knack of putting a convincing alternative before their peoples. Because of this ambivalence, unfortunately, it is being left mainly to the military people to prop up the make-believe empires which give them their livelihood and sense of importance.

Many statesmen seem so imbued with the arrogance of power—"Peace through Power" is the slogan—that they rarely talk about peace and security except as a by-product of military might. Yet we are living on borrowed time. The harnessing of ever greater nuclear destructiveness to the obsolete war machines of a previous century presents the human race with the choice of total peacemaking or total perishing.

Hence, this book tells quite a different story from what the NATO generals are briefing their public relations officers, as they try to put Humpty Dumpty together again. A novel experiment is in operation around the earth today that is not receiving its due in high places, nor is its public image being given the place it should have by the mass media. In turning to the second half of this book, therefore, we are exploring what is still *terra incognita* for many people. That is, how to build peace in the world.

For two decades or more a generation of politicians and publicists have created a simple black-and-white dichotomy that the Cold War is somehow good for us. This has been especially true of the United States, where this author has passed the best part of those twenty years. It is, in his view, less true of Britain, with its traditional institutions favoring open-minded dissent, and the deliberate opposition techniques encouraged in parliament and press and developed by the B.B.C. (Barely a dozen cities in the United States run competitive newspapers, and the myriad of TV stations across the land compete for syndicated commercials, but not for independent ideas.)

Nonetheless, the Cold War attitudes which are contested so strongly in this book have been frozen for so long into the texture of governmental policy and public rhetoric, especially by the mass media in the English-speaking world, that the author has felt compelled to give chapter and verse for the massive evidence that can be adduced to the contrary.

Those readers who have not followed the NATO versus U.N. debate at all closely will indeed be surprised—we trust agreeably—that so much of the contemporary material presented in this book flatly contradicts what professional columnists and editorial writers have been presenting and politicians and broadcasters have been saying for the last twenty years.

At first sight, U.N. peacekeeping may appear a shaky affair at best. The U.N. itself has run into all sorts of obstacles recently. Most people think that it gets nowhere near resolving the problems which the mammoth alliances were set up to resolve, such as meeting "Communist aggression." Only a handful of world-minded leaders, in fact—and we shall cite them often—seem to have grasped the true significance and long-term implications of what is taking place at the U.N. But, unless this relatively new factor in world relationships becomes a normal way of life for mankind, and that quite soon, there will be no Twenty-first Century to enter.

★　★　★　★

Our enquiry will take us into several areas of foreign policy, bearing on what is euphemistically called "national defense." A number of immediate queries demand an answer. For example, is it not too late, with an arms race escalating between these decaying alliances, to put things into reverse? And, since modern armaments involve so much of a nation's economy, will not a switch to a genuine peace program be bitterly resisted by the military-industrial complex?

Then, there are some basic problems of definition. High-sounding words in daily use don't mean what they appear to mean. Take the term "policing." Statesman A says: "Our marines landed in Zorrombia this morning as a police precaution to protect the lives of our nationals." Statesman B insists that: "Our navy is the natural policeman of the Pacific." Russian generals restore "order" in Prague.

This peace-through-power attitude has become second nature with certain Great Powers; but military action taken by one state against another state can never be "police" action in the context of world order. Foreign military interventions, whether to prop up an unpopular government, put down a revolution, or otherwise—be it Lebanon or Hungary, Dominican Republic or Egypt, Syria or Israel, Czechoslovakia or Vietnam—are acts of war. As such, they are prohibited by the U.N. Charter and are a violation of international law. The U.N. was set up under its Charter as the protector of international law; as such, it was designed to take over alleged "police" duties from its members on the *world* level.

A policeman in civil life is called "an officer of the peace." He cannot legally take sides; he should not employ more physical force than the situation requires; he must not deliberately kill people; he is the servant of the whole community, subject to its laws, its courts, its administrative procedures. It need hardly be added that he never uses force against a whole nation.

The analogy is not a perfect one, but U.N. peacekeeping is of that order. It is founded on the police function as it is normally understood and practiced in advanced societies. It has taken hundreds of years to reach that point in international life. But we are now there. *The U.N. system is not an extension of national military policy; it is a repudiation of it.* The fact that the U.N. is holding up a standard of international conduct that may still be years ahead of the practice of some governments is no excuse for them to flaunt it.

The U.N. is not a super-military alliance; it is a world peace organization. It has evolved all kinds of built-in techniques for *keeping* the peace, of which the police function is only one, and a marginal one at that. For that reason, the attempt to give outside military alliances an aura of respectability by bringing them under those provisions of the Charter permitting the establishment of "regional agencies" has very doubtful legal validity at best and has failed lamentably in practice. The truth is that NATO and the rest of the outside alliances are *not* sanctioned by the Charter; they are incompatible with the Charter.

A clear understanding of this basic disparity between the functions of a war system and of a peace system is so vital for the human future that the author offers no apology for stating it and re-stating it so emphatically in this book. The war mechanism of the modern sovereign state would seem at times, alas! to be so over-sophisticated that plain men might well despair of ever replacing it by an entirely different system of international peacekeeping. Yet the unmistakable crumbling of today's alliances should at least give the concerned citizen a fresh stimulus to investigate what the World Organization can offer by way of an acceptable alternative.

*　　*　　*　　*

To turn now to some of the most obvious roadblocks, we are first confronted with an extraordinary doctrine called "containment." The origins and demise of NATO—and how much actual "containing" it has done—will occupy the first two chapters. The American diplomat who is popularly credited with having conceived the "containment" of the Communist world in Europe is George Kennan, former ambassador to Russia. A fellow-diplomat, Harry Byroade, is said to have proposed a similar buffer-state policy to be applied to Asia. CENTO (then called the Baghdad Pact) was envisaged as a block of Moslem states on the southern borders of Russia and China, to act as a military "shield" for the United States.

Both these authorities firmly agree today—Kennan publicly and Byroade privately—that the buffer-state-containment policy is unworkable and outmoded. Why they and other diplomatists have drastically changed their minds on NATO we shall also study in Chapter 2. The inventor of SEATO, John Foster Dulles, is no longer with us; but the unparalleled disaster he left behind him in Southeast Asia will receive documented analysis in Chapter 4.

More important, perhaps, than these personal errors of judgment have been the technological and economic developments in the West which, along with similar changes in the Soviet world, have convinced more and more people that the Cold War alliances not only are obsolete, but have become a distinct liability to everybody. Military technology—the topic of Chapter 3—has run away with chess-board diplomacy.

Furthermore, the growing worry of both the United States and Britain over the dead-weight costs of their military commitment in Europe has been for a long time propelling NATO toward a total revision. The NATO Ministerial Council's last discussion held in Paris in December 1966—after General de Gaulle had given it notice to quit—centered not on defense against Communist aggression, but on *détente* with the Soviet Union and Eastern Europe. This line was carried further in December 1967 when some of the NATO governments began to put out timid feelers as to how to carry the shattered remains of NATO into the 1970's.

In fact, when the NATO ministers met at Brussels at the end of 1967 to put forward to their governments a blueprint for a revised NATO, following France's withdrawal from its so-called "integrated military structure," the *New York Times* made this salutary comment: "The North Atlantic Treaty Organization has lost an ally and an adversary. Now it is looking for a role . . . But these were precisely the problems the NATO

xiii

ministers did not—and perhaps could not—face at Brussels last week; instead, they whistled loudly to keep up morale, then went home."

Not only in the United States, but in Britain too a conspiracy of silence seems to have been prepared to persuade the public, when the hour of decision arrived, that NATO should be kept more or less intact. Some evidence of this behind-the-scenes maneuver came to light in February 1968, when Sir John Hackett, the British General in charge of the NATO Northern Command, took the unprecedented step for a British serving officer of writing a letter to *The Times* urging the continued existence of the Alliance. Instead of repudiating this grave lack of decorum in violation of Army regulations, the Government admitted that General Hackett's arguments "coincide with the views of Her Majesty's Government."

Rumors at once began to circulate that the Americans had started to negotiate a new treaty to replace the old one and that Britain's future role had become a major worry to the Pentagon planners—especially now that Norway, Denmark, and other smaller partners had serious misgivings about entering a new pact. At the same time, nearly two hundred Labor and Liberal M.P.'s signed a motion in the House of Commons to substitute instead an all-European East-West peace treaty. But, with a "dump NATO" campaign developing among the smaller countries, the Anglo-American compromise plans to revamp NATO as a sort of old generals' active duty club were still kept under wraps at the North Atlantic Council meeting in Reykjavik in the late summer of 1968.

In any case, Britain has no lasting commitment to keep 57,000 British troops in West Germany and Berlin. What is now wanted is a phased withdrawal on the same sort of basis as the withdrawal from East of Suez. By the early 1970's a total withdrawal of B.A.O.R. from Germany and withdrawal from Berlin would contribute significantly to disengagement in Central Europe. In the next financial year Britain could make a token withdrawal of about 10,000 men. This could be the first step toward the withdrawal of all foreign troops from West Germany—British, American and the remaining French forces, coupled with the phased withdrawal of Soviet troops from East Germany, Czechoslovakia and Poland. Such disengagement could lead toward a genuine European security arrangement under Article 52 of the U.N. charter to replace NATO and the Warsaw Pact.

The time has come, therefore, to challenge the orthodox military patchwork repairs that are being devised in secret and to set against the revisionists' guesswork some of the radical alternatives which our global society demands. Now is the time to make that attempt. It was not possible in the political atmosphere of the 1940's. But it is possible, and desperately needed, in the 1970's.

*   *   *   *

The reason why the present book falls into two parts is precisely because the instrinsic contradictions of the military alliances and the nuclear strategies exposed in the first part can never be remedied within the existing order of military "necessity." At the time that some authorities were debating the use of tactical nuclear weapons by the United States for the "limited" purpose of relieving the garrison at Khesanh in the spring of 1968, one general was publicly quoted as saying: "Why not? What the hell do we spend all that money on them for, if we never intend to use them?" But a noted physicist immediately replied to him explaining exactly why such weapons could never be used even against a tiny non-nuclear state, since "crossing the nuclear line" left no place for escalation to stop short of an all-out nuclear war.

It will doubtless astonish some readers to discover how far the disintegration of the alleged "defense" system, on which their very existence is said to depend, has already gone and how futile it has become to try to patch it up. The fact that the Western governments cannot seem to make a clean break from international makeshifts which their expert advisers confess are no longer viable is the gravest part of our modern dilemma.

Take, for instance, one very elementary question: What is the *use* of nuclear weapons? French political philosopher Raymond Aron put this point well in *The Great Debate* (1965): "Under what conditions should thermonuclear weapons be employed? Who, within the framework of the Atlantic Alliance, should have the choice of *when, where,* and *how* to use them?" During the last fifteen years, he says, innumerable studies on nuclear strategy have been carried out in America, but the results have often been misunderstood abroad, just as many Americans misunderstood France's desire for its own nuclear force. These questions have come closer to splitting the West than has any maneuver by the Russians, he concludes: "The complexities are so enormous that debate often degenerates into total confusion." That is exactly the position taken up in the following chapters—except that we reject total confusion as a workable foreign policy.

★ ★ ★ ★

Luckily, the main post-war alliance (NATO) specified the year 1969 (plus one year's notice) for its own dissolution or revamping—although NATO's present Secretary-General has referred to it as "timeless." Hence the crescendo of frantic efforts now being put forth by its erstwhile sponsors to justify it or, at least, to save as much as they can from the wreck and so fit together the pieces for some future use.

For example, the best recuperative prospect for NATO, SEATO, and CENTO—it has been urged—is to develop the non-military co-operation of their members, especially in the economic field. Thus, an amorphous "Atlantic Community" makes its recurrent appearance on the world stage of pleasing phantoms: that is to say, a "broader alliance" based on NATO —after it has crumbled.

To make up for the deficiencies of SEATO (the main subject of Chapter 4), a wider Southeast Asian grouping, it is claimed, might bring the relatively backward nations of that area into a closer relationship with Japan and India, and so put all of them—in the eyes of Washington—in a stronger position to deal with Communist China. Accordingly, in the spring of 1967, the United States President toured various capitals in pursuance of a short-lived "Johnson doctrine," labeled the Southeast-Asia Associated States; and while Vietnam peace-feelers were operating in the spring of 1968, Secretary of State Dean Rusk was even then presenting to the SEATO Ministerial Council Meeting in Wellington, New Zealand, a yet more excellent plan for establishing a "collective security organization for Asia and the Pacific region." But the U.S. President and the Secretary of State were still chasing the will-o'-the-wisp of containment; while Edwin O. Reischauer, former U.S. Ambassador to Japan, declared quite bluntly in March 1968: "Once again, the chief concern in Japanese minds is the threat to Japan of the American alliance, not the dangers to Japan of an unstable East Asia."

If, however, the root and branch rejection of the theory and practice of military containment in the following pages may sound too drastic at times, an aphorism which appears in Dag Hammarskjold's *Markings* is singularly appropriate:

The madman shouted in the market place. No one stopped to answer him. Thus it was confirmed that his thesis was incontrovertible.

These partial attempts to contrive *ad hoc* peace-and-security systems, now fitfully proceeding in Western foreign offices, call instead for a return to first principles. This is how the U.N. President put it in closing the Emergency Session of the General Assembly in July 1967, which called a halt to the Arab-Israeli War:

This session again has demonstrated to the whole world that, as in 1956, the United Nations can rise promptly to safeguard the peace even in the most precipitous emergency . . . It has been said that the United Nations is the last hope of peace. It *is*—when men gambling with other ways *make* it the last. When the time comes that men realize, as they realized in 1945, that there is no substitute for a total approach to the problem of peace, they will make it the *first* hope of mankind.

*　　*　　*　　*

Where have the Western alliances taken us since the U.N. Charter was signed? The United States has ringed the Asiatic mainland with bilateral and multilateral alliances, all aimed at the containment of "Chinese aggression." These include bilateral defense treaties with South Korea, Japan and the Philippines; while Nationalist China is still protected by the

Seventh Fleet. Under SEATO, tenuous mutual security arrangements were made on paper with Pakistan, the Philippines, Thailand, Australia, New Zealand, Britain, and France.

To shore up all these "local" efforts, directed solely against the Chinese, the U.S. has for over a decade provided large-scale military aid to India, South Vietnam, South Korea and Nationalist China. Four hundred American military bases and costly installations stretch from the Bering Straits to Thailand. Year after year the nuclear-armed Seventh Fleet patrols the sea off North China's coast—even colliding at times with ships of the Soviet navy, legitimately stationed in the Sea of Japan along the Russian coastline. The "Pueblo" incident off North Korea in 1968 pointed to the powder-keg character of some of these skirmishes.

Yet, despite these mounting threats of military intimidation, China is less isolated today than ever before. Peking has already broken through many of the political and economic barriers raised against it. It has steadily improved diplomatic and trade ties with France and other Western powers and has closer ties today with Pakistan and Japan. In 1966 its imports from Western Europe rose by 25 per cent over 1965 and its exports to Western Europe no less than 36 per cent. Most significant of all, in direct response to the Pentagon's open challenge, the peasant-dominated pre-Mao China has burst out of its age-long domination by the West, equipped with a thermonuclear arsenal of intercontinental ballistic missiles of rapidly increasing deadliness and range.

★　★　★　★

Seen against this darkening backdrop of political ineptitude and military miscalculation, the attempted take-over (at *three billion dollars* per month) of tiny Vietnam might have seemed to the military-industrial mind to be mere child's play, were it not for the fact that Vietnam has proved to be the Achilles heel of this gigantic gamble of containment. If Vietnam goes, the whole gamble is lost. Hence, the desperate mood of the interventionists in clinging on there, when private wisdom and public morality alike have urged speedy withdrawal—as the U.N. Secretary-General (a Southeast Asian by birth) pleaded from the very start.

In more senses than one, Vietnam has become a proving ground. The real test is whether an internal social revolution is to be subjected to the pretensions of an external military empire. It is too late for empires—military, ideological, or otherwise. The remedy for revolutionary nationalism is not neo-imperialism, but international co-operation.

In a recent address to the Asia Society in New York U Thant pointed out: "The desire for independence and national identity is one of the most potent forces of our time. It should not be confused, as too often it is, with the East-West ideological conflict. I have said on several previous occasions that nationalism—the desire for national independence and a sense

xvii

of national identity—and not any political ideology, is still the most potent force in the life of a people."

What are described as "wars of liberation" are likely to proceed across the developing countries for some years to come. These inevitably violent revolutions cannot be lumped together as Communist-inspired "subversions," to be deterred or crushed by outside military intervention.

But in 1954, the United States, barely recovered from the frustrating Korean stalemate, would not accept this view of current reality. Dulles flatly turned down the Geneva settlement and "went it alone." In *This Lost Revolution,* Robert Shaplen, a long-time observer in Vietnam, reminds us of the official mood at that time:

Although some people in the State Department still spoke occasionally of the need to complete the process of Vietnamese independence . . . Secretary of State John Foster Dulles foresaw victory by the end of 1954, and others, including Vice-President Richard Nixon, declared that it was impossible to think of anything but victory.

★   ★   ★   ★

We have therefore to come to grips (in Chapter 5) with one of the most tantalizing elements of the Cold War: a social neurosis of startling proportions called "anti-Communism." This grotesque misreading of world history so distorts normal discourse that every social upheaval in the life of a backward people anywhere on the globe is depicted as a threat to the peace and security of the United States.

Since the early Twentieth Century, the ideology and practice of Communism have been associated with the overthrow of some discredited or bankrupt political order. "Anti-Communism" is, in that sense, a double negative. It doesn't deal with the causes of the original problem—it compounds them. Yet it has been so exploited by military careerists and political office-seekers and by the demagogues of mass media that it has been paraded in the United States as a way of life—or, rather, of death.

"Anti-Communism" has developed into a kind of ethnic reality in itself. It has produced its own jargon, its own hierarchy of self-appointed heroes, its own network of vested interests, and its own sinister momentum. To have attempted to build a foreign policy on such a dubious foundation has become not only a disaster to the United States, as is now so evident, but also a threat to genuine peacemaking everywhere else. As the plain-spoken former Ambassador Edwin O. Reischauer has said: "Our concept of Communism as a great wave threatening to sweep over the dike we were desperately trying to build in Asia is quite false . . . Asian states do not need military dikes so much as good economic land-fill."

★   ★   ★   ★

"Weapons," Dr. Ralph E. Lapp, the noted physicist, charges in his outspoken book, *The Weapons Culture* (1968), "are tending to dominate our lives, to envelop our economy and to ramify into almost every niche of our society." Can we continue these increasing outlays for national defense, he asks, which give the military more and more power over our lives, without warping the very character of the nation? Although we can only skim the surface, in the following chapters, of this "new writing" in the field of defense-planning, enough has been published to demonstrate how the public—and politicians as well—have been fooled by the generals and their backroom strategists who still want things their own way, irrespective of the economic and social damage our weapons culture has already inflicted.

At long last, however, the irrelevance and tragic waste of the Cold War, with its ridiculous military postures and "Maginot" mentality, stretched across the wide oceans and open skies to "contain Communism," are seen in the setting of the dire needs of today's desperate world. That barely a fraction of the human resources being drained away on war-preparation to a global total of 150 billion dollars annually cannot be transferred to the urgent tasks of peace-preparation is one of the dark mysteries of our time.

This is the real war—to which we turn in Chapter 6. Ritchie Calder, social scientist, has written: "I have been in most parts of the world in recent years and there is no place where I have been where the awareness of a new world has not penetrated. The confrontations are no longer East versus West, but North versus South. The issues are between the highly advanced nations and the less developed nations—a collision which has nothing to do with Communism and Capitalism."

The emergence of this "Third World" is making nonsense of both Communist and Western pretensions. In Africa, not a single "new" country has set up a Communist government. But it does not follow that Western-type liberal democracy can succeed there either. Nor has one of the "new" countries joined NATO or its ugly sisters, or the counter-alliances which grew up in counterpoint. But they are relying more and more on the operative organs of what is known as the U.N. Family.

These expanding agencies, institutes, projects, missions, are aimed, not at the refinements of future warfare but at the cultivation of present welfare. And it may surprise some readers, once again, that so many significant advances in the earth's common life have come about so silently and in so short a time, within the ever-expanding framework of the World Organization.

★　★　★　★

How, then, can we escape from this thraldom to the military ethos? No single answer can be given. The remedies need to be as far-reaching as the evils to be cured. For example, the U.N.'s primary task as "Peacekeeper" (Chapter 7) has already replaced the warrior with the policeman at some of the world's worst danger spots. And all this has happened in barely a dozen years. Formidable obstacles still stand in the way; as Albert Einstein pointed out: everything has changed except our minds. But a workable basis now exists for a universal peacekeeping system—if we want things that way.

Resort to war anywhere undermines world order everywhere. Yet the rule of law bides its time. Saner forces are all the while pushing their way past the military-compulsionists. It is astonishing how human institutions grow, slowly and fumblingly at times, to meet the demands of a new society (Chapter 8). The beginnings of World Law are clearly discernible and the time has come to implement them.

If this book has to leave for future assessment so many of the rich possibilities touched upon in the second part, it is because man's reach must ever be beyond his grasp. Carlos P. Romulo told the U.N. Tenth Assembly:

We are not working with slide-rules here, but with the measureless flow of history itself.

Perhaps the pursuit of peace may appear at times as impossible as a poet's dream. Even so, says Shelley, standing at the beginning of an earlier Age of Change: "When the voices of war and hate grow higher, then the voice of the poet must be raised higher still to call the tune of the future."

JAMES AVERY JOYCE

New York
August 1968.

PART I

THE PAINTED CORPSE

"Look yonder, friend Sancho Panza, where thou mayest discover somewhat more than thirty monstrous giants, whom I intend to encounter and slay; . . . for it is lawful war, and doing God good service to remove so wicked a generation from off the face of the earth." "What giants?" said Sancho Panza. "Those thou seest yonder," answered his master, "with long arms . . ." "Look, sir," answered Sancho, "those which appear yonder are not giants, but windmills; and what seem to be arms are the sails, which, whirled about by the wind, make the mill-stone go."

—Cervantes in *Don Quixote*

1 SETTING THE STAGE

> "There was a touch of drama in the defense of the
> land of Thermopylae and Marathon against an inva-
> sion more dangerous because more insidious than that
> of ancient Persia."
>
> —James T. Shotwell, *historian*.

When Melina Mercouri, the film actress, was deprived of her
Greek citizenship by a military junta in Athens, her many fans throughout the world did not realize—or were not told—that this act of ridiculous
tyranny was due to NATO.

In fact, not many people realize today what a threat NATO has become
to their peace and well-being. When the Greek colonels pounced in the
spring of 1967 on what was left of parliamentary government in the very
birthplace of democracy, the official reaction in the West was neither too
shocked nor too resentful at what had happened. One British newspaper
made the casual but typical comment that the new Greek leaders presumably felt that they were entitled to the same degree of toleration that
has been accorded Dr. Salazar, another anti-democrat, since Portugal had
joined NATO. The same paper continued:

NATO cannot afford to wash its hands of the whole unfortunate affair. Not
only did the conspirators use NATO weapons to seize power, they also based
their operation on a NATO plan drawn up in case of war with a Communist
country.[1]

With this simple thread in our hands we can seek to find our way
through the shabby intrigue by which the usurpers of Western democracy
put NATO into practice on their own soil. The same pattern may emerge
at any time on other soils of the unsuspecting "free" world. The special
interest of this particular revelation, however, is that Greece was the birth-

[1] *The Scotsman,* May 6, 1967.

3

place of NATO. The wheel of coincidence having swung full circle, this modern Greek tragedy moved toward its sinister *dénouement*.

The passing comment of one American correspondent contained more than a grain of truth: "Does this mean that we shall now send abroad another half million American youths to save democracy in its very birthplace? Or will we merely shrug our shoulders and say: 'But they are only Fascists'?"

Yet there were low comedy aspects, too, in the junta's behavior. These reached their lowest point when—in addition to abolishing beards and miniskirts for incoming tourists—a Government order was issued to theater managers prohibiting all plays and other public spectacles which might "disturb public order" or promote "subversive theories." This order, emanating from the new Prime Minister's office a few days after the *coup*, revived a law passed in 1942, while Greece was under Nazi occupation, to set up a theatrical plays control board. All scripts of proposed plays must now be reviewed by the board, which has authority to insist on deletions —or no play.

The primary objectives of the take-over succeeded only too well: namely, to suspend constitutional guarantees, close down Parliament and abolish local representative institutions, send from five to eight thousand persons into imprisonment and exile, and purge the civil service, the judiciary, and the Church; then proceed to try "political" prisoners—including Andreas Papandreou, American-educated son of the former liberal Prime Minister, and himself a potential Prime Minister—by military tribunals.

Suppression of all except Government-supporting newspapers became complete. H. J. Bradley, President of the International Federation of Journalists, announced that Brigadier Patakos, Minister of the Interior, had denounced as "communists" the board of the Athens Union of Journalists, and that "the Greek press has lost all freedom and three hundred journalists are unemployed." A ban was imposed on the music of Mikos Theodorakis, a Member of Parliament and composer of enormously popular songs—including the music for *Zorba the Greek*. He was later arrested.

This is to say little of the sheer ineptitude of the military junta as a modern government, their lack of a viable economic and social policy, and their total disregard for those fundamental precepts of popular representation which have been the pride of our Western civilization and which ancient Greece bequeathed to us all.

"The Greek colonels and brigadiers have no ideas on what to do with the country," commented the *New York Times* in retrospect: "They know how to suppress and censor, how to spy and conduct kangaroo courts— they are skilled at trapping and jailing citizens for playing the forbidden music of Mikos Theodorakis—but they are barren of plans for bringing the promised political reconstruction and the restoration of parliamentary democracy."[2]

[2] *New York Times,* September 10, 1967.

4

When the King fled the country in December with his household, the future of his personal counter-coup—apart from its mismanagement and ill-timing—only served to entrench the regime more firmly. Yet the regime's apprehension was reflected in many ways, such as in the savage five-year prison sentence inflicted in August 1967 on the former Greek Foreign Minister, Evangelos Averoff, for holding a meeting of more than five people at his home—although Averoff insisted that it was purely a social gathering. The *Times* observed: "A different conclusion that might be drawn from the charges made against men of Mr. Averoff's reputation is that the junta show all the signs of nervousness. By their wholesale arrests of the Left-Wing leaders and many in the center, the military men have assured themselves against assault on their authority from that quarter."[3] With the belated flight of the King, however, the isolation of the beleaguered colonels was complete.

While Greece's NATO partners stood back a little nonplused from this right-wing brand of subversion—which the NATO organization was hardly equipped to tackle—the regime's theatrical policy proved a great deal more embarrassing to the military government itself than could have been anticipated. The "purification" changes they directed to be made in the ancient plays selected for the 1967 festivals brought down on them the united condemnation of the artistic and cultural world. Most ancient Greek plays touch with a perennial freshness on such political ideas as monarchy, democratic ideals, free speech, and political exile. But the purified program of ancient drama performances in Athens, Epidaurus, and Delphi deliberately omitted some of the best known comedies of Aristophanes, such as "The Birds," "The Clouds," and "The Frogs." The Government also ordered that Euripides' "Phoenician Women" and "The Suppliants" be replaced by his innocuous "Ion." Sophocles' "Ajax" was dropped, as was Aeschylus' "Prometheus Bound."[4]

The unexpected irony of this last piece of clumsy censorship was that the code name of the military coup itself had for years been listed in NATO's secret dossiers as "Prometheus." The lame excuse which the junta gave, in reacting to the spontaneous outburst of world-wide indignation, was that the plays they had proscribed were nowadays accompanied by "Communist-composed music." (This was a degree of "guilt by association" far beyond the late Joseph McCarthy's intellectual comprehension.)

Be that as it may, outraged world artists hit back with a unified voice, in a campaign initiated by Melina Mercouri in the United States. One group, including Edward Albee and Leonard Bernstein, decided to boycott the Athens music festival. Isaac Stern, the violinist, canceled his engagements and Jean-Louis Barrault's Theatre de France withdrew from the same festival. According to a press account: "Mr. Stern canceled an

[3] The London *Times,* August 17, 1967.
[4] *New York Times,* June 25, 1967.

5

earlier appearance in Athens with Eugene Istomin, the pianist, and the cellist Leonard Rose, on the ground that the three musicians were 'indisposed.' Instead, the trio went to Israel and gave concerts there." The text of Mr. Albee's protest ran:

The lights have gone out in Greece. Greece, the birthplace of the democratic concept, is presently under the heel of a military dictatorship. Constitutional government and the rights of the people and the press thereunder have been repressed.[5]

Expatriate Greeks who repudiated the armed subjection of their land and spiritual heritage were branded by the Government—along familiar lines—as turncoats or "Communist agents." The expatriates accused by name were Melina Mercouri, herself the daughter of a liberal Greek deputy, and George Vandalis, former embassy official in Tokyo and son of a Center Union deputy. Interior Minister Stylianos Patakos declared: "They may have been born in Greece, but they never loved their country, because their hearts did not keep pace with the nation's heartbeat. These traitors have denied their own country . . . They are Communists or paid foreign agents." To which Miss Mercouri is reported to have replied on the way to her stage dressing room in New York City: "I was born a Greek and will die a Greek. Patakos was born a fascist and will die a fascist. If he wants to make me into a Joan of Arc, that is his business."

Reminiscent of Mussolini's program in the 1920's, the proclaimed aim of the junta was to "purify" the corruptness of national politics—while accepting military aid from across the Atlantic amounting to sixty or seventy million dollars a year. In "The Frogs" the proscribed Aristophanes had a rejoinder to this kind of double-faced asceticism:

But under his rags he is wearing a vest, as woolly and soft as a man could wish;
Let him gull the state, and he's off to the mart; an eager, extravagant buyer of fish.

Monroe Doctrine for the World

The history of dictatorship in modern Greece is too long and complicated a story to be told here. But it is relevant to the general theme of this book to recall that the first King Constantine, who was married to the Kaiser's sister, aligned Greece on the German side in World War I. Between the Wars, King George II, uncle of the present King, turned to General Metaxas for help, and so ran the country as a dictatorship until World War II broke out. Then came the Nazis and the War.

Soon after the end of World War II, the Truman doctrine brought NATO to Greece and so kept the country in the thrall of dictatorship. And

[5] *New York Times,* July 14, 1967.

6

the late Professor James T. Shotwell outlines the post-war sequence with pleasing clarity in *The United States in History:*

On March 12, 1947, in a message read to both houses of Congress, President Truman met the challenge of Communist imperialism by a counter-challenge destined to realize the vision of Woodrow Wilson in the creation of a "Monroe Doctrine for the world," extending the guarantee of freedom to all peoples . . . Both Congress and public opinion in the United States gave overwhelming support to President Truman when he proposed to take over the very task for which Great Britain had been so severely criticized. It took Congress only ten days to translate the message into law. Immediately, American military and civilian personnel left for Greece and Turkey . . . There was a touch of drama in the defense of the land of Thermopylae and Marathon against an invasion more dangerous because more insidious than that of ancient Persia.[6]

David Horowitz in *The Free World Colossus,* however, with the advantage of hindsight, puts a different construction on the post-war situation in Greece and suggests: "In order to understand the events of the year 1947, which proved to be the decisive turning point of the post-war period, it is necessary to view them against the background of the civil war in Greece. For it was this civil war which provided Truman with the occasion to declare that the world was divided between alternative ways of life."[7] Among the leaders of the E.A.M., which was then in control of nearly the whole country, were many liberals and social democrats, although the Communists were dominant. But the E.A.M. was not allowed to reap its victory, says Horowitz, because aligned against them were not merely the discredited monarchists, but also the British forces.

"The decisive factor in the ensuing struggle for power was the British Army, which entered the country as the Germans left," confirmed the seasoned British historian Hugh Seton-Watson in *The Pattern of Communist Revolution* (1960): "This was a defeat for the Greek Communists, and it was *not* due to factors within Greece, but to British intervention: without British action Greece would have had the same regime as Yugoslavia." It seems all too obvious now that the British were determined to break the E.A.M. and install in power the discredited monarchy and its rightist supporters. Thousands of patriotic young men fled to the mountains and others fled into Yugoslavia for protection. Elections of a sort were held in March 1946 and the monarchists won. Seven months later a referendum restored King George to the throne.

A renewal of civil war was inevitable, and the social and economic misery of the Greek people was complete. United Nations relief agencies reported that while seventy-five per cent of all Greek children were suffering from malnutrition at this time of transition, half of the new Tsaldaris Government's expenditures was on army and police, and only six per cent

[6] J. T. Shotwell: *The United States in History,* Simon & Schuster, New York, 1956.
[7] D. Horowitz: *The Free World Colossus,* Hill & Wang, New York, 1965.

7

on reconstruction. This was one of the "free peoples" that Truman declared "it must be the policy of the United States to support."

A few days before the 1967 coup, at a ceremony in Washington, the Ambassador of Greece presented a Sixth Century B.C. Athenian helmet to Secretary of State Dean Rusk on the occasion of the twentieth anniversary of the Truman Doctrine, and Secretary Rusk accepted the token on behalf of President Harry S. Truman, "whose statesmanship and vision helped Greece resist totalitarian servitude in 1947." This pleasant little ceremony was followed by a "Salute to Freedom" dinner.

United States aid to Greece since the inception of the Truman Doctrine in 1947 totals 3.5 billion dollars, divided about equally between economic and military assistance. In 1966, however, economic aid was cut to 6.8 million dollars, while military aid, to help Greece as a NATO ally, totaled over 78 million dollars.

Yet despite these twenty years of continuous subsidy, the military junta at once urged the United States to help floundering Greece's economy "to prevent the country from falling to the Communists." This was an all too familiar note. Colonel Makarezos, one of the ruling triumvirate, touchingly said: "I hope the Americans will realize the importance of helping Greece again without being asked." The moment is ripe, the Colonel explained, for the United States at least to announce an increase in military assistance because the *coup d'état* had placed Greece "more firmly than ever inside the North Atlantic Treaty Organization."[8] (Incidentally, the preamble of the NATO Treaty states that its members are: "determined to safeguard the freedom, common heritage and civilization of their peoples, founded on the principles of democracy, individual liberty and the rule of law.")*

In these circumstances, Washington wrestled with the political problem of how to reconcile the continuation of relations with a regime they viewed with some distaste but considered crucial to the military preparedness of the Western alliance. *"With the interests of the North Atlantic Treaty Organization's military command uppermost in policy considerations,* the Johnson Administration decided to continue its shipments of small arms, ammunition and military replacement parts to the Greek armed forces." (Italics added.)[9] In June 1968 the new Secretary of Defense, Clark Clifford, announced that, "as a NATO ally," full military aid to Greece would be resumed by Washington. So the Greek colonels had won again. The Defense Secretary told the Senate Foreign Relations Committee that "the obligations imposed on us by the NATO alliance are far more important than the kind of Government they have in Greece."

[8] *New York Times,* May 6, 1967.
[9] *New York Times,* December 15, 1967.
* In April 1968 the junta urged the NATO Nuclear Planning Group meeting at the Hague to consider placing nuclear land mines along their border with Bulgaria. The Group agreed to "study the idea."

It will be observed that both Britain and the United States fathered the original plan to defend Greece. But the justification for NATO's continuance into the 1970's must surely rest on something more persuasive than the belief that Russia is about to take over physical possession of the West—a topic we shall pursue in the next chapter.

If we take the Cyprus dispute as a concrete test question, the speculation of a Communist take-over, on which the very existence of NATO is based, could hardly be seen to be more irrelevant. And, as we shall observe later on, the world today is full of "Cyprus" questions, for which the NATO syndrome is equally irrelevant—if not a distinct peril.

What has happened to NATO in Greece has, in fact, given rise to serious misgivings as to its consequences for other countries, caught between the upper and nether millstones of the Cold War. The London *Times* wrote at the time:

What happens now is not just a Greek concern. Greece is a member of NATO and has been growing economically closer to Western Europe. If there ever is a federated Europe, Greece would be a logical member of it. This makes it all the more unfortunate that Greece should be the first NATO country where Parliament is sent packing . . . The Turks will be looking anxiously to see whether more strident nationalism over Cyprus is going to be part of the new Greek regime's policy, and they are not the only anxious watchers.[10]

Unwittingly, the protestors also reveal the use to which Greece is being put. Dean Alfange, President of the American Hellenic Educational Progressive Association, has said: "Beginning with the Truman Doctrine twenty years ago, the foreign policy of Greece became increasingly subservient to American interests. With the advent of NATO it became a corollary of American policy and ceased almost entirely to serve indigenous interests. During this whole period, the United States Embassy, the American Military Mission and the Central Intelligence Agency virtually dictated the foreign policy of Greece. . . . All this they were able to do thanks to prodigious grants of military and economic aid."[11]

But the attitude of the present rulers of Greece toward Cyprus can bring little consolation to any one of its NATO partners. It seriously provoked Turkey at a time when both secret diplomacy outside and the U.N. peacekeeping forces inside had been quietly doing their healing work on an island which has so conspicuously revealed the inner contradictions of NATO policy.

It will be recalled that communal strife broke out on Cyprus in December 1963, following changes in the Cypriot constitution which the Turkish minority felt would reduce their rights. Four-fifths of the inhabitants are

[10] The London *Times,* April 24, 1967.
[11] *New York Times,* December 24, 1967.

9

Greek Christians, while most of the remainder are Turkish Moslems. Under a United Nations Security Council resolution in March 1964, an international peacekeeping force (UNFICYP) went into action and both sides eventually accepted a U.N. cease-fire. The deplorable fact was, however, that Turkey had been using U.S. fighter-bombers against its NATO "allies," the Greek Cypriots. It was U.N. intervention that then saved NATO's skin, as well as the Cypriots'.

Cypriot opposition to incorporation of their island into Greece has grown since the military take-over in Athens. The military leaders of Greece were rumored to be plotting to topple President Makarios, and a sizeable Greek military force remained stationed on the island, ostensibly to resist the threatened Turkish invasion, until it was partially withdrawn in December 1967.

When the U.N. Secretary-General's Special Representative in Cyprus, B. F. Osorio-Tafall, arrived in Athens direct from Istanbul on a special mission in July 1967 "to establish personal contacts with officials dealing with the Cyprus problem," a further step was taken to set up a conciliation mechanism to protect the island's independence. But when in November that same year an attack on the Turkish-Cypriot enclaves was led by the Greek General George Grivas, with the object of clearing a crossroads for military use, the new crisis engendered could have had terrible consequences not only for Cyprus, but also for Greece and Turkey. It was then that, once again, the Security Council stood between the contestants, and what was described in the Western press as "the brink of war" was circumvented.

In June 1968, Greece and Turkey agreed at last to serious negotiations over their tangled minority problems and asked Mr. Osorio-Tafall to arrange for a site for their talks, which he accordingly did in Beirut, Lebanon.

Naturally, the United States has a big stake in preserving peace in Cyprus, if for no other reason than that the Turkish military establishment too has been almost entirely supplied by the United States and the North Atlantic Treaty Organization. A halt in military aid to Turkey would hurt the preparedness of the Alliance almost as much as it would hurt the Turkish Government. A Washington view was reported as follows: "The alternative would be two long-time allies using their American-equipped armies against each other. The entire Turkish Air Force of 53,000 men is assigned to NATO. So is the 390,000-man army. . . . In case of a war with Greece, these units would be removed from the NATO command."[12]

"Cold is the heart, fair Greece, that looks on thee today," wrote Byron. The troubles of NATO in Greece over Cyprus did not begin, however, with this latest dictatorship. Writing from Athens some years back about what he described as "Crumbling on NATO's Flank," that much-traveled journalist C. L. Sulzberger of the *New York Times* closely documented

[12] *New York Times,* November 24, 1967.

10

in a series of reports the fact that the Turkish armed forces and the Greek armed forces had recently been prepared more for war against each other than against any NATO enemy. "The erosion that has been undermining NATO gradually since Stalin's death has been accelerated," he asserted, "and what was left of the eastern flank shows further signs of crumbling. The Turks appear to think they can make some kind of deal with the Russians to get their backing on Cyprus. And the Greeks, alarmed as they are by this attempt, seem unable to prevent their own self-destruction." That was written in Athens in 1964, while the U.N. Security Council in New York was establishing the U.N. Force in Cyprus (UNFICYP) and so kept the local situation well in hand to the great benefit of all parties involved.

Prometheus Unbound

Within three hours on April 21, 1967 a handful of Greek officers seized power and rounded up their opponents without bloodshed. But what was the coup that was code named "Prometheus"? It was a NATO general staff contingency plan envisioning war with a Communist country. It foresaw the need for swiftly arresting Communist leaders to prevent underground subversion, and for moving into key administrative and communications centers to forestall sabotage.

The insidious character of what happened in the spring of 1967 is evidenced by the fact that when "Prometheus" was first drafted in 1950 it was intended to prevent a *coup d'état,* not promote one. C. L. Sulzberger in Athens talked at length with each of the triumvirate—Patakos, Papadopoulos, and Makarezos—who had conceived the coup, and he relates how:

The triumvirate hit upon the brilliant device of using Prometheus, which automatically entailed seizure of strategic points and subversives who might lead to countermoves or go underground. They merely added their relatively short list of non-leftists. Twenty hours before striking, they accepted nine officers into their conspiracy, forming a special executive committee of twelve. Fourteen hours before the coup, which came at 2 a.m. Friday, April 21, approximately twenty others were informed.[13]

Apparently, Spandidakis, then Chief of Staff, was kept in the dark till the last moment, as he could not be relied upon to act without the King's knowledge; but Sulzberger concludes his on-the-spot revelation of this long-planned conspiracy by asserting that "the coup succeeded totally all over Greece and in three hours, only because orders for executing it had been issued by the Chief of Staff himself. All he had to do was command the application of Prometheus. He did—as the tanks of Patakos moved."

[13] *New York Times,* May 3, 1967.

Some time later, General Spandidakis insisted that the coup was the work of the *entire army*. But he conceded that five members of the Supreme Military Council were retired immediately after the coup because they had not taken part in it. "They were not very informed," he said: "They did not understand what everything was." According to other sources, General Spandidakis agreed to take part in the hope of representing the King's interests. Many other "unreliable" officers were retired later in the year.

As a result of the coup, the Defense Minister declared that "Greece is now even more firmly in the North Atlantic Treaty Organization than before." In fact, "We belong in the West and will stay in the West at all times," Spandidakis added. And since Greece's membership in NATO had been "strengthened" by the coup, the time was opportune for the United States to *increase its military aid*. This being obviously the kind of action that "strengthens" NATO, the chief paymaster should foot the bill. But, alas, it is difficult to do something for Greece without doing the same for Turkey. So the United Nations was again helping the U.S. out of its dilemma by mediating between the two rivals.

While some observers believe that the coup came as a surprise to King Constantine, it could not have come as a surprise to Washington. Many foreign correspondents and diplomats had been warning for months that the military, with the approval of the throne, was prepared to seize the Government if democratic forces won the May elections, or if they even appeared on the verge of winning. The resurgence of former premier George Papandreou, leader of the liberal Center Union Party, was the real thorn in the flesh of the military clans who, for two decades, had fed themselves so well on the Truman dollars.

The election of a liberal-democratic government in Greece would, at last, have clipped the wings of the bloated military—but not only in Greece. The unsuccessful efforts of the earlier Papandreou regime to attempt this clean-up of the Augean stables, and the ambivalent conduct of the King in blocking the May elections, may be left to the historians to appraise; but it is germane to the present account of how NATO became involved to recognize that, for these twenty years, the Greek army, like the Turkish, has been virtually a branch of the U.S. armed services. One commentator goes as far as to assert that: "The Greek army is a satellite army. It is inconceivable that it would have acted without the knowledge, if not the direct approval, of American officials in Athens. By clear inference, Washington knew what was planned and did nothing to avert it."[14]

In the opinion of Maurice Goldbloom, who served with the U.S. economic mission to Greece in the 1950's: "For its part, the United States, through its initial acquiescence, has given the junta the time it needed

14 *The Nation*, May 8, 1967.

to dig in. In other words, the junta, though not noticeably more popular, does seem to be more solidly entrenched . . . Because civilian political groups—*including the weak and demoralized Communists*—were prepared only for electoral activity, there was no popular resistance."[15]

Who Killed Democracy?

The truth is that ever since the Truman Doctrine of 1947, U.S. military men have been moving in to direct war against Communists. There has been a continuously intimate association between Greek and American officers. Yet there is no evidence which would convince any intelligent European that it was Communism, and not corruption and incompetence, that threatened Greece during this time. A close British observer stated that the present regime "claims to have saved Greece from an organized Communist take-over, which would have happened if the Papandreou-dominated election had been allowed to take place as planned last month. But there is still no convincing evidence that this danger existed. On the contrary, it is arguable that the elections . . . would have been the first step towards a return to political normality after two years of crisis."[16]

Five months after the coup, the former Premier, Panayotis Canellopoulos, whose right-wing Cabinet was deposed by the army on April 21, courageously told Greece's ruling officers to "clear out of power." This defiant sixty-four-year-old conservative leader called for an immediate restoration of political freedom in Greece. The former Premier was forthright in condemning Stytianos Patakos, now Minister of the Interior, and said bluntly: "The brigadier is not speaking the truth . . . If he continues to have some dignity as a former Greek officer, who served repeatedly under my orders in time of war, he will understand that it is impossible for me to stop being a free Greek."

Safe and sound across the Atlantic, General James A. Van Fleet, a retired United States general who advised the Greek Army on how to stamp out the Communist revolt some seventeen years ago, publicly lauded Greece's military regime for "sparing the United States another Vietnam." Van Fleet was, in fact, chief of the U.S. Military Advisory Group in Greece in 1948 to 1950. The (censored) Greek press has reported him as saying that Greece had been heading toward *neutrality* before the April coup, so he was "extremely delighted" to hear of the army take-over. To the benighted general, "Communism" was equated with "neutrality"! This is indeed the mentality which drags the United States into Vietnams across the world.[17]

[15] Maurice Goldbloom: "How the Military Rules 8 Million Greeks," *New York Times Magazine*, September 24, 1967.
[16] Leslie Finner: *The Observer*, London, June 11, 1967.
[17] *New York Times*, October 1, 1967.

Writing from Copenhagen in March 1968, an expatriate Greek, N. J. Zaronikos, put the general into context: "If a new Vietnam is created in Europe, the responsibility will fall squarely on United States shoulders. For if American support were to be drastically withdrawn, the junta, having no popular base of support whatsoever, would simply collapse."

Even though any serious Communist threat was overcome long ago, American military aid has continued at the rate of 60 million dollars or more a year. The guns, tanks, and planes that were used to overthrow the constitutional government in 1967 were supplied by the United States. Thanks to NATO, it was not Communism but democracy which lost out in Greece.

Perhaps the ally which registered the sharpest critical reaction to these happenings was the second ancient home of our Western civilization, Italy. An appeal signed by the professors of several leading Italian universities, following up their Government's official protest, could not have been more explicit:

One aspect of recent events in Greece is particularly disturbing because it points to a possible threat to our own country as well . . . How is it possible for an army which is a part of NATO (as is our own) to be used by a partisan faction of officers to suppress the very freedom it was supposed to defend? . . . We have always believed that NATO was designed to defend us from tyranny, but episodes such as this—and Greece was only the most recent and most shocking incident of a series—cannot fail to erode our trust in NATO and thereby in its most powerful member: the United States of America.

An enormous amount of misplaced idealism has, unfortunately, been invested in NATO by private citizens. For example, a so-called "DECLARATION OF PARIS" reads: "We, the citizen delegates to the Atlantic Convention of NATO nations, meeting in Paris, January 8-20, 1962 . . . submit this Declaration of our convictions." Having declared that "The Atlantic peoples are heir to a magnificent civilization, the signatories call on the (then) Greek Government for the *Reconstruction of the Acropolis* and "decide that the Acropolis shall become the symbol of our culture and the shrine of our Alliance and call upon governments to consider how this resolution might be given concrete form."

If this well-meaning NATO Convention had postponed their Declaration but a few short years, their hopes would have been dashed, for by then Paris had walked out of NATO and the Acropolis was no longer available for democratic assemblies.

Notices to Quit

By way of sharp contrast to the somewhat peripheral problem of Greece, there is France, where NATO built its magnificent Headquarters and stored most of its hardware—until General de Gaulle issued his stern notice to quit in 1966. The bulky bag and baggage of NATO was removed in early 1967, at a cost estimated at about 700 million dollars, to less salubrious accommodations thirty miles from Brussels. One section of NATO actually moved to a disused coal mine, in order to bury its top secrets well underground.

This sorry treatment of a super-safeguard of the Free World by its host country is by no means unique. We shall witness this undignified form of exit again in a later chapter when we look at what remains of the original Baghdad Pact, which was re-allocated elsewhere and re-christened CENTO when Baghdad also issued its notice to quit—and quit itself. There are, moreover, valid grounds for believing that one of the results of the involvement of SEATO in the universally discredited Vietnam War will be its voluntary dissolution or total disintegration, since its gradual dismemberment is already well advanced. "SEATO is a bad joke," writes the distinguished historian Henry Steele Commager, and adds: "NATO included most Western European countries, served for some years a useful purpose and was always respectable; SEATO included only one Southeast Asian country, has served no purpose, and is disreputable."[18]

The defection of France from NATO, however much its crucial importance has been played down in both the British and the United States press, has undoubtedly been the most cruel blow struck at the whole system of alliances since World War II. For France is not a marginal power, but lies at the heart of the Atlantic Community.

It is difficult to separate this act of major policy from the personality and philosophy of the French President himself, but considerations of space require that our survey be confined to the basic facts behind the French Government's decision. Let it be said, in passing, that the editorial —if not the senatorial—reaction to General de Gaulle in the United States has been as peevish and extravagant as it has been toward any of the other foreign monsters who have, from time to time, refused to carry the Stars and Stripes dutifully. Incredible though this may sound, Representative L. Mendel Rivers, Chairman of the House Armed Services Committee, asserted that the United States Government should disinter the thousands of American dead in France and bury them at home; and he said of the French President: "He is the most ungrateful man since Judas Iscariot betrayed his Christ."[19]

Yet the General's attitude has been consistent since he became Head of State. Alfred Grosser, professor of politics at the University of Paris, for example, has sought to explain that the Gaullist behavior which has so irritated his allies can be accounted for by the General's resolute determination to induce Washington to take France seriously.

His campaign to accomplish this had gone through several phases. First,

[18] *New York Times Book Review,* July 14, 1967.
[19] *New York Times,* December 8, 1967.

he tried to win for France her "proper" place within the framework of NATO. This began with his 1958 proposal for a nuclear directorate consisting of France, Great Britain and the United States. On the side, as it were, in 1963, he first vetoed British membership in the Common Market. The second phase consisted in the wooing of the underdeveloped nations of Latin America, Africa and Asia, in an attempt to influence events in Vietnam. The third phase has shown a tendency to align France on Moscow's side in international disputes. (By stepping into France's vacant shoes in Vietnam, the Americans have only shown that the French knew at least when the going was good.)

In all these initiatives three elements have been revealed, which have, unfortunately, rarely gotten past editors to the general public. First, de Gaulle has shown himself to be a realist-statesman. As Régis Débray, the young revolutionary philosopher, has called him: "A big man, a man with high style in comparison with all the mediocrities around him." And, again, "He is one of the men for whom I have the greatest admiration," André Malraux, the old revolutionary philosopher, has said, "and it isn't in my nature to admire people." Secondly, he happens to be a Frenchman, not American or British. Thirdly, practically all of France, from right to left, is behind him—at least on *this* score.

This was demonstrated in April 1966, for example, when Premier George Pompidou addressed the National Assembly and contended that United States nuclear strategy "condemned Europe to destruction" and was adopted in violation of a unanimous decision by the fifteen members of NATO. The Premier asserted that the presence of American military headquarters on French soil could make France a "target for nuclear attack." Pompidou's address was intended as a complete vindication by the French Government of General de Gaulle's decision to take France out of the integrated Western defense system and to insist on the removal of American and other foreign military installations. The Assembly gave its overwhelming approval to President de Gaulle's policies on NATO. A motion of censure against the Government's handling of the NATO crisis received only 137 votes out of 482.

In March 1968, sixty-one percent of French voters approved of President de Gaulle's foreign policy and 13 per cent disapproved of it, according to an opinion poll conducted for the newspaper *Le Figaro* by a private polling organization. By a strange coincidence, a similar poll taken in the United States that same month arrived at almost identical figures approving or disapproving of the President's policy in Vietnam—except that the figures were reversed. In June 1968, for the first time in French parliamentary history a single party—de Gaulle's party—won an absolute majority in the National Assembly in one of the most dramatic elections of modern times.

French disengagement from the integrated system did not preclude agreements between France and the United States or with the fourteen allies, the (then) Premier explained. There was nothing in the French decision that need disquiet the allies; and an independent France need not be a negligible ally. The heart of the matter was that if the United States continues to plunge so recklessly into unpredictable military adventures, France would be running a grave risk by having American headquarters for Europe and the whole complex of NATO bases on French soil, since NATO was merely a secondary outlet for Washington policy.

Change But Not Decay

The French decision to get NATO out of France and to give advance notice of getting France out of NATO has, of course, thrown out of gear the fantastic apparatus of so-called integrated defense which the missile-minds have so carefully elaborated since World War II. Only a brief summary of their old frustrations and their new problems can be attempted.

The original U.S. monopoly of atomic weapons comes at once to mind as one instance of how the United States had attempted to tie its allies legally through NATO. In December 1957, Secretary of State Dulles first offered to make available atomic weapons to the allies, but made the offer conditional on an *integrated NATO command*. When the Eisenhower Administration wanted to amend the Atomic Energy Act in 1958, he emphasized that atomic weapons were being made available only through NATO. Now that France is out, the President could presumably make a separate legal arrangement with France, outside NATO. Yet there would appear to be no intention to do so, either way. Even if the President chose to do so, the agreement would have to be submitted to the Joint Atomic Energy Committee of the Congress, with easily foreseen results.

France's withdrawal from the integrated NATO command has been felt in West Germany most of all, for the United States will almost certainly be obliged to withdraw the U.S. nuclear weapons made available to the French forces there under American control. The French withdrawal has, therefore, pointed up a very important lesson for Britain and the other allies. It has reversed the whole trend of American policy to control its allies. Its allies are now beginning to control the United States, by withdrawing.

As the United Kingdom comes to appreciate this fact, it too will be able to exercise an increasing restraint on those military adventures which so many U.S. citizens themselves earnestly desire to reduce. The present runaway situation, however, calls for some resolute outside ally to stand up to the military careerists inside the United States. Britain has a key role to play in the rebuilding of world peace, which has been jeopardized by subservience too often to an American defense "posture" based on emo-

17

tional and doctrinaire attitudes toward Communism long since discarded by the rest of the Western world.

At the first news of the French walk-out, the British Government preferred to look the other way. Common Market aspirations had reached such a pitch of confusion and delay by 1966 that to have the French out of NATO was almost a relief. Talk of "toughness" against the rebel seemed pointless—you can only really be "tough" with an enemy. Yet toughness was just what de Gaulle was himself displaying toward his *soi-disant* friends. A Conservative opinion at the time might have stood for the Labor Government equally as well: "France's partners in the tightest peace-time alliance in history have watched paralyzed and complacent while she sloughed off one commitment after another and made no bones about her imminent intention to drop the lot."[20]

So the Government tactfully passed over all the hard core misgivings that the real patient, NATO, might actually be approaching *rigor mortis*. They announced the understatement of the crisis on March 18, 1966: "The British Government welcome the evidence which the Declaration, published today by fourteen Heads of Governments, provides of the continued solidarity of the Atlantic Alliance. We are glad that General de Gaulle has made clear that he intends to remain the ally of his allies . . . At the same time, those of us who believe in the need for an integrated defense organization, which has already proved its worth as a deterrent to aggression, are determined that it shall continue."

This phlegmatic view has been continued ever since. It can be compared with the French Government's note to Washington in that same week:

The conditions prevailing in the world at present are fundamentally different from those of 1949 and of the following years. Indeed, the threats weighing on the Western world, in particular in Europe, which motivated the conclusion of the Treaty, have changed in nature . . . In particular, France is equipped with atomic armament, which by its very nature is excluded from integration. The nuclear balance between the Soviet Union and the United States, substituting for the monopoly held by the latter, has transformed the general conditions of defense of the West. Finally, it is a fact that Europe is no longer the center of international crises. This has been shifted elsewhere, notably to Asia.

Thus, de Gaulle confirmed the fear that he expressed with studied frankness at an earlier historic press conference, when he declared: "While the possibility that a world war may break out in Europe is receding, at least to a certain extent, there are other conflicts in which America is involved in other parts of the world—as once in Korea, yesterday in Cuba, and today in Vietnam—that could escalate to a general conflagration, in which Europe, *whose strategy in NATO is the same as America's,* would be automatically implicated, even if it had not wanted it." (Italics added.)[21]

[20] *Daily Telegraph,* April 14, 1966.
[21] *New York Times,* February 22, 1966.

The statesman-realist will have no more of a "U.S. protectorate over Europe" (his phrase) nor be dragged automatically into an Asian war, since NATO's strategy "is the same as America's." What man of sense would choose otherwise? The humiliating role of an American satellite was far too dangerous now that the self-proclaimed world policeman insisted on having the last word over everyone's nuclear weapons.

Feet of Clay

The somewhat muted attack which followed on the Grand Old Man of Europe from the Western board of directors made interesting reading, but it never made much sense because, underneath, his most ardent critics knew he was right in getting out. It was *where* he was going which became the important question. It is on this point that the present book parts company from both the General and also from his many traducers in asking whether, by escaping from the frying pan, he had not cast France into the fire?

The General's three unoriginal sins stand out conspicuously and unashamedly in all that he does, namely: nationalism, militarism, and isolationism.

To take them in order, it should by this date be obvious that no national statesman can be truly a *world* statesman if he gives way, as de Gaulle has persistently done, to the antiquated concepts of an Eighteenth Century foreign policy, usually to the last fading strains of *La Marseillaise,* wherever he goes. And he travels freely from Moscow to Quebec. There is an essential place for enlightened and enthusiastic nationalism, especially in a country like France, bearing in mind the renewed moral incentives which were called for, following the bitter years of physical and psychological depression under the Occupation and succeeded by the calamities of Algeria and Southeast Asia. But what could he have meant when he declared at another historic press conference: "On the whole, the question is to restore a normal situation of sovereignty, in which everything that is French, on the ground, in the air, and on the seas, and every foreign element stationed in France, must be under the sole control of French authorities. As you can see, this is in no way a break, but a necessary adaptation."

What he does mean is "adaptation" back to the past. But, "there is no greater delusion than the feeling that we can solve our common problem on the basis of adventures in military nationalism," Prime Minister Harold Wilson had declared at the NATO Ministerial Meeting held in London on May 11, 1965. And as U Thant has counseled: "Surely, in the third decade of the United Nations, when the very survival of humanity can no longer be taken for granted, there is no room for the out-dated concept

19

of narrow nationalism." U Thant has also said: "With each nation-state relentlessly pursuing what it considers its 'place in the sun,' . . . international co-operation is no longer just a desirable ideal; it is an imperative if we are to avoid collective suicide. Nationalism must adjust itself to this over-riding reality; it can have true meaning only if it seeks fulfilment in stronger international co-operation."

Coming, next, to that inveterate fetish of militarism, it can today be categorically denied that national armaments—however nuclear they may be—will ever do the job of keeping a Third World War from France's soil. We listen to his flamboyant boast, multiply it around the nuclear and prospective nuclear powers, and then ask where it leads us: "As our country becomes a nuclear power herself by her own means, she is led to assume the political and strategic responsibilities which that implies—responsibilities whose size and nature are obviously impossible to reject." We are now back in the international anarchy which led up to and produced World War I—but without hope of any national survival next time. The way back is not the way out.

Isolationism, of course, runs through all this earnest struggle for national identity. But the Twenty-first Century, not so far away, can guarantee national identity only in terms of the world community. Yet the foundations of this wider perspective have received little underpinning from de Gaulle recently. The French seat has been vacant at the 18-Power Geneva Disarmament Conference (publicists now refer to the "17-Power Conference") and the Nuclear Test Ban and Non-Proliferation Treaty have been ignored by France. There is no rational excuse for this irresponsible boycott. Again, when the General Assembly debate in 1965 on members' obligations under Article 19 of the U.N. Charter produced the "payments crisis"—still unresolved—France was second among the major defaulters. Then, the French delegation offered ingenious proposals for setting up a new Finance Committee, but not the money France owed for past peacekeeping operations. General de Gaulle has shown his respect for the World Organization by being the only considerable figure in world affairs never to visit its headquarters in New York.

General de Gaulle has, however, moved much further than President Johnson or any American President has done to negotiating peace settlements—both with Russia and with Germany. This penchant for conciliation actually began with Algeria, when he assumed the Presidency in 1958. Only those who knew France well in the 1950's—and watched especially the tragic drain this colonial war was exacting from its youth—can appreciate the nation-wide gratitude the French people bear for the General's courageous withdrawal from that tortured country and his firm handling of the reactionary generals who found it "impossible to think of anything but victory." When the French Foreign Minister told the General Assembly in November 1966 that the U.S. might well learn how to

20

deal with Vietnam from the experience of his own country, the contrast between the superior statecraft of his President and that of the U.S. President was not lost on that Assembly.

De Gaulle's direct overtures to the Soviet Union, as far as France is concerned, put an end once and for all to those bitter years of Cold War bluff, blunder, and simulated war-scares, which had produced the North Atlantic Treaty in the first place. Fear of Russia has been the obverse side of the counterfeit coin called NATO. One result of de Gaulle's position in banishing NATO is that, in proportion as NATO diminishes further, the Federal Republic of West Germany becomes less beholden to the West, while the so-called "satellite" countries become less beholden to the Soviet Union. (This steady loosening of the Warsaw Pact we shall pursue further in the next chapter.) The fact is that France has gained more in real security from its rapprochement to Russia and Eastern Europe than de Gaulle's gesture of nuclear isolation could ever achieve.

Again, France's vastly improved relations with her immediate neighbor are making the remnants of her occupation army in West Germany an empty mockery. It should be recalled that two divisions that had been stationed in West Germany were withdrawn during the Algerian war, but no unit was reintegrated in NATO; while French ground forces which remained under the NATO command in Germany were limited to two divisions. France withdrew her NATO forces in the Mediterranean in 1959. In early 1964, she withdrew her naval forces in the Atlantic from the control of the Alliance, and three months later all French naval officers were withdrawn from integrated NATO staffs. France's position on the future of Germany, however, was explained by the Foreign Minister as unchanged. France had no present intention of recognizing the Communist Government of East Germany.

Apart from de Gaulle's gracious undertaking to remain "an ally of the allies," why should either France or Britain perpetuate the occupation charade a moment longer? Twenty years after Germany's total defeat, the two remaining European allies who are still patroling German soil would appear to be staying on merely to justify the American presence, even though Vietnam priorities have been steadily reducing the U.S. effectives in West Germany. NATO's war games must go on. But why?

Sick World, Sick Men

In all that has been said above in terms of the General's unique personality and unquestioned leadership, one factor of primary importance has been omitted so far from the political equation which will color so much of what follows. What sort of men are these master-builders of the NATO-conditioned world? Can the human race really afford them?

21

On May 22, 1949, one of them, James Forrestal, America's First Secretary of Defense, plunged to his death from the sixteenth floor of the Bethesda Naval Hospital, where he was undergoing psychiatric treatment. Just two months earlier President Truman had awarded him the Distinguished Service Medal for his services to the nation. What were the facts about his final collapse—since Washington refused to admit the real nature of his illness, even after his death? Did his personality disorders affect basic decisions regarding international policies? To answer these questions, Professor Arnold A. Rogow has probed deeply into Forrestal's private and public life in his remarkable biography.[22]

He explored Forrestal's childhood, his estrangement from his family and his rejection of Catholicism, his meteoric rise in Wall Street, his contacts with "the power elite" in Washington, and his government career as Navy Secretary and finally Secretary of Defense. The agonizing story of his last months in office, his "resignation under fire," and his private war with Communism is closely documented throughout this remarkable book. One commentator has tersely remarked: "The story of James Forrestal is truly an American tragedy." On the day following the suicide, Representative Paul Shafer told the House: "James V. Forrestal hated the Communists. He hated the thought of their undermining this land of ours, in which he had been able to work himself up from a poor man to one of wealth and high position . . . There is every reason to believe that the dangers of Communism and the manner in which so many of our citizens overlook those dangers preyed on his mind, until, finding a weak spot, the pressure caused his collapse which ended in his tragic demise."

Arnold A. Rogow, Professor of Political Science at Stanford University, tells the personal story in great depth. His account raises the gravest questions about the consequences of mental illness in high government office, and especially the kind of judgment a Secretary of Defense exercises in shaping his nation's attitude to Communist countries. The author asserts frankly that his interest in Forrestal "relates less to the fact that he was a distinguished American public servant—he was certainly that—than to his significance in any study of the relationship between personality, especially personality disorders, and politics. While not the first high official to become mentally ill, Forrestal is the highest ranking American official to have committed suicide. The tragedy that ended his life in May 1949 underscores the observation that we need to know much more about the tensions and frustrations of high office. And if it be doubted that the Forrestal case proves the point, perhaps it is enough to refer briefly to some other officials whose medical histories reflect stress and strain in high office."

[22] A. A. Rogow: *James Forrestal: A Study of Personality, Politics, and Policy*, Macmillan, New York, 1964.

22

Rogow proceeds to do this, and adds: "There is a body of opinion which holds that illness and exhaustion affected decisions made by Presidents Woodrow Wilson and Franklin D. Roosevelt during their last years in the White House. More recently ulcers, hypertension, coronary disease, and 'exhaustion' have affected or terminated the political careers of Generals George C. Marshall and Walter Bedell Smith."

Pursuing this same strain, Cornelius Ryan's *The Last Battle* records that: "Roosevelt and Churchill met once again in Quebec in September 1944. Roosevelt had changed visibly. The usually vital President looked frail and wan. . . . The campaigning, the diplomacy at home and abroad, the strain of the heavy burdens of the War years, were fast taking their toll. It was easy to see why his doctors, family and friends were begging him not to run again. To the British delegation at Quebec, Roosevelt appeared to be failing rapidly . . . We knew the shadows were closing in."[23]

Of course, "tension diseases" are not exclusively American. Allan Bullock's *Hitler: A Study in Tyranny* stands at the head of a class of scientific biographies which should by this date have also warned the common man against the type of uncommon man who talks seriously of such abominations as massive retaliation and who practices brinkmanship with the lives of untold millions.

The British list of those recent leaders who have suffered physical or mental illness while in public office includes Anthony Eden, Ernest Bevin, Stafford Cripps, and Neville Chamberlain; to which has been added the provocative commentary on the life of Winston Churchill, written from the private diaries of his personal physician, Lord Moran. Russian victims of acute mental stress that come readily to mind are Andrei Vishinsky (duodenal ulcer) and, of course, Joseph Stalin (hypertension and paranoia). Stalin's daughter Svetlana Alliluyeva, who fled to the West in 1967, described her father's lingering death from asphyxiation in 1953 after a brain stroke in her book, *Twenty Letters to a Friend*. Her first chapter pictures Stalin as a man dissociated from reality and prescribing his own medicines.

So it has been seriously asked: Is the fate of the modern world safe in the hands of sick men? Can the secret malady of a statesman be more disastrous than his secret diplomacy?

"There will be other Forrestals and other wars if attempts are not made to prevent, detect, treat, and cure those illnesses that affect rational mental processes in decision-making environments. . . . More knowledge, more discussion, and more case studies are necessary if citizens everywhere are to have some assurance that the policy process does not suffer from the contamination of illnesses that affect the mind," is the sensible advice which Arnold A. Rogow leaves us to ponder.

[23] Cornelius Ryan: *The Last Battle,* Simon & Schuster, New York, 1966.

Still following this line of enquiry, one further case should come before our scrutiny of critical disease in relation to national policy decisions, especially as the diplomatic activities of the unhappy sufferer, John Foster Dulles, receive detailed study in later chapters. It will suffice here to call evidence—and that friendly evidence—from two witnesses of the final stages of the career of the irrepressible Secretary of State, who once insisted: "I am forced to the abyss. I do not go there of my own volition. But when I am there, I am not willing to retreat. I have proved it at Quemoy." Thus, Dulles is alleged to have assured Chancellor Adenauer: "I have proved that I am not ready to retreat, and I will not do so at Berlin."

In *Berlin, The Wall Is Not Forever,* Eleanor Lansing Dulles engages in a prodigious defense of her late brother to show that "Berlin continues to be one of the vital interests of the United States—the key to any lasting peace in Europe and one of the major problems to be settled before the United States and Soviet Russia can terminate the Cold War."[24] As one follows this one-sided story of the beleaguered city, one's mind goes once more to Cornelius Ryan's *The Last Battle* and recalls how the gallant defender of Stalingrad, with four million Russian dead and ten million other casualties and a third of his homeland lying devastated behind him in the final German retreat, had entered the shattered city as its captor. One wonders what effect such a myopic display of chess-board assertiveness over the physical possession of Berlin could possibly have on such a Russian victor as this—or on the younger Russian mind that is growing up today.

Be that as it may, Eleanor Lansing Dulles' own portrait of the last days of John Foster Dulles are probably more revealing than she intended, for his notoriously obstructive tactics on every world issue he touched drove not only his enemies but also his allies to despair. Many seasoned diplomats believed that, but for Dulles—tormented in mind and body as this intimate account shows—both British and French military forces would have been out of West Germany long ago. Berlin would probably have been re-integrated as an internationally "protected" city under U.N. jurisdiction or under the kind of joint-guarantee which the Soviet Union had long stated its willingness to join and which has been pressed for again and again at the United Nations.

In September 1967, Chancellor Kurt Georg Kiesinger declared that his Government was ready to conduct negotiations with East Germany at a high official level "to help alleviate the misery of German partition." This was the first time that a West German Government, turning its back momentarily on Washington, had made a concrete proposal for high-level talks with the East German regime. Chancellor Kiesinger's offer to East

[24] Eleanor Lansing Dulles: *Berlin, The Wall Is Not Forever,* Chapel Hill, 1967.

Germany was in fact a guarded reply to a letter he received from Premier Willi Stoph, who had proposed a treaty to establish normal relations between the two Germanys and recognize the existence of East Germany, accept the Oder-Neisse border between Germany and Poland as permanent, and recognize West Berlin as an independent "third German state." At least, this was to be a beginning.

Six months later, in March 1968, Foreign Minister Willy Brandt broke another taboo by calling for "recognition and respect of the Oder-Neisse line" as one of post-war Europe's "realities." What shall we then say of the wasted years?

Addressing the Royal Geographical Society in London, Professor E. Friedensburg, a member of the German Federal Parliament, Vice-Mayor of Berlin from 1946 to 1951, and the last Acting Mayor of the *undivided* city, stated: "For more than twenty years, the strange political fate of this city has made the headlines in papers all over the world. I do not think that I am exaggerating if I say that the ultimate result of the quiet battle within and around that city will have a decisive influence, not only upon the relations between Russians and Germans, but even upon the political future of all the countries involved in one way or the other in the struggle between West and East . . . The less we give way to the comprehensible desire to look into the actual political implications of the Berlin situation, the easier and the better we will recognize the indestructible roots of the strength of the city and its inhabitants."

This unquestioned German authority drew the only conclusion which sane men everywhere would have drawn from the plain facts of life years ago, namely, that Berlin, "situated in the middle of the province of Brandenburg, in the middle of Germany, in the middle of the European Continent," had to become, by its very nature, a uniting and not a divisive factor in European and world affairs:

It is neither an Eastern nor a Western city. Its population is composed of elements from all sides. If the present division of the city had not such an ugly political meaning, it could serve as a classical symbol of the position of the frontier between both parts of the world. . . . West Berlin will continue to thrive. But it would be foolish to obscure the fact that the present situation is unnatural and therefore a source of innumerable incidents and frictions of which our citizens are the victims and, what is still more urgent, which form a constant threat to peace in Europe.[25]

But Eleanor Lansing Dulles explains why this could not happen: "In Washington and in the Paris meeting of NATO, Secretary Dulles hammered home the determination to hold the line, and in early 1959 he made his last visit to Europe. He knew that his speculative statements about methods of reunification and the possible acceptance of East Germans as agents of the Soviets had troubled leaders in Bonn and Berlin. He also

[25] *The Geographical Journal,* Vol. 133, Part 2, June 1967, London.

thought it essential to demonstrate the continued unity of the Allies in their firm position in defense of Berlin. . . . It was on his return to Washington on February 11 that he had his last interviews in his office. The doctors had told him at noon that he must enter Walter Reed Hospital at once."*

In fact, a follow-up conference on Berlin was interrupted in Geneva during May of that year so that the ministers could attend Dulles' funeral in Washington. Eleanor Lansing Dulles continues her essay in self-opinionated and uncalculating rigidity: "The results were equivocal in that the Soviets may have thought our position was weakened (by Dulles' death), whereas the United States insisted there were no compromises."

In closer detail, observers who were near to Dulles at this final period of his life describe how "Dulles stirred the hearts of Europe's most urbane diplomats when, in intense pain, he made his final odyssey to Europe with the shadow of death upon him . . . to grapple again with the Berlin crisis." They report that:

At the Palais de Chaillot, it required a major exertion for Dulles to see the conference through. After the second NATO plenary session, he looked haggard. . . . His purpose, in his final appearance at NATO, was to make clear beyond a doubt to the other fourteen Western allies that Berlin was a matter of war or peace to the United States.[26]

To the American Ambassador to France, Amory Houghton, say the authors, it was "the most amazing performance of separation of mind from matter." Couve de Murville said later: "It hurt us all to watch him. He was very tired. We knew then that he did not have very long to live. De Gaulle admired his courage. We all did."

To which we make emphatic rejoinder: Must the shadow of death ever lie athwart man's thorny path to peace? Has human courage no larger hope to offer mankind than the projections of paranoid or weary leaders and the neurotic strivings of tormented minds divorced from reality? Can the defense of freedom be left any longer to the irrational hostilities of fear-ridden protagonists facing each other across a tiny planet which was meant to house and protect one world community? Perhaps we are awaiting a new breed of statesmen to ensure that life continues on this earth?

[26] Roscoe Drummond & Gaston Coblentry: *Duel at the Brink,* Doubleday, New York, 1960.
* See also: Eleanor Lansing Dulles: *John Foster Dulles, The Last Year,* Harcourt, Brace and World, New York, 1963.

2 NUCLEAR SHADOW BOXING

The great wish of some is to avenge themselves on
some particular enemy, the great wish of others to
save their own pocket. Slow in assembling, they devote a very small fraction of the time to the consideration of any public object, most of it to the prosecution
of their own objects. Meanwhile each fancies that no
harm will come of his neglect, and that it is the business of somebody else to look after this or that for
him; and so, by the same notion being entertained by
all separately, the common cause imperceptibly de-
cays.

—Thucydides (Pericles on Alliances)

The Maginot Line still stretches undamaged along the German
frontier just inside France, almost thirty years after the German troops
invaded France through Belgium and rolled up the Maginot forts behind
it. It cost half a billion dollars to build and it is still intact, too solidly colossal to move. A proposal—not meant ironically—to use it as a NATO
storage depot came to nothing. Across the frontier, its rival, the Siegfried
Line—earmarked for speedy demolition by the victorious Allies—is still
largely untouched, except that farmers store hay in its deserted bunkers,
when tourists are not being shown around.

The NATO Line has been somewhat more flexible, geographically
speaking, but infinitely more expensive in upkeep. When General de
Gaulle foreclosed its picturesque headquarters at Fontainebleau in early
1967, "that pyramid of staffs and budgets" (as he unkindly termed it)
moved to its present site at Casteau, near Mons in Belgium. This site has
since been functionally planned for three separate military families,
namely, Americans, British, and "internationals." The new living facilities
reflect the different tastes of the three groups—showers for the Americans,
long baths for the British, and presumably an amalgam of both for the

27

"internationals." Added to basic necessities are clubs, chapels, a 750 seat theater, schools for 2,250 students, recreation halls, and a covered swimming pool. United States General Lyman Lemnitzer, the Supreme Allied Commander in Europe, has his office in the main command building, linked by a corridor to the windowless concrete "top secret" operations center where NATO strategy is mapped out.

The civilian departments of NATO had likewise to move to Belgium from their ten million dollar "palais" in Paris. In all, 70,000 U.S. servicemen and civilian employees and their families had to get out of France at the same time. There were 770,000 tons of military supplies (enough to fill 50,000 railway cars) to shift from nearly 200 military installations on French soil—warehouses, offices, schools, hospitals and an oil pipeline to West Germany. The question has been asked: "What will the United States and NATO get back from this multimillion dollar investment? The answer is: not very much. 'The simple fact is that much of what we have built has little value to the French,' explains a senior American officer. 'A lot of our buildings are in open countryside, too far away from towns to be of much use except for military storage, and too expensive or impractical to convert' . . . some U.S. air bases will be ripped up at American expense and restored to farmland."[1]

Moving into a new home has been no simple matter—for NATO is dispersed across the globe, with one focus in Washington (to which most of the military aspects have naturally gravitated) and the other focus in and around Brussels. NATO's seven-million-dollar provisional headquarters in the suburb of Evere moved in during the autumn of 1967, thus providing working space for the 900-man staff of the Secretariat, and for some 750 officials working for the permanent delegations of the fifteen member countries, as well as the 400 officials of the Military Committttee that were to be transferred from Washington. These provisional headquarters will be used until a proposed twenty million dollar permanent complex is built on the Heysel plain (site of the 1958 world's fair) around 1980—if NATO lasts that long.

NATO's armed forces strength was listed in 1966 as follows: America 2,847,310; France 513,698; Turkey 480,000; Britain 419,567; West Germany 402,000; Italy 400,000; Greece 162,000; Portugal 148,000; Netherlands 123,500; Canada 111,500; Belgium 110,000; Denmark 52,000; Norway 32,200; Luxembourg 1,800. This comes to a total of nearly six million personnel (more than the total population of Denmark, Luxembourg, Iceland, Alaska and Nevada put together). The total cost at the 1966 figures was 60,852 million dollars for North America and 21,317 million dollars for European NATO members—a global total of just over 82 *billion* dollars.

In a world so desperate for money, men, and materials to save its

[1] Don Cook in *Reader's Digest,* April 1967.

impoverished millions from hunger and fear and despair, these bare figures speak nothing less than a blasphemy against the human spirit and are a measure of the degradation of Man. The often repeated pretext that they represent a necessary price for human freedom on this planet is a demonstration of the absurd, and this shallow philosophy will be scrutinized in depth in later chapters.

No one would have imagined that this pyramid of staffs and budgets could possibly have proliferated from the Treaty itself, which is both short and simple—perhaps too simple. (The complete text will be found in Appendix 2.) Historically speaking, the North Atlantic Treaty grew out of the Treaty of Brussels, signed in March 1948, by which Belgium, France, Luxembourg, the Netherlands and the United Kingdom pledged themselves, in case of *aggression,* to give each other "aid and assistance by all the means in their power, military and other." The earlier Treaty, establishing the Western European Union, was the West's immediate reaction to the installing of a Communist government in Prague the month before. In June of that year, the Vandenberg Resolution brought American delegates hurrying across the Atlantic to Western European Union meetings. As a consequence, the North Atlantic Treaty was speedily formulated and signed on April 4, 1949 at Washington by twelve signatories (later increased to fifteen).

The Treaty contains five points of importance:
(1) It applies to a wide geographical area defined as Europe (which includes Turkey), America, and "the Atlantic" north of the Tropic of Cancer;
(2) It can take effect only in case of "armed attack";
(3) All members are to be the judges of their own type of participation;
(4) All have a duty to increase "their individual and collective power to *resist attack"*;
(5) It may be modified after ten years and abrogated after twenty years —with one year's notice.

Following a specific undertaking to abide by the U.N. Charter,* the main article (No. 5) provides that "the Parties agree that an armed attack against one or more of them in Europe or North America shall be considered an attack against them all." This does not carry an automatic engagement of all or any of the members, for a little further on a limitation appears: "if such an armed attack occurs, each of them . . . will assist the Party or Parties so attacked by taking forthwith . . . such action as it deems necessary, including the use of armed force . . ." Thus the Treaty does little more than express very broad and vague principles of co-operation.

* Article 1 reads: "The Parties undertake, as set forth in the Charter of the United Nations, to settle any international dispute in which they may be involved by peaceful means in such a manner that international peace and security and justice are not endangered, and to refrain in their international relations from the threat or use of force in any manner inconsistent with the purpose of the United Nations."

The Alliance itself has, in fact, been filled in gradually in the *application* of the Treaty.

A foremost French authority on NATO, General André Beaufre, served on the NATO staff in various capacities for a number of years. "I was in Indo-China when General de Lattre asked me to join him at Fontaine-bleau," he writes. (In Indo-China, of course, the French were then staging their abortive colonial comeback.) His book, *NATO and Europe*[2] throws a revealing light on NATO's internal affairs. He records that: "Two contradictory tendencies appeared in the negotiations: the Europeans, hoping to benefit from an unconditional American guarantee, demanded a statement of total engagement, as in the case of the Treaty of Brussels; while the United States, desirous of maintaining its freedom of action, was willing to accept only an engagement in principle."

It was upon this engagement "in principle," however, that the mammoth superstructure was erected. As General Beaufre says: "The Americans were bound to have the lion's share of the commands and the general staffs, and all facilities would be given them for stationing their troops in Europe." From that point on, Parkinson's Law seems to have progressed in geometrical ratio—until de Gaulle's Law began to operate instead, in inverse ratio.

In outlining the main structure of NATO, assisted by the accompanying diagram, we might take warning from André Beaufre's further comment: "The military organization is still more complex and tentacular, probably because of the influence of the Pentagon, that Kafkaesque monster which employs forty thousand people."

It should be explained, however, that the French General's spirited account is by no means resentful; he is thoroughly in favor of NATO as a European-based organization, which he ardently hopes will one day "progress towards European Union." But he was disturbed from the start that NATO was "submitting to the cumbersome American administrative machinery, which perceives organization only in the form of highly complex diagrams."

Political Façade

NATO is composed, first, of a supreme political organ, the North Atlantic Council, comprising the fifteen Allied states, represented either by their Ministers or more usually by the Permanent Representatives of their governments. This Council meets in plenary session twice a year, presided over in turn by Representatives of each member country. Second, a Permanent Secretary-General prepares the working papers of the Council and runs the International Secretariat—now located near Brussels, as

[2] André Beaufre: *NATO and Europe* (Translation), Vintage, New York, 1966.

30

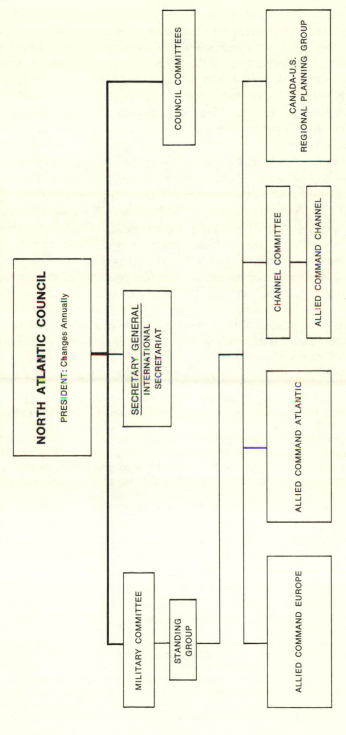

NATO'S CIVIL AND MILITARY ORGANIZATION

NORTH ATLANTIC COUNCIL

PRESIDENT: Changes Annually

SECRETARY GENERAL
INTERNATIONAL
SECRETARIAT

COUNCIL COMMITTEES

CANADA-U.S.
REGIONAL PLANNING GROUP

CHANNEL COMMITTEE

ALLIED COMMAND CHANNEL

ALLIED COMMAND ATLANTIC

MILITARY COMMITTEE

STANDING
GROUP

ALLIED COMMAND EUROPE

we have seen. Third, at the apex of the military organization is the Military Committee, composed of the chiefs-of-staff of the fifteen countries, which meets formally twice a year, while between meetings a standing committee of military representatives of the chiefs-of-staff is at work in Washington all the time, and is appropriately called "The Military Committee in Permanent Session." (Incidentally, since Iceland has no army, it sends a civilian representative to these meetings; but no doubt feels safer from Russian or Chinese or Cuban invasions by having NATO bases installed on its shores.)

Fourth, the Military Committee has set up a Standing Group composed of the United States, Britain, and (formerly) France.* The somewhat disillusioned André Beaufre explains that: "In the initial conception of NATO, the Standing Group was to have been the military brain of the Alliance, and at the beginning it was composed of military leaders of the first rank who, because of their prestige, were able to exert an influence over the Council as well as over their own governments." But, alas! Washington "began to over-emphasize the role of the Military Committee in Permanent Session," and also "the British, during this period, preferred to treat with the Americans privately on affairs of importance. The result was that the Standing Group, when I was assigned to it in 1960, was only a system of wheels without power, revolving almost uselessly around questions of routine."

The main problem, as General Beaufre saw it, was one of authority:

But if the military organization of NATO has become virtually a body without a head, it is because the major subordinate commands, entrusted to American generals and admirals, have tended to become independent of the inter-allied hierarchy, while depending directly on the Pentagon in their capacity as commanders of American forces. It is this very situation . . . that has altogether falsified the original plan of NATO and placed practically the entire defense organization under the close control of the American general staff.

This subordination of what was essentially a European alliance to Washington's global strategy was particularly revealed in what are known as the military commands. Again, our description must be minimal, though NATO's telephone directory is an elephantine polyglot series of volumes. SHAPE (the Supreme Allied Command Europe) is perhaps the most shapeless of all the commands, extending from North Cape to the Caucasus, including the Baltic and the Mediterranean, with various subordinate commands with headquarters stretching from Oslo to Malta. "This

* To illustrate how over-simplified is the foregoing version of NATO complexities, we can designate some of the military agencies attached to the Standing Group alone, such as MAS (Military Agency for Standardization), AGARD (Advisory Group for Aerospace, Research and Development), AMCEC (Allied Military Communications-Electronics Committee), ALLA (Allied Long Lines Agency), ARFA (Allied Radio Frequency Agency), ANCA (Allied Naval Communications Agency), ACSA (Allied Communications Security Agency), and the NATO Defense College.

enormous machinery," comments the French General, "which is supposed in case of war to have under its orders some sixty divisions and some two thousand planes (in other words, half of the total Allied forces in France in 1940), is in fact very closely controlled by SHAPE and SHAPE has generally been headed by American generals of strong personality, who are also in command of American forces in Europe and therefore directly under the American general staff."

It is not surprising, therefore, that our much disturbed French analyst should come to the conclusion that:

From a strictly logical point of view, this proliferation and Americanization of the Supreme Command in Europe constitutes an error in technique—and from the political point of view, an error in judgment that explains in large part the recent reactions of the French government.

To complete the present survey, the same situation can be said to exist in the Supreme Allied Command Atlantic—to which is allocated, by the way, the protection of Portugal, "founded on the principles of democracy, individual liberty and the rule of law" (to quote the Treaty's preamble)— with its assorted subordinate commands, and the Canada-U.S. Regional Planning Group and others. Among these, the Allied Command Channel, which is British, seems out of place somehow because no one has yet decided whether the English Channel belongs to Europe or the Atlantic. What is certain is that it does not flow into Chesapeake Bay.

"A Gaping Hole"

Of course, no one would suggest that all this lopsided growth just happened. Perhaps future historians will assess NATO as one of the worst psychological hangovers of the two World Wars. Certainly, the pattern of hate and violence and the moral vacuum left by a war which destroyed half of Europe and culminated in Hiroshima could hardly be expected to provide fertile soil for the tiny seeds of future peacemaking to flourish in. Wars breed wars. There can be no doubt that the dragons' teeth that all nations sowed so recklessly during those violent years sprang up as armed men as soon as the original fighting had stopped.

But apologists for NATO have never seen things that way; they have been dedicated almost unanimously—in the Niagara of words which has since swept all before it—to a black-and-white theme: "Hitler's Germany, conquered in 1945, left the center of Europe a gaping hole in which Soviet armies were engulfed. For the first time in history, conquering Russians occupied Berlin and Vienna." No one could have put the issue in a briefer form than these words from General André Beaufre's apology. Yet, even in this thumbnail sketch of post-war history, the two ways of international life stand out in clear contrast. The West got the Russians out of Vienna by a sensible peace treaty of compromise and mutual guarantee; Vienna thereby escaped both NATO and the Cold War. Why could not Berlin have been handled this way?

No one country could really be blamed for the unholy panic which, hardly was the ink dry on the United Nations Charter, sent many of the Western leaders scampering back to the Nineteenth Century, with an atom bomb on their consciences.

Every NATO General regards himself as an authority on Russian and Chinese (and now Cuban, North Vietnamese and North Korean) perversity. He must fall back on a pre-conditioned orthodox interpretation of Communism or his *raison d'être* disappears. Mountains of pro-NATO books and speeches all follow the same party line. Brigadier General Monro MacCloskey, for instance, has written two such recent text books, to which we shall refer in some detail below. Both are based from start to finish on premises which—even if the General never noticed it earlier— are now being shaken to bits all around the world. The following passages may be taken as characteristic of these elementary NATO polemics:

The direct threat having failed to bring about the collapse of the West, the USSR pushed the struggle into other areas . . . In pursuing these aims, the Soviets exploited such issues as the relaxation of international tensions, disarmament, suspension of nuclear tests, and suppression of nuclear weapons. They have also endeavored to neutralize a part of Western Europe to perpetuate the status quo in Eastern Europe and have pursued their policy of economic penetration of African, Asian, and Central American countries.[3]

Every variant has been played on this common theme—fear of Russia —without any effort being made to consider alternative explanations or discover non-military remedies, least of all to practice what the originators of NATO preached in Article 1 of their own Treaty: namely, to settle international disputes in accordance with the U.N. Charter and "to refrain in their international relations from the threat or the use of force."

In this endemic approach, the facts of the last War and its brutal legacy are ignored. The Nazi occupation, following on the pre-war ramshackle dictatorships in Eastern Europe, are forgotten, while the blunders and miscalculations of the Western powers are excused and their high motives are exaggerated. Hence, a spurious black-and-white pre-selected picture emerges as justification for what is virtually a continuation of the last war by very much its same general staffs. Only the enemies have changed, not the slogans. Monro MacCloskey, for example, expounds the motivation of NATO in these simplistic and romantic terms:

When World War II ended with the surrender of Japan on September 2, 1945, the Western democracies fervently hoped that an era of peace and security had begun. They demobilized almost all their armed forces and pledged their

[3] General Monro MacCloskey: *Pacts for Peace* and also *The North Atlantic Treaty Organization,* Richards Rosen Press, New York, 1967 and 1966, respectively.

34

faith in the United Nations for the settlement of international disputes and the maintenance of world peace . . . Confronted by the inability of the United Nations to halt the territorial aggrandizement of the USSR, the Western countries had no means of ensuring their own security other than by uniting together for their common defense.[4]

So familiar is this holier-than-thou line that has flowed from parliaments, presidents and press for two decades that our present survey might best be devoted to some of the more subtle aspects of the Great Confrontation. We can therefore give attention to three related, but not always consistent, schools of NATO thought which have been emerging over the questioning years and which will undoubtedly beckon more appealingly as the "re-shaping" develops. This is how they might be listed:

Number One: "The Status Quo for Ever."

Number Two: "The Great Success Story."

Number Three: "If You Don't Succeed the First Time, Try Again."

Regarding "The Status Quo for Ever" it has to be admitted that the Bourbonists in our midst, who have learned nothing and forgotten nothing, will be a tough obstacle in the path of those who want to re-shape the Alliance. But even those who, like General MacCloskey, are still thoroughly convinced about "the continuing Soviet Communist threat to the peace and security of the world" have to concede some minor changes, because (as he himself states) "in the early months of 1965, we find the Alliance partners in a bewildering predicament. In terms of military might, wealth, resources, and population, the Western countries have never been so strong. The West is far ahead of the Communist countries by every accepted standard. Nevertheless, with such tremendous strength, the West is losing ground in the world." His chief worry, however, seems to be outside Europe altogether, where "even former friends of the West have joined the Communists and others are infiltrated by them." And to bolster his pessimism he makes the quite astonishing assertion: "Additional nations have joined the Communist Bloc, including Algeria, Cambodia, Ceylon, Egypt, Ghana, Indonesia, Sudan, and Yemen."

The myopic General would appear to have not the least inkling of the aspirations or even the existence of independent African and Asian peoples outside his rigid categories. "United States policy against trade with Cuba," he opines, "is being completely undercut by our Alliance partners who trade with Castro. In the war in South Vietnam, are the Alliance partners providing any assistance?"

We can, alas, do little to reassure the professional NATO-ist who assumes the Pentagon's inherent right to re-shape the earth in its own godless image. Ronald Steel's *The End of the Alliance* is a factual exposé of how NATO, like the bullfrog in the fable, inflated itself with pride, until

[4] *Ibid.*

it burst. As a former U.S. Foreign Service official, he explains that the primary purpose of NATO "was to give the Europeans the assurance that the United States would protect them while they proceeded with the work of economic recovery, which we agreed to support under the Marshall Plan. Originally designed to last twenty years, NATO was a simple guaranty pact which would tide the Europeans over until they were sufficiently prosperous and self-reliant to defend themselves."

Ronald Steel goes on to trace NATO's expansion into something that became its own justification. An alliance conceived as an instrument for achieving certain ends was soon transformed into an end itself. "Every Soviet action was treated not in terms of the world power balance, but upon its significance for NATO," he states: "If the Russians appeared to falter, it was only to catch the West napping. If they blundered, it was to confuse us. If they compromised, it was only to seduce us." And so on; and in doing so NATO created its own *raison d'être*. "Built on alarm and nourished by emergency, NATO developed a vested interest in the perpetuation of that very state of emergency." This self-perpetuating and self-justifying complex of vested interests became less and less what it was supposed to be and more and more what it is today, "an end in itself."[5]

Let us listen, then, to the official voice of NATO today: "The year 1969 is often mentioned as the next obstacle to be overcome," stated NATO Secretary-General Brosio in November 1967: "From many quarters we hear the refrain that the Treaty of Washington is due to be renewed or even re-negotiated at that date. I believe that I am on record for having repeated *ad nauseam* that the Treaty is timeless, that it is not bound by a 20 years' span, which comes to an end in 1969. The year 1969 simply marks the maturing of the right given each government by Article 13 to announce its withdrawal from the Treaty in the following year."

This attitude explains why so many people swallow the status quo. Hugh Jenkins, M.P., put this very neatly when addressing a Conference in London of the Labor Peace Fellowship (an organization including over sixty Members of Parliament) in 1967: "The strategy of NATO is still based on the imminence of a Soviet attack on Western Europe. In the event of conventional weapons being used by the East, NATO plans a nuclear response. This policy would, in fact, destroy everything in Europe that it pretended to defend. The end product would be the wiping out of European civilization . . . During my recent visit to NATO headquarters, it was clear that its publications were continuing with Cold War propaganda and a one-sided analysis of world problems designed to justify NATO's continued existence. Today NATO is dangerous and totally evil . . . *But both the permanent officials and NATO collectively have a vested interest in continuing war-based policies.*"

[5] Ronald Steel: *The End of the Alliance,* Viking, New York, 1964.

36

Scotching a Myth

"The Great Success Story"—*Number Two*—rests on what went before, for, as the *New York Times* naïvely declared under this very slogan: "The greatest threat to the Atlantic Alliance now, ironically, is its own success." The psychological springs of the Cold War can be left to later examination, but, since all the pro-NATO studies we have referred to above have been based on the *assumption* of an expected Soviet take-over of West Europe, a direct refutation of that thesis should be registered here.

When Winston Churchill, as leader of the Opposition, came to the United States in 1946 to make his famous Fulton speech, Britain's century-old control of the Mediterranean had been considerably loosened as a result of the War, and guerrilla groups were pictured as moving into the chaos which was Greece at the instigation of Russia. So the wily old campaigner begged the United States to take over the precious burden from him. "Nobody knows what Soviet Russia and its Communist international organization intends to do in the immediate future," he confided to the apprehensive Americans: "It is my duty to lay before you certain facts about the present situation in Europe . . ." Then the Iron Curtain came clattering down.

This is how one of the strident new voices, however, calling for a sense of balance and sanity in his own country, epitomized America's swift reaction to Churchill:

This was the call we had been waiting for. We hitched up our pants and were off. This gave us a clear mandate to exercise our missionary spirit and save the world for Christianity. A myth was born, that Russia and its armies stood ready to overwhelm West Europe. *There is no evidence at hand that the Soviet Union was capable of smashing clear to the Pyrenees, as the Pentagon was suggesting.*[6]

Let us take this point further. It should be recalled that, in spite of its successful onslaught on Berlin, the Russian Army was seriously depleted by the War, suffering far more in casualties than all the rest of the allies put together. There were no discernible plans at that period for a European conquest or any build-up of bases for such an attack. In fact, the Russians have never shown enthusiasm for fighting away from their soil, except to throw back the invaders—which they had already done. It was now a question of holding them back.

Moreover, no nation had more cause to welcome peace so desperately and thankfully than did the Russian people in 1945. For years afterwards, Soviet literature and films and poems and speeches have been filled with this sense of escape and liberation from the "German War," as they saw it. To have started an open-ended global war against their well-equipped allies—with the U.S. at the height of its industrial strength and possessing

[6] Tristram Coffin: *The Armed Society, Militarism in Modern America,* Penguin, London and New York, 1966.

37

an immense uninjured war-machine—would have been sheer lunacy. But the myth was born.

The French historian Raymond Aron went deeper into this Churchillian fantasy in his *Peace and War Between Nations*. He pointed out that: "The Russian leaders do not have a biological concept of history. They are not fighting the American people. They have no desire to murder or enslave them. They believe in the inevitable and progressive advance of a system of government whose first model they themselves created. They are convinced that the winds of history will fill the sails of their assumptions and hopes. Why should they place everything they have created in deadly jeopardy simply to hasten a process that they regard as inevitable?"

According to Tristram Coffin, again:

Russia's postwar policy was simple: to make the U.S.S.R. impregnable from attack from the West by building a great military strength, following Trajan's example, by creating a vast buffer area in the west, and splitting Germany in two. There never was any secret of this intention. Stalin in his conversations with Djilas showed a negative reaction to Communist moves, outside of this strategy, which might arouse the West. He was far more interested in Mother Russia than the Communist International.[7]

Three years after the Fulton speech, and two years after Truman had launched his Monroe crusade, none other than the late John Foster Dulles, speaking in 1949 before the National Conference on Churches and World Order, said: "So far as it is humanly possible to judge, the Soviet Government under conditions now prevailing does not contemplate the use of war as an instrument of its national policy. I do not know any responsible high official, military or civilian, in this government or any government, who believes that the Soviet Government now plans conquest by open military aggression." What happened to Mr. Dulles' thinking after 1949 is a matter of tragic record; but, in any case, the Truman Doctrine was then gaining momentum and Dulles was yet to become Secretary of State and so brought into the Cold War system—just as his health began seriously to deteriorate.

George Kennan, formerly ambassador in Moscow, calling for basic changes in U.S. foreign policy some years later, deplored the common impression which had triggered the Truman build-up: namely, "that Stalin was a man of war aiming to launch a military onslaught against the non-Communist world and deterred only by our atomic armaments. . . . Although Stalin's intentions toward ourselves were strictly dishonorable," Kennan insisted, "nevertheless, those intentions, I am convinced, did not include the determination to unleash a third World War in the grand manner. The image of a Stalinist Russia poised and yearning to attack the West, and deterred only by our possession of atomic weapons, was largely a creation of the Western imagination."[8]

Meanwhile, from being a poor and backward society of the early Revo-

[7] *op. cit.*
[8] *Harper's,* August 1956.

lutionary years—as is still depicted in much current political literature of Darkest America—Russia had become a relatively wealthy, literate, advanced and highly industrialized society, a master of nuclear energy and space technology. Along with this rapid material transformation, the progressive liberalization of Soviet society—in the Western sense—and the emergence of a new pattern of peaceful co-existence have come steadily in sight. These new insights have, of course, been making their way to the surface of public debate in America—but too late to undo the harm of two decades of Cold War psychosis, which sustained, and still does sustain, the orthodox militarists' position.

In terms of this unyielding orthodoxy, on the one hand, we note that General Monro MacCloskey has the temerity to proclaim (and presumably he believes) that: "Few would deny that, but for NATO, the Berlin wall would now be on the English Channel instead of in Germany. For the past sixteen years, NATO has been the major peacekeeping force in Europe and it must be preserved for the deterrent force that it is. It has been the most successful defensive alliance in modern history."[9]

On the other hand, one of those who would flatly deny this is another professional soldier, who was a top U.S. administrator in Germany at the time and who maintains: "No Soviet plans have ever been discovered for a military move west of the positions defined by the armistice of May 1945. None ever existed. I was stationed in Germany between September 1945 and November 1947. I had many talks with most of the leaders of all four occupation zones, as my principal office was located in Berlin. Never once have I met anyone among these leaders who really believed the Soviet Union to pose a military threat. . . . She was emaciated and eager to rebuild, and heal her wounds. She was anything but ready or willing to depart on military adventures."*

We shall cite, in the course of this book, the outspoken opinions of a number of ex-military professionals who, like General Hester, have come right out from The System and who call for international solutions which their own experience has proved can never be secured by military means. General Hester presents, moreover, some cogent reasons why the NATO complex was put together so hurriedly during the post-war period, on the pretext that the West was in peril. This unusually liberal General's reasons throw a lurid light on the real motivation for keeping NATO alive today. We cite them here exactly as he penned them so tersely in his earlier statement:

NATO was organized for several purposes: (1) to prevent by *whatever means* any left-wing front from coming to power in the areas under Western military control; (2) to re-arm West Germany as the U.S. Government's chief ally

[9] *op. cit.*

* From a privately published statement of Brigadier General Hugh B. Hester (Retired), 1942-45 Director of Procurement of Military supplies for General MacArthur's forces under Lend-Lease Agreement with Australia; and, in 1945-47, the Administrator of the U.S. Food and Agricultural Program for Germany.

in Europe; (3) to ensure American and West German hegemony over West Europe; and (4) to pose a threat to the Soviet position in East Europe.

"Ah, yes!" responds the pro-NATO partisan, as his precious myth is steadily deflated by the accumulating evidence; "but it is *subversion* that we fear, not Russia's armies—it is the attack from within, not the attack from without that matters!" So into the language of the Cold War we observe that the term "Communist oppression" is slowly being replaced by "Communist subversion." But those who seize on this newer weapon do not see that it cuts both ways. (The scandalous antics of the C.I.A. are sufficient proof of that.) The towering superstructure of NATO was never designed to deal with "subversion," as recent events in Greece have shown. No sane person employs a steam-hammer to repair a malfunctioning watch. NATO faces outwards, not inwards. When the ground of the argument is shifted from external aggression to internal subversion (which term is usually left undefined) the whole NATO contraption falls flat; for subversion (whatever it is) calls for political—and maybe juridical—procedures, not military ones.

How to Succeed by Trying

Turning now to *Number Three*—"If You Don't Succeed the First Time, Try Again"—we are on more difficult ground, because re-shaping NATO covers virtually the whole scope of foreign policy across the globe, and, what is more important, it reveals the basic philosophies of the reformers themselves. The main graduations in this attempt, as we shall now examine them, move from (1) the "bravado" attitude, to (2) the *sauve-qui-peut* approach, to (3) the "disengagement" plan, and finally to (4) the "European Unity" concept.

Starting with the lowest denominator of sheer "bravado" as a way to face such complex problems, we find ourselves back with the status quo supporters, trusting to military power alone and believing that a stable international order can be based on superior force rather than on compromise and consent. As a case in point, at the end of his own analysis in *North Atlantic Treaty Organization,* General Monro MacCloskey arrives at the following penny-in-the-slot conclusion: "The defense policy of the Atlantic Alliance is to avert war by making it unmistakably clear to any potential aggressor that war with the West *will not pay."*

That all sounds reasonable and so very familiar. But we have italicized the last words because this "will not pay" syndrome is the underlying fallacy of the militarist solution. Every alliance has been based on it from time immemorial. Now we face nuclear annihilation because of it. If anything "will not pay" it is just what General MacCloskey advocates. To stand firm is praiseworthy—except when standing on quicksand, with the tide coming in.

Three summary answers can be given here rejecting the MacCloskey

40

thesis—a thesis which represents the gist of so much contemporary literature and professional opinion supporting the NATO case, repeated *ad
nauseam*. Later pages will be devoted to their elaboration, namely:

(1) NATO's "unity" neither exists today nor is it feasible at any time;
we are, in fact, farther away from it than ever;
(2) The international role ascribed to Communism is both over-
simplified and exaggerated; in any case, this is not the major
threat that we are facing today;
(3) The existence of NATO has itself become a major threat to peace;
worse, it is a roadblock to the World Organization on which world
peace *does* depend.

Coming now to the *sauve-qui-peut* approach, this was well illustrated
when a Republican group of Congressmen in August 1967, alarmed by
NATO's growing decay and worried by the absence of any lead from the
White House, urged the following steps: (1) a new NATO strategy council should be created to give the European allies a "genuine" role in
determining Atlantic defense policy; (2) the fifteen-member Atlantic
Council should be revitalized to act as the "principal instrument for
allied political decision-making"; and (3) the Council should be authorized to seek inter-allied agreements on East-West trade, on disarmament,
on German reunification and Central European security, and on aid to
underdeveloped countries.

The Congressmen pointed out that under the present organization the
NATO Council can debate, but can take no initiatives in foreign policy
not specifically allocated to it by member governments. They also urged a
more equitable distribution of command positions, including the appoint-
ment of a European as the Supreme Allied Commander in Europe. (This
post has been held by Americans ever since General of the Army Dwight
D. Eisenhower became the first Supreme Commander in 1951.)

This *sauve-qui-peut* appeal to the U.S. Administration was obviously
meant to show that, even if the Democratic forces came up with nothing,
while the Pentagon was biding its time, the opposition party, with the
1968 Presidential election in mind, wanted to put up a show of concern.
But the trivial and superficial nature of these proposals—from politicians
who had nothing to lose—is one further proof that the United States, while
holding tight to the past, has nothing whatsoever to offer its NATO allies
for the 1970's, except a dose of the same nostalgia.

The non-political but colorful General James M. Gavin took this rather
watery face-washing process a little further, however, when he said:
"NATO was conceived and brought into being at a time when we believed that we were confronted with a world-wide Communist conspiracy.
NATO has served us well (*sic*) and the importance of its role has been
emphasized time and again to the American people, indeed to the extent

that today *to question NATO is to seem almost unpatriotic.* Yet the facts are that, today, conditions in Europe are entirely different from those when NATO came into being." (Italics added.)

He was speaking before the Senate Foreign Relations Committee on February 21, 1967, and continued: "We are no longer dealing with fifteen separate countries; we are dealing with the United States and Canada on this side of the Atlantic, and the European Economic Community and other states who are seeking to find some relationship with that community on the other side of the Atlantic. NATO today must recognize this fact and set as one of its goals a reorganization that will reflect the changing components within NATO itself."

General Gavin went so far as to urge that "the United States' troop commitment to Europe is far in excess of today's needs. In fact, it could be argued that its very existence in Europe acts in a manner inimical to the long-term military interests of Europe." Reassuring the Senate Committee that "with an improving society at home and an outgoing approach to dealing with the problems abroad, we shall have no fear whatsoever for our own place in history," this unusually outgoing General concluded his evidence thus:

The NATO organization should ultimately assume the character of a small planning group, organized in a manner to hold together loosely the resources of Europe and North America. Ultimately the European forces should have as much independence of action as those of the United States and be an equal independent partner.

Again, a plan for "the political and economic rebirth of NATO" was proposed by twenty-one other Republican members of Congress in October 1967. They suggested an end to the division of Germany and *a progressive trading policy with East Europe.* NATO should negotiate with the Warsaw Pact; and a North Atlantic Parliament should be set up. Washington's obsession over President de Gaulle, they said, was holding back NATO evolution from a purely military pact into something wider. "By allowing its fixation on de Gaulle to shape policy within NATO, the United States has tended to divide Europe rather than unite it, and to deny the relevance of everything he has said."*

Their proposals were issued in anticipation of the NATO report to be presented to the NATO Ministerial meeting in December of that year, which the group thought was "as important as any peace conference ever held." (They were to be gravely disappointed in the event.) While the

* Some of these proposals were expanded in a book by Nelson Rockefeller, Republican Governor of New York, published later in 1968, under the title: *Unity, Freedom & Peace,* as a plank of his political platform, when running for the Presidency. In it he wrote: "We need a sense of full purpose—a dream, if you will. We need such a dream in order to live the waking life in this troubled world. For without such a sense of purpose—such a dream—we could only be a nation of sleepwalkers, stumbling toward an ever deeper darkness." His point was well made.

alliance still is necessary for defense, they stated, a re-shaping of goals is needed to treat "the problems and opportunities of the 1970's. If we expect the NATO of the 1940's to provide in the 1960's the unity of the 1940's, the North Atlantic Community may come to an end as a constructive force in world politics."

But what is remarkable about these last minute conversions is that there is a consistent reluctance on the part of the re-shapers to say outright: "The military might of NATO is dangerous and wrong and must *go*; and this is the way we propose that it should be dismantled!" All these nibblings at the shadow of NATO's future evade the dual issue, which lies at NATO's base, and that is radical disarmament measures and reliance on U.N. peacekeeping alternatives instead.

Typical of the continuous flow of apologetics in this field—most of which comes from the perimeter of the salaried defense personnel—is Timothy W. Stanley's *NATO in Transition*. This is another long study by one of the (new) lost generation, an author who is described as "professionally associated with the Department of Defense," and who manages in over four hundred pages, devoted ostensibly to "the future of the Atlantic Alliance," to include five very slight and casual references of a few words each to the existence of the United Nations. True to the bi-polar thinking we have deprecated throughout the present book and in spite of the plain facts of life, and also, as he states, "the special dilemmas . . . that have tended to sap the vitality of this partnership between North America and Western Europe," he nonetheless assumes that NATO can move forward, beyond its defensive-alliance past "born of military necessity and cemented by fear"; and that in a world of profound and rapid change, made additionally uneasy by nuclear proliferation and the contest of ideologies, NATO's goal can still be that of a fully co-operative partnership leading the way toward a stable and relatively peaceful world order.[10]

In spite of that rhetorical flourish, the book's central focus is on purely military and strategic make-shifts which will presumably govern the future —a future where the peacekeeping functions of the United Nations are completely ignored and where self-centered super-governments continue to play games with I.B.M.'s, balancing megatons against megatons—and call it security. If NATO scholarship comes no longer to praise Caesar, it need not bury him under a surfeit of out-of-date fatuities.

Breaking the Engagement

The "disengagement" approach is, of course, a far more radical attitude and it has been coming from Americans outside the military ranks, thus

[10] T. W. Stanley: *NATO in Transition—The Future of the Atlantic Alliance,* Praeger, New York, 1965.

43

deflating the whole NATO philosophy. The fact is that one cannot have both engagement and disengagement at the same time; they run in opposite directions.

The very presence of NATO has blocked serious discussion of disengagement on the governmental level over the years. "An East-West détente in Europe is now the key to world peace," says a well known banker and publicist, James P. Warburg: "There can be no such détente so long as NATO remains the pillar of our European policy, because NATO's very life depends upon continued East-West tension. Nor can the troublesome problem of Germany be settled so long as our policy demands keeping part of a partitioned Germany in NATO."[11]

Says Warburg: "Instead of patching up NATO and trying to solve a political problem by some military device, we should seek the achievement of an all-European security agreement in which, *within the framework of the United Nations,* the nuclear powers and all the nations of Europe would undertake to prevent the spread of nuclear weapons and to suppress all military aggression, whether emanating from East or West. Such an agreement would be directed against no 'enemy' bloc or nation. Unlike the confrontation of hostile alliances, it would promote rather than obstruct the abatement of tensions, the settlement of divisive issues and the beginning of disengagement and disarmament."

Let us take Warburg's point further. Negative though the idea may seem, such a policy could become a positive program for all Europe. Broadly speaking, "disengagement" calls for the mutual withdrawal of foreign military forces by international agreement, thus relaxing East-West tensions and achieving a first-step disarmament agreement. Here, London and Paris working alone—freed from Washington's strong-armed men— could do more for the stability of Europe than all the combined NATO partners could. With the mutual withdrawal of foreign military forces, an agreement to keep hands off the area becomes possible. This has already happened with Austria, with distinct success—the four occupying armies simply got out. Has anyone heard of the Austrians clamoring to get back under the "nuclear umbrella"?

A more specific type of disengagement is, of course, "de-nuclearization": the establishment of as many nuclear-free zones as possible in which nuclear weapons of any type would be banned. Guarantees would also need to be exchanged that nuclear weapons would not be used *against* the area. This program offers no Utopia; but it is being pressed constantly for both Africa and South America, and the U.N. has naturally been the forum for such advances in true security. A General Assembly resolution which was adopted, over the opposition vote of the United States, on

[11] James P. Warburg's testimony before the Senate Committee on Foreign Relations, March 22, 1966.

44

December 18, 1965, can be taken as typical of this forward-looking policy. It reads, in part:

Recognizing that the de-nuclearization of Africa would be a practical step towards the prevention of the further spread of nuclear weapons in the world, *calls upon* all States to respect the continent of Africa as a nuclear-free zone, and to refrain from the use, or the threat of use, of nuclear weapons on the African continent, and to refrain from testing, manufacturing, using or deploying nuclear weapons on the continent of Africa, and *urges* those States possessing nuclear weapons not to transfer nuclear weapons, scientific data or technological assistance to the national control of any State, in any form which may be used to assist such States in the manufacture or use of nuclear weapons in Africa.

At the 1967 General Assembly, a similar resolution was passed covering most of Latin America. So disengagement and neutralization are not new ideas, though disengagement was first considered primarily with reference to Central Europe, *viz,* the mutual withdrawal of American, British, Russian, and other foreign military forces from East and West Germany. Such terms are similarly being used more frequently nowadays with reference to the Middle East and directed at slowing down the perilous arms build-up by both Israel and the Arabs, in spite of the confusion and unsettlement left in the wake of the June 1967 War.

James P. Warburg began his personal campaign in 1949. Similar proposals have been advanced by many influential people. But their plans have always split on the NATO rock. Now that the NATO rock is itself split, this is surely the time to put disengagement to work. In short, a practical alternative to NATO would consist of a phased withdrawal of all foreign troops from Germany and eventually from Europe, and for U.N. supervision of a neutralized Germany, or, at least, of Berlin.

In Great Britain and France disengagement proposals have been pressed by leading statesmen like Anthony Eden (Lord Avon), Hugh Gaitskell, Denis Healey, Pierre Mendès-France, Jules Moch, and many groups of prominent citizens over the years. In fact, disengagement as a viable *alternative policy* to NATO gained wide publicity in Europe as a result of George Kennan's lecture series over the B.B.C. some years ago. But this sensible initiative achieved no support in the United States, because the arms men would not listen to it. They even exploited the favorable response coming from the Communists as an argument *against* it.

The most detailed of the disengagement plans have, in fact, come from the Communist side. For over ten years, Foreign Minister Adam Rapacki of Poland has appealed regularly at the United Nations General Assembly for the "de-nuclearization" of a central zone in Europe. Under the Rapacki plan no nuclear weapons would be permitted and guarantees would be exchanged by the nuclear powers not to use such weapons against any territory in this zone. Each year, Poland and other Communist "satellites" renew this plea to the West, but the NATO powers have so far managed to evade it.

Is it not obvious that the "satellites" should by this date want the Russians off their necks? Yet Western opposition has been adamant in binding the peoples of East Europe to the Soviet yoke, on the specious ground that it would weaken the "defense posture" of the West. A former Secretary of State, Dean Acheson, contended recently that such a mutual withdrawal "would make our military position weaker, and that as a result our forces would be *less desired wherever they may remain,* and that withdrawal from one area would spread to all overseas areas, thus weakening our entire defense system." (Italics added.)

He was correct. Any form of "disengagement" in Europe—or any-where else—would knock the bottom out of the alliance system; it would mark the end of U.S. military hegemony over the weaker nations of the world. No one could have put this in blunter language than one of NATO's co-authors. Now that the "entire defense system" is in such disarray—for quite other reasons than what Acheson feared—the Rapacki Plan and others like it can no longer be swept under the Washington rug. The collapse of NATO, like disused scaffolding, has allowed the light to enter windows which for twenty years the general public never knew existed.

Humpty Dumpty Cut in Two

This brings us to what is called "European Unity" as a cure for NATO. We meet with a paradox immediately. It is the essence of the NATO case for survival that the Alliance is a step toward European integration. Yet the obvious failure to attain unity within NATO itself results in post-poning the hope of European integration still further. NATO is now caught in a vicious circle. "NATO's effectiveness has been reduced by the withdrawal of French troops and facilities, for the Alliance is now *cut in two* by the so-called neutral belt of France, Switzerland, and Austria."[12]

If NATO, with the advantages of men, money, and motivation that it has enjoyed for twenty years, *had succeeded* in integrating its fifteen members, then the foundation of European Unity might have been firmly laid. But not only has NATO split militarily, not only has it completely failed to build a political or parliamentary structure, not only has it erected no economic superstructure (the Sixes and Sevens juggle within it), but it has kept the continent of Europe at loggerheads and kept Germany divided for twenty years. Only now, with its approaching dissolution, are there faint hopes arising that the twenty-nine countries that make up the real "Europe" can come closer together.*

12 *The Scotsman,* April 1, 1967.
* The word "integration" is used in this context in the journalistic sense. The term is by no means a simple one to define—see particularly E. B. Haas' monumental *Beyond the Nation State,* Stanford University Press, 1964.

46

NATO's increasing disunity is particularly evident in the field of policy. In a collection of studies, appropriately entitled *NATO in Quest of Cohesion,* Hans J. Morgenthau of the University of Chicago and a consultant to the Department of State has no hesitation in stating that: "The Western alliance has ceased to be an instrument for policies to be pursued in common by its members. A *tour d'horizon* of the world scene presents a shocking picture of disintegration. There is not a single one of the outstanding issues of world politics on which all members of the Alliance see eye to eye. The United States stands alone in its policies vis-à-vis China, South Vietnam, and Cuba . . . As concerns the German question as a whole and the over-all relations between the West and the Soviet Union, irreconcilable divergencies of interest and policies have made abstention from initiative and a passive commitment to the status quo the order of the day . . . The members of the Western alliance have only one obvious interest in common: protection from Communist aggression and subversion."[13]

Professor Morgenthau then proceeds to show, by example after example, how the "balance of terror" theory has become obsolete and that the one theoretical "common protection" which does remain can never be achieved by military means. How much further must Humpty Dumpty disintegrate before all the King's horses and all the King's men despair of putting the scattered pieces back on the wall again?

Even the dictator Premier Antonio de Oliviera Salazar has warned the Western powers that they will not get "automatic co-operation" from Portugal, a founding member. He has described NATO as totally "inadequate" for present needs and a source of "disastrous results." In place of NATO, Premier Salazar has proclaimed a policy of bilateral co-operation with countries that are "ready to co-operate fully with Portugal." Fortunately they can't be many in view of the tightening boycott agreed upon at the U.N. in response to Portugal's misdeeds in Africa. At the same time Salazar has openly accused Washington of "undermining the worldwide positions of its allies," notably of Portugal.[14]

The fact that anti-democratic Portugal also wants to throw off the Washington yoke takes us back to the base of NATO's problem—before de Gaulle upset the apple cart—namely, "how to circumscribe the dominance of the United States." Yet to shake off "the dominance of the United States" is not a call to join some artificial counter-balance in divided Europe, but, simply, to join the human race instead.

"Is it realistic to try to apply to modern conditions a concept of the past, a concept that has proved itself wrong again and again? We cannot solve the problems of international conflict without changing the context

[13] Hans J. Morgenthau: *NATO in Quest of Cohesion,* The Center for Strategic Studies of Georgetown University, Praeger, New York, 1965.
[14] *New York Times,* March 17, 1967.

from which they arise," so states one of the acknowledged leaders of the European Unity movement, Jean Monnet, president of the Action Committee for the United States of Europe, who actually assisted Robert Schuman in preparing the coal and steel plan which led to the formation of the first European Community. Yet he goes on to say: "I am more than ever convinced that world peace can be safeguarded only by the formation of larger entities in the world, meeting and discussing problems inside common institutions. . . . Ultimate success will depend on many things: on the continuance of the efforts of the nations of Europe to achieve unity, on the economic development of the other parts of the world, on the policy which the United States pursues towards a uniting Europe, and on the Soviet Union. Only in a climate of peace developed by the United States, the U.S.S.R., and a uniting Europe can the other nations of the world achieve their aspirations." He asserts that this is "the truly realistic policy"; but he does not seem to realize that the very forces that have rendered the nation-state obsolete as a self-contained or self-centered economic unit have also rendered his artificial "larger entities" equally obsolete. Nowhere in the Monnet philosophy, as he pleads for a start to be made on "economic co-operation between the Common Market and the U.S.S.R.," is there a grasp of, or even mention of, the basic reality of a *world* society where the supranational functions of his assumed "entities" have already found a habitation and a home within the U.N. family of agencies and institutions.*

Of the many fallacies underlying the much publicized European Unity concept, we select two for brief comment. It is to be noted that books and most political speeches about "European Unity" do not even define what "Europe" is. Its proponents assume that it is some vague amalgam of *Western* European peoples who can be somehow "integrated." The nearest actualization of this concept is probably the Council of Europe. Its Assembly and offices at Strassburg and its various appendages— Euratom, Human Rights Commission and Court, and so on in other European centers—have extremely useful functions *inter se*. They are not to be criticized on that score. But these partial Western European institutions (which this author has frequently visited) do not answer the basic needs of genuine "European Unity," least of all offer a solution, in principle or practice, to eventual NATO integration.

This author has followed the evolving complexity of "European Unity" questions ever since he listened as a young man to the impassioned tones of Aristide Briand, with his unkempt lion's head and magnificent gestures, expounding to the League of Nations Assembly in Geneva in the 1930's his grand design of a European Union. But it is a fact of history that the Briand Plan floundered on many shoals, two in particular.

Perhaps the most important of these was that no vital European issue

* Jean Monnet in *European Community,* No. 108, January 1968, Washington, D.C.

—security or disarmament, colonies or trade, international finance or balance of payments—could be solved within Europe itself. Every major European problem was seen, in practice, to be a universal problem, demanding international techniques beyond the geographical confines of the European Continent. The world was small and compact enough, even in those times, to impose global solutions for global problems. Tomorrow, it will be even more so.

Since Briand's days, however, the original Schuman Plan and the emergent Common Market have paraded their wares, and their temporary successes, in the garments of European Unity. This, of course, is a clear misnomer, for they have set barriers across Europe, but not bridges. In response to the plea of the European unionists, this author has drawn attention elsewhere to the beginnings of a permanent and more stable experiment in economic co-operation—under the United Nations, not in extension of a military alliance:

So intense has been the concentration of Cold War publicists on the virtues of "The Six" (three big and three quite small countries) that it will come as a complete surprise to most people that for fifteen years the United Nations, under several brilliant economists and administrators, like Dr. Gunnar Myrdal, has been endeavoring to construct a truly *continental* program of economic co-operation and human welfare on all levels, which has peace instead of conflict as its external goal. ECE (Economic Commission for Europe) and EEC (European Economic Community or "Common Market") may look alike, but in essence they are poles asunder, moving in opposite directions and motivated by contrary philosophies. Their juxtaposition reveals how far we have diverged from the straight path of genuine European "unity," while playing on the hopes and expectations of many generations.[15]

Fraying at the Edges

One of the most intractable obstacles among the permanent disabilities of NATO has been where to find its edges. And that was the other unanswerable objection to Aristide Briand's imaginative "Union of Europe" in the 1930's. No one could ever discover where "Europe" left off. Now, in the jet age, Europe doesn't leave off anywhere. It is one thing to regionalize down from a world organization; it is quite another thing to provincialize up from sovereign states.

"There is another danger in the Mediterranean which may in time be more important than the present danger to the independence of Turkey, Greece, and Italy of an aggressive Russian government," warns Drew Middleton, a peripatetic cold-warrior always in search of trouble spots. He continues: "This danger is the increased nationalism of the nations along the southern shore of the sea from Egypt to Morocco"; and he

[15] J. Avery Joyce: "Europe Meets at Geneva," *The Contemporary Review,* London, August 1962.

49

presses his point thus: "The political danger is that if the West fails to reach agreements with these aroused peoples, agreements which must be more than large scale hand-outs and the retention of quasi-colonialism, North Africa will drift from aggressive nationalism into anarchy." He wrote this before the 1967 Arab-Israeli War had made co-operation between the West and the southern Mediterranean so much more precarious.

In any case, the hopelessness of the "Atlantic Powers" doing anything useful at all seems apparent from the fact that, as he says:

You cannot defend Europe without defending the Mediterranean. But you cannot defend the Mediterranean by defending the northern half of it . . . And because in North Africa the Atlantic powers will have to deal with peoples holding political and religious beliefs totally different from theirs, the political job in North Africa will be as complex and as difficult as any facing the Atlantic alliance in Europe.[16]

NATO is admittedly at a dead end when it comes to North Africa, since the Africans want to be left alone, as we have seen. Moreover, the implications of the Middle East war for NATO were pinpointed at the time in the *Frankfurter Allgemeine Zeitung* as follows: "The crisis and the war give the Atlantic allies of the United States a good deal to think about, for the new planning in NATO is based completely on the strategy of crisis management." The manner in which this particular crisis was "managed" is within the public memory. If NATO had intervened, the crisis would have become a world disaster. So NATO merely looked on and held its breath—while the U.N. again struggled with the realities. It is, every time, the U.N. which lifts the impossible burden off NATO's shoulders.

Let it be added, as a general comment, that *The Defense of Western Europe* is typical of the scores of books in this field which have followed like bubbles in the wake of the good ship NATO as it has zigzagged across two decades; more bubbles will follow as it sinks. They make depressing reading, because they offer no way out for the dilemmas they pose. They can't give the right answers, because they don't ask the right questions. They seek to apply medieval remedies to a Twenty-first Century problem. The alliances they admire are no longer a substitute for the world order they so studiously neglect.

It is easy, perhaps, to forget the confidence which, but a short time ago, simply oozed out of NATO. Said Lord Ismay in an adulatory foreword to *Atlantic Democracy,* by Charles d'Olivier Farran (who was awarded a NATO fellowship for his study):

During the five years that I had the honor of being Secretary-General to the North Atlantic Treaty Organization, I preached in season and out of season that unity among the fifteen countries of the alliance was at once their most powerful and their most essential weapon, and I believe that that view is shared by all the Governments concerned.[17]

[16] Drew Middleton: *The Defense of Western Europe,* Appleton-Century, New York, 1952.
[17] Charles d'Olivier Farran: *Atlantic Democracy,* Praeger, New York, 1957.

It is somewhat ironic that Dr. Farran should remark: "It is a tragedy of the Twentieth Century that ideas have been warped by the manipulation of the words which represent them," for on the same page he asserts that "we seek to show that the NATO member states have something more in common than merely a shared fear of possible Soviet aggression. They are, rather, united by the prevalence in them of true (i.e. parliamentary) democracy."

Perhaps the unfortunate problem of Greece on the east and Portugal on the west is just a minor fraying on the edges? NATO weapons have become both the symbols and instruments of modern dictatorship and colonial domination. What the Greek exiles or the Africans of Angola and Mozambique think of parliamentary democracy, as practiced within NATO, is doubtless an unkind question. Meanwhile, in January 1968, napalm and phosphorus bombs marked "Made in U.S.A." were reported in responsible U.S. newspapers to have been dropped in African villages, according to numerous eyewitness reports and photographs which appeared to be genuine. The villages were part of Portuguese Guinean territory wrested from Portuguese control by nationalist forces fighting for their freedom.

Dr. Farran's book is symptomatic of that vast bulk of NATO books which have appeared on both sides of the Atlantic. They begin, as his does, by dividing the globe neatly between the good guys and the bad guys. Having adopted a divisive premise at the start, they run on through the subsequent syllogisms without noticing the widening gap between fact and fallacy, as the argument proceeds on a closed circuit:

Asia and Africa are awakening. More than two-thirds of Mankind lives in them. On their eventual choice of Communism or real Democracy, not only their future, but also ours, emphatically depends. At this cross-roads of History we must use every effort which lies within our power to explain to the uncommitted peoples, as well as our own populations (not all of whom are so securely averse to Communism as we may care to imagine)—even to those now living in Eastern Europe under Communist regimes—exactly what it is for which we stand.

If it is true, as Dr. Farran says, that "the older call of exclusively patriotic loyalty is not yet dead, but it is dying," and that "supranational ideological loyalties are very rapidly taking its place," then why doesn't this recognition of a wider loyalty mean something more than the fortuitous mixed bag of "good guy" nation-states inspired by "a shared fear of possible Soviet aggression," which is what NATO is? If, as the writer states, the world stands in need of parliamentary democracy, then why does he not look to that actual achievement of expanding parliamentary democracy on which the Western world has labored long and finally produced in the United Nations Charter? Why not tell us how to shape it more effectively so that the bad guys are educated to become better guys?

"It is not enough for us to label ourselves anti-Communist,'" he rightly insists. How sensible it is, too, that "a cause flourishes by what it stands for; not by what it opposes. We must be 'pro' something, and something far more attractive than Communism. Now is the time to make clear to the World what that something is."

Exactly! But how disappointing that the writer's acceptance of a shrinking globe and of the fact that world peace is one and indivisible, does not lead him to discover the evolution of parliamentary democracy beyond the nation-state? Does not the Charter itself, with its "We, the People," its World Assembly, its World Council, its World Court, its World Secretariat, convey to the normal educated mind some idea of a *World* Parliament? If a shift of loyalty is now called for so desperately, then why not to *World Loyalty?* How can a "NATO loyalty," on the facts as we know them, have any tangible meaning to anyone—except, perhaps, to its salaried officials?

We have looked carefully into Dr. Farran's book not merely because it is typical of the academic studies which are being officially sponsored by NATO, but because its search for an undefinable entity called "The Atlantic Community" and its insistence on a continued Cold War in which Asian, African and other peoples *must* take one side or the other is as dangerous as it is unrewarding. "While Democracy is an Idea, it is also machinery," the writer asserts; but while "the idea is universally the same, the machinery varies in accordance with national conditions and circumstances." Yes, but he completely misses the point that the machinery must also be *universal,* and adapted as time goes on to the varieties of national life and social conditions and the international needs which go to make up the human race which is universal.

The Rot Spreads

Now that criticism is mounting, there are two main lines of responsible reaction to NATO: one says that NATO was an enormous blunder from the beginning (a view taken in this book) and the other says that it was the right thing to do in 1949, but it is now obsolete—or fast becoming so (a view we shall now examine). In either case, both sides say the time has come to re-shape NATO and look afresh at the Alliance system as a whole. Of course, those who take the first view are more likely to call for drastic and wholesale changes, if not outright abolition. Even those like former Prime Minister Sir Alec Douglas-Home, who blithely said in Washington sometime back that "NATO has done its job—extremely well," might still be persuaded that it has served its turn and can now be honorably discharged.

Quite apart, however, from NATO's intrinsic weaknesses, some new facts about the Communist "enemy" have come into the discussion which were not present or obvious enough when NATO was devised. This new evidence can be summed up under two headings: (a) The Communist World is split from top to bottom and so no longer presents the monolithic conspiracy against the West which dominated the thinking of political leaders in the 1950's; and (b) The new face of China as a nuclear super-power, in spite of its "containment" by the United States, calls for a world program for bringing the Communist and non-Communist peoples to-gether to save them from a common grave. Long-range programs of co-existence between the alleged "two worlds"—assuming Russia has not changed sides meanwhile—gain momentum from today's swift techno-logical changes and particularly from the emergence of the Third World, with a mind and will of its own.

In *The New Eastern Europe,* Professor J. F. Brown of the Manchester and Michigan Universities, examines in detail the fascinating story of how, in the last decade, the satellite states of Eastern Europe began to move away from Stalinist uniformity and the absolute control of the Kremlin, toward a position of increasing diversity and even autonomy. Studying each state individually, he evaluates, for example, the influence of Yugo-slavia's revisionism and Rumania's success in developing policies inde-pendent of the Soviet leadership, and, what is most interesting of all, the varying responses of the East Europeans to the challenge of the Peking regime, on the one hand, and to the East-West détente, on the other. In the future, contends Professor Brown, the force of economic circumstance and the clear needs of an industrial and technical world will bring both greater freedom to these nations and also many more reasons for working with the advanced Western nations. Generally speaking, he says, referring to the East European states, "their various schemes for economic reform have provisions to free foreign commerce from the more crippling kinds of bureaucratic interference. The stultifying effect of bilateralism is also understood, and the first gropings toward a multilateral trading system have been made. There are attempts to study Western market conditions and to adapt East European industry to them."[18]

Since he wrote these words the process of liberalization has accelerated. Even the U.S. Secretary of State has shown himself willing at times to notice the bare existence of this new set of facts. But he has a unique way of turning the facts on their heads, so as not to disturb the military status quo. This flair was well brought out in an address that Dean Rusk gave to the Council of Foreign Relations in New York on May 24, 1966, when he stated:

Significant changes have occurred within the Communist world. It has long ceased to be monolithic, and evolutionary influences are visible in most of the Communist states. But the leaders of both the principal Communist nations are committed to promotion of the Communist world revolution—even while

[18] J. F. Brown: *The New Eastern Europe,* Praeger, New York, 1966.

they disagree bitterly on tactics . . . The clearest lesson of the nineteen thirties and forties is that aggression feeds on aggression. I am aware that Mao and Ho Chi Minh are not Hitler and Mussolini. But we should not forget what we have learned about the anatomy and physiology of aggression.

So that closes the newly opened book with a bang! Whatever Dean Rusk might or might not have learned about "aggression"—a term still undefined in international law—he must have known that there was not a single Chinese soldier in Vietnam at the time he spoke, yet half a million American soldiers were there, fighting the Vietnamese in their own country. This Alice-in-Wonderland terminology becomes more transparently dishonest as time goes on, for it subverts the facts themselves. For example, Dean Rusk noted modestly that "the solidarity of NATO has had a good deal to do with reducing the 'sense of threat' from Eastern Europe." The truth is exactly the opposite. It has been the impending break-up of NATO that has led directly and very quickly to the loosening of the Eastern bloc— hence to a lessening of its own "sense of threat."

It is not to be expected that the NATO Generals—or their Secretaries —are going to accept anything like this. NATO's present Secretary-General, Manilio Brosio of Italy, has dubiously said: "The doctrine of peaceful co-existence was formulated not to end the struggle, but to shift it to the less dangerous arena of political pressure and diplomatic maneuver. Not only does the political threat in Europe remain, but the Soviet Union is actually gaining ground in the steady, deliberate struggle she is waging against the cohesion and strength of Western Europe."

The promising "liberalization" of the Communist regime in Czechoslovakia might well have evolved normally during 1968 but for the fact that some of the Warsaw Pact members interpreted it as a NATO attempt to weaken their cohesion further. In the result, Czech people were ground to the dust between the millstones of the Cold War. But was NATO ever intended to consolidate the Communist World?

"What NATO originally meant was above all an American commitment to Europe—an essentially unilateral guarantee in the guise of an alliance of equals—sufficient to deter the Soviets from aggression. Everything else was mainly supplementary and, it was hoped, not too expensive burden sharing," says Bernard Brodie in *Escalation and the Nuclear Option,* and he adds: "The other side of the coin is that the Soviet Union has for a long time seemed to most Europeans to be offering no serious threat of aggression. There is still, to be sure, a deep ideological cleavage between the Soviet Union and the NATO Powers, and there is the continuing territorial division of Germany. Yet even in these respects the situation today looks somehow less grim than it did only a few years ago."[19]

Yet Brodie (another RAND product) plays down the strategic importance to the West of the Sino-Soviet split and he suggests: "Each side needs, no doubt, to be in competition with the other to prove that it is

[19] Bernard Brodie: *Escalation and the Nuclear Option,* Princeton, 1966.

orthodox in its support of 'national liberation' movements; but how does the split affect the *risks* that each is willing to take in offering that proof?" For it is an essential part of Brodie's thesis, as we shall note later, that nuclear strategy is still worth its exorbitant cost. He does not want the West to "weaken" on account of the fractionalization of the Communist world, for Professor Brodie is an expert on escalation and it would be a severe intellectual jolt to find the escalator running down instead of up. He regrets that the deterrent effects of America's gigantic nuclear capabilities have already been "diminished" by public statements of reluctance to *use* them.

Realism sometimes makes strange bed-fellows. Even the White House, it can be recalled, was reluctant to castigate General de Gaulle's decision. The latter had set in motion many similar defections, both ways, East as well as West. It is more than likely that the restrained White House approach in 1966 to the North Atlantic upset was partly motivated by mounting Rumanian and similar Eastern discontent with Soviet domination of the Warsaw Pact. Violent denunciations of "military blocs" were being made at that time, for instance, by the Rumanian Communist leader Nicolae Ceausescu.[20] It was NATO's lack of solidarity which was reducing the "sense of threat" from Eastern Europe. So why regret it? Why oppose it? Why not take full advantage of it?

Since the United Nations is a "mirror to mankind," as U Thant has repeatedly said, it is not surprising that it has been in U.N. circles that the disintegration of the Communist World was early reflected. The movement of Communist-governed states away from the Soviet orbit by no means began with the discovery of a rival solar system in the New China. Tito of Yugoslavia had already proved that point many years back.* Yet neither rebel Yugoslavia nor little Albania, nor even harassed Hungary, at any time sought in any way whatsoever the protection of NATO's "nuclear umbrella" against Russia—nor would they have received it, if they had done so. Nonetheless, the Soviet Union, which was alleged to be poised ready to swoop against the West at fifteen minutes' notice, was successfully held at bay by Yugoslavia over the years. Nor is it a coincidence that the Russian intervention in Hungary in 1956 happened at the very moment when British, French, and Israeli bombs were falling and their troops were being landed in Egypt. Far less was it a coincidence that the Russian hawks pounced on Czechoslovakia when their chief adversary was enmeshed in the jungles of Vietnam.

Regarding tiny impoverished Albania, let us listen to the Foreign Minister of this thoroughly red-dyed Communist country addressing the U.N. General Assembly's Special Session on June 26, 1967, when he contended that "the world had categorically condemned" the recent meet-

[20] *New York Times,* May 20, 1966.
* *See* especially J. C. Campbell: *Tito's Separate Road,* Harper & Row, New York, 1967.

ings of the leaders of the United States and the Soviet Union—the two States "primarily responsible for the situation in the Middle East." This collaboration between the U.S. and the U.S.S.R. was "a sign of new imperialist-revisionist plots" against all peace-loving peoples, he went on. The Soviet request for the convening of that Assembly was intended to "camouflage the treachery" of the Kosygin Government toward the Arabs and to provide "an opportunity for bargaining and plotting by the leaders of the two Powers, at the expense of the peoples of other States, *for their policy of world domination.*" (Italics added.)

The Albanian Foreign Minister then asked why the United States fleet remained in the Mediterranean and what the Soviet fleet was doing there too. Whom were they defending, and against whom? "The fleets of the imperialists and the revisionists are called peace fleets; but we can confirm that they sought to divide the booty gained from their plots." But, he continued, "You are in no position to frighten anyone." The peoples were resolved to die fighting, and one of them was Albania.

When he condemns the Soviet Union, however, for preventing the People's Republic of China from regaining its rights in the United Nations, because they (the Russians) feared to lose their monopoly over the decisions of the Organization, and when he prophesied that "the People's Republic of China will gain its seat here," the patent injustice and absurdity of his attack was apparent to all, since it has been the Soviet Union and not pro-Chinese Albania which has, day in and day out, campaigned for China's "legal rights to be restored" (as the phrase goes) at the U.N.

This basic split over China is so obvious a clash of ideology that it requires no detailed argument in this book. But the Arab-Israeli crisis in the summer of 1967 revealed other long-standing fissures in the Communist front. "The sharply contrasting reactions of the Yugoslav and Rumanian Governments to the Middle East crisis have provided a new perspective on current Eastern European politics," said a *New York Times* editorial at the time: "Yugoslavia followed the Soviet line on the Mideast as dutifully as if it were still a satellite; Rumania gave new evidence of its insistence on truly independent sovereignty."

Yet this potent disunity has not altogether pleased the Pentagon planners who, like the makers of silver shrines at Ephesus, are suspicious of this new teaching. As *The Spectator* of London put their dilemma (March 29, 1968):

"Each successive stage in the disintegration of the Communist monolith brings anguished regrets from Washington that the West does not offer a more cohesive pattern to appeal to the East. But, in fact, it is the diversity of attitudes and policies in the West that has contributed largely to the diversity of attitudes in the East."

56

A Forthcoming Marriage?

It might be useful to recall some of the phases of this growing diversity. The Warsaw Pact has eight members: the Soviet Union, Poland, Czechoslovakia, East Germany, Hungary, Rumania, Bulgaria and Albania, though Albania is now understandably inactive. The total armed forces of the six others, excluding the Soviet Union, are estimated at just over a million men, of which 890,000 are ground troops, 49,000 are in naval service, and 139,000 are in the air force. Communist China, North Korea, North Vietnam, and Mongolia usually attend Pact meetings as observers. But the Political Consultative Committee of the Warsaw Pact is so snarled over its own problems of "unity" that it has not met since January 1965.

Soviet troops were withdrawn from Rumania in 1958, but they are still stationed in East Germany, Hungary and Poland. This position was expressed by Nicolae Ceausescu, the outspoken Chief of the Rumanian Communist party and now Head of State, in these terms: "One of the barriers in the past to co-operation among peoples are the military blocs and the existence of military bases and troops of some states on the territories of other states . . . The existence of these blocs, as well as the dispatching of troops to other countries, *represents an anachronism that is incompatible with the national independence and sovereignty of the peoples and with normal interstate relations.*"[21]

In July 1968 Czechoslovakia had called for a basic revision of the Warsaw Pact, "to ensure genuine equality of its members." The Czechoslovak Communist party's chief for military affairs charged that representatives on the pact's joint command had been limited by the Soviet Union to liaison roles. Part of the proposed revision would be rotation of the top command among the member nations.

The same trend has been obvious in the economic relations of the East European group, which are focused to some extent in Comecon. Michael Kaser, British economist, makes this observation: "The dispute over Comecon's future, made frankly public in 1964, was politically centered on a new Rumanian nationalism in the context of the Soviet clash with China. The economics of the dispute are, however, rooted in the origins of the organization . . . The principle of sovereignty was entrenched in Comecon's founding declaration of 1949, when Soviet leadership was undisputed, but since 1956—the year of the assertions of Hungarian and Polish nationality—the autonomy of members as such has become a reality. In 1958 Bulgaria, and in 1963 Rumania, made Comecon the testing-ground for particular demonstrations of independence."[22]

It is perhaps a token straw in the wind of change that in August 1967 the Foreign Minister of West Germany (Willy Brandt) visited Bucharest

[21] *New York Times,* May 17, 1967.
[22] M. Kaser: *Comecon,* Oxford University Press, London, 1967.

and received Rumania's promise to support West Germany's entry into the seven nation Danube Commission as a full member. Germany was a member before World War II, but was not readmitted when the Commission, which regulates Danube River traffic and navigation projects, was reconstituted in 1948. Since the Danube originates in West Germany, its Government has a vital interest in membership; the other members being Austria, Bulgaria, Czechoslovakia, Hungary, Rumania, the Soviet Union and Yugoslavia.

But only four of the Warsaw Pact powers, Russia, Czechoslovakia, Poland, and East Germany, met in East Berlin recently—as these countries feel most directly threatened by West Germany—to discuss a reorganization of Soviet forces along the borders of Germany. Such a reorganization, however, as we saw in August 1968 did little to resolve the Pact's inner stresses.

The truth can be recalled on the plain evidence of dates and documents that the Warsaw Pact had its origins solely as a military response to NATO. Its ramshackle existence has owed more to NATO than to its Communist designers. Professor Kaser sums up the vacillating nature of the Treaty over the years thus:

The signature of the Treaty in May 1955, by the same states that were then members of Comecon, took place within a framework of existing bilateral treaties with the U.S.S.R.—again, as with Comecon in 1949. For its first six years the Organization had little more than a paper existence, and served only to formalize relations with the dominant partner, who regarded the armed forces of the others as the extension of its own defense system.

Let two later examples suffice. At the time that MLF was under attack at the U.N. General Assembly in December 1964, the Foreign Minister of Bulgaria argued—as, in fact, events proved later: "The establishment of multilateral nuclear forces presents a direct danger to the security and the further improvement of the situation in the Balkans and the Eastern Mediterranean through the involvement of the South Balkans in the dangerous military and political plans of NATO. The Balkan peoples need tranquillity and mutual confidence and not the presence of NATO nuclear forces, which can only be factors of tension and of menace."

The second example comes from another reluctant member of the Warsaw Pact, Poland itself, whose Prime Minister told the U.N. Special General Assembly in June 1967: "We are faced with the policy from the position of strength in a new, by no means improved, edition. Its aims are the same as in the time of the late Mr. Dulles: American domination of the world . . . These methods, reminiscent of the Dulles years, are, in spite of the large application of computers, even less exact in their calculations. I am afraid that the more the present leaders of United States policy become convinced of their abilities to control the course of events, the more they become slaves of the chain-reaction which they themselves have unleashed. Here Vietnam serves as an example, as an ever more ominous memento."

When, therefore, the Communist party leaders of Eastern and Western Europe met in Czechoslovakia in April 1967 and signed a declaration upholding present frontiers in Europe, thus hoping to persuade the West to abandon NATO in favor of an "all-European security system," they were not just hatching another "Communist plot" to subvert the West, but seeking, as experienced and nationalistic-minded leaders of long standing in their countries, to gain a form of security for their own people more durable than the Soviet umbrella could ever offer them. The Chinese problem apparently did not come up at the public sessions; but the chiefs of the twenty-four Communist parties specifically urged an all-European conference on European peace and security in place of Western plans for renewing NATO. Furthermore, when the Soviet Politburo chiefs and the Czechoslovak Presidium met face to face on Slovak soil early in August 1968, after months of shadow-boxing, the outer shell of the Warsaw Pact had already cracked beyond repair.

And from *inside* NATO the doubters are changing their tune. "The German Government, the German Bundestag, and the overwhelming majority of German public opinion," said Erik Blumenfeld, West Germany's delegate to NATO at its Brussels session in November 1967, "wishes to continue its efforts to bring about a real and lasting *détente* and understanding and good neighborly relations with our East European neighbors, and also with the Soviet Union, in spite of the fact that they seemingly have turned down the hand that has been stretched out."

"In the current atmosphere of a prosperous Europe, expanding its contacts with Eastern Europe," wrote Don Cook from Paris, as he watched the departure of the NATO officials, "there is no point trying to pretend that NATO forces have to be kept at double the manpower of forces in East Germany in order to maintain peace. It is difficult to feel that war is in the offing when Fiat of Italy and Renault of France are building automobile works in Russia, and when the West Germans and the French are jointly installing a diesel-engine factory in Hungary."[23]

The following opinions in the British liberal *Guardian* would seem to sum up tidily the attitude adopted in the present book on the current relationship of NATO with the Warsaw Pact. Discussing a recent NATO Foreign Ministers' meeting in Brussels, the journal also reported a contemporaneous meeting of the Warsaw Pact countries in Warsaw, and asks: "Why can't the members of both alliances meet together?" Even admitting that "events in Southeast Asia have temporarily disrupted East-West relations . . . and Russian diplomats are fully occupied by their quarrel with the Chinese," what is more important is that:

[23] Don Cook: *Reader's Digest,* April 1967.

Nobody now thinks that the Russians are intending to launch a military attack against the West. Nobody in Moscow, one may also assume, genuinely believes that NATO is planning to roll back Communism in Eastern Europe, with the West German *Bundeswehr* in the vanguard. Why, then, is it proving so difficult to wind up the two alliances? . . . *This can be done when Ministers from the rival alliances meet together, and not in separate cities.* (Italics added.)

The General Assembly in 1967 saw for the first time a Communist diplomat elected (with only one negative vote) to preside over the Forum of the Nations. This did not mean an ascendancy of Communism at the United Nations, as some Cold War critics rushed to proclaim. Of the 123 members, only 11 have Communist governments. Ten years back, with less than 60 members, 10 were then Communist—only Cuba has become (if it really has) "Communist" since. This lack of specific Communist votes at the U.N. and its steady proportionate diminution over the years has been a difficult fact for the cold warriors to swallow, for the U.N. has always been a main target on their battlefield.

When Corneliu Manescu of Rumania became United Nations President in 1967, NATO received its *coup de grâce*. "The General Assembly's decision," he said, "to elect the representative of a socialist country as President for the current session is a recognition of the need for an equal participation by the various regions and systems in the work of the United Nations. No one could objectively review the history of this Organization without acknowledging the part played by the countries of Eastern Europe in its founding and development, and their active role in international life as a whole."

Britain at the Crossroads

That NATO should have developed into a minor branch of American global supremacy has been increasingly recognized and resented in Britain by both Labor and Conservative opinion. Said the London *Times*: "It is a poor commentary on the fertility of American military thinking that the hierarchy's only reaction to problems in Vietnam has been to ask, like Oliver Twist, for more." *The Times* then poses a very important question: "Is this the same military machine which guides NATO in sophisticated matters of global nuclear strategy and crisis management?"[24]

Is it not indeed invidious that the external relations of fifty-five millions of free people who live in the British Isles, with its cementing role in the external relations of the whole Commonwealth, should remain at the mercy of those "bright young aides" whom Robert S. McNamara, ex-doyen of General Motors, brought in with him to work in the Pentagon "planning systems analysis" and who, equipped with the most modern complex of computers, have been making up the minds of NATO's generals ever since?

[24] The London *Times,* July 14, 1967.

"Have we arrived at that technocratic utopia where judgment is a machine product?" asked a Senate Sub-Committee recently. One cannot argue with a computer; yet a cursory review of what has come out of Mr. McNamara's and his successor's punch-cards in Vietnam since 1961 should keep any British Government as far away as possible from (to quote the same Senate Sub-Committee) "the risks and dangers of relying too heavily on computer analysis in defense and policy matters."[25]

Two token examples of the moral revival of Britain as an influence for peace can be given here—for they point to a re-emerging military independence and international leadership, which had disappeared to vanishing point under the previous Government and continued to do so during the 1964-66 phase of Harold Wilson's treks across the Atlantic to ensure Britain's financial stability at the price of the moral support he appeared to give to the Washington view of the Vietnam War. Since then, it is the U.S. which, with the world's gold market still in London, is desperately seeking financial stability.

First, we recall that, at the 1966 U.N. General Assembly, Foreign Secretary George Brown spoke for his Government in a language almost as severe as that of his French counterpart, Couve de Murville, who preceded him at the rostrum of the nations, when he insisted that there could not be, nor should there be, a military solution to the Vietnam conflict, but that the bombing of North Vietnam by United States and South Vietnamese aircraft should cease, and that a pledge should be given that bombing would not be resumed unless and until a Geneva-type conference had met and failed. "As soon as is practicable the High Command of each side should simultaneously give orders that their forces would not initiate any new aggressive actions and the present International Control Commission should be strengthened by the addition of representatives of other Powers and have at its disposal an international Peacekeeping Force." This continued to be Government policy. The Foreign Secretary's speech gave no aid and comfort to the escalationists, but opened the way for an even stronger British initiative.

Second, Britain's permanent delegate at the U.N., Lord Caradon (who announced his first appearance with the simple affirmation: "I am a U.N. man"), had this to say:

What does this mean for each of us? It means a conscious decision by all Member States to use this Organization not for the peddling of selfish and shortsighted national interest, but in order to create an international rule of law. We have taken our decision. Britain now has a Government which fundamentally believes in the United Nations and which has, time and time again in this past year, been prepared to make sacrifices, some of them far from easy, to help forward the purpose of the United Nations.

[25] *New York Times,* August 21, 1967.

With this healthy trend affirmed and with the demise of NATO in sight, the time has surely come for Britain to consolidate its new found leadership and carry with it, as it should, all the thirty or more Commonwealth countries—even if Australia and New Zealand may take a little longer to learn the tragic lesson of Pentagon commitmentship in Vietnam.

"Change is our ally. In this, as in other fields, we must not only not be afraid of it, we must be active in welcoming it. NATO must be kept up-to-date, firm, yet flexible. But this can only be done by each one of us turning our eyes beyond national frontiers, national defense ministries and national considerations." Such was Prime Minister Harold Wilson's peroration at the NATO Ministerial Meeting in London in May 1965. We cannot agree more with his concluding sentence—in fact, it cancels out the penultimate sentence altogether. The really important question is: How *much* change?

Making Political Sense

How has this trend evolved since in Britain? A brief recapitulation is pertinent. An entertaining dialogue between the Government and itself appeared in the Statement on Defense issued February 22, 1966 under the title of "Britain's Military Role," as follows:

Defense must be the servant of foreign policy, not its master. Military forces must be designed accordingly . . . We are compelled to plan the main features of our defense policy a decade ahead; it takes at least ten years to develop and introduce a major new weapon system, and at least five years to produce base facilities abroad . . . Defense policy, therefore, has to be based on assumptions which must be constantly revised and are less certain the further we look ahead.

From this important confession we learn three basic truths: (1) Defense is a branch of foreign policy—not *vice versa;* (2) Foreign Policy must be planned ten years ahead; and (3) Nothing can be certain—we are all at sea as to what can happen in ten years! (Presumably this applies to all the other fellow members of the U.N. too?) Hence, the Statement continues: "the Government must take some firm decisions based on the best predictions it can make . . . Above all, the Government can and must decide in broad terms what sort of role Britain should play in the world *in ten years' time,* and what part its military forces should play *in supporting that role.* In short, it has to decide what sort of military capability *is likely to make political sense."* (Italics added.)

The point at issue could not have been put more clearly. The Government sensibly insists: "Recent history underlines the importance to Britain, as to all other countries, of strengthening the United Nations as *the main instrument for keeping peace.* Britain is already making a major contribution to the United Nations forces in Cyprus, and has offered further units for logistic support of a United Nations force, whenever this is required in future." (Italics added.)

It should be noted that this valuable piece of insurance in Cyprus is put into the peace force of the U.N.—not NATO's. And although, continues the Government, political disagreements have "set limits to the United Nations' authority for peacekeeping, it remains a major aim of British policy to enable the United Nations to take on more in the years to come." This is all to the good. But is it really sufficient to leave good enough alone for ten years? That "more" is needed *now*, and should be spelled out in policy terms.

The Government recognizes, meanwhile, that "most Great Powers now realize that their own security can only be safeguarded in the long run by halting the international arms race. The trend of military technology suggests that the survival of humanity itself will soon depend on making progress towards general and complete disarmament. But this will not be brought about overnight . . . The most urgent and immediate problem is to stop the further spread of nuclear weapons. We accordingly aim to internationalize our nuclear strategic forces in order to discourage further proliferation and to strengthen the Alliance."

There we arrive at the snag in the ten year program. Does "more" really mean "to strengthen the Alliance"? Alas! It would seem so, for the Government says: "We must be ready to continue living in a world in which the United Nations has not yet assumed effective responsibility for keeping the peace, and the arms race has not yet been halted." But how can the U.N. become effective, so long as an arms race, conducted by rival alliances, goes spiraling up with impunity?

The spectral voices of the Nineteenth Century creep into the Government's dialogue: "In such a world the first purpose of our armed forces will be to defend the freedom of the British people. The security of these Islands still depends primarily on preventing war in Europe. For this reason, we regard the continuation of the North Atlantic alliance as vital to our survival . . . Broad guide-lines governing the possible recourse by NATO to nuclear weapons in self-defense were agreed at the Athens meeting of the NATO Council in 1962; increased participation by officers of member countries in nuclear planning and control was approved at the Ottawa meeting in 1963 . . ."

The time-worn argument proceeds: "To deter aggression in Europe," a Special Committee of Defense Ministers met for the first time in November 1965 to "reduce to the minimum any uncertainty" on the foregoing issues. But has it done this? We have, continues the Statement, "urged on the Alliance that it should abandon those military preparations which rest on the assumption that a general war in Europe might last for several months. At the same time, NATO must maintain enough conventional forces to deal with small-scale conflicts in the European theater without automatic resort to nuclear weapons, when the origin of the conflict may be uncertain and the intentions of the enemy obscure."

Do the British people really understand—and accept—that their survival rests on this fragile guesswork? With escalation proceeding before their eyes in Southeast Asia and more subtly in the Middle East, does their security "primarily" depend on "preventing war *in Europe*"? That is what the Government seemed to be insisting on in 1966: "A direct threat to our survival seems less likely outside Europe. Although we have important economic interests in the Middle East, Asia, and elsewhere, military force is not the most suitable means of protecting them, and they would not alone justify heavy British defense expenditure." If this is so, then why should military force be the more "suitable" means for Europe, of all places? Is not this the dark hand of NATO again? It doesn't make sense otherwise. Who is pressuring Britain?

The ramifications of this exercise in sophisticated guesswork, as propounded by the Government, need not be pursued here, but one conclusion is obvious: a defense policy based on (a) the continued arms race and (b) the assumption of a take-over of West Europe from East Europe could carry no conviction with any sensible person today. It just does not "make political sense." In truth, no British Defense Minister can any longer make political sense at all—military technology outpaces him every three years. His weapons are obsolescent before they leave the drawing-board and obsolete before they leave the factory. Only by replacing NATO by true mutual security and insisting on a disarmament agreement can he make political sense; and this means, among other things, acting as an efficient broker between the Americans and the Russians. France does not want to do this; West Germany cannot; but Britain can and must!

A contemporary appraisal of some of the White Paper's financial implications is perhaps germane. Although the proposed 1969-70 defense budget will be reduced by 400 million pounds to 2,000 million pounds, and Britain will be spending 6 per cent instead of nearly 7 per cent of the national income on defense, this is still a considerable amount for a Britain facing the economic challenge of the 1970's. "It compares with 5 per cent in West Germany, and less among some of the smaller NATO allies, and with only 3.5 per cent in Australia. But the difference is less startling when compared with the United States (8.9 per cent) and when one remembers that most of our allies have conscription."[26]

On this last question, the British have had another important talking-point with their American allies, who are finding the conscription of more and more of their young manpower as onerous as it is controversial. (Toward the end of 1967 churches across the United States were offering their premises as "sanctuary" for draft card burners.) So the clipping off of "foreign commitments" in the British White Paper pointed to a salutary

[26] Andrew Wilson in *The Observer,* February 27, 1966.

moral for others, namely: If you want freedom for your young men, don't try to become a global gendarme! Self-defense today does not need resort to the press-gang, but building a world-wide military empire certainly does.

Affluent America, too, is slowly beginning to learn from austerity Britain in terms of the warning voice of Roy Jenkins who said in the spring of 1967, even before he became Chancellor of the Exchequer: "Britain continued to believe it our duty to police large parts of the world, to defend our former dependencies . . . *I do not believe that the attempt has worked.* It has produced twenty years of severe overstrain, with grave effects upon our economic performance. And these effects have themselves undermined the object of the exercise."

The Observer military commentator quoted earlier offers a further observation, which we shall pursue in a later chapter: "Britain's ultimate participation in an international peacekeeping force is to be welcomed. By requiring us to discard the concept of self-contained forces all over the world, it can lead to our meeting the real need which peacekeeping imposes: the provision of logistic and other specialized units, perhaps surplus to purely national needs, but essential to United Nations operations, such as those now in Cyprus . . . Looking further ahead, to a possible permanent U.N. peacekeeping organization, it seems almost inevitable that the part of Britain's forces available for tasks outside Europe will have to develop more and more into a kind of military Meccano set—a series of parts, constantly interchangeable to meet unexpected needs in *ad hoc* task forces." It is toward this kind of transition from the myths which have dominated NATO to meeting the "real need which peacekeeping imposes" that Britain can contribute so much during the 1970's.

In this direction, more and more parliamentarians are moving in support of U.N. initiative—as when the British Parliamentary Group for World Government set down on July 6, 1966 in the House of Commons time-table the following motion:

That this House, recognizing that the current meetings of the U.N. Special Committee on Peace-Keeping may lead to a radical reorganization of the structure of the Organization, calls on Her Majesty's Government to propose the establishment of a permanent peace-keeping fund to finance future peace-keeping operations; . . . and calls on Her Majesty's Government for its part, to reorganize the machinery of Government so that peace-keeping and disarmament activities, which are so intimately connected, are dealt with by a single department of the Foreign Office.

Government in a White Sheet

In the 1967 White Paper, the Government announced a plan for the progressive withdrawal of British forces from the historic life-line to the

Far East—from Malta to Hong Kong—and also, incidentally, the reduction of manpower to NATO on the Continent. This carried with it the transformation of the Royal Navy to a minor "policing" function. These important changes will be "phased" over the next decade. However, there will presumably be enough left to play some part in the "defense of Europe" and to contribute to "stability" in Southeast Asia. (These assurances were no doubt included to meet attacks from the Tory benches and complaints from the United States that Britain was selling the Alliance short.)

"Far-called, our navies melt away," prophesied Kipling in 1897. Yet the Navy will still perform "a valuable peace-keeping function outside Europe by the unobtrusive and flexible exercise of maritime power," the White Paper states modestly. Aircraft carriers are to go, and what is left of the Navy "will rely for support upon Royal Air Force land-based aircraft." The abandonment of the big base at Aden in November 1967 was to be followed by a complete withdrawal of British forces in the Southeast Asian complex in the early 1970's by the progressive reduction of forces in Singapore and Malaysia. By implication these "obligations" will be left to Australia, New Zealand and the United States under SEATO—if SEATO lasts that long.

Such drastic changes in the disposition of the Old Empire seem to have worried the Americans a great deal more than the British themselves. It is untrue that this withdrawal has been militarily feasible only because the United States' umbrella is there to protect the Asian people deprived of the Union Jack. The facts are quite the opposite. Washington has long discouraged withdrawal of British forces and in some cases (from Singapore, for example) prevailed on London to stay longer than was first proposed, only to be disappointed when it came to a showdown early in 1968.

There simply must be major changes in Government policy with the aim of saving some 1,000 million pounds (approximately two and a half billion dollars) by 1970, insisted the most conservative and pro-American among the financial pundits: "Defense is one obvious candidate. Government expenditure here has been one of the fastest growing debit items in the balance of payments during the past decade or so . . . The rest of the world, the Americans included, can hardly expect Britain in its present economic situation to go on bearing the remnant of its imperial role, which before the last War was borne almost entirely by the Indian and Malayan budget."[27]

The new situation was tersely summed up by the Defense Correspondent of the London *Observer* as follows: "Defense is in the melting-pot. If the Government makes the drastic cuts necessitated by the economic crisis,

[27] *The Financial Times,* London, January 4, 1968.

major British commitments—to Europe or to the countries East of Suez—will have to go. Some commitments, *such as those of the Southeast Asia Treaty Organization, are relatively easy to terminate.* Others, to Malaysia and Singapore, for example, are more difficult."[28] (Italics added.) The point about SEATO's demise was made in the previous chapter—now, necessity becomes the mother of intention.

Coming to 1968, "The foundation of Britain's security," said the White Paper on Britain's defense, published in February 1968, "now as always lies in the maintenance of peace in Europe." *The first priority must be* "to give the fullest possible support to the North Atlantic Alliance." In fact, Britain's contribution will increase as British forces are brought back from Southeast Asia and the Middle East and assigned to NATO command in Europe and the Mediterranean. Denis Healey, Minister of Defense, had this to announce about the concentration of British forces in Europe and beyond:

Over the next four years we will be withdrawing our forces from the Persian Gulf and from Singapore and Malaysia . . . but as a result we shall be making a bigger contribution to the defense of Western Europe . . . I believe that our ability to make a bigger contribution in Europe in the 1970's will prove to be of great political importance to our relations not only with our European neighbors, but to our position in the world as a whole."

To which a direct reply can be given in these simple terms, as amplified later in this and subsequent chapters: Britain's most important political contribution to the defense of peace (of which "Western Europe" is but an arbitrary geographical segment) in the 1970's will be, on the negative side, to repudiate the continued Southeast Asia military intervention of the Americans and to disengage completely from NATO in Europe; and, on the positive side, to initiate mutual security undertakings both with Russia and with China and to transfer step-by-step, financially and organizationally, United Kingdom one-time "policing" functions to the World Organization.

Reacting to the unwelcome news of the British 1967-68 cut-backs, U.S. political commentators automatically opined that the basic reason for this retrenchment was that the United Kingdom's "socialistic economy" was not strong enough to support the social services upon which the British people have become dependent or to sustain "what it takes" to be a major world power. "What it takes" is presumably a nuclear "punch" to knock out the whole planet and half the solar system as well, even though a nation bankrupts itself in the process. So Britain can be written off—a victim of socialism and no longer a "world power" on that account. Yet the example, limited though it is, that Britain set for America, of reduced defense spending to improve its balance of payments position without

[28] The London *Observer*, December 31, 1967.

cutting into the welfare of its own population—who, incidentally, are not put into military uniform unless they volunteer—instead of intruding into impoverished countries to save them from Communism, will repay rich dividends before the decade is out.

The British example, so far as it goes, is not to be gainsaid. There are already signs that Britain's deliberate phasing out from the Cold War—which has been generally welcomed in Canada and the other Commonwealth countries, as well as its more realistic contribution to the U.N. arms debate—has put a subtle pressure on the Pentagon planners, who can no longer place Britain in a forward position on their global chessboard.

Britain's Peace Commitment

A great deal more is required of Britain, however, if defense is actually to become a branch of the foreign policy of phased disengagement. Lest it be thought that the more advanced proposals which follow are "unrealistic" or Utopian, let us sum up the implications of the world role to which Britain is already committed as a result of the 1967-68 arms cuts.

First, as regards Europe, there must be no nuclear weapons for West Germany. The Prime Minister declared in 1964, when the present Government was formed: "We are utterly and unequivocally opposed now and in all circumstances to any suggestion that Germany, West Germany or East Germany, directly or indirectly, should have a finger on the nuclear trigger or any responsibility, direct or indirect, for deciding that nuclear weapons are to be used." There was behind him then, and more so now, a Government pledged to the hilt to reject any form of international nuclear force which included Western Germany.

This has not been the case in the United States, where every kind of pressure had been practiced to give nuclear arms to the Germans—under U.S. control, of course. The British stand has since been vindicated by the general acceptance of the non-proliferation agreement in the spring of 1968. Moreover, the Government is further pledged to support the establishment of nuclear-free zones in Africa, Latin America and Central Europe. As the 1968 Non-Proliferation Treaty forbids the direct or indirect transfer of nuclear arms, the U.S. commitment to the treaty has meant scrapping any NATO deployment of nuclear arms under shared control with West Germany. But the Eastern European countries consider ratification by West Germany to be essential for a meaningful treaty.

It might be recalled, too, that the European allies—starting with the like-minded Social Democratic Governments in Norway and Denmark, and, at the time, Belgian Prime Minister Spaak, the Dutch Government, and the Left-Center coalition in Italy—were opposed to the MLF for the

68

same reasons, but they were waiting for a lead from the British Government. They got it and MLF was dumped. Now it is NATO's turn. Moreover, the 1967 meetings of NATO witnessed strong protests (led by the Scandinavians) against further Greek participation. If Greece insists on remaining in, Britain has even more reason to get out. The others are certain to follow, for it is Britain, not West Germany, which nowadays holds NATO together.

Second, regarding Asia, Britain and most of the Commonwealth recognize China, legally and factually—while Washington still pretends to look the other way. The French ex-colonies in Africa have also for the most part followed the Metropolitan lead. Thus, an ever-widening conciliatory element has been introduced into East-West relations which can be used to turn the edge of the Cold War to the advantage of world peace, in spite of the unrelenting campaign which pervades much of the American press and mass media magnifying every passing incident, however dubious or trivial, in the current Chinese experiment with a so-called "cultural revolution." The manner in which, without panic or timidity, British police action in Hong Kong, during the "Communist-inspired" riots of 1966-67, both kept the peace locally and stabilized relations with Peking, provided an example of administrative acumen and political sobriety on how best to handle similar "Communist-inspired" problems in Southeast Asia.

The winning back of the people of China to the world community, where they belong, with all that it will mean for world peace, not least the progressive participation of the Chinese inventive genius in the constructive programs of the U.N. Family—economic, scientific, technological, cultural—would be one of the outstanding triumphs of Twentieth Century statesmanship. With the Third World forming every day more sophisticated links with China, and with the menace of the Vietnam débacle becoming a more worrying concern of the whole world community, it is within the bounds of possibility that, by the end of the century, China will have truly re-joined the human race.

In such an achievement the British and Commonwealth role could be more crucial than that of either France or the Soviet Union. If the Cold War can be de-fused by the conscious spread of such attitudes, the British Commonwealth, with probable French and Russian collaboration, and the steadily mounting support of the Third World at the U.N., could be decisive in breaking down the Chinese wall, without awaiting the advent of global maturity in the United States. One great priority of the 1970's is for British policy toward China to shake off the shackles imposed by the "contain-Communism" dogmas that still linger across the Atlantic.

In short, an evolving British foreign policy which relegates orthodox "defense" to a minor role, while promoting bolder U.N. techniques for policing the earth's danger spots, is incompatible with Britain's ball-and-chain servitude to NATO. Escape from this twenty years' self-sentence would give Britain back the freedom of choice which it lost in 1949, when it followed the Leader of the Opposition into President Truman's Cold War. If, as Churchill himself declared during the infancy of NATO, "we armed to parley," and if, as daily becomes more evident, the Russians are ready to parley, then what are we waiting for?

Happily, some tentative but timid steps seem to be in prospect on the Government level toward a post-NATO program. At the last NATO Council to be held in Paris, Lord Chalfont, occupying the imaginative post of Minister for Disarmament, confessed that NATO held little future as a purely military alliance. For eighteen years NATO had waited for an attack that never came. They still waited, nuclear-armed to the teeth, for a type of attack that few people, even in the Pentagon, honestly expect will ever come. So Lord Chalfont quite simply spelled out the advantages of using NATO as a *negotiating* agency with the Russians. Many parliamentarians and diplomats seem to agree with him. One of them, Raymond Fletcher, M.P., has said: "If de Gaulle's view that settlements with the East are possible is grafted on to Chalfont's view that NATO as a whole should begin exploring the possibilities, we have the beginnings of a concept around which NATO can be re-shaped." From a traditional point of view, this course might seem to have much in its favor. "We have no eternal allies and no perpetual enemies," said the shrewd and calculating Lord Palmerston: "Our interests are eternal and perpetual and those interests it is our duty to follow." Would any modern Foreign Secretary be prepared to contradict him?

But is this enough? Palmerston left things a little too vague. In *The Future of NATO* Alastair Buchan, Director of the Institute for Strategic Studies, London, concludes that "NATO has achieved its primary objective, the creation of stability and security in Europe, though it may have failed in a secondary objective, namely, laying the foundations of an Atlantic political system." He thinks that NATO should be viewed "not as a series of institutions, but as a form of inter-state obligations and relationships between the United States and Western Europe, . . . a cocoon from which some new arrangement will emerge during the 1970's."[29] Once again, we are presented with a frank explanation of *why* NATO has ceased to function, but no convincing case for its further existence. Not all Cold War cocoons produce butterflies.

This was certainly the case when fourteen of the fifteen Western allies —France naturally did not participate—held a number of meetings in Brussels in November and December 1967 to draw up a blueprint to alter the basic nature of the North Atlantic Treaty Organization and reform the

[29] Alastair Buchan: *The Future of NATO*, International Conciliation, Carnegie Endowment, New York, 1967.

alliance—so it was announced—"to face new diplomatic tasks foreseen for the nineteen-seventies." Leading policy-makers from the NATO capitals were in fact proposing, on paper, to convert what has been essentially a military alliance into "a political unit capable of arriving at an Atlantic consensus on policies to be pursued in other parts of the world."

The Brussels meetings, however, came to nothing. Why? Because, once again, the military experts won hands down. In short, while the Defense Ministers rejected as completely "unrealistic and unconvincing" the concept of massive retaliation for any Soviet aggression against any NATO country, they substituted a three step "flexible response" and invented a new strategic doctrine which looks to the maintenance of "sufficient" non-nuclear forces to respond to a "variety of potential Soviet military thrusts," initially with conventional weapons. At some point, left vague, the new strategy—still on paper—calls for resort to "small" battlefield nuclear weapons in the hope of persuading the Russians that "continued aggression threatens to spread beyond the zone of combat." Finally, if all fails, nuclear missiles will be directed against targets in the enemy's homeland.[30]

One military planner at the Brussels meeting declared with evident elation: "For years most members of the Alliance had been disenchanted with the old strategy. Nobody really thought the Soviets could be deterred from pushing hard on Berlin or elsewhere simply by the bluff of massive retaliation. But we didn't have a new strategy. Now that we do, the military men will find it easier to make more realistic plans based on the new doctrine."

That is exactly the point: however abortive Brussels was in producing the faintest outline of a constructive political settlement or even a military détente, the military-minded men got their way once more. As one of them remarked: "We have to create a strong uncertainty about the point at which conventional war might turn into nuclear cataclysm in the Russian mind."

This is how NATO has entered the last phase of its embalming process. All splendor without, all decay within: a painted corpse.

A Bid for Posterity

The fiasco at Brussels will surprise no one who has followed the argument so far; it will become even more obvious as we probe more deeply in the pages that follow. No doubt much Thames water will flow under Westminster Bridge past the House of Commons while this "re-shaping" takes place; it may take years. But, if mere re-shaping, rather than escaping, becomes the end-all of British action, then the five-sided Castle of

[30] *New York Times,* December 13, 1967.

Doubt on the Potomac River will dictate its own terms, for it has most to lose. A post-NATO program calls for something much vaster than reshaping a military alliance; it calls for remaking a peaceful world.

Anatol Rapaport argues a very significant point in his *Strategy and Conscience:* "The relations between the United States and Canada, between Denmark and Norway, between Switzerland and Italy *are of a different sort* from those of the United States and the Soviet Union."[31] It is hardly likely that Danish spies are spending much energy in Norway or that Italy is preparing for a Swiss invasion, he says. Likewise, for Britain to use a U.S. yardstick for its "defense" is to be saddled with all the surplus "hardware" that the Pentagon needs on British soil to implement its calculated and continuing hostility toward Russia. At best, this hostility does no useful service to the U.S., so why should Britain be an agent for extending it?

When de Gaulle said: "I cannot permit U.S. protection anymore on our soil—it is too dangerous," he was not any less a devotee of self-defense for himself; he was saying in effect: "Franco-Russian relations involve the Franco-Russian type of defense—not the U.S.-Russian type." When Britain decides to live up to the Prime Minister's solemn announcement that "defense must become a branch of foreign policy," instead of vice versa, no longer will British planners be forced to serve as an appendage of Pentagon strategy against the Soviet Union—or against China, for that matter.

In *The End of the Alliance,* Ronald Steel reminds us that France is not the only NATO country intent on going its own way. The others have not gone so far, that is all. The recent anger with de Gaulle served only to distort the real issue. Far more significant than the General's diplomacy were the necessities of military technology. "Although American officials are understandably reluctant to admit it," writes Ronald Steel, "the United States, under the impact of changing technology and national interest, is clearly moving towards a 'Fortress America' defense, resting on intercontinental missiles and on mobile infantry brigades which can be quickly airlifted to trouble spots around the world." He then makes the important point:

The prerequisites for nuclear disengagement in Europe have now been laid: the closing of overseas bases, the downgrading of battlefield atomic weapons, the discouragement of national nuclear arsenals, and the demand for a large European conventional army. Only one more step remains to be taken to ensure that the power of decision between peace and war remains in American hands: the retirement of American soldiers from Europe.[32]

If this is substantially true, we have yet another reason to account for the moderation of U.S. official criticism of the General—however loud

[31] Anatol Rapaport: *Strategy and Conscience,* Harper & Row, New York, 1964.
[32] Ronald Steel: *The End of the Alliance,* Viking, New York, 1964.

and rude the politicos and editorial writers have been. Steel's book aroused a storm of controversy in the United States, to which Senator Fulbright's recent contributions have added political realism. But *The End of the Alliance* has even greater cogency for British NATO-ites. The recent annual defense statements, unlike actual U.S. procedures, would definitely rule out "mobile infantry brigades" flying to the defense of all and sundry around the globe.

Obsessed with de Gaulle's defections, however, the London representative of the *New York Times* wanted his American readers to believe that: "London finds itself taking the lead in re-shaping the Pact without de Gaulle." The mantle had fallen on Britain rather than America "not because the British want the role, but because it has fallen to them by a process of elimination." A United States lead might be interpreted as "American dictation," while "the Germans' history excludes them from this kind of leadership, and the other countries are too small."[33]

For these and the more cogent reasons already advanced, the only honest course for the British Government to take is to deposit the required year's notice of withdrawal and to announce an alternative program based on the growing peace capacity of the Commonwealth and its allies, centered on the U.N. That, in essence, is where the foregoing argument leads us. Such a clear-cut initiative would stir the hopes of more millions of fearful people throughout the world than any tinkering with NATO, and would certainly elicit a far more positive response from United States citizens than its cold warriors are at present able to appreciate. There is much to be done, if defense is actually to become the servant of foreign policy. But time is of the essence, and that time is NOW.

New possibilities reveal themselves at once. How to strengthen peace in Europe—and beyond? By abandoning NATO a breakthrough can be made on German unification—whatever form it takes. The neutralization of Berlin under some form of U.N. trusteeship, at least for the time being, becomes feasible, without "selling out to Communism." The complete dissolution of the Warsaw Pact may well follow. Since France and Britain are by no means alone in developing Eastern conciliation programs, increased trade and political adjustment will doubtless bring Europe closer together and facilitate the Rapacki type of disengagement, as modified in terms of the one-time Gaitskell Plan and other British proposals.

Moreover, technical rapprochement with the Communist satellites in East Europe would greatly strengthen the structure of the U.N. Economic Commission for Europe, with its sensible "non-discrimination" policies for all of Europe's twenty-nine countries. This truly European development will in time aid the Six and Seven in joining up together in post-de Gaulle Europe. Past over-emphasis on the so-called Common Market had too many "security" strings tying it to NATO. The withdrawal of

[33] *New York Times*, May 9, 1966.

73

unwanted British men and costly equipment from West Germany should evoke a profound sigh of relief from the Chancellor of the Exchequer with his thousand million pounds axe, as well as from the citizens of East Germany, longing to see the backs of the Russians. At last, an All-European Non-Aggression Agreement could be realized. Though no one imagines that Rome can be rebuilt in a day, the spirit of *Pacem in Terris* is closer to the hearts and minds of ordinary people than NATO's balance of terror.

As soon as the NATO menace is removed from the Continent of Europe, the countless stores and barracks and air strips and camp grounds and tons of useless lethal equipment that it has accumulated at public expense can be contributed toward European economic and social betterment. NATO's nuclear weapons—hidden away under secret locks and keys—can be disassembled; some could be put on public exhibition (alongside their Russian counterparts perhaps?) at selected sites along the tourist highways as peace memorials symbolizing mankind's escape from strategic insanity. General de Gaulle, caught between the Devil and the deep blue sea, lost this chance. But why should Britain pass up the same chance of assuming the moral leadership that Europe awaits?

The British Government has a unique responsibility for formulating an entirely new approach, in view of the failure at Brussels in December 1967. In opposition, the Labor Party sought to reduce the danger of having any incident in Europe escalate to the nuclear level by abandoning the "independent" deterrent altogether and developing within NATO a strategy of reliance on conventional forces. Now in power, Labor has nevertheless kept the bomb. Nuclear forces—V-bombers and the Polaris submarines—are being maintained at a cost of well over 100 million pounds annually. In the 1967 Defense Debate, Denis Healey told the House of Commons that "NATO would be compelled to resort to nuclear weapons within days of attack."

If it can be convinced by its own arguments when in opposition, the present Government—which once liked to regard itself as the "Peace Party"—can escape from the dilemma which it inherited, by first escaping from its place on the chain-gang. It should stop all further work on Britain's own nuclear weapons and their means of delivery, and cancel the Polaris program, as well as the purchase of more military aircraft from the United States.* It should refuse to contribute Britain's existing nuclear weapons toward a new Western European "deterrent"—or as a price for entry into the Common Market. Above all, it should open negotiations with Russia, Poland, and other European states to pave the way for an All-European Security Pact based on East-West disengagement and a nuclear-free zone covering initially Central Europe and ultimately the whole of Europe.

* This proposal was, in fact, put into partial effect, following the adoption of the 1968 budget.

Such a plea for a genuine British leadership is frequently voiced in the House of Commons and was tersely summarized some time back by one of the Labor Party's independent journals thus: "The creation of a new international atmosphere, within which peaceful negotiations can gradually replace the brandishing of deterrents as the normal means of settling differences between States, requires the abandonment of nuclear weapons altogether. One great power must give the lead. We insist now that Britain should be that power."[34]

This could be effected in stages, if the Government genuinely declined to make defense the master of its foreign policy. For example, as interim measures, Britain could:

(a) Refuse to have any part in "re-shaping" NATO until we have sat down at the Conference Table with Russia and the other Warsaw powers.*

(b) Make clear to other Allies that, as NATO should only be invoked in cases of unprovoked aggression, the British commitment to NATO is dependent on the easing of provocative policies.

(c) Plan to remove, after due notice, American bases from Britain and withdraw the forces from Germany, while exploring with Soviet Russia a treaty of mutual non-aggression and conciliation.

"We Shall Not Lose America!"

One of the harshest reactions in Washington to this bid for British peace leadership would be likely to be that it would endanger traditional Anglo-Saxon concord, and even promote hostility between the British and the American people. On the contrary, it is the abortive Atlantic Alliance mystique which stands between the British and the American peoples. This was particularly demonstrated when the U.S. military went into Southeast Asia, and lost British, as well as French and practically all other NATO moral and material support, with a few isolated exceptions in conservative quarters. Because of that unilateral act of military intervention, deplored by reasonable people across the globe, a "creditability gap" has never been wider across the Atlantic. The mounting opposition in the States have looked increasingly to British sympathizers in their effort to rescue their country from such shameful predicaments.

This "loyal opposition" in America has brought together for the first time in American history a mass movement of spectacular proportions. Public personalities of eminence in all fields of national life have joined

[34] *Tribune,* March 11, 1960.

* "What is at stake is our ability to convince our neighbors, those with whom we must negotiate for a relaxation of tension, that our aims are genuinely defensive, not aggressive or *révanchiste,* and that our methods, so far from encouraging the spread of nuclear weapons, are designed to prevent it."—From a speech of Prime Minister Wilson to the NATO Council on May 11, 1965.

hands to save the peace and prestige of America as never before. For example, Senator J. W. Fulbright, author of the 1967 bestseller, *The Arrogance of Power,* castigating the U.S. War Lords, heads a group of like-minded Washington's top Congressmen; Professor Quincy Wright, doyen of international lawyers; Robert Hutchins, educationalist and director of the Center for the Study of Democratic Institutions; and medical authorities like Dr. Benjamin Spock make common cause with the top-ranking scientists who have expressed their consistent opposition to the official policies in such outspoken journals as the *Bulletin of the Atomic Scientists.* Across the United States, civic and religious leaders in local communities have organized petitions and demonstrations and protests, sometimes numbering a quarter of a million participants at one time.

This "other America"—outside and above the contest of the formal political parties—has no use for the NATO generals. It is reading, discussing, arguing so vehemently, that, in default of leadership from within the American Establishment, a radical program of peaceful change from across the Atlantic will find in it eager and ready response. The true voice of the English-speaking world becomes daily more insistent in its opposition to Cold War adventures, while the United Nations offers a forum and instrument for the wider mobilization and diffusion of these same attitudes.

"I am very concerned about my country," Senator Fulbright has said: "I have never felt this way before. I wake up at nights, and I think, we are capable of so much progress, so much good, and we toss away men, money, resources, goodwill like pennies into a savage war—for what? This could have been the beginning of the golden age of America."

The permanent bonds between the people of Britain and the people of the United States were never closer or more promising than they are in this day of great peril *from within*. United States charity to stricken Europe following the Second World War received considerable and deserved acclaim. The opportunity now occurs for Britain to recompense the American people in their own time of dire need—not materially, but spiritually—for our next chapter will attempt to show how tight has become the stranglehold of the military controllers over the whole range of American life.

3 DEAD END

"I've always admired the United States and I thought I knew it very well. But I just don't understand what's going on there now. Tell me, gentlemen, is the Statue of Liberty standing on its head?"

—Ho Chi Minh

"Make no mistake about it," said André Malraux, "modern civilization is in the process of putting its immense means at the service of what used to be called 'the Devil.' " By "the Devil" the talented French Minister of Culture obviously meant something morally bad. But the public relations techniques of the nuclear war-machine are so efficient—and so well-oiled with public money—that even the Devil has been transformed into an Angel of Light. A Special Forces Prayer has been prepared for the use of chaplains conducting religious services in camp, which reads: "Go with us, the men of the Special Forces, as we defend the defenseless and free the enslaved . . ." But Donald Duncan, a former Master Sergeant in the Special Forces, describes in all its sickening horror in *The New Legions* the brutality, sadism, and bestiality of this modern brand of sophisticated killing.[1]

The biggest impediment in getting rid of the ball and chain described in the previous chapter is undoubtedly this illusion that war (our particular war) is good and that God likes it. The Devil is always the other fellow. It is not only the Statue of Liberty which is standing on its head—"Oh Liberty, what crimes are wrought in thy name!" echoed libertarian John Stuart Mill—but the distorted moral order which sustains the war system under which we live. The freedom of man depends no longer—if it ever did—on the pursuit of war, but on its abolition.

Some of the war programs (i.e. "national defense") that we shall review in this chapter are so obviously bad for the human race—and par-

[1] Donald Duncan: *The New Legions,* Random House, New York, 1967.

77

ticularly for the people of America, who seem to have got themselves entangled in them more than anyone else—that we cannot at first understand how it has come about that presumably intelligent political leaders should be devoting their lives and talents to such asinine policies. There must surely be some elementary explanation of this endemic contradiction between private principles and public practice, between national pretensions and international behavior? How has it come about that "My Country, Right or Wrong" should have become resurrected today as an accepted standard of state activity, following a century of mass education and world-wide communication?

James H. Breasted's classic work on ancient Egypt, *The Dawn of Conscience,* contains a part-answer, where the historian remarks:

Everyone knows that man's amazing mechanical power is the product of a long evolution, but it is not commonly realized that this is also true of the social force which we call *conscience*—although with this important difference: as the oldest known implement-making creature man has been fashioning destructive weapons for possibly a million years, whereas conscience emerged as a social force less than five thousand years ago. One development has far outrun the other; because one is old, while the other has hardly begun and still has infinite possibilities before it.[2]

Professor Breasted wrote these words in 1933. Since then mankind has created and undergone the biggest of all internecine wars, and from the ruins of the last so-called victory produced a nuclear war-machine which makes any future "victories" obsolete—because man himself will then become obsolete. In studying, therefore, in this chapter, some of the errors and terrors of atomic diplomacy and the queer notions of the people who nurture and fondle it, the seeming severity of our judgment at times must be set against this time-lag between mentality and mechanics, between law and war, between conscience and chaos.

It was Ralph Waldo Emerson who epitomized so well this gap in human evolution in his Essay on Politics:

We think our civilization near its meridian, but we are yet only at the cock-crowing and the morning star. In our barbarous society the influence of character is in its infancy.

In focusing the present chapter on the role of conscience, however, we at once run into some harsh realities. For one thing, atomic diplomacy has vastly widened the evolutionary gap since the NATO type of mentality took over the Western mind. For another thing, *mechanization* of the war-machine itself, with its feed-back devices, has replaced human brains by computers and produced a bastard science of "strategy," which, under the inspiration of such men as Herman Kahn and Edward Teller, leaves no place at all for compassion or conciliation and very little place even for the free play of normal intelligence. The callous dogma of "deterrence"

[2] J. H. Breasted: *The Dawn of Conscience,* Scribner's, New York, 1933.

is one of the off-shoots of this de-humanization of war. Finally, the ridiculous geo-political domino theory, invented apparently by State Department planners to circumvent the inconvenient social revolutions of Southeast Asia, is wedded to a global strategy of nuclear weaponry which treats the earth as one satanic chess-board where ambitious generals play their war-games under the guidance of pseudo-scientists who seem to have lost contact with the human condition, while the politicians who instigate them have put power before people and the Great Society before the Good Society.

Fortunately, however, social and behavioral scientists are beginning to play a more vital part as critics of this Theater of the Absurd, where military minds manipulate their manikins of fear and retaliation. For by no means have all scientists sold their souls to the Devil. One of them, Eugene Rabinowitch, editor of the *Bulletin of the Atomic Scientists,* sets our present frame of reference when he states: "The world in which nuclear forces are on the loose is a world in which man cannot survive by the same kind of endurance, cleverness, and luck which have permitted him to survive in the 'chemical' world of yesterday . . . Man can survive in this world of incredible violence only by similarly spectacular progress in social and political wisdom."

Yet, to read the published works of the nuclear strategists or listen to their liturgies on missilry and deterrence and mass damnation is to plunge beneath the surface of normal discourse into a nightmarish nether world. But it is a nightmare which is always shifting—not merely because of the technological revolution in weaponry, but also because of the colossal errors in strategic thinking which each new strategist discovers in his predecessors and fellow-travelers—and in his own previous works.

The real trouble with the nuclear strategists is that they do not understand the present global conflict at all, least of all how to deal with it. To attempt to do so not only would lose them, in many cases, their incomes and comfortable niches in the "think tanks" of modern missilry, but it would require something like a religious conversion in their day-to-day thinking. The Cold War has proliferated a breed of faceless and often rootless men—a sort of sub-species, the Neanderthal Scientist—who, though living with the rest of us, are shut off from the past, present, and future by a robot-minded ideology born of fear and pride, and subsidized without limit by an outmoded nationalism.

Professor Anatol Rapaport, a brilliant behavioral scientist, believes that normally intelligent peoople can barely get through to this problem-group at all, for they suffer, he says, from a "functional deafness" to any discourse carried on in "other than the strategic mode." He concludes:

Consequently, if someone wants to *reach* the strategists, to induce them to listen seriously, he must either gloss over the moral issues or lay them aside altogether. . . . Someone moved by a passionate concern for human values,

79

but with no understanding of the intricate strategic issues and their highly proliferated ramifications, may as well be speaking a dead language.[3]

There is, perhaps, a background explanation of this "functional deafness" of the Neanderthals in our midst. After all, they have had a very long history all to themselves. We can turn back for a moment to James H. Breasted to explain the gap in their development as full humans:

Man became the first implement-making creature not later than the beginning of the Ice Age, probably a million years ago, and possibly earlier. At the same time he also became the first *weapon-making creature*. For perhaps a million years therefore he has been improving those weapons; but it is less than five thousand years since men began to feel the power of conscience to such a degree that it became a potent *social force*.[4]

Breasted urged—and this was even before weapons became atomic—that the moment had come for the modern world to catch something of the true significance of this slippage between weapons and morality: "It is time that it should become a part of modern education. It is therefore the purpose of this book," he says, "to set forth the historical facts and to present the leading ancient records from which they are drawn, showing that we are still standing in the gray dawn of the Age of Character." The author of the present book might add to these profound sentiments his own belief that in the race between education and disaster, the language of religion—in its broadest sense—as well as the language of science is needed to provide the guidelines for the defense of the common peace.

Military men themselves are sometimes to be seen searching desperately for a way of escape from the awful dilemma which modern science has imposed upon them. "It may be that the problems of accommodation in a world split by rival ideologies are more difficult than those with which we have to struggle in the construction of ballistic missiles," General Omar Bradley has said, "but I believe, too, that if we apply to these human problems the energy, creativity, and the perseverance we have devoted to science, even problems of accommodation will yield to reason." To General Bradley, once commander of the Twelfth Army in Western Europe and later Chairman of the U.S. Joint Chiefs of Staff: "The central problem for our time—as I view it—is how to employ human intelligence for the salvation of mankind. It is a problem we have put upon ourselves. For we have defiled our intellect by the creation of such scientific weapons of destruction that we are now in desperate danger of destroying ourselves."

Let it be stated once and for all that the *motivation* for this vast military autocracy is invariably described as the defense of democracy and the preservation of freedom. No one can quarrel with these aims—the bibliography at the back of this book offers ample evidence of the weighty

[3] Anatol Rapaport: *Strategy and Conscience*, Harper & Row, New York, 1964.
[4] *op. cit.*

moral justification accorded to these alliances by their defenders. Many dedicated national leaders see things just that way. But the plain fact is that *the ends have changed places with the means*. The hierarchy of military might has developed a momentum of its own and has become its own motivation. Freedom and democracy have become its victims, not its beneficiaries or even its justification.

That is why General de Gaulle, himself an unabashed military man, has seen the folly of submitting his country to the centralization of power in the hands of his opposite numbers at Washington. His unwillingness to be caught unawares in open-ended "anti-Communist" wars at any spot on the globe that the Pentagon planners select as their next showpiece of freedom and democracy is held against him as an attack on American ideals and uprightness. The very virulence of the personal attacks upon him is proof of how subtly the Pentagon establishment has succeeded in controlling the means of public persuasion in the United States, even while the systematic destruction of the Vietnamese people has produced an irrefutable case study of what the defense of democracy actually means when power proceeds, as the Chinese would say, from the barrel of a gun.

Ronald Steel sums up this downward drift of American foreign policy over the past decade as follows: "John F. Kennedy saw America playing the role of watchman on the walls of world freedom, protecting the weak from aggression and keeping the enemies of democracy at bay. Lyndon Johnson ordered the watchman to come off the walls and plunge into the mêlée below. But in becoming the defender of everyone's freedom, America has come perilously near to compromising her own. By defining freedom as the absence of Communism she has allowed herself to be drawn into fights on behalf of tyrannies not much better than the Communism to which she is opposed."[5]

Computers and Orgtalk

A student of linguistics visiting Washington had this to say on his return to London:

Stroll down a corridor of the State Department, and you will overhear an argot that blends the unhappiest features of Madison Avenue and the Pentagon, turning a rich language into an Orgtongue. "Have you been to the debriefing given by Smallbore?" says the gossipy official. "Politicalwise, he says China and Chicom tension is increasing among the Asian LDC's because bloc technicians are infiltrating and the infrastructure is weak. Topside wants me to flesh out a memo with a few positive inputs so that we can be plugged in when the paperwork is finalized."[6]

[5] Ronald Steel: *Pax Americana,* Hamilton, London, 1967.
[6] Karl E. Mayer in the *New Statesman,* August 17, 1962.

81

Interpreting this casual specimen of Orgtongue, the visiting linguist understood that the civil servant in question was enquiring about Small-bore's report on his trip and noted that there had been more conflict between Chinese Nationalists and Chinese Communists in Asian countries. (LDC referred to "less developed countries.") Soviet agents had been making mischief in vulnerable places. The official's chiefs wanted him to draft a memorandum with a few concrete suggestions so as to have a voice when a final policy paper is written.

Granted that Orgtalk is confined neither to America nor to the world's military establishments across the world, our visitor nonetheless goes on to say: "As befits the largest office building in the world, with 27,000 persons tucked into 1,000 cubicles, the Pentagon has developed a vocabulary outstanding for acronymous plenitude and euphemistic boldness. Each service has its own dictionary, but the master volume is a 299 page book known as JD, which is short for *Dictionary of U.S. Military Terms for Joint Usage* and which has inputs ranging from Abort to Zuni. It is doubtless a useful and necessary document not intended for outside lexical criticism. But it serves as a necessary tool for the student of Orgtalk." Among some of the choice specimens from JD appear the following:

CEP—Circular Error Probable (an indicator of the accuracy of a missile).

COMHAWSEAFRON—Commander, Hawaiian Sea Frontier.

COMPHIBTRAPAC—Amphibious Training Command, Pacific Fleet.

CONELRAD—Control of Electromagnetic Radiation.

CRYPTOSYSTEM—Associated items of cryptomaterial which provide a means of encryption and decryption.

DASH—Drone Anti-Submarine Helicopter.

FABMDS—Field Army Ballistic Missile Defense System.

JANAP—Joint Army-Navy-Air Force Publications.

NUDETS—Nuclear detonation detection system.

TACCGRU—Tactical Air Control Groups.

A Senate subcommittee asked the Pentagon recently how many committees it had going, and received back in reply a book the size of a big city's telephone directory. Among more than nine hundred such committees was the Helium Policy Committee: "To study national policy to prevent the loss into the atmosphere of any appreciable part of the country's helium which has not first served the purpose of helium."

The Sub-Committee on National Security and International Operations, referred to above, criticized the application of systems analysis in two recent Pentagon decisions on the propulsion of new aircraft carriers and on the selection of the F-111 swing-wing fighter bomber. Systems analysis, the Sub-Committee said, "was used to justify the purchase of a 277 million dollar oil-fueled aircraft carrier that was obsolete before it was launched."

The same technique was also employed, according to the Sub-Committee, "to rationalize the choice of an airplane whose costs are soaring, if not its performance." It is almost amusing to learn that systems analysis was more readily applicable to decisions on alternative weapons systems than foreign policy questions. They say: "Defense deals in large part with end products that one can see, touch, measure, test-fire and ride in. But the State itself has virtually none of that; it deals mainly with the battle of ideas and interests called diplomacy."[7]

But the Senate Sub-Committee was actually confronted with a far more serious issue than with a battle of ideas between the U.S. and countries outside it. A President had obviously become a prisoner of computers which were giving him the wrong answers because they were being fed the wrong data. Worse, he had really no one else to rely on. Bogged down in Vietnam as a direct result of such bad computering, there was no way out, except to get out. A promising East-West détente had been brought to a standstill, and money desperately needed to meet the drain on the dollar through a worsening balance of payments and also to control the accelerating racial revolutions at home was being poured into the Mekong river. He was virtually standing alone in a manner almost unique in a modern political democracy.

The Washington Correspondent of *The Times* has aptly remarked: "The separation of powers isolates the President from parliamentary debate, and indeed makes debate in Congress a rare occurrence. The Cabinet is a misnomer for a group of departmental heads who do not share collective responsibility for policy. The President must look elsewhere." Never was the constitutional problem in the United States brought out more strongly—unlike a British Prime Minister and his departmental chiefs, all directly responsible to the House of Commons and their constituents—than by this terrible loneliness, and pressured all the time as he is by an amorphous fourth arm of government, which has no constitutional validity at all.

Moreover, the President has inherited a system that provides a dangerously mechanistic view of international affairs. Writing in the *Bulletin of the Atomic Scientists,* Professor William Polk of the University of Chicago, a former member of the Policy Planning Council in the State Department, said that the mechanistic approach associated with the RAND Corporation had spread from military planning to politico-military affairs. In its war-games approach, foreign problems are reduced to scenarios. "Antagonists are pitted against each other and logical responses to given moves are analyzed and escalated to a showdown."

These "war-games" fanatics have sought to provide the President with a complete theory on how to develop and use nuclear weapons which will, in practice, put the American system in politico-military control of

[7] *New York Times,* August 21, 1967.

83

the earth. But, as Professor Polk shows, the *actual* war situations which are likely to arise from time to time, such as Vietnam, are slipping through the fingers of Superman—reflected, if not created, by the infantile comic strips fed into the Pentagon computers and relayed to the millions on mass media. As the world knows perfectly well by this time, the mechanistic approach to foreign affairs is disastrous and can never work.

When the British Trades Union Congress in the autumn of 1967, by a big majority vote, defied their own leaders and urged Her Majesty's Government to "disassociate itself" formally and openly from the U.S. war programs in Southeast Asia, the nine million members of organized labor in Britain were, in effect, declaring that Britain should escape while there was time from the computerized inhumanities of the Pentagon, and give Britain back to its own people. When the Labor Party Annual Conference was held a little later on, the same thing happened—the rank and file outvoted the official Party policy and refused to be associated in any way with U.S. war gambles. This was 1776 in reverse. In 1968, British policy did actually change in these terms, though other reasons also prevailed.

From the American side, too, an informed and lively opposition is arising to the computer control of foreign policy. As a contribution to the United Nations observance of 1968 as Human Rights Year, a group of authorities on international law drew attention to the potential threat to individual freedom posed by computers, wiretap and eavesdropping devices and genetic controls. The Commission to Study the Organization of Peace issued a study entitled "The United Nations and Human Rights," drafted by Louis B. Sohn, Professor of Law at Harvard. The report calls for establishment by the United Nations of a body that would "study the implications of scientific and technological developments for human rights." It states that: "There is a cumulative danger involved in the march of technology and science without adequate consideration of the social effects of their findings." Noting modern man's growing dependence on computers, the report declares: "There is a grave danger that actual decisions will be no longer in the hands of duly-elected representatives of the people, but instead in the hands of *those who feed the data to the computers on which decisions are based and who are the interpreters and implementers of the answers given by the computers.*" The report also urges that "arrangements will have to be devised to control the precious few who know how to run the machines, and on whose wisdom and impartiality the fate of mankind may depend . . . Many military decisions already depend on answers given by computers."

Nor must it be assumed that all science is the stooge of the military planners. There is a growing ground swell from the scientific world against the misuse of their discipline and the abuse of their confidence. One of the contentions at the Annual Congress of the American Association for the Advancement of Science in 1966 was that political and military pressures were eroding the integrity of science. Dr. Margaret Mead, curator in Ethnology at the American Museum of Natural History, cited instances where there has been a clash between the peaceful programs of modern science and the scientific procedures promoted by the military.

One Starfish project consisted of a hydrogen device exploded in space by the United States to study the effects on the Van Allen radiation belts surrounding the earth and thus give the military some idea of the disruptive effect on radio communications. There was also the Project West Ford, when the Americans put into orbit a belt of copper needles to reflect radio signals. Both these projects were condemned by scientists everywhere because they interfered with the earth's natural environment, but also because the experiments were carried out without consultation with the international scientific community. Both Starfish and West Ford experiments showed that the civilized procedures which must govern scientific investigations to further the accumulation of knowledge could be disrupted by an irresponsible military clique. Again, Operation Apollo (flying a man to the moon) was primarily undertaken as a political decision. The Apollo project did not appear to be based on the orderly extension of scientific investigation, the Congress report stated. Commenting on the so-called space race, the Congress declared that the pattern of development in this terribly expensive field had been distorted significantly by political decisions.

A year later, the National Academy of Sciences joined with British scientists in protesting a proposal to establish a British military airfield on Aldabra Island in the Indian Ocean—an island rated by the Academy as a "biological treasure house" of bird and plant life. The Academy recorded that both it and the Royal Society in London "have urged their Governments to exert every effort to eliminate this threat of incalculable damage to one of the world's unique resources for scientific investigations." Naturalists hoped that the British Government would have the sense and decency to give the "twelve endemic species of birds, including the flightless rail, and eighteen or more unique species of higher plants," which enjoy the peace of the Indian Ocean, a more secure future than the less fortunate gooney birds and sea gulls have suffered off the shores of Alaska. Happily—due to the arms cuts announced in November 1967— these rare races, including the pink-footed booby, were saved.

A Mushy Thing

If the mad-hatter scientist were the main problem child in the Alice-in-Wonderland of military technology, the natural growth potentials of our democratic institutions might give the ordinary citizen cause for optimism. The fact is, however, that the mobilization of man's vast technical resources pays and pays well. The gold rush of the 1960's is on. Former U.S. Secretary of Defense McNamara has publicly stated that NATO is stronger in manpower and firepower than the Warsaw Pact, has more troops in Western Germany than the Russians have in the East, and that "the danger of a Russian invasion hardly exists." Why, then, this fantastic over-insurance against the thing least likely to happen? The explanation is that the American arms program has developed a vested interest of its own. Promoted by the collusion of the arms manufacturers and service chiefs, it is paid for by a subservient public, who are represented in Congress to a great extent by military-industrial complex men who exhibit no obvious desire to resist this appalling momentum. Their voting record speaks for itself.

"To fight an amendment by Senator Church to curtail gun sales to poor countries," reads a typical press report, "Senator Jackson, *whose state subsists largely on defense contracts,* is leading the fight against the Church amendment. Senator Gore read from a record which showed that the Pentagon agrees with General Eisenhower that politicians know nothing about fighting wars. One Latin American country, unnamed by Pentagon request, received 5 million dollars for miscellaneous army, navy and air force equipment. Senator Fulbright says that the power of the military-industrial complex has never been greater than it is today, and that the General himself may have forgotten his famous warning."[8]

"More and more, as the nation's principal business becomes military or paramilitary, the Defense Department has established itself as the dominant branch of the United States Government," says Nora Beloff, who made a special study of the relations of the military and Big Business: "In Washington the Pentagon is not just the largest, but also overwhelmingly the most conspicuous and most talked-about Ministry. As the principal provider of federal funds, jobs, favors, contracts . . . it controls installations—and patronage—in every American State, and its territorial possessions stretch over an area roughly the size of all England."[9]

"The top management of the Defense Department now includes not only the directorate of the largest military establishment in the world, but also the central managing office over the largest aggregation of industrial operations in the United States," states Professor Seymour Melman, Professor of Industrial Engineering at Columbia University. It need hardly be added that, working in constant collaboration with the Defense Department, America's biggest buyers are the munition-makers, the producers of intercontinental missiles, thermonuclear warheads, nuclear submarines, helicopters. They represent unprecedented concentrations of money and resources. For what end? One B-52 can carry greater ex-

[8] *New York Post,* August 15, 1967.
[9] Nora Beloff on "Juggernaut or Jelly-Fish," in the London *Observer,* September 1962.

plosive power than all the aircraft that ever flew in World War II, including the ones sent over Hiroshima and Nagasaki. These genocidal and
suicidal planes are literally "worth their weight in gold." But for what
end, we ask? Yours and mine?

Half a dozen giant corporations share a quarter of the missile business
for Government orders of up to 1,000 million dollars. Since the complexity and secrecy of most of the new weapons systems rule out open-market
bidding, what is left of American free enterprise? Nobody bothers, because the gigantic profits are there anyway—and that is just what free
enterprise has come to mean in practice. A retired Admiral from one of
the Los Angeles firms, when asked who took the day-to-day decisions on
production questions, replied: "The lines of authority are a mushy thing."

"The producers are compelled to remain intimately dependent on the
Pentagon, which is their only buyer," Miss Beloff points out: "In fact, the
personnel in the public and private sectors are often more or less interchangeable: modern businesses are full of retired officers and former
Civil Servants, recruited for their intimate knowledge of what Washington
wants and will pay, and the top levels of the Administration itself are full
of businessmen and technicians who first made their mark, such as former
Defense Secretary McNamara himself, in private business."

As Colonel W. H. Neblett (whose very lively book we shall notice
below) affirms: "Every large business in the United States engaged in
making some form of war material has one or more retired generals or
admirals in high executive positions. These retired military men, turned
corporate executives, are entirely unacquainted with business or business
principles, but they are super-lobbyists at the Pentagon for the sale to our
military forces of the obsolete weapons and supplies the companies they
represent are tooled up to make."

Treadmill to Oblivion

When Senator Eugene J. McCarthy drew attention to the fact that
35 billion dollars' worth of arms exports were undermining U.S. foreign
policy, he also put his finger on new political implications: "Supplying
arms opens the way to influence on the military and also on the political
policies of the recipient countries. Experience has demonstrated that when
an arms deal is concluded, the military hardware is only the first step.
Almost invariably, a training mission is needed and the recipient country
becomes dependent on the supplier for spare parts and other ordnance."[10]

As a boon and blessing to the private arms manufacturers and their
henchmen, NATO has proved a superb investment over and over again.
One of the smaller arms firms' private sales agents, who claims that his

[10] *The Saturday Review,* July 9, 1966.

annual sales come to "under 100 million dollars," says: "Our biggest headache is getting policy from the State Department. I was recently approached by a Latin American country for the delivery of fifty light American M-41 tanks. These are good tanks which NATO considers obsolescent, so that NATO nations want to unload them . . . I have the NATO powers' approval for the sale. But at State they've been stalling since June." Such are the casual business grumbles of private arms salesmen such as Samuel Cummings, who works out of his apartment in Monaco—like Sir Bazil Zaharoff before him, who sold arms to both sides in the Boer War and built up the rival armies of Greece and Turkey. Mr. Cummings is on record as frankly abetting the morality and legitimacy of profiting from (his term) "our treadmill to oblivion."[11]

Meanwhile, all this means jobs for workers, as well as profits for bosses. The Vietnam War created more than one million jobs in the United States, recorded the U.S. Labor Department's comprehensive report in 1967. The sharp rise in employment, because of the military build-up, amounted to some 23 per cent of the total increase of more than four million new jobs in the United States economy since 1965. In fact, the number of civilians and military personnel whose jobs stemmed from the Vietnam War and other defense commitments totaled about 7.5 million, or nearly 10 per cent of the total labor force. About 18 per cent of all the nation's engineers were in defense work, as were some 22 per cent of electrical and electronic technicians.

Fed by, and feeding, the military-industrial complex, says Miss Beloff, are the universities, whose science faculties are now more than three-quarters financed by the defense budget. Both Harvard and Princeton have refused to take secret work on their campus, but most state colleges and technical schools need the government money too badly to argue about terms. It is depressing to think that the vast majority of science graduates in America find their way, through teaching or research, into the military pipeline.

Dr. Jerome Wiesner, chief scientific adviser to the President, recently told a Congressional Committee that research will go up to 12,300 million dollars—more than the Federal Government contributed to research in the entire period from the American Revolution to the end of the Second World War. Scientists unwittingly welcome the rapid enlargement of the number of students each year going into what some of them call "the slaughter machine."

The fact is that the Cold War has taken the choices out of the American future. In Cold War America, young people have been for years more and more forced to choose careers that fit them into niches in the Cold War establishment—thus perpetuating the system. The recent scandals, which became front-page news, of how the C.I.A. had penetrated into the stu-

[11] *New York Times Magazine,* September 24, 1967.

dent associations and subsidized a wide range of educational organizations are a sinister witness to this subversion of American youth to serve "the slaughter machine."

David Riesman in *Abundance for What?* describes how the Cold War has narrowed the whole range of political opinions in the United States. It has made it hard for any normal citizen to take a dispassionate view of Russia or Castro or to judge Communist China by rational standards. The Open Society has given place to the closed mind. The gigantic slaughter machine cannot be kept running otherwise: it *must* have enemies—and victims. As Riesman describes him, the cold warrior perceives Russia as an unchanging antagonist, and the United States in frozen posture of deterrence and retaliation.[12]

The cold warrior blinds himself to the evidence of rational Russian development or the need for co-operation with China or Cuba—and to the possibility of changing American policies. The Cold War has long become a substitute for creative thought and an excuse for the postponement of social action, with disastrous results for the much overdue anti-poverty and civil rights programs. "The slaughter machine" is running away with the human being.

This subordination of man to computerized military technology is paralleled by the steady erosion of the democratic society. In *The Passion of the Hawks,* Tristam Coffin illustrates with a wealth of documentation how the military hierarchy "are turning the American eagle into a vulture that feeds on democracy." He cites instances of how courts martial become kangaroo courts, of how the military exercise a stranglehold over scientists and scientific research, and of the military's planned interference with a democratic press. Coffin's factual analysis of the Pentagon in relation to its allied industries uncovers some disturbing examples: how "Big Business-at-Arms" absorbs 78 per cent of the national budget, how the Navy squandered nine million dollars in Massachusetts during Senator Saltonstall's campaign, how the Academies have become second-rate engineering schools for permanent adolescents, how the draft solves the servant problems of the Big Brass, and how "Old Soldiers" fade off to the Far Right, or, as Coffin pointedly says: "Gold Braid becomes Lunatic Fringe."[13]

Coffin recounts how the vested interests of the military-industrial complex are not only eating out the heart of American democratic processes, but making it impossible for America to finance vitally needed civilian projects at home. In the Soviet military high-command the same dangers operate as in ours, he says, but they are directed to America, not at their own people. In this regard, many Western observers who have intimate ties with the United States have long been deploring "America's political

[12] David Riesman: *Abundance for What?*, Doubleday & Co., New York, 1966.
[13] Tristram Coffin: *The Passion of the Hawks,* Macmillan, New York, 1964.

and moral isolation," as Gunnar Myrdal, the Swedish economist, recently described it. He remarked in a speech in New York: "We ask ourselves how far has the erosion gone of the system of checks and balances, so carefully thought out by the founders of this great democracy, when power over life and death of hundreds of thousands, and in the further course of this war perhaps millions of peoples, is put in the hands of a small group of men in Washington."

Filling the Bottomless Pit

The assertion is frequently made that the Cold War was forced on the United States soon after World War II by aggressive outsiders. But no one seems to have calculated what would have happened to U.S. industry if the U.S. reaction had not come so swiftly into the Cold War at the time it did, starting, of course, with the Marshall Plan. Within the first decade, the Defense Department spent 26 *billion* dollars in military equipment, mostly under NATO. The Far East came second, regionally, with a total of 6 billion. The Mid-East and South Asia ranked third regionally with about 4 billion, and Latin America received about the same. But that was only a start. For the second decade of Cold War, ending 1970, the United States will have spent a third of its national budget on overseas *military* projects (including Vietnam), estimated at least at two hundred billion dollars.*

Describing the gathering of the business bees around the national honey-pot in January 1966, for example, fiscal statisticians showed how billions of taxpayers' dollars were being fed into the big corporations as military orders. The Boeing Company had slipped from second position to seventh, while the General Dynamics Corporation moved up to the runner-up spot behind Lockheed, which had the jackpot for that year. The McDonnell Aircraft Corporation held third place, the General Electric Company went from sixth to fourth; and North American Aviation, Inc., dipped to fifth place from fourth. The next five largest contractors, in order, were the American Telephone and Telegraph Company (which one does not think of as a major factor in defense), Boeing Company, Grumman Aircraft Engineering Corporation, Sperry Rand Corporation, and the Martin Marietta Corporation. Then follow a hundred or more lesser companies in a seemingly endless list.[14]

* The United Nations report to the Geneva meeting of the Economic and Social Council in July 1968 showed that the United States balance-of-payments deficit was "adversely affected by the eruption of hostilities in the Middle East and the escalation of the Viet-Nam conflict." It also stated: "The foreign exchange cost of United States military operations in Viet-Nam . . . accounted for about 40 per cent of that country's entire 1967 payments deficit."

[14] *New York Times,* January 16, 1966.

And the (alleged) "improvements" in the apparatus of killing follow fast on each others' heels. The new C-54 transport, which will be able to transport hundreds of troops across oceans at jet speeds, illustrates the increasing emphasis the Pentagon has been placing on mobility in what are described as limited warfare and "brush-fire" conflicts—although many people would question whether Vietnam has been either limited or brush-fire. Then there is a new type of naval vessel known as the fast deployment logistics (FDL) ship, which will serve as a floating depot loaded with weapons, vehicles and communications equipment, to be positioned at sea close to trouble spots.

This summary collation of "limited warfare" commitments reminds one of the dilemma of the boy in the Sunday School class who asked his teacher: "What happens to a man who falls into the Bottomless Pit when he comes out the other end?" No doubt the answer would be that he will still be looking for trouble-spots in the Cosmos while policing the Universe.

Sweet Dreams of Girlhood

As his part in the Vietnam conflict shows, General Maxwell Taylor regards himself as an authority on small wars. In an extraordinary article on defense, written in 1956 for the quarterly *Foreign Affairs* but suppressed because of objections by the State and Defense Departments, General Maxwell Taylor, then Chief of Staff of the United States Army, attacked what he called the "fixation on the overriding importance of the one big war . . . The avoidance of deliberate general atomic war should not be too difficult," he wrote, "since its unremunerative character must be clear to the potential adversaries."

A nation need only be reasonably sure that an opponent had some high-yield weapons, *no matter how indefinite their exact number,* to be impressed with "the possible consequences of attacking him." It will be seen that the ex-chief of the U.S. military establishment abolishes at a stroke the "balance of terror," the missile race, and possibly even the Moon Race. Just a handful of atomic bombs will do the trick.

General Taylor rejected the assumption that general atomic war was the only war worth preparing for, or that it would begin with a crippling atomic attack on America. In such an event America would be unable to support her forces abroad or even help her allies. Logically, therefore, her forces should be brought home *now* and her commitments to allies reduced. But the dilemma was that this would alienate her allies, increase their reluctance to allow bases on their territory, and also "encourage trends towards neutralization." From this result he thought that it would be a short step to the abandonment of the present strategy based on NATO, and the U.S. would return to "entrenched isolation."

It is significant that the State Department objected to the publication of these pessimistic conclusions by one of its top advisers on the grounds that they displayed a "lack of faith in *deterrence*," and also that "this kind of speculation *is not for public discussion*." (Italics added.) (This heretical article, together with the official objections thereto printed as an appendix, has since been published in General Taylor's *The Uncertain Trumpet*.) But when General Taylor advocates strengthening conventional power, so no one would be tempted to use the nuclear weapons, he arrives at a remarkable conclusion, for he says that so long as "traditional weapons" alone are used, "war finds its justification in the creation of a better world after the close of hostilities." In other words, let us have smaller wars, without using nuclear weapons, so that we can have a clean finish to them—and something left to live for afterwards! This simple naïveté in so big a general elicits the sort of comment which Tristram Coffin makes about it in *The Armed Society:* "This sounds like a woman longing for the sweet dreams of girlhood. It is the general longing for a return of the romantic and chivalrous concept of war."

Similarly, Professor Urs Schwarz has pointed out in *American Strategy: A New Perspective* that a revolution in warfare came with World War II, as well as the lessons he believes some of the generals learned later in the Korea and Vietnam conflicts. The stockpiling of nuclear weapons by the United States and the Soviet Union, and the subsequent discovery that this "balance of terror" did not eliminate other forms of *limited and local war* —added to the fact that small wars might lead to big ones—has inspired recent studies of the ways and means of *avoiding* universal destruction. Professor Schwarz explains how he believes this can be done: "Diplomacy, signals given to the other side, proposals for arms control, statements of policy, doing or not-doing, disclosure of secrets to the other side, and penetration into the secrets of the potential enemy, had to be understood as being quite as important as weapons." Nuclear weapons, in fact, were now "out"![15]

Private research corporations in America, rather than the soldiers and professional diplomats, have consequently been turning their minds to such unresolved conundrums as: "How effective is strategic counter-force? How really credible is a first strike capacity? How can war be terminated if deterrence fails? What is the effectiveness of civil defense?" All these grotesque speculations would appear to affect the *technique* of deterrence. Yet Urs Schwarz believes that the shift in "American strategic thinking in the mid-sixties . . . has permitted the creation of a national defense establishment in the modern sense, directed toward the use of all the nation's resources for the mastery of the infinitely complex problems confronting it."

[15] Urs Schwarz: *American Strategy: A New Perspective*, Doubleday & Co., New York, 1966.

92

All, that is, but one. And that one is a national resource that the professional generals and underground strategists cannot bother even to think about—*how to make peace*. This elementary resource for *avoiding* universal destruction does not lie within their field of military dialectics or spiritual discernment. This is what we mean by *un*thinking the thinkable. Yet strategy was once defined by General Albert C. Wedemeyer as "the art and science of employing all of a nation's resources to accomplish objectives defined by national policy."

Chasing after the red herring of "war-substitutes," the think-tank experts of the *Report from Iron Mountain* fall constantly into the same dilemma: i.e., the war system can be eliminated only by an effective war-substitute (and they enumerate half a dozen "models"); but no viable war-substitute can be brought about while the war system is still in effect.[16] They can no more resolve this dilemma than a man can hoist himself up by his own bootstraps. We shall attempt, however, to resolve the dilemma for the Iron Mountaineers later in this book.

Wrong policy means wrong strategy—however expensive the military and scientific brains producing it. Since a "nuclear exchange" (a current euphemism for deliberately transforming the earth into a charred radioactive shell) is definitely "out," while smaller wars, social revolutions and territorial disputes are still going to remain the lot of mankind, what shall our overall national policies be? For an answer to that question, we have to listen to the counsels of wiser men than the generals and strategists who led their nation into the swamps of Vietnam, but could not get it out again on their own terms.

"There is no *technical* solution to the paradox of growing military power and decreasing national security," declared Senator J. W. Fulbright: "A nation's security depends upon its overall position in the world—on its political and economic strength, as well as its military power, on its diplomacy and foreign trade, its alliances and associations, and on the character and quality of its internal life."[17]

But can these wiser counsels ever prevail as national policy? A professional historian has uttered a timely warning: "The attempt to get back to the days of knighthood and establish rules for war which will permit us to use our nuclear plenty in carefully graded doses to impose our will upon the Communists, and to get force and war back into usable instruments of diplomacy, runs directly counter to the deadly progression of this Century, the ever faster acceleration of the technology of destruction." So states Professor D. F. Fleming, who continues: "The lethal fact is that we are in the grip of a runaway military technology, which turns out 'ultimate' weapons in rapid succession—each much faster and more fabulously expensive than the last one." While Professor Fleming maintains that "the

[16] L. C. Lewin: *Report from Iron Mountain,* The Dial Press, New York, 1967.
[17] J. W. Fulbright: *Old Myths and New Realities,* Random House, 1964.

acceleration in killing has long since passed the point of control," he does not despair. He repudiates the infantile day-dreams which are fed into the Pentagon's computers and embellished in its publicity releases, and concludes thus: "The gadgets of destruction have escaped all bounds and they will infallibly destroy man, unless he pushes on to the making of peace and the organization of the world community."[18]

Generals Out of Control

No one can disguise the fact that, whatever Communism might have meant in the mid-century years, the major threat to civilized life on this planet in the last third of our century is old-fashioned militarism. In the smaller or "new" countries in Latin America, Asia, and Africa, its results have been all too evident during the past decade. In Africa alone, since the independence movements failed to produce stable civilian governments, a dozen countries came under the control of military governments during the 1960's. But even where the military men have not taken over the government of a country completely, every day produces a fresh instance of the inroads they are making. Writing of "the system of garrison commands that has become entrenched in Indonesia over the years," a London commentator remarks: "Most of these commands, though not necessarily disloyal politically, have got used to supervising the trade of their area and taking a suitable rake-off. Corruption in the army is no less than it used to be among the civil servants they have displaced."[19]

The present book, however, cannot pursue the cause of this lamentable relapse into military government in the developing areas. We are concerned with the course and phases of this same phenomenon in the most powerful country in the world, the United States. For if the military domination of civilian life is inimical to the people of a small country, its emergence can be disastrous to the people of a big country, for then the danger becomes worldwide. In fact, the growth of military power in the United States, whatever its causes or motivations, is no longer just a national issue for Americans, but an international peril of immediate concern to all peoples.

For into the hands of a new race of Nuclear Supermen modern technology has placed life and death power over the total planet. One of these living giants has been described in precise terms as follows:

Few military men on earth have as much destructive power within their grasp as has Admiral Ulysses Simpson Grant Sharp, commander of all United States forces in the Pacific area. From his beautifully situated headquarters high in

[18] D. F. Fleming: *The Cold War and Its Origins* (2 vols.), Doubleday, New York, 1961.
[19] The London *Times,* August 8, 1967.

the Hawaiian hills above Honolulu, he controls an armada of ships, planes and men that packs an almost incomprehensible wallop. It is a force that could blow a good-sized piece of a small country like North Vietnam off the map.[20]

About the same time as this terrifying description appeared, the *New York Times* publicized a chilling editorial drawing attention to the serious issues of civilian versus military control over defense and diplomatic policy which were then being raised by "the public campaign of some of the nation's top generals for an extension of the bombing of North Vietnam"—a campaign that had brought them favorable Senate response, seeing that the Senate was dominated by a huge majority of inveterate "hawks." The newspaper continued:

The spectacle of General Greene, the Marine Corps Commandant, talking from an American Legion podium to tell the country that the war in Vietnam is more important than the plight of America's riot-torn cities is the latest and most grotesque distortion of the traditional role of the military in American life.[21]

Yet another philosophy was quietly at work while the veteran general announced his own distorted standard of values to his fellow citizens. A scholar and world-minded statesman from distant Afghanistan, Abdul Rahman Pazhwak, presiding over the opening meeting of the 122 nation General Assembly in New York at that time, spoke in the name of our common humanity when he said: "In many areas and on many levels the psychology of force has swept the minds of men and nations, and where once the virtues of peace were extolled, today the efficacy of force is openly flaunted and even exalted."

With the approach of the 1968 Presidential election and because of the primitive urge—so often met with in politicians hoisted on the petard of their past mistakes—to "get it over with," the President was surrendering initiative more and more to this unrepresentative and unelected fourth arm of government. "This has not been the first Administration surrender to military pressure," asserts the foregoing editorial; it listed the surrenders one by one and concluded: "Responsibility for this tragic miscalculation undoubtedly belongs to the President more than to any other man. Yet, the military leaders who advised him—and have failed dismally to produce any military improvement for this huge investment—are now the chief opponents of . . . a political solution."

"Many Americans," states Senator J. W. Fulbright again in *Old Myths and New Realities,* "have come to regard our defense establishment as the heart and soul of our foreign policy whose effectiveness depends, not only on its size and variety, but also on the skill, and restraint, with which it is used." It will be noticed that this courageously outspoken voice of

[20] *New York Times,* August 10, 1967.
[21] *New York Times,* September 1, 1967.

95

the New America echoes the thesis of the previous chapter with respect to Britain, namely, that defense must be the servant and not the master of foreign policy. Senator Fulbright continues:

The trouble with the American technological bias is that it can conceal but not eliminate the ultimate importance of human judgment. Like any other piece of machinery, our military establishment can be no better than the judgment of those who control it . . . The American people are not now exercising effective control over the armed forces; nor indeed is the Congress, despite its Constitutional responsibilities in this field.[22]

But many Americans, in all walks of life, are becoming desperately concerned with the recent growth of this "Caesarism," as a leading religious journal described it: "One of the gravest dangers posed by war is its power to turn a free people's government into a vast, inhumane Caesarism. Gradually, almost painlessly, a government at war steals from the people their inalienable rights of self-determination . . . the government determines what is the national will and purpose, substitutes propaganda for truth and compels a supine people to adopt codes of morality that flout religion and human decency. The brainwashing that occurs when a combatant falls into the hands of the enemy is a minor crime compared with the brainwashing a resolute and authoritarian government can impose on a whole people in wartime."[23]

Unfortunately, the world has seen too often, each in its own setting of history or tradition or culture, the problem of the generals claiming to "save" democracy or the national destiny. Writing of a pre-Atomic General, in *Tojo: The Last Banzai,*[24] Courtney Browne considered that General Hideki Tojo should be the last of his kind anywhere—an insensate soldier carried away by visions of victory and notions of national grandeur. But gradations of his prototype still exist in our midst, East and West. General Tojo's ascent is set within the context of Japan's gradual submission to a military shogunate that strove to make Japan dominant in East Asia. (This could have been called Japan's "Johnson Doctrine"— except that the Japanese happen to live in East Asia.)

Such men as Tojo would rather lead the country into an interminable war than accept the frustration of that purpose. As things worked out, they resisted surrender till all was in ruins. Courtney Browne's book describes, again in the Japanese context, the methods resorted to by extremist civilian groups who backed up the military organization and how groups of extremist military officers could in time of war gain full control of the destiny of the country. They treated the peace opposition not only as unpatriotic, but as fit subjects of assassination.

[22] *op. cit.*
[23] *The Christian Century,* May 8, 1967.
[24] Courtney Browne: *Tojo: The Last Banzai,* Holt, Rinehart & Winston, New York, 1967.

96

Wages of Fear

One of the most unorthodox critics of the "dead-enders" is the author of *No Peace with the Regulars*. Colonel William H. Neblett is no visionary, but a professional soldier who learned his trade the hard way from over thirty years of military service, both as a commander in the field, on General MacArthur's staff, and in the higher echelons of the Pentagon. Colonel Neblett talks as an insider when he raises a really startling point on the domination of the new military over the old politicians:

There is no way our general staff can keep our great and useless military forces in being except by holding the control of the politics of the country. We have recently been treated to the spectacle of the Soviet head men destroying, or attempting to destroy, the memory of Stalin. . . . The correct interpretation of the move of the generals now in power in Russia for the destruction of Stalin's memory would be to view it as a move to put the army in a responsible position in politics. All of the heads of the government are former generals. They worship nobody's memory; only their own careers.[25]

This viewpoint represents pretty strong meat for the generals who have been saving democracy in Southeast Asia, Lebanon, or Central America. William H. Neblett's personal history, as recorded in *Who's Who in America*, includes many worthy accolades acquired in field service. He propounds a direct and simple thesis when he maintains that "the struggle for peace is made doubly hard by the militarists who are, today, in absolute control of the principal governments of the world."

It would seem that he has both his own country and the Soviet Union particularly in mind when he reminiscently states:

The misunderstanding between Russia and our country . . . delays peace and keeps us and the Russian people in constant fear of war. Our young Air Force generals openly boast that our Air Force is ready at a moment's notice to wipe Russia out of existence by the application of massive retaliation . . . Assuming that our Air Force could, what then?

That this picture is not far-fetched was borne out when the Strategic Air Command (SAC) announced that it had succeeded in placing one-third of its nuclear-armed bomber force of more than 2,000 planes on a fifteen minute ground alert. This meant that more than 600 aircraft could get into the air "for retaliation" in less than fifteen minutes after the report —true or false—of any enemy missile or bomber assault. "For all practical purposes, this goal in readiness status had been achieved earlier than expected, and might soon be exceeded," was the statement issued by General Thomas S. Power, then head of the Strategic Air Command.

But what is the effect of this dangerous posturing on the world outside? As Jack Raymond says in *Power at the Pentagon,* the image of the United States abroad is *all military:* bases, alliances, pacts—everywhere and as

[25] W. H. Neblett: *No Peace with the Regulars,* Pageant Press, New York, 1957.

far as the human eye can reach, all military. He ingeniously argues: "United States forces are deployed in an effort to make it possible to evaluate a situation that may appear to be an attack; to make it possible also for the enemy not to fear the fears of the United States, and the United States not to fear that the enemy fears its fears. For in the Pearl Harbor psychology of the United States, such fears might well trigger instant retaliation that would afterward be regretted."[26]

Within this self-induced psychosis, even "disarmament" is envisaged as a means of re-armament. At the Pentagon, says the same writer, military professionals as well as civilians devote themselves to questions of disarmament with great intensity. They ask themselves not merely: "What can we accept in the way of disarmament and arms control without weakening our security?" but also: "What can we suggest that will *add* to our security?" Little wonder that the Geneva discussions of the 18-Power Disarmament Conference have proceeded year after year in a descending spiral of futility, as the leading negotiators look at every proposal in terms of this stronger defense. Setting military minds to think creatively about disarmament is "like asking a priest to work out campaigns for spreading atheism," explains Mr. Raymond; he points out that: "Military men are more receptive to the term 'arms control' than to disarmament. This term accepts the military professional's premise that true disarmament is not possible and not necessarily desirable, but that mutually agreed controls over arms build-ups can satisfy *national security requirements.*" In the logic of the Pentagon, he says: "military preparedness and arms control are two sides of the same coin."

Disarmament does not primarily rest on an *international* agreement, as we are so often told; it rests on a *national* decision to be master in one's own house. The interests of the people of the Soviet Union and the United States are identical—to stay alive together. But the interests of the cynics of disarmament are to ensure that they don't. Senor Salvador de Madariaga, once head of the Disarmament Section of the League of Nations, remarked about the First World Disarmament Conference between the World Wars: "They all come to Geneva to disarm—each other!" To get results, international statesmanship must be primarily concerned with how to make the switch, psychologically and technically, from warmaking to peacemaking *within* each nation—not between the nations. It is a simple but basic fact that arms are *national*. The will to disarm must be national, before it can be translated into an international treaty. Disarmament can only begin at home. How long will it take our leaders and spokesmen to learn just that?

So now we know why disarmament rarely happens, in spite of the legends that national politicians so piously recite in their own favor that all they want is "peace." The outspoken Colonel Neblett characterizes as follows the civilians who, as Secretary of Defense and Secretaries of the

[26] Jack Raymond: *Power at the Pentagon,* Harper & Row, New York, 1964.

98

Army, Navy and Air Force, are *in theory* the heads of the military establishment: "These Secretaries have no real power; they are figureheads; they exercise no more authority over the General Staff than Queen Elizabeth does over the British Parliament; they march to the generals' tune and do and say what the generals and admirals want them to do and say." In consequence, the United States Arms Control and Disarmament Agency has made such a pitiable contribution either to the peace of the world or to the permanent security of the United States.

It must be remembered that the more disastrous the war situation, the more political the generals tend to become. In outlining his objectives in Vietnam for 1968, General Westmoreland, just before his recall back to the States, defined his second objective as a *political* one in the following words: "Extend the secure areas of South Vietnam by co-ordinated civil-military operations and assist the Government of South Vietnam in building an independent *viable non-Communist society."* (Italics added.)

It should be recorded, however, that Professor Raymond's well-documented analysis of the encroaching powers at the Pentagon contains some favorable appraisal of the rare human types who, he says, "do not fit the stereotype of trigger-happy Pentagon militarists that so often pops into disarmament discussions." This observation brings up a disturbing thought. George Steiner expresses it thus: "We now know that a man can read Goethe and Rilke in the evening, that he can play Bach and Schubert, and go to his day's work at Auschwitz in the morning . . . Does some great boredom and surfeit of abstraction grow up inside literate civilization, preparing it for the release of barbarism?"

The Mark of the Panzer

Another of America's retired rebel generals brings our narrative back directly to the question of *who* is running NATO. General Hugh B. Hester stated in 1962: "The U.S. Government's German policies become more incredible. Not only is the convicted war criminal General Foersch in command of West German Armed forces, Nazi General Hans Speidel in command of NATO ground forces, including U.S. troops, and 'major war criminal' General Adolf Heusinger in charge of NATO planning, but Admiral Gerhard Wagner, Hitler's naval planner, commands the Northern Naval Sector of NATO, and Hermann Goering's aide Ernest Kusserow heads the air defense staff of NATO air forces in Central Europe . . . All these men served Adolf Hitler and his murderous purposes loyally until it became obvious to all that he could not win. Some twenty-odd other generals, admirals, and civilian co-conspirators were hanged by order of a world court for crimes against humanity."[27]

Be that as it may, the shock and indignation felt by so many British and

[27] Hugh B. Hester, Brigadier General U.S. Army (Retired), in a privately printed statement, December 12, 1962.

American citizens—and no doubt Frenchmen too—could hardly be contained when, on June 28, 1966, a German ex-Panzer commander, veteran of the conquests of Poland and France, was formally named Commander-in-Chief of Allied Forces in Central Europe, the most important post to be held by a West German in the NATO Organization. As such, General Johann Adolf von Kielmansegg directs half a million United States, British, and West German air and ground troops, serving from Bavaria to North Germany. He took over the command headquarters, then at Fontainebleau, from General Jean Crepin of France, at the time that all French forces were withdrawn from NATO.

It is significant that with the military departure of the French from NATO, the choice of a Central European commander fell to Bonn *as contributor of the largest forces in the sector*. The new commandant will be responsible, of course, to Supreme Headquarters Allied Powers in Europe (SHAPE) under General Lyman L. Lemnitzer of the United States. Apparently his big qualification is that, after serving on the Russian front, he joined the German Army's General Staff, and, as a friend of those who tried to assassinate Hitler in 1944, he was jailed by the Gestapo for two months. General von Kielmansegg was summoned after the war to work for Bonn's first Defense Minister, who was then preparing to resurrect the German army—which had been specifically outlawed by the Potsdam Agreement.[28]

The shaky Potsdam Agreement is sometimes cited in the West as evidence of the Soviet Union's bad faith in not observing international obligations—without its being noticed that the Western parties have beaten a roadway across it by the horses and coaches they have been driving through it ever since. Is it not a greater mystery that British forces should be compelled to remain a moment longer in this invidious and subservient relationship? The more logical French have moved themselves out and removed the ex-Panzer chieftain safely beyond their frontiers.

But behind this brass facade lies the question that nobody in or out of NATO can ever answer. "The argument about *when* nuclear weapons can be used," says Leonard Beaton in *The Struggle for Peace,* "has dominated all military thought and planning in Europe and North America for about fifteen years. There has always been a 'tripwire' school of opinion which has insisted that all that was needed to secure Western Europe from the Soviets (and no doubt Eastern Europe from the NATO powers) was a light force which could make sure that any enemy attack was determined and genuine. There has also been the landpower school which has said that nothing less than a full capacity to defend would do. Into this has been fitted, with great uncertainty, the idea of using nuclear weapons locally to stop an aggressor or to destroy his supply lines."[29]

28 *New York Times,* June 29, 1966.
29 Leonard Beaton: *The Struggle for Peace,* Institute for Strategic Studies, London, 1966.

Now we know—"with great uncertainty"—on what the safety of the human race depends: that nobody does, in fact, know! The same writer continues: "This issue has never been satisfactorily worked out. Governments have not been able to see their way clearly. In the face of a crisis, they increase their conventional power and their nuclear threats. In the end, both sides have obviously decided that there are severe limits on what 'the deterrent' can be relied on to do."

How, then, *should* nation-states develop and use their national military power? "To raise this question," states Professor Klaus Knorr, who is Director of the Center of International Studies at Princeton University, "is surely appropriate at a time when the leaders of many states, including the United States and the Soviet Union, have flatly declared that war—at least nuclear war—has ceased to be a national instrument of policy, when official declarations on matters of arms control and disarmament have become frequent, and when, indeed, arms control and disarmament have become the subject not only of a large and growing literature on their principles, techniques, and practicality, but also of numerous and protracted conferences among governments."[30]

Discussing the "vast complexity of the subject matter" involved in the use of nuclear weapons, Klaus Knorr concludes:

It demands attention to far more aspects of human behavior, many only dimly understood, than any one author is competent to exercise. Thus, part of the problem concerns uses of military power, and their consequences, regarding which there is no experience to draw on. Since Hiroshima and Nagasaki, no nuclear weapon has been fired in war, and no major military powers have been directly at war with one another. About such contingencies we can only speculate.

This, then, is the rarefied atmospheric level to which strategic scholarship has climbed in speculating on *how* governments should use their "nuclear capability," as the missile-men term it. Even searching the present and past, social scientists and historians have still not assembled the needed basic information, the author asserts, nor have they produced the supporting literature "that would permit many aspects of the problem to be put into proper perspective."

Herman Kahn, mathematician, physicist, and former master strategist of the RAND Corporation, in his later book, *On Escalation: Metaphors and Scenarios,* attempts to answer the escalating questions as to *when* governments should use nuclear bombs, by reducing the arms race to a simple "competition in risk-taking." The intensification of this race can be depicted according to Kahn by means of a theoretical "escalation ladder." Ascent of the ladder's rungs brings opponents closer to all-out war. But the climb is not inevitable. At each rung, he asserts, decisions must be made from numerous choices before the climb proceeds higher. "These choices may well avoid the dreaded extreme of total annihilation

[30] K. Knorr: *On the Uses of Military Power in the Nuclear Age,* Princeton, 1966.

and the equally dreaded alternative of total surrender." On the other hand, "the statement that 'there is no alternative to peace' is misleading. If it means anything, it must be a call for peace at any price—any kind of peace."[31] However, "a very undesirable peace might have consequences," he says, "worse than those of many wars—even (some) thermonuclear wars."

But we have yet to learn from Professor Kahn's brilliant guesswork what *could* be worse. This circular reasoning reminds one of the aphorism that there *are* worse things than war, but war includes them all. The greatest danger we face, Professor Kahn asserts, is that a steadily intensifying crisis will culminate in war—because no country would initiate war today unless it were so desperate as to prefer war over all the other alternatives. Herman Kahn asks us to face squarely and unemotionally the terrors of a world fully capable of suicide. Thermonuclear annihilation is unlikely to come out of the blue, he suggests, but nations may elect to climb the ladder (did he mean downwards?) to hell. But we, his perplexed readers, have an ultimate question to ask: How did *homo sapiens* ever get involved with such a queer coterie of governmental advisers and "thinkers of the unthinkable"?

The question of both *how* and *when* governments should act rests on an answer to the prior question of *why* they should act. And that is not a military question, but a moral and political one. "Clausewitz's definition of war as the continuation of politics by other means remains valid, but modern warfare has now become a very intricate process and the strategic planning and control of operations calls for an unprecedented input of thought and study," says Michael Golovine in a highly technical work: *Conflict in Space.* He asks but does not adequately answer: What are the "factors contributing to the continuation of the present state of tension"? He does well to remind us: "The picture is complicated by the fact that, in addition to national interests and aspirations, ideological motives and impulses exert a considerable influence upon the general psychological environment. Thus, political doctrines of the Communist and Hitlerite type sharpen the aggressiveness of hidden nationalist aims. The primeval urge to aggrandize the tribe, community, or nation originates conflicts which are rendered more acute by ideological fanaticism fostered by irresponsible leaders."[32]

Of course. But does not this very argument include yet another category of fanatical doctrines—i.e. the nuclear strategists with their genocidal programs? Who can say that their open repudiation of traditional moral values, their fixation on mass-killing and uncalculated arson does not make *them* far more vicious and dangerous to our global society than Communist and Hitlerite types? Eichmann was tried and executed (os-

[31] H. Kahn: *On Escalation: Metaphors and Scenarios,* Praeger, New York, 1966.
[32] M. N. Golovine: *Conflict in Space,* St. Martin's Press, New York, 1962.

tensibly) because he carried out his government's orders. He possessed only limited means to destroy his tens of thousands. What kind of men are they who would destroy tens of millions, if their government so ordered?

Mini-Weapons and Over-Kill

Turning for a moment to the "local" school—i.e. using nuclear weapons "to stop the aggressor" or "force the enemy to the conference table"—what do we learn about what are casually called "tactical weapons"? Firstly, we discover that these mini-weapons are several times more destructive than Hiroshima and Nagasaki put together. Representative L. Mendel Rivers is reported to have said that it would be "immoral and un-Christian" not to use nuclear weapons "if needed to save our men at Khesanh." How "local" can nuclear devastation be? That is the real question. Secondly, we learn that in "escalating" any local war, nobody can be sure that "some mad or drunken officer will never throw one of these tactical weapons at the enemy in a brush-fire skirmish. Will the enemy fail to throw one back sooner or later? And where will the exchange then stop?" So asks Ralph E. Lapp, in a chapter appropriately headed "Accident, Miscalculation, or Madness" in his astoundingly frank work, *Kill and Overkill*.

The outspoken nuclear physicist underlines what every rational person ought to know when he hears hawkish politicians advocating the "limited" use of tactical weapons:

Many military men, as well as civilians, regard "tactical" nuclear weapons as a still more dangerous Pandora's box of accidents and miscalculations. The manufacture of these weapons, and the Pentagon proposals to use them in limited engagements, are the height of irresponsible nuclear gamesmanship. The first firing of a nuclear weapon in anger, no matter how small the weapon or how remote the battlefield, would enkindle alarm and panic throughout the world.[33]

Even General Lauris Norstad, one-time Commander of NATO, asserted in 1959:

I do not agree with those people who say that you can control the size of this fire . . . once it starts. I think that it is the most dangerous and disastrous thing in the world. I think that you must prevent the thing from starting in the first place, because once it starts in a critical area, such as the NATO area, it is more likely than not, in my opinion, to explode into the whole thing, whether we like it or the Russians like it or anybody likes it.

For that reason alone, what has become modestly known as the "presence" of the U.N. in brush-fire situations becomes more and more indispensable. There are two special reasons for this, as we shall go on to ex-

[33] R. E. Lapp: *Kill and Overkill*, Basic Books, New York, 1962.

plain in Chapter 7. First, because of the mutually restraining effect of its central debate on the rights and wrongs of the contestants—as happened in June 1967, when Israel's sudden attack on her Arab neighbors *might* have led to a bitter war of attrition involving the nuclear giants—and also by the local deployment of U.N. mediators or observers or actual peace-keeping forces. It is tact, not tactics, which stops wars. Moreover, it is easier for the alleged aggressors to climb down when the U.N. is seized of a violation of its Charter; but no one can climb down from a mushroom cloud.

This speculative uncertainty about nuclear missilry is known to the few, but it has so far done little to check the Pavlovian reaction of the many. Hanson W. Baldwin, the well-known military correspondent, said, when Russia had followed the U.S. example, in the usual way, and started some few years ago missile tests in the Pacific: "There is some obvious flexing of the Soviet missile muscle involved in the new rocket shoot in the Central Pacific, with the United States fleet, surfaced and submerged, not far away. The announcement creates an undeniable political and psychological impact—for the Russians are moving in to an open-ocean area hitherto ruled only by gooney birds, sea gulls and ships and planes of the United States Navy."[34]

So what is to be done? One would have imagined that, now the Russians had again caught up, this would be an ideal moment for the missile men to say "quits" or, at least, "let's stay put." But no, the mad race must accelerate. So the military expert advises: let us go one better; he says: "The utilization of Alaskan soil for intelligence purposes is paralleled by an extensive network of United States radar warning stations in the forty-ninth state, and a huge ballistic missile early-warning station is at Clear, Alaska. But what Alaska lacks is a missile 'punch,' or, in fact, any offensive power. The paradox and the tragedy of Alaska, one of the most strategic areas in the world, is that we have spent and are spending billions there for defense, in an age when the only good defense is a strong offense." That provocative arm-chair advice was given in 1960. Today the deed is done and billions more spent—while the Cold War itself begins to thaw and look more and more ridiculous in warmer climes.

No Exit

Most pathetic, perhaps, in the reelings of NATO from pillar to post was the short-lived episode which went under the initials "MLF." We recount the episode here because the NATO story is made up of many such stupid and wasteful ventures. Its proponents had claimed that, while adding little to Western military capability, it would at least hold together

[34] *New York Times,* January 11, 1960.

a disintegrating NATO and prevent Germany from obtaining nuclear arms. This multilateral nuclear force died without a whimper at five years of age on December 21, 1965, when the President of the United States and the Chancellor of West Germany, representing the only Governments still interested in the venture, buried it while nobody else was looking.

Volumes had been written about the idea. It was yet another footling fancy born of the State Department's policy planners. Conceived and publicized as a diplomatic necessity, MLF quickly grew—on paper, tons of it —into a mammoth military proposal to float a 5 billion dollar fleet of 25 surface ships bearing 200 Polaris missiles—enough to blow up the earth several times. This gigantic Atlantic Bubble was to be jointly financed by four or more Western allies and manned by mixed crews of *multilingual officers and men* from the national navies of the co-owners. The nuclear weapons were to be fired only upon order of the President of the United States, plus two or more participating Commanders-in-Chief.

The object of the plan was simple. When it came before the NATO Council in December 1960, its merits were proclaimed as "to share the burden and sense of ownership." The United States could thus preserve its nuclear monopoly over the West, while letting its European allies have the feeling of sharing in the management and operation of the ultimate weapons. Mixed-manning would prevent its withdrawal or unilateral use, and floating it on sea would spare the embarrassment and political pressures that would come with nuclear bases on land.

But, like the perfect crime, it never quite came off. The Americans hoped by these means to keep the French from building their own nuclear force and to persuade the British to surrender theirs, and so, by slowly strangling their two chief allied forces, it was imagined that no German Government would be tempted to copy them. The planning continued until 1962, when the British Air Force suddenly felt itself threatened by the Pentagon's cancellation of the promised air-to-ground Skybolt missile. In 1963 France signed a treaty of co-operation with West Germany, which set off fears that Paris and Bonn might secretly co-operate on atomic weapons. So MLF then became the bait to buy off the Germans.

Unfortunately, the Communist nations were so ill-advised as to imagine that this was the first step toward West German control of nuclear weapons. In fact nobody really liked MLF, and even the Pentagon accepted it as a second best. So, in December 1965, President Johnson proposed a Christmas holiday that proved fatal.[35] This capsule account of the birth and demise of MLF is given here to show, once more, that nuclear weapons can be acclaimed and accumulated as a "diplomatic necessity"—but nobody knows what to do with them after that.

Coming to the latest phase of this "no exit" program, the same computerized compulsionists are now urging that America should develop,

[35] *New York Times,* December 23, 1965.

stage by stage, an antiballistic missile system. Even Conservative opinion in Britain and Europe was shocked at the prospect of yet a new spiral of the Moscow-Washington race—a sort of three-legged race with a third competitor coming up to the front. "A Russian anti-ballistic missile defense against the Chinese and an American against the Chinese would be indistinguishable from a defense against each other. So, in the absence of a foolproof system of reciprocal inspection, both Moscow and Washington would become involved in an anti-anti-missile race, and would have to expand their offensive potential in the hope of having enough missiles to saturate the other's defenses."[36]

Yet, in the summer of 1967, a United States Senate Committee recommended that a "limited" anti-missile system should be set up immediately, to be described as a defense system against nuclear attack from *China*—the cost of which, incidentally, would be equal to that of the entire British defense budget. (Similar defense against Russia would cost ten times as much.) To announce a new "yellow peril" and to proclaim as stridently as possible that the country's safety in the 1970's is threatened now became the routine task of the immense public relations warning system of the Pentagon, so that the anti-missile money will be steadily forthcoming from the frightened taxpayer as ABMs proliferate their progeny. Wasn't he assured, a few years ago, that the nuclear deterrence packed into the first Polaris submarine was to be his ultimate means of salvation? Healthy negotiations with the Russians will recede yet further, for how could they be persuaded that the new screen is merely an anti-Chinese one, painted yellow, not red?

When former Secretary McNamara addressed the United Press International in September 1967 on what he described as "the gravest problem that an American Secretary of Defense must face: the planning, preparation, and policy governing the possibility of thermonuclear war," he explained to the world how the United States would now begin to take on China—without having even first disposed of Russia. The Nike-X system, as conceived by Pentagon planners, he said, would rely on long-range radar to pick up approaching enemy missiles thousands of miles away. Within four hundred miles of the target, Spartan missiles would be exploded in their path. If some of the invading missiles slipped through, Sprint missiles would be fired at them from within fifty miles of the target. The press and glossy magazines accordingly went to work on neat little diagrams drawn to scale, showing exactly how this latest war game would be played.

This is the voice of the sacred computer again. But, although anti-missile technology has improved substantially, the former Defense Secretary confessed "it is important to understand that *none of the systems at the present or foreseeable state of the art* would provide an impenetrable

[36] *The Yorkshire Post,* August 8, 1967.

shield over the United States" against an all-out Soviet attack. Nobel prize winner Dr. Hans A. Bethe and other noted nuclear physicists immediately denied that anti-missilry would protect American cities, but that the avoidance of war would.

A short and speedy answer to this further flight into futility was given by the Canadian-American Assembly, which met at Toronto in June 1967. Emphasizing that "the military value of anti-ballistic missiles is debatable," these friendly neighbors came to the following conclusion:

A race between the Soviet Union and the United States involving ballistic missile defense systems is incompatible with the hopes resting on the adoption of a non-proliferation treaty, and would seriously inhibit any progress toward nuclear arms control in the near future. It is urged that the United States and the Soviet Union agree, formally or tacitly, to forego a new arms race in defensive and offensive missiles.

When the defense chiefs of six NATO nations met at Ankara, Turkey, a few weeks later, McNamara confidently told them that this "limited" anti-missile deployment was "aimed" at China and not at the Soviet Union, so no "balance" would be upset. But the British Defense Minister, Denis Healy, expressed his own country's unhappiness at the timing of the plan's announcement. Other NATO nations were even more upset because they were only notified—not even consulted—when the decision was made. If protests were not louder, it was because everybody knew that this "limited" anti-anti venture was downright fatuous anyway. No one has yet leaped a chasm in several jumps.

True to form, this living embodiment of the military-industrial complex recounted in his next press statement that: "The road leading from the stone ax to the I.C.B.M.—though it may have been more than a million years in the building—seems to have run in a single direction." He might have been asked in what "direction" did he imagine the road would run, with so many McNamaras urging their governments along it? It strikes almost as an impertinence, at the end of a discourse presaging a vaster acceleration of the nuclear race, to be assured that: "In the end, the root of man's security does not lie in his weaponry. In the end, the root of man's security lies in his mind."[37]

State Within a State

This state within a state has become daily more demanding since the Vietnam intervention began. It seems almost as if an open-ended war were essential to win the support of both legislators and public as the fantasy of defense grew more unreal. To be appreciated fully, military "posture" has to be seen in action. Hanson Baldwin, Military Correspon-

[37] *New York Times,* September 19, 1967.

dent of the *New York Times,* recently described under the revealing caption: "The Disappointed Military," how the President's relatively restricted plans for the Vietnam operations were regarded in the Pentagon as a temporary or "stop-gap" measure only. They wanted so much more and they set about getting it. Champing at the bit, says Baldwin, "the military men recognize that base, harbor, and logistics facilities and airfields in Vietnam are inadequate for a big build-up and much construction and engineering work needs to be done." He pointed out with military triteness: "They feel it [victory] could be accomplished much more quickly if there were sufficient funds and a sense of urgency commensurate with what many regard as the increasing seriousness of the military situation."

It is not only for the Pentagon's own wars that pressure is exerted on the Administration. Pentagon officials have been quietly promoting among key members of Congress a plan to enable the Defense Department to continue selling arms to underdeveloped countries on easy credit terms through the Export-Import Bank. Previous authority, which had made possible over half a billion dollars' worth of arms credit sales to fourteen developing countries within the previous two years, had been killed by a recent Senate vote of 46 to 45. Yet the Administration assumed that the House would approve the Pentagon's arms credit sales authority as requested, for "the Administration contends that unless the credit sales authority is revived, it will be unable to bolster the defenses of pro-Western Middle East governments, and it also says it would be unable to meet 730 million dollars in *obligations to United States arms suppliers,* resulting from overseas commitments already made." (Italics added.)[38]

The Pentagon sales to foreign countries, largely to NATO allies, continue to make a major contribution to solve the United States' worsening balance-of-payments problem. Past arms sales have met from 40 to 50 per cent of the foreign exchange costs of United States overseas troop commitments outside of Southeast Asia. Such sales will reach a combined total of at least 4.5 billion dollars to 4.6 billion dollars over 1968 and the next two fiscal years.[39]

The art of selling itself has been developed to the point where the Pentagon has the most efficient and expensive public relations service anywhere in the United States—or the world for that matter. "The American Military Establishment spends 31 million dollars on public relations, as compared to the State Department's 1.5 million dollars. Public relations is an amiable phrase for controlling or shaping the news. The press release is the simplest and most rudimentary; the military puts down the information it means to give and in its own words. There is no appeal."[40]

[38] *New York Times,* August 20, 1967.
[39] *New York Times,* January 5, 1968.
[40] Tristram Coffin: *The Armed Society,* Penguin, London and New York, 1964.

It has been estimated that the military establishment publishes annually over a thousand newspapers and a mountain of magazines, press and mass media releases, and other Cold War publicity. It is perhaps most prolific in the "movie" field; the Pentagon runs the largest movie studio in the eastern United States. How much of this vast output is wasted or futile nobody will ever know. But it is a pretty certain guess that on any night of the week any person anywhere across the United States can flick his television dial and find a program with live American military personnel and current equipment fighting either real or fictitious battles, with Japanese or Germans, Chinese or Russians—the transposition of the "enemies" from one race or period to another is secondary, compared with the fact that the current "enemies" are there on the visible screen facing the viewer daily in his own home.

Thus, the flood of violent and sadistic films—wars and assassinations, murders and gun fights—which provide the major evening entertainment for the millions is supplemented by this continuous stream of military indoctrination, for which the American taxpayer has handsomely paid— though the T.V. industry still inflicts on him the banalities and indignities of its uninhibited commercial advertising.

Outside the home, the spate of "war" films in the movie theaters knows no limit, either of subject matter or degree of depravity, adding to the pre-conditioning of the average citizen. He finds it ever more difficult to distinguish fact from fiction, since the film industry normally plays down to the lowest passions and most arrogant type of nationalism.

One commentary must suffice, since the scandal of our modern film catalogue of sadism and violence is not hid under a bushel. Describing one of these "slaughter-house films," Bosley Crowther says: "Take this picture 'The Dirty Dozen,' which is a brazen and brutal account of how a group of American military prisoners, condemned for murder, rape and other major crimes, are taken from a military prison in England in World War II and secretly trained as a team of commandoes to mop up a chateau-full of Nazi officers on the eve of the assault on the Normandy coast. . . . If one could find in the structure of this picture, or in the way it was angled and staged, the slightest hint of intentional, sardonic comment upon the fundamental nature of war—the slightest glimmer of revelation that all killing is essentially criminal—then the hideous brutality of it might be regarded as subtle irony, and the glorifying of its felons as a tragic travesty."[41]

In addition to systematic coast-to-coast brainwashing of the American citizen, "the American military has 250 radio and 34 T.V. stations overseas," records Tristram Coffin, "with an eavesdropping audience of foreigners twenty times that of the Voice of America English-language

[41] Bosley Crowther: "Movies to Kill People By," *University* (No. 34), Princeton, 1967.

broadcasts. These stations are the principal entertainment media for fourteen million Japanese. The West Berlin military radio, a clear channel station, is heard all the way to the Dnieper . . . Major hotels overseas regularly use the local American military station as one of the pre-selected channels for room radios. The German radio-T.V. magazine described the American military network as 'the most popular station with the young people in half of Europe.' " This imposition of Cold War mass-communication on NATO countries is exemplified by the fact that American forces radio stations have been set up in Turkey, in spite of a Turkish law banning broadcasting outside the nationally operated radio network. Apart from its great expense to the American people, all this mental pressuring of the rest of the world might be regarded as fair game and legitimate, but for the fact that several U.N. resolutions have been adopted deploring this systematic invasion of other people's airspace. In the experience of the present author, this intrusion on the average European home listener is frequently resented and its influence greatly overestimated—certainly it can rarely have won a single convert to Americanism.

No Paper Tiger

It must not be assumed that all this tonnage of wood pulp and film-footage poured across the Atlantic turns NATO into a paper tiger. Its *raison d'être* is, of course, deterrence; and the essence of deterrence is publicity. But deterrence is not just a paper doctrine. "The range of our weapons," reported Captain Eugene Hinterhoff in a typical eulogy in the official journal *NATO's Fifteen Nations* in 1964, "varies from the half-kiloton warhead of the Davy Crockett mortars to the Redstone, Pershing or Mace, which have a several hundred-mile range, far in excess of the real requirements of a battlefield zone." As far as deterrent weapons of the United States are concerned, there were 90 Atlas missiles then and 120 by the end of that year. "Next year there will be 54 Titans," he continued. "By the beginning of 1965 there will be 950 Minuteman missiles and 650 Polaris missiles, all able to hit the Soviet Union." Since then, this stockpile of super-genocide has steadily expanded. But, as Professor Seymour Melman has pointed out, this means an "overkill capacity" of monstrous proportions. If all the megatonnage aimed at the Soviet Union hit that country it would be wiped out 1,250 times over.

Yet the suicidal doctrine of deterrence cannot be considered intelligently by one side only—it needs *acceptance* from the other side, i.e., the fellow to be deterred. But he may not want to accept what *we* tell him is good for him. He may look on it as an avoidable nuisance and do either of two things: get out of it by some escapist trick or set up a counter-deterrence to deter the deterrers. In either case, the deterrence doesn't come off. So we must set out again to deter the anti-deterrence. This is just what has happened and always will happen. The Maginot Line produced the Siegfried Line, as we noticed earlier. As their modern equivalents, NATO produced WARSAW. Now we have reached the anti-anti stage in nuclear defense—which can no longer *defend* us anyway. Playwright John Galsworthy expressed in the form of a modern Greek-Trojan tragedy the human waste involved in this kind of military futility and chose as the title of his play: "X = 0."

Secretary of Defense McNamara estimated shortly before he left the Cabinet in 1968 that American strategic forces could deliver up to 4,500 nuclear explosives against a Soviet capacity of about 1,000. In the next few years the United States will add missiles capable of putting into space a number of individually targetable warheads. Yet, the military equilibrium between the two nations is now based on the realization that any nuclear war between them would be mutually suicidal. This insane numbers game is described by NATO spokesmen as "the European shield." Walt Rostow, Chairman of the Policy Planning Council, spoke more truthfully than he realized back in 1963 when he said: "We understand why our friends in Europe may not be content, when threatened, merely to say to Moscow: Washington will protect us."

There are two simple and related answers to the fallacy of deterrence. The first answer is that it doesn't *pay;* and the second is that it doesn't *deter.* But any definition of deterrence rests for its sanction on *fear.* In another recent work entitled *Deterrence and Strategy,* General André Beaufre attempts to make this point clear:

The object of deterrence is to *prevent* an enemy power taking the decision to use armed force . . . This psychological result is the product of the combined effect of a calculation of the risk incurred, compared to the issue at stake and of the *fear* engendered by the risks and uncertainties of conflict.[42]

Other protagonists—and certainly the less responsible type of politician —insist on the threat being *real,* not theoretical. This is the way in which it was expressed some years back by one of the British co-authors of the doctrine, Air-Marshal Sir Victor Goddard (Retired), in his book, *The Enigma of Menace:*

The philosophy of deterrence is constantly bedevilled by misunderstanding of the meaning of it. The deterrence is not in the bomb, but in the determination behind it. Bluff may work for a while, and on occasions, but if there is no determination, there can, in the long run, be no deterrence.

In the same tradition, General Maxwell D. Taylor, when Army Chief of Staff, concluded an appeal for a more confident reliance on nuclear weapons by declaring: "We must have faith in deterrence and live by that faith if we are to have the power which assures the peace." But Amitai Etzioni, a Fellow of the Center for Advanced Study in the Behavioral Sciences, in discussing Bernard Brodie's *Escalation and the Nuclear*

[42] A. Beaufre: *Deterrence and Strategy,* Praeger, New York, 1966.

111

Option, advocating a "first strike" policy, draws attention to the grievous error in this philosophy when he states: "It is not only the odds which must be taken into account, but the magnitude of the disaster if one misjudges them. A sensible person may risk a few dollars even if the odds are against him, because he finds the prize attractive; but he would be quite senseless if he were to gamble all his possessions, let alone his life, even under much more favorable odds. Since the stakes of all-out nuclear war are high beyond comprehension, any policy that advocates risking the first round on the grounds that it may not lead to higher ones, is reckless."

Bernard Brodie had argued that a system of threats, on which true deterrence is based, requires the *occasional realization* of a threat if its credibility is to be preserved. But his critic responds: "Why couldn't the Russians, too, bolster the credibility of their threats with the occasional dropping of nuclear bombs?" It is a comfort that the behavioral scientists are with us also to correct the false analogies of professional soldiers and Iron Mountain strategists who still believe that nuclear missiles are weapons of national defense that can somehow be swung into position like Nineteenth Century cannon to win victories over an advancing foot soldier.

The top RAND expert in this field is probably Professor Herman Kahn, whose book *On Thermonuclear War* is (or was) regarded as the modern classic on the theory that nuclear war can somehow "pay," provided it is run in accordance with the American rules of the game. Professor H. Stuart Hughes asks whether Kahn, like Clausewitz before him, aspires to be "the master military strategist" of the age. Professor Hughes asserts that, unlike the inspirer of the Prussian juggernaut,

Kahn underestimates the effects of frightful devastation on the emotions of the survivors. Despite his efforts to convey to us the notion of thermonuclear war as a present reality, he is unconvincing in his suggestion that a nation such as our own, after losing its great urban centers and a third of its people, would go briskly about the task of picking up the pieces.[43]

Kahn has correctly pointed out that the sheer horror of these results has produced among military men and policy-makers the contemporary all-or-nothing stance—the conviction that the U.S. and the Soviet Union are linked by a "mutual suicide pact." Kahn believes that, theoretically, there are other choices available; but the mentality of our "defenders" is such that none of them is willing to abandon the actual policy of thermonuclear deterrence. Deterrence remains at the center of defense thinking and planning, although nobody really believes it *will* work. In fact, Kahn himself cites the cynical comment of one Pentagon official: "If these buttons are ever pressed, they have *completely failed* in their purpose! The equipment is useful only if it is not used."

[43] H. Stuart Hughes: *An Approach to Peace,* Atheneum, New York, 1962.

Bombs Among the Cargo

The basic fallacy of the deterrence myth has been summed up elsewhere by the present author in the following terms:

We are confronted with the spectacle of a race of the Nuclear Powers towards a war of mutual extermination, spurred forward by the most fantastic doctrine ever known to man. The "nuclear deterrent" is a spurious offspring, born of "massive retaliation" and sired by "negotiation from strength" . . . Both these highly abstract defense policy terms, "retaliation" and "deterrence," have been used as if they had a concrete meaning—like a medieval suit of armor, or a wall around a beleaguered town. They are, of course, nothing of the sort.[44]

To this general warning can be added the certainty that the present "balance of terror" cannot stay as it is. For one thing, more super-powers may arise before the end of the century to upset the balance, the Non-Proliferation Draft Treaty notwithstanding. Mao has said that men are more important than weapons, but he clearly has not overlooked the latter either. Weapons have, in fact, run away with men. To build national defense on deterrence between two pre-selected "sides" is like two ship-wrecked sailors pulling each other down in panic and desperation instead of swimming together to the shore. There *must* be an alternative to oblivion!

Not only are the Big Powers involved. The urgency of the agreements sought by the Committee of Seventeen at Geneva cannot be gainsaid. The high significance of the 1968 Non-Proliferation Treaty was underlined some years ago when the present Minister of Defense, Denis Healey, wrote in a pamphlet entitled *The Race Against the H-Bomb* as follows: "A country which wants atomic weapons for bullying an enemy with poor defenses and no atomic weapons of its own may be satisfied with a few kiloton bombs and a primitive delivery system—two nominal atomic bombs exploded in the holds of cargo vessels in the harbors of Haifa and Tel Aviv could destroy Israel as a State . . . Once atomic weapons begin to spread into the Middle East, Africa, and Asia, there will be greater danger that nuclear striking power may be used, not just as a deterrent, but for aggression."[45]

If nuclear weapons spread geographically with the inevitability of a chain reaction, as they may, so does the peril. The belief that a world-wide "balance of terror" can preserve peace proceeds from completely erroneous premises. No such "balance" can be held or ever will, because it is the nature of military research to *upset* the balance. And, when the whole world becomes one vast powder-keg, ready to explode from a single careless spark, no one knows who will be responsible.

How easily and unexpectedly that spark can be ignited—when all reasonable precautions in the world had been taken and there was no

44 J. Avery Joyce: Chapter entitled, "The Myth of Deterrence and Nuclear Weapons," in *Capital Punishment, A World View,* Thos. Nelson, New York, 1963.
45 Denis Healey: *The Race Against the H-Bomb,* Fabian Society, London, 1960.

enemy in sight to upset the works—can be illustrated by quite recent events. The first fell as a sudden warning of what might happen elsewhere on an infinitely bigger scale one day soon, when in July 1967 in the Gulf of Tonkin, 150 miles off war-wracked Vietnam, an inferno of fire and explosions swept through the mighty U.S.S. "Forrestal." A Skyhawk bomber, taking off on a bombing mission against North Vietnam, spewed flame around it in what is known as a "hot start." The flames struck a nearby missile, intended for the "enemy"; the missile tore loose and struck the fuel tank of another plane. The fuel ignited and spilled over the deck. More and more flames spread as a river of fire entered the bowels of the ship through the holes ripped in the decks by explosions. Men rushed to other rockets, which might have exploded at any moment, and heaved them over the side. But more than 130 of their shipmates were doomed. It all happened in spite of every precaution.

By way of less tragic contrast, we might review the far more serious incident that did *not* occur just a month earlier, in the actual words of Defense Secretary Robert S. McNamara, who stated: "Take the case of the Liberty last June," he said. (The Liberty was that ultrasophisticated electronic intelligence ship that was suddenly attacked by Israeli warplanes in the Mediterranean.) "I thought the Liberty had been attacked by Soviet forces. Thank goodness our carrier commanders did not launch immediately against the Soviet forces who were operating in the Mediterranean at the time."

The Pueblo incident a few months later came as another reminder of how quickly the Cold War could become a hot one. The state of instant readiness for war is so definitely dangerous, because there are few rights and wrongs about such incidents; nor do moral or legal issues have time to operate. Both sides are spying on each other all the time. All claim they are operating in international waters, or on their own side of the frontier, keeping the law. Before another Pueblo spark reaches the powder keg, the only sane way to peace and security is through United Nations supervision on control of the danger spots. We have to come back to that alternative every time.

The Korean crisis over the impounded spyship in January 1968 proved that neither bilateral diplomacy nor the threat of war could have brought the release of the Pueblo and its crew. There was no conceivable use of force against North Korea which could achieve its object or even command world support. The Americans could not drop bombs on North Korea because that would be more likely to cause the death of the Pueblo's crew than their release. The presence of the nuclear aircraft carrier stationed off North Korea was more likely to defeat its own purposes, because nobody seriously believed that the Americans were going to use this giant hammer to crack the miniscule nut. The world would have been horror-struck if they had done that. The London *Times* observed: "The contrast between their gigantic military resources and their very small immediate political aim, and their inability to match the two, is infinitely frustrating for the Americans . . . That is why the Security Council—and indeed all governments—must do all they can to ease the situation." [46] So, today, the plain fact is that in crises the U.S. seems to need the U.N. more than the U.N. needs the U.S.

The Pueblo dilemma, it will be recalled, followed close on yet another scandal which occurred off the coast of Greenland late in 1967, during the course of an illegal flight of a U.S. warplane which crashed in flames and deposited its nuclear bomb load on the floor of the polar sea, to the peril of other ships and planes.

The lesson is never learned, yet the list of offenses accumulates. Just a year earlier, Tad Szulc tells in *The Bombs of Palomares* of the consequences of the collision over Spain in January 1966 between an American bomber carrying four hydrogen bombs and the tanker from which it was refueling. Again, no enemy in sight. No attack. But the aircraft disintegrated in flames over a sleepy seaside village called Palomares. Three of the bombs fell on land, and one in the Mediterranean. The first problem was to locate the bombs, and an enormous American task force was sent to the area and soon managed to discover three of the bombs. But the fourth bomb was not recovered until two months later, when it was found perched on the edge of a deep ravine at the bottom of the Atlantic sea. Detonations of the trigger mechanisms of two of the bombs, however, had caused the release of plutonium in the area; so an immense decontamination exercise was set in motion by the senior partner of NATO. (Spain is not a member of NATO, but enjoys its benign protection.) Compensation has been paid and the Palomares crops appear to be growing again; but there is no known method of assessing the long-term effects of plutonium poisoning. So the case is not closed. [47]

Nobody knows when or how it will happen, or how quickly it will spread, but nuclear destruction and nuclear contamination today hang like a common plague over mankind. It might be the careless handling of a single tactical weapon in one of NATO's innocent little war games, or the wrong interpretation of a flight of gooney birds across a radar screen in Alaska that brings down that plague upon us. Some start must be made to avert the mathematical certainty that the balance of terror can *never* balance. And that start *must* include the dissolution of NATO, whatever other steps are necessary to de-escalate the armed anarchy that NATO symbolizes and perpetuates.

The True Defense of Peace

The same Denis Healey quoted above and who is now the British Cabinet member responsible concerning these questions has stated: "The

[46] The London *Times,* January 27, 1968.
[47] Tad Szulc: *The Bombs of Palomares,* Gollancz, London, 1967.

strategic concept under which the NATO commanders have to work at present is many years out of date. It is absurd to expect that NATO could fight, or even more win, a general war in Europe lasting for several months after nuclear exchange had started. It is just not 'on.' " So confessed the British Minister of Defense in the House of Commons on March 3, 1965; and he added a few seconds later: "President Johnson told the American people last September that in the first nuclear exchange 100,000,000 Americans and more than 100,000,000 Russians would all be dead. In any so-called tactical nuclear battle in Europe, the damage and casualties would be no less catastrophic. Organized society would cease to exist. In such circumstances, even the idea of organized warfare is a blasphemous mockery."

What kind of double-talk, then, is this? Have both sides of the Atlantic gone mad? Presumably, the more than 50,000,000 British subjects in between would also disappear on their unsinkable aircraft carrier? NATO ensures that they will. *Without* NATO 100,000,000 Americans and 100,000,000 Russians and 50,000,000 Britishers would have a better chance, on the known facts, to stay alive. And so on around the NATO family circle.

For what, then, are we waiting? There is a tide in the affairs of men which can be taken at the flood when the Treaty expires. The 1970's can become the Decade of Détente instead of the Débacle of Deterrence.

Interestingly enough, Italy, a NATO voice which does not get the lion's share of publicity in European defense questions, was heard recently. Guiseppe Saragat, in his inaugural address as President of Italy, made some statesmanlike observations which might well underline the purport of this chapter: "Technology has rendered possible," he said, "the construction of monstrous weapons which, if used, would make every trace of life disappear from our planet. *Thus, the defense of peace is the first duty of legislators, men of government, and chiefs of state* . . . Peace, which today is guaranteed by a balance of force, a balance to which Italy contributes in participating in the defensive Atlantic Alliance with the great democracies —must become inviolable with progressive, simultaneous, and controlled disarmament." This could be brought about, Italy's Chief of State declared, by a relaxation of international tensions and through talks between governments representing diverse political, economic and social systems "in understanding and tolerance."

So we are back once again with the United Nations and with "understanding and tolerance"—or, as the Charter prescribes: "a center for harmonizing the actions of nations."

4 THE UGLY SISTERS

"I hope that you will not consider it presumption for me to say that the integrity of these alliances is at the heart of the maintenance of peace."

—Dean Rusk at 1967 Annual Meeting of Chamber of Commerce.

When the Geneva Conference on Indo-China closed on the afternoon of July 21, 1954, the author was standing at a third floor window of the European Office of the United Nations (which had housed and serviced the Conference) watching the exhausted delegates emerge onto the central plaza. A colleague nudged me and asked: "But where is Dulles?" Someone from behind replied: "He's gone out the back door!"

John Foster Dulles, chief U.S. delegate, had, in fact, boycotted the Geneva proceedings some weeks earlier, embittered and frustrated, after a token attendance of a few days. From the start he had realized that this Peace-in-Southeast-Asia happening was not his cup of tea. In Geneva, the Anglo-French alliance was on all fours with the Russian-Chinese bloc. Poor Dulles was a fifth wheel on the chariot of peace. He had made desperate attempts earlier in the year to dissuade Anthony Eden and the successive French Prime Ministers to drop the whole idea. But Eden was adamant and Mendès-France had staked his political career on winding up the French débacle in Vietnam. Both Westerners were astute and seasoned diplomatists, while the other two negotiators confronting Dulles were none other than Molotov and Chou En-lai. Unfortunately for Dulles, both of them had solid reasons of their own for winding up the French colonial war.

For the first time, the master of brinkmanship was stopped in his tracks. But only for a brief time, as we shall note. Dulles was conducting a personal war against *Communism;* but the other men around the Conference

117

table had come to Geneva, with the rare backing of both Eastern and Western worlds, to restore peace to the peoples of Southeast Asia by means of a reasonably negotiated settlement after two decades of foreign invasion and bloody war.

"Three or four centuries ago, when Reformation and Counter-Reformation divided Europe into armed camps, in an age of wars of religion, it was not so rare to encounter men of the type of Dulles," said Sir Oliver Franks, former British Ambassador to the United States: "Like them, he saw the world as an arena in which the forces of good and evil were continuously at war."

The Conference, after dragging on for nearly three months, turned out to be an unexpected and unexampled triumph. It owed much to the tactful steering of joint-Chairman Eden, no less than to a series of mutual compromises between the Communist giants and France, supported by Britain. The delegate who made most concessions was Ho Chi Minh's representative; he was in a strong position to do so because the forces under Ho Chi Minh had just soundly defeated the Western interventionists (France backed by the U.S.) and he stood head and shoulders above the local and provincial leaders who all owed much to Ho's brilliant leadership and political sagacity.

Nearly twenty years of continuous warfare in Southeast Asia was more than enough. The sense of relief in Geneva was never more evident than at the conclusion of the Agreements. Prime Minister Nehru was typical of world-wide reaction when he praised them as "the most valuable international accomplishment since the end of the Second World War."

U Thant, addressing a correspondents' luncheon in New York in 1967, recalled this universal acclaim when he stated:

These Agreements, the first of their kind to be arrived at between all great Powers, were probably one of the most important achievements in the field of international relations since the end of World War II. If there is a willingness to return to the situation envisaged by these Agreements, then the way would be open for new, imaginative and constructive steps towards peace.

But Dulles had already flown off in a rage. His strong aversion to having any direct contact with Molotov was well known, and while in Geneva he did his utmost to avoid even passing Chou En-lai in the U.N. corridors. Indeed, when he found he could no longer block the Geneva plan, he was already in his Washington office drafting the rival document, which he presented exactly six weeks later at Manila as the text of the "SEATO" Treaty. Meanwhile, he persuaded his deputy, General Bedell Smith, to occupy his Geneva seat. It was the Under-Secretary of State who, therefore, on the next to the last day (July 20) uttered those fateful words which were to account for the presence of over half a million American fighting men in Vietnam ten or twelve years later. These were his words: *"My Government is not prepared to join in a Declaration by the Conference* *such as is submitted."* And he continued: "The United States makes this unilateral declaration of its position. . ."* Then follows the one and only "commitment" which the United States Government has ever officially made about Vietnam—if the word commitment means a commitment to somebody other than to oneself. The Geneva text reads:

"The Government of the United States of America declares with regard to the aforesaid Agreement and paragraphs that:
(i) It will refrain from the threat or the use of force to disturb them, in accordance with Article 2 (Section 4) of the Charter of the United Nations . . . and
(ii) It would view any renewal of the aggression in violation of the aforesaid Agreement with grave concern and as seriously threatening international peace and security."

Here we have a prime example of the Dulles diplomacy. After backing the "aggressors" (i.e., the French) for nearly a decade and having spent an estimated two billion dollars to help re-establish their pre-war colonial administration, the one and only United States commitment—squeezed out of the State Department at the tail end of the agenda—is to get out and to stay out of Vietnam.

Note that this belated declaration was made *unilaterally*. This means that, irrespective of what any other party did or did not do, the United States had pledged itself to respect the terms of the Agreement. When the renewed Vietnam conflict had been fully taken over by the United States and began to turn into a vicious holding operation and American casualties began to mount in 1965, the White House became aware of what the rest of the Western world had long been urging and began itself to advocate "a return to the Geneva Agreement," but without withdrawing American troops in accordance with the Agreement. In other words, a double-faced policy developed over 1966 and 1967, escalating the war still further; but calling on everyone else to seek a solution on the basis laid down in 1954. Yet, by the very terms of the United States' own freely chosen commitment, no one else was strictly involved or obligated in any way. The United States did not have to wait for anyone else to do something first or mutually. "Reciprocity" was ruled out by the United States' voluntary unilateral declaration in 1954.

The origins, atmosphere, and conditions which prevailed at this historic Conference should be recalled, for it may well prove the turning-point between the way of life and the way of death for this century. Rarely have the two roads stood out in clearer contrast: a negotiated settlement which,

* The official minutes of this vital Conference were published at the time in the United Kingdom, Command Paper No. 9238 (London, 1954), but were never, it seems, generally available for the American public, until the War had escalated to such an extent as to release the flood of books which has since appeared, such as *Vietnam: History, Documents and Opinions,* edited by Marvin E. Gettleman, Fawcett Publications, New York, 1965.

119

in spite of all its imperfections and dangers, could have set Southeast Asia on the road to peace, on the one hand, and a continued war which has become a road to Calvary for the Vietnamese people, on the other hand.

Walter S. Robertson, Assistant-Secretary of State for Far Eastern Affairs, who also sat in at the Conference, spoke candidly to the Dulles brief. He made such violent attacks on the other delegates that Anthony Eden in his memoirs refers to him as "so emotional as to be impervious to argument or indeed to facts." This irate and badly informed gentleman told the Geneva Conference that three hundred thousand men were still anxious to fight for Bao Dai—the French-supported playboy Emperor who had collaborated with the Japanese against the Viet-Minh—if only they had U.S. "support and encouragement."

He had testified to a House Appropriations Committee earlier that same year as follows, and his words reveal very clearly why Dulles had no use for the Geneva Conference:

The heart of the present policy toward China and Formosa is that there is to be kept alive a constant threat of military action vis-à-vis Red China in the hope that at some point there will be an internal breakdown. . . . In other words, a cold war waged under the leadership of the U.S., with constant threat of attack against Red China, led by Formosa and other Far Eastern groups and militarily supported by the United States.

So the Chinese cat slips out of the Vietnam bag. The Vietnamese people were not to be allowed to have their country back, after two decades of continuous national struggle. Another half-country was preferable to a united and independent country on China's southern frontier, friendly to its powerful neighbor. Looking back over the years, it cannot be said that the United States has ever repudiated that view of China as a territory to be surrounded with hostile governments and military bases.

In pursuance of this pernicious doctrine China now faces a Maginot line of military might from north to south. The United States has sent 40,000 troops to Japan; 60,000 to Korea; 50,000 to Guam and Okinawa, 50,000 to Formosa; 40,000 to the Philippines; 35,000 to Thailand; and 50,000 are in the Seventh Fleet; while over half a million have been fighting in South Vietnam, and air attacks on North Vietnam have frequently threatened the borders of a China that has not (at this time) a single soldier or military installation outside its own territory.

When the U.S. President came under increasing pressure during 1966 and 1967, both from responsible political leaders like Senator Fulbright, Chairman of the Senate Foreign Relations Committee, and from leaders of Western countries and from the Secretary-General of the United Nations, he again and again insisted: We are in Vietnam because the United States *and our allies* are committed by the SEATO treaty to "act to meet the common danger" of aggression in Southeast Asia. Similarly, Secretary of State Dean Rusk at many congressional hearings—as the

120

legal and moral position became more and more untenable—categorically cited the Southeast Asian Treaty Organization as the real source of President Johnson's *legal* authority for sustaining the war in Vietnam. This alleged legal authority, in fact and in law, we shall now examine.

How Geneva Was Sabotaged

Before Dulles tried his luck again at Manila, the contemporary records (such as Eisenhower's published memoirs and Dulles' own flamboyant speeches) make it clear that the Geneva results—especially the call for country-wide elections by July 1956—were to be discreetly buried as soon as the Conference broke up. "Dulles fathered SEATO with the deliberate purpose, as he explained to me," wrote C. L. Sulzberger in the *New York Times,* "of providing the U.S. President with legal authority to intervene in Indo-China. When Congress approved SEATO, it signed the first of a series of blank checks yielding authority over Vietnam policy." Meanwhile, a Catholic Mandarin named Ngo Dinh Diem had been quietly rescued from three years of exile in a New Jersey monastery after his retreat to Paris, and installed in Saigon. He was most generously accompanied by U.S. plain-clothes military advisers and "counter-subversion" agents who began to arrive in greater numbers to bolster his dictatorship. A security police training program at Michigan State University and other C.I.A. subsidized institutions were rapidly called in aid.

When Diem arrived, amid the Catholic versus Buddhist wrangles and post-war confusion south of the Geneva temporary cease-fire line, his authority did not run far beyond his palace walls. How could *he* win a state-wide election against Ho Chi Minh, the George Washington of his people who had succeeded to the presidency of *all* Vietnam before the French staged their abortive comeback in the South, and whose sensible land reforms, carried out from the ancient seat of Hanoi, were the hope of the impoverished peasantry everywhere?

By the time the plain-clothes "advisers" had done their work thoroughly in the South, there were supposedly 600,000 men under arms—trained, equipped and paid for by Diem's only sponsor, the United States, not by the people of Vietnam. The variegated assemblage of opposition leaders—Buddhists, liberal Catholics, socialists, Communists and other sects—were by end of the 1950's either executed or in jail, or had fled to Paris or to the mountains to join the National Liberation Front. Some 700,000 Catholics ("refugees from Communism") were transported by U.S. transport from the North to give Diem a strong footing politically and to counterbalance the Buddhist opposition. This steady and unpublicized infiltration into the South by the United States military and their supporters was consolidated before even the term "Viet Cong" came into popular use on

American T.V. and radio or "aggression" by the North had become the *raison-d'être* of U.S. official policy.

But it was SEATO which was designed to give the real *coup de grâce* to the Geneva Agreement. The date of the signing of the Pact, namely, September 8, 1954, is itself significant, following so speedily on the heels of Dulles' defeat at Geneva. Eden has told in his memoirs why he refused to look at Dulles' design for a Southeast Asian alliance until the Geneva Conference was over, in case it should prejudice the Geneva decisions. Certainly, Dulles had great disappointments awaiting him at Manila, too, especially when he came head on, once more, with British obstinacy and French war-weariness. Let Richard Goold-Adams, Dulles' biographer, continue the story:

Although the British were willing to consider and eventually sign a mutual defense agreement covering Southeast Asia, they did not particularly relish the idea, and they certainly did not feel that it should be put into writing before the end of the Geneva negotiations. A fair section of American opinion, on the other hand, still felt keenly about military agreements. . . . Accordingly, in spite of all the acrimony and misgivings, Dulles worked steadily forward during the summer of 1954 to achieve a Southeast Asian security pact.[1]

Dulles reached Manila in the Philippines on September 6 for the Conference. Representatives from seven countries, Britain, France, Australia, New Zealand, Pakistan, Thailand, and the Philippines, soon joined him there. It was a brief and streamlined affair, the cards having been carefully stacked during Dulles' itinerant discussions around the earth during the previous five months. This was Dulles' concrete response to Geneva. And "what a thing of rags and tatters" it proved to be!

Many leading nations of South and Southeast Asia flatly refused to come to Manila. India, Burma, Nepal, Indonesia, and Ceylon, as well as the recently neutralized nations, Vietnam, Cambodia and Laos, sent specific rejections of the proposed pact. All these absentees from Southeast Asia were (or were soon to become) members of the United Nations—except unfortunate Vietnam, which had still to await its reunification under a legally elected government before it could participate as a sovereign state in events pertaining to its own survival. Even pro-Western Malaysia and Singapore, when statehood came to them later on, refused to join, though the door had been left open for them; their armed forces were not to be regarded as part of SEATO, and no SEATO operations were to be carried out from bases on their soil. Dulles could do nothing about the major absentees. All of them were outspoken opponents of his plan. But he had cleverly netted the three minor absentees in his ingenious Protocol.

Before the Manila meeting had even begun, Prime Minister Nehru had

[1] Richard Goold-Adams: *John Foster Dulles: A Reappraisal,* Appleton-Century-Crofts, Inc., New York, 1962.

declared on August 8, 1954, that India, Burma, and Indonesia had stated their opposition to SEATO "in unambiguous terms." He added that:

We have expressed our inability to participate in this meeting because it seems to us that it is likely to reverse the trend of conciliation released by the Indo-China settlement. Collective security, according to our belief, can only come by resolving world tensions and developing the pattern of collective *peace*. . . . The proposed Southeast Asian collective organization will in the present circumstances do more harm than any good that it may hope to do in the future.

Nehru foresaw what we now know to have been lamentably true. Opening a foreign affairs debate in the Indian Council of States that same month, the Prime Minister elaborated on their decision to stay away from the SEATO meeting: "We came to the conclusion . . . that this particular move, more especially at this particular juncture, was unfortunate. It was likely to change the whole trend toward peace that the Geneva Conference has created by its decisions on Indo-China."

That is exactly what did happen—and what the veteran cold warrior from the West intended should happen. It was at this period that Dulles publicly pronounced Nehru's neutralism as "immoral." (Toward whom? we might ask.) The chairman of the Indonesian Parliament's Foreign Affairs Committee declared in similar terms that Indonesia's foreign policy was opposed to all military pacts. Membership in the proposed SEATO alliance would mean "siding with one of the blocs in the Cold War," and that was what his country was trying to avoid.

But Dulles, obsessed with his falling dominos, never took "No" for an answer. He told the Manila Conference that the 7,000 mile distant United States had "a sense of common destiny" with countries concerned in opposing *the spread of Communism,* whether by open aggression, subversion, or indirect aggression. Against the first of these dangers, he said, it would be impossible to ensure defense by stationing adequate land forces at selected points, since the "free" nations could not match the vast land armies of the Communist Powers. The U.S. would therefore think in terms of mobile striking power with strategically placed reserves.

The two related factors which predominated in Dulles' mind were Communism and a *military* response to it. He regretted the absence of Cambodia, Laos, and *South* Vietnam from the Conference, but hoped that some "mantle of protection" could be thrown over those states as a result of Manila. This line of argument was a direct repudiation of the Geneva decisions, which had plainly stipulated a neutral and "unified" Vietnam and had laid down the specific electoral and supervisory machinery for securing it. (The Geneva text runs thus: "The military demarcation line is provisional and should not in any way be interpreted as constituting a political or territorial boundary.") Naturally, the British and French (second-ranking) representatives at Manila—though giving the U.S. Secretary of State his day in Court—were nettled by this strong-armed attitude, and they took a back seat at the conference.

Prince Wan of Thailand associated himself with Dulles' arguments and even urged a pact along the lines of NATO. He offered Bangkok as the headquarters of the new regional organization and advocated the inclusion of Cambodia, Laos and (note again!) *South* Vietnam in such regional security arrangements. This fact should be borne in mind, for ten years later, Thailand has been virtually taken over militarily by the United States as its main base. (The speeches of the Thai representative at the SEATO routine council meeting which took place in New Zealand in April 1968 make pathetic reading amidst the dreadful silences of the other delegations who failed to come or failed to speak.)

No official statement was issued until the final terms of the Treaty were disclosed on September 8. Divergent opinions had arisen from the start as to whether the pact should be directed only against "Communist aggression," or against *any* form of aggression from whatever quarter. The latter was not only the emphatic British and French positions, but it represented also the opinion of all the other parties. Dulles continued to insist that the Pact should be of an exclusively anti-Communist character. But as the others would not give way, the implacable Secretary of State informed the Conference that his delegation would have to include a special reservation in the Treaty expressing the U.S. Government's view that it was specifically *directed against Communists*. Thus, on September 8, with the signing by the seven other delegations of the Treaty, the final text was accompanied by—in addition to the ingenious Protocol—a *unilateral declaration* by the United States that the Pact was directed against "Communist aggression." It is claimed that this was how Dulles managed to get the Treaty through the U.S. Senate.

This second "go it alone" gesture came barely six weeks after the Geneva *unilateral declaration,* namely, that the United States would get out and stay out of Indo-China. It can hardly be wondered, with so much unilateralism in the mid-1950's, that the United States should have found itself by the mid-1960's practically alone in the Western world, bogged down in an essentially colonial war, contrary to its solemn United Nations and international obligations, pitted against an Eastern people who had never asked for U.S. "protection" or injured its vital interests in any way.

Until February 1966, when Dulles' successor at the State Department disinterred it—to defend U.S. policy from increasing attacks from within and without—the Manila Pact (as it first was called) had been largely forgotten. Occasional peregrinations of military planners and information officers to keep it before the public were all the notice it received for over ten years. One critic, describing what he termed "The Sudden Rediscovery of SEATO," said pointedly:

The citation by Secretary of State Rusk of the Southeast Asian Treaty of 1954 as the fundamental source of President Johnson's authority to commit the

United States to whatever expenditure of manpower and treasure he deems "necessary" to sustain the war in Vietnam, was a shift of emphasis by the Administration. And the reason is as plain as the ground is weak . . . Senatorial voices were rising in protest against the Administration's oft-reiterated claim that the President's open-ended commitment in Vietnam derives from the so-called Gulf of Tonkin resolution approved by Congress in 1964.[2]

A more significant shift of emphasis, in fact, has been the transformation of this horrible war—in Washington—from a rebellion against an imposed "colonial" government to an aggression from outside. Rarely has the Big Lie technique been more ruthlessly applied or exposed. We can contrast, on the one hand, Dulles' statement of 1950 that: "This is a civil war in which we have, for better or worse, involved our prestige—that is why we must help the government we back" (i.e. France); with the assertion, on the other hand, of General William C. Westmoreland at a press conference in New York on April 25, 1967 that, "What we have is not a civil war. It is a massive campaign of external aggression from North Vietnam." In an official statement issued in New York by the Permanent U.N. Observer of the Republic of Viet Nam on December 13, 1967, the National Liberation Front was described as *"outlaws rebelling against a legitimate and legal government."*

Amid these self-assertive voices which have for so many years deafened the American public with their blatant falsehoods and shabby excuses, how refreshing it is to listen for a while to some of the new men who are trying to salvage the American Dream. Such a voice is Senator Eugene McCarthy's when he suggests: "There is never a totally painless way to pull back from either unwise, ill-advised, or outdated commitments. But throughout history, mighty nations have learned the limits of power."[3]

General Maxwell D. Taylor, U.S. Ambassador in Saigon in 1964-65, perhaps more than any other individual, carries the heaviest moral and advisory responsibility for this mounting tragedy. Yet the former Chairman of the Joint Chiefs of Staff and President of the Institute for Defense Analyses had the temerity to state when a return to the Geneva Agreements became official Washington policy: "In such a contest for such stakes, as President Kennedy said in 1961, 'We cannot stand aside.' Having taken sides, this side can and must prevail." The General made nonsense of the President's ostensible offer to negotiate *on the basis of the Geneva Agreements,* when he stated: "We must not yield to the specious slogan: 'Let's stop shooting and start talking.' It will be essential to keep up the military pressure while we negotiate."[4] How did he expect any enemy to negotiate while under continued attack? The Geneva Agreements themselves are based on precisely the opposite—a cease-fire and military pullback. The farcical proceedings of the so-called Paris "peace"

[2] Arthur Krock: *New York Times,* March 6, 1966.

[3] Eugene J. McCarthy: *The Limits of Power,* Holt, Rinehart & Winston, New York, 1967.

[4] *The New York Times Magazine,* October 15, 1967.

negotiations in the summer of 1968 were a living exhibition of the Taylor formula, accompanied as they were by an increased bombing of North Vietnam.

Lip Service and Other Lapses

As with NATO, the SEATO treaty opens with routine lip-service to the Charter of the United Nations. In past centuries international treaties opened by evoking the name of God. Today God has been replaced by protestations of adherence to the principles of the Charter. The practical outcome, however, is not conspicuously different. The genuineness of this initial declaration of loyalty to the United Nations can be contested in various ways. Firstly, SEATO seeks to bypass the United Nations by a diplomatic subterfuge. It evades the basic principles of the Charter, prohibiting the use or threat of force without recourse to the Security Council, and it attempts to substitute a military alliance based on principles directly opposed to the Charter.

According to its chief architect, SEATO's prime purpose was to "supplement" the Geneva settlement by discouraging future Communist expansion. Yet it should be noticed that each of the seven parties (Great Britain, France, New Zealand, Australia, Pakistan, Thailand and the Philippines) already had ample military ties with the United States. No party is obliged to do anything under the Treaty, except to take *individual* action—which it would take anyway.

Secondly, SEATO recognizes the limitations—since it was drafted in the U.S.—of restricting executive war-making power, as embodied in the United States Constitution. These legal limitations, contained in the SEATO Treaty itself, could not have been more strongly described than in the words of Chairman George of the Committee on Foreign Relations, when the Treaty came up for discussion in the Senate, as follows:

The Treaty does not call for automatic action: it calls for "consultation" (with the other signatories). If any course of action shall be agreed . . . then that action must have the approval of Congress, because the "constitutional process" of each signatory government is provided for . . . I cannot emphasize too strongly that we have no obligation . . . to take positive measures of any kind. All we are obligated to do is to consult together about it.

Uncertainties in its voting procedures are indicative of the absence of any real political consensus within the Alliance. Unlike NATO, its organizational structure is virtually non-existent. The Treaty added nothing to anyone's security. That is one reason why, for over ten years, nobody bothered about it—until, that is, the Vietnam *war* had to be accorded the appearance of legality.

In the event, SEATO turned out to be merely a set of bilateral arrangements between the seven countries and the United States. Its fundamental weakness was never put more succinctly than by Professor Peter Lyon, in a study entitled "Seato in Perspective":

SEATO was born an ailing alliance. Conceived at leisure and delivered in haste, with the United States its harassed and impatient father, and Thailand its partially pleased but worried mother, the first draft obituaries for this infant alliance soon began to appear. They have continued to do so ever since.[5]

The only "ally" to which SEATO has meant anything is Thailand. The result is that today Thailand is in an extraordinarily unenviable and perilous position. For in Thailand the usual pattern inevitably followed. By 1958 Thailand had suffered a military dictatorship, when Field-Marshal Sarit Thanarat overturned the Government and suspended the 1952 constitution and parliamentary assembly with the stock excuse of combating Communist inroads. "The historical influence of the United States in Siam's affairs is most interesting, as it explains the background of the May 1962 landings of U.S. Marines," explains Prof. J. S. Roucek in an article, "Thailand in Geopolitics," on his return from that country: "The American-equipped Thai army played a major role in the September 1957 *coup d'état,* which enabled Field-Marshal Sarit Thanarat to seize control of the government."[6]

Since then, the virtual Pentagon take-over of Thailand, with its five colossal air fields (a sixth is under construction) and several U.S.-built harbors and its incredible network of military roads and stations, has become the major base of attacks against Vietnam.* And now, more and more Thai troops are there. Ten thousand were pledged by the end of 1967. Meanwhile, pockets of "Communists" in the North-Eastern provinces—where peaceful Chinese "immigrants" have lived for several generations—have grown in direct ratio to the impoverishment of the peasantry who make up most of the population. The latter have gained nothing from the rapid inflow of dollars to the American installations, which has knocked the bottom out of the rural economy.

The Philippines, together with Australia and New Zealand (via their own ANZUS Treaty with the U.S.), were also brought into line. Philippine President Magsaysay declared that his Government was prepared to join with other nations in warning Communist China against "further aggression" in Southeast Asia and that the Philippines was prepared to accept in principle the U.S. proposal for a united front against Communist aggression in Southeast Asia. A similar relationship was attempted with Pakistan in 1953, but this did not bring the Pentagon such useful dividends.

In fact, the Philippines was the only power that managed to exact a

[5] Peter Lyon in *Yearbook of World Affairs,* London, 1965.
[6] J. B. Roucek in *Contemporary Review,* London, August 1962.
* "We have just installed one of the most elaborate communications networks anywhere in the world which links the new port, the air bases, Saigon, Bangkok, Manila and the U.S. in a 150,000,000-dollar system." (*New York Post,* October 19, 1967.)

price *from* the United States by joining SEATO. Its delegation insisted at Manila that United States assistance would be available, whatever happened under SEATO, and the Philippines has since received all its arms from the United States. Much has been in the form of direct gifts, so its expenditure on defense, in terms of national income, remains one of the lowest in Asia. In early 1967, for instance, Philippine President Marcos returned to his country with further largesse from a fruitful trip to Washington—no doubt an extra reward for being the *only* SEATO Asian partner backing the U.S. militarily in Vietnam, until the Thai troops were brought in late in 1967.

The two other Asian "allies" pressed into the Vietnam War—South Korea and Taiwan—were U.S. military protectorates anyway. Yet both are specifically *excluded* from the SEATO provisions by reason of a latitude stipulation. Pakistan, though a formal treaty partner, is as outspokenly opposed to the war as her sometime rival India. Recognizing Peking and flatly opposing the Vietnam War, France has taken no part in recent SEATO sessions.

"The actual birth of the Southeast Asia Collective Defense Treaty, SEATO, in September 1954 was wholly the result of United States initiatives and persistence," according to Prof. Peter Lyon. He adds:

> SEATO was thus brought into being hastily between April and September 1954. It was a product of the acute crisis brought about by the French collapse in the Indo-China war, and by the need to *underpin* the Geneva settlement of 1954. Its membership and structure were in large measure a legacy of the not clearly resolved friction between the United States Secretary of State, Mr. Dulles, and the British Foreign Secretary, Sir Anthony Eden, about how to deal with the Chinese Communists and their associates.[7] (Italics added.)

The word which the present author has italicized in the foregoing quotation could more aptly be rendered as "undermine," since there were essential differences, as we have seen, between the views of Britain and France, on the one hand, and the strategic intentions of the United States on Southeast Asia in 1954, on the other hand. The French were desperate to wind up the costly war following their defeat at Dien Bien Phu in May, and the British were highly perturbed by military pressures which were mounting in the United States to try out nuclear weapons in Indo-China or against China. They were most anxious for a general *political* settlement, based on a guaranteed neutrality for *all* Southeast Asia. Since the Geneva accords in July were regarded only as a *beginning** in the stabilization of that area, it was natural that France and Britain should try to agree on some formula to placate Dulles' public defeat at Geneva. Dulles' own

[7] *op. cit.*

* There were hopes in 1954, later developed in conversations between their respective governments, of a wider *neutral* confederation of the states of Southeast Asia, including a unified Vietnam, Cambodia, Laos, Thailand, Malaysia (later Malaysia and Singapore), Indonesia, and, possibly, the Philippines and Burma. But all these sensible trends toward a neutralized and economically viable Southeast Asia were blighted by the American military intervention.

dangerous game of dominos had therefore shifted to Manila—and World War III loomed into sight.

What Is "Self-Defense"?

As the complete text is set out in the Appendix, the following commentary on some legal aspects of the Manila Treaty can be kept to essentials. But the issue mentioned above—the conflict between the Treaty and the U.N. Charter—must be given space, first of all, since it is perhaps the central aspect of the controversy. The same basic principles are involved in regard to NATO and other military alliances. They are well stated in Article I of the Treaty, as follows:

The Parties undertake, as set forth in the Charter of the United Nations, to settle any international disputes in which they may be involved by peaceful means in such a manner that international peace and security and justice are not endangered, and to refrain in their international relations from the threat or use of force in any manner inconsistent with the purposes of the United Nations.

This opening gambit in the NATO, SEATO, and other defense treaties is obviously intended to legitimize such treaties, since all parties are committed to observe their obligations under the Charter. Moreover, there is an oft forgotten article in the Charter—Article 103—which runs as follows:

In the event of a conflict between the obligations of the Members of the United Nations under the present Charter and their obligations under any other international agreement, their obligations under the present Charter shall prevail.

There are three other articles of the Charter which have a direct bearing on the Alliances. Supporters of the defense pacts contend that two of them—Articles 51 and 52—provide legal authority to set up outside organizations like these. But opponents of the Alliances say (like this author) that the Charter, in both spirit and letter, gives little or no validity to them and, further, that it is an abuse of the Charter to try to stretch its meaning to justify international wrongs committed in its name.

About the first of these basic articles, least need be said. Its clear import runs like a golden thread through the whole Charter. It is Article 2 (fourth paragraph) and it reads:

All Members shall refrain in their international relations from the threat or use of force against the territorial integrity or political independence of any state, or in any other manner inconsistent with the Purposes of the United Nations.

The other two articles, however, are the ones generally relied on by supporters of the alliances. The first—Article 51—is about "self-defense." But it will be seen at once that it is "self-defense" with all sorts of qualifications surrounding it, and it is these latter which have given rise to a

129

considerable legal debate.* Article 51 comes at the very end of a Chapter dealing with "Threats to the Peace," and it runs:

Nothing in the present Charter shall impair the inherent right of individual or collective self-defense if an armed attack occurs against a Member of the United Nations, until the Security Council has taken measures necessary to maintain international peace and security. Measures taken by Members in the exercise of this right of self-defense shall be immediately reported to the Security Council and shall not in any way affect the authority and responsibility of the Security Council. . . .

It should be noted that this wording does not *confer* a right or duty on any member-state. It merely recognizes that an "inherent right" already exists. Being *inherent,* it obviously does not require any treaty or Charter to authorize it. Indeed, this so-called "inherent right of self-defense," inserted in Article 51, was taken from the customary law of the Nineteenth Century. It was never intended to override the main purpose of the Charter, which prohibits altogether the use of force and the threat of force in international disputes, as noted above. In any case, this "inherent right" may be exercised under Article 51 only *if* "an armed attack occurs." Even then, local military action is subject to the "authority and responsibility of the Security Council."

Says Professor Ian Brownlie in the *International and Comparative Law Quarterly* (October 1959):

The very terms of Article 51 preclude a view that its content is special and not general; it refers to "the inherent right" and it is not incongruous to regard the Article as containing the only right of self-defense permitted by the Charter. Its narrow terms are explicable against the background of the general prohibition in Article 2, paragraph 4, and the general assumption made at San Francisco, and evident in the text of Article 51, that the Organization was to have a virtual monopoly of the use of armed force.

What this really means is that, first, an existing right of self-defense for an individual nation is not to be taken away by what is previously stipulated in the Charter on behalf of the U.N. as a whole; and, secondly, there might arise occasions when, *before* the Security Council could act, a state which is under attack may still legally enjoy its "inherent right" to defend itself. It was a device to tide over the situation *until* outside help came.†

* *See,* for example, the following basic treatises (each of which gives ample references to other sources):
Hans Kelsen: *Law of the United Nations,* Praeger, New York, 1950.
Arnold (Lord) McNair: *Law of Treaties,* Oxford University Press, 1961.
D. W. Bowett: *Self-Defense in International Law,* Manchester University Press, 1958.

† It should be mentioned, however, that there are other legal opinions on this issue. For example, a well-known Australian jurist, Dr. J. G. Starke, states in his textbook on International Law: "It appears that consistently with Article 51, the North Atlantic Powers could legitimately enter into their Regional Security Treaty of April 4, 1949, and create the machinery beforehand for collective self-defense should any one of their number be exposed to an armed attack." But the learned author adds: "A matter of current controversy is whether, under Article 51, nuclear and thermonuclear weapons can legitimately be used in self-defense against a non-nuclear armed attack."

Hans Kelsen, one of the greatest legal minds of this century, has suggested that it may be that "the framers of the Charter did not take into consideration the possibility of organizing collective self-defense through regional arrangements, *since they recognized the right of self-defense only as a provisional measure to be taken within the short period of time between the occurrence of an armed attack and the putting into operation the machinery of collective security by the Security Council.*" (Italics added.) Professor Kelsen goes on to emphasize:

The use of the term "until" and the obligation imposed on the Members to report immediately to the Security Council the measures taken under Article 51 show that the application of this Article is intended by the Charter only as a temporary measure; not as a substitute for the collective security to be realized by the Organization.[8]

Again, the apparent contradiction implied in the term "collective self-defense" has, admittedly, given rise to uncertainty. How can *self*-defense be "collective"? This term is nowhere defined in the Charter. Perhaps the shortest clarification has been given by Dr. D. W. Bowett, when he states: "Collective self-defense, as used in the Charter, does no more than recognize that members may exercise collectively what is their individual right; it does not create new rights, nor, by permitting the use of a legal fiction, convert action unauthorized by a competent organ of the United Nations into action in the exercise of the right of collective self-defense."[9]

The point, again, is that the Charter does not authorize or confer a special collective right on some of its members; it merely accepts that self-defense in an emergency situation can also be collective. What the Charter does do is to insist that this ancient customary practice must from now on be subjected to the new rules laid down in the Charter. It was to say the least interesting to listen to the Soviet delegate in August 1968 defend the occupation of Prague under Articles 51 and 52!

Yet in spite of the patent illegality, or doubtful legality at best, of NATO, SEATO and other permanent military organizations which have been built upon this verbal pretext, their spokesmen have long made a habit of stringing together, for the benefit of simple folk, lip service to the U.N. along with praise for NATO and the other alliances. The U.N.'s universal peacekeeping functions have been distorted so as to provide a cloak of respectability to cover the legal and moral nakedness of their illegitimate protégés.

The other article in the Charter usually cited as justifying the military alliance is Article 52. We, again, note its negative form as merely a "savings" clause:

Nothing in the present Charter precludes the existence of regional arrangements or agencies for dealing with such matters relating to the maintenance

[8] Hans Kelsen: *Law of the United Nations*, Praeger, New York, 1950.
[9] D. W. Bowett: *Self-Defense in International Law*, Manchester University Press, 1958.

of international peace and security as are appropriate for regional action, provided that such arrangements or agencies and their activities are consistent with the Purposes and Principles of the United Nations . . .

Although SEATO and some of the others might pass the geographical test of being called "regional," the sophistry of calling NATO a "regional arrangement," consistent with Article 52, becomes a *reductio ad absurdum* if one merely looks at the map. Any schoolboy can see that a military alliance that stretches from the Hawaiian Islands or the Bering Straits to Istanbul is not a "regional arrangement" at all. But, even if it were, the Charter clearly states later on (Article 53) that military action can take place only under the authority, again, of the Security Council.

NATO merges geographically with CENTO in the Middle East, and CENTO reaches out to SEATO in Asia, then across the Pacific to the recent unfruitful attempt to set up a regional *army* under O.A.S. Thus, a preposterous meaning has been given to "regional arrangements," which are a direct affront to the U.N. collective security system. Furthermore, no honest or sensitive observer could accept this campaign of creeping militarism as "consistent with the purposes of the United Nations." The choice between the two ways of conducting the world's affairs could never be made plainer than by watching this multi-headed python coiling its sly way year by year around our tiny planet to stifle the life of "We, the Peoples" as it swallows 150 billion dollars annually of the earth's sparse resources.

No Obligation

By Article II of the SEATO Treaty the signatories agreed "separately and jointly, by means of continuous and effective self-help and mutual aid," to "maintain and develop their individual and collective *capacity* to resist armed attack and to prevent and counter subversive activities directed from without against their territorial integrity and political stability." (Italics added.) This means, of course, more armies and military aid and arms sales, and more C.I.A. and similar "anti-subversion" assistance —made familiar to everyone in the "Ugly American" film tradition. Yet no party is obligated to *do* anything under this Article, except to take *individual* action.

In Article III co-operation to promote economic progress and social well-being is stressed. But, in 1964, the SEATO Public Information Office issued a statement which said, in part: "SEATO does not attempt to compete with the other arrangements, but rather seeks to complement them. Little in fact is required in this field because of the extensive co-operation carried on in other ways."

Now we come to the important Article IV. In the event of armed attack against any of *their territories* in the treaty area or against the territory of any State listed in the Protocol to the Treaty whose government has invited or consented to their intervention, each signatory agrees that it will "act to meet the common danger in accordance with its constitutional processes" (paragraph 1).

The "treaty area" is defined in Article VIII as the general area of Southeast Asia, including the entire territories of the Asian Parties. But the area north of latitude 21° 30' north is specifically *excluded*. This wording was designed to exclude Hong Kong and Taiwan. (The British and French would never have swallowed putting them in!) But it also cuts out Japan, South Korea, and much else. What, then, do the parties undertake to do in the event of threats to the peace within this area? They undertake to *consult* on measures for common defense (paragraph 2). *That is all SEATO's collective defense amounts to.*

The Protocol names the "new" states of Cambodia, Laos, and "the free territory under the jurisdiction of the State of Vietnam" (presumably a pseudonym for *South* Vietnam). These three countries had the distinction of being inscribed, without their consent, in the annex to the Treaty. Could international duplicity have gone further? The first two states so named had been neutralized but six weeks earlier. Vietnam had also been neutralized *as a single state,* but had not then entered statehood, for its unification—made a specific condition in the Geneva Agreements—could only happen after nation-wide elections had actually been held in 1956. (We now know why those elections were never held.)

As concerns Laos, its ineligibility to become a sleeping partner of SEATO was reinforced and guaranteed at the later Geneva Conference of 1962. Its resistant—even if shaky—government is still headed by a resolute neutralist, Prime Minister Prince Souvannaphouma—one of the most astute statesmen of Asia, for he has managed to keep his country, unlike unhappy Thailand, out of the Vietnam War, although he has both Communist and right-wing reactionaries to handle at the same time, as well as American incursions. Likewise, Cambodia rejected SEATO's "protection" in 1954 in even more specific terms. Its open hostility toward the Alliance has since been compounded by Prince Sihanouk's frequent appeals to the United Nations and to the International Control Commission for protection against his erstwhile protectors. But his penchant for maintaining good relations with his giant neighbor Communist China and full diplomatic relations with North Vietnam has hardly earned him the gratitude of Washington.

Secretary of State Rusk has been prone at news conferences to refer to the "Protocol States" as though he were conferring on them some sort of high favor. Cambodia's insistence on retaining its independence and neutrality, in spite of being systematically squeezed between two "allies" in the Vietnam War, was emphatically reaffirmed by Huot Sambath, Cambodia's delegate to the 22nd Annual Assembly in 1967, in these terms:

My country will not accept any compromise when its independence, its neutrality, and its territorial integrity are at stake. Our people, guided by

Prince Norodom Sihanouk, enjoys the regime of its choice and is profoundly attached to its monarchical institutions, to its Buddhist religion and to its millenary traditions. *Foreign ideologies, whatever they may be, do not attract us at all* . . . We threaten no one and belong to no organization or military alliance.

Finally, what has this "protection" meant to Vietnam, which, unlike Laos and Cambodia, has never been in an independent position to secure the direct protection which the other two enjoy as full United Nations members? A short historical answer was given by Professor Lyon thus:

South Vietnam has been a "protectorate" of the United States since American influence helped Ngo Dinh Diem to power in 1954; and, just as he was brought to power by United States influence, so the removal of United States support in the second half of 1963 prepared the way for his deposition and death in November of that year. In the fifteen months following President Diem's overthrow, there were seven major government upsets in South Vietnam. All this time the Vietcong systematically extended and tightened their grip on the countryside, while the towns, and the capital Saigon in particular, seethed with dissension as army officers plotted and counter-plotted . . . [10]

"Only an Internal Dispute"

SEATO specifically lays down in Article IV that a Protocol State must *request* assistance before SEATO can intervene. The designated "Foreign Minister of South Vietnam," Phan Huy Quat, who attended the Manila meeting in 1954 as an observer, however, was persuaded not to table a proposal for SEATO assistance against North Vietnam. And, despite all the disasters since, no Saigon "government"—under either Diem or the shifty military despots who succeeded him—has exercised its right to request the intervention of SEATO against alleged North Vietnamese "aggression" or "subversion." In fact, at the early Council meetings of SEATO, such participants who attended regarded the troubles in Vietnam as (to quote from the minutes) "only an internal dispute between factions."

Addressing the General Assembly on October 13, 1967, Australia's Minister of External Affairs (Mr. Hasluck) had his own special interpretation of current history: "Australia had no part in the earlier events. We hoped that the Geneva Accords would lead, with the good offices of all Powers that could play a helpful role, to a new course ending in political stability, security, and perhaps eventually the reunification of Vietnam (*sic*). . . . It was only when North Vietnam created the National Liberation Front, when it promoted guerrilla war and terror, and when it sent the regular divisions of its own army into the South . . . that Australia an-

[10] *op. cit.*

swered the request of the Government of South Vietnam for support in its defense and gave military aid."

The factual accuracy of these sweeping assertions is open to grave dispute and it is germane to point out that Australia had already committed itself to U.S. policies in Southeast Asia by the ANZUS Treaty of 1951, Article IV of which became merely an echo in SEATO three years later and reads: "Each Party recognizes that an armed attack in the Pacific area on any of the Parties would be dangerous to its own peace and safety and declares that it would act to meet the common danger in accordance with its constitutional processes."

The following question and answer exchange in the Canberra House of Representatives on May 4, 1966 indicated the almost casual manner in which the issue of a legal commitment under SEATO was swept aside. Mr. Hasluck was asked by the Opposition (which has remained bitterly hostile to the Government's Vietnam involvement): "If the Right Honorable Gentleman claims that the Government's action in Vietnam is justified or required by its SEATO obligations, why has the Government not cited SEATO in the notification to the Security Council, and why has the Government not sought the authorization of the Security Council to take enforcement action under this regional arrangement, as is required by the United Nations Charter?" The Minister's reply was: "We quoted comprehensively our international obligations in notifying the Security Council, and our international obligations include those under SEATO and those under the United Nations Charter."

There is, in fact, no public evidence that South Vietnam has ever made a request for SEATO's assistance. Nor would it have received it if it had. Bulletins issued after each SEATO meeting have been studiously vague, and the one issuing from the 1968 meeting was the most pointless of them all, with France and Pakistan not even voting. So how could it have been the Treaty which has put the Americans in this tormented land?

General Eisenhower emphasized when President his belief that "the Communists must be stopped in Vietnam." But he insisted later on that his letter to President Ngo Dinh Diem of October 1954—often quoted by President Johnson as the basis of his own action—was a pledge of foreign aid, *not military involvement.* He stressed that he never made a unilateral military commitment to South Vietnam; only a multilateral engagement through the Southeast Asia Treaty Organization. "It was," according to the *New York Times* (August 19, 1965), "a unilateral decision by President Kennedy in 1961—not a SEATO decision—that launched the program of massive American military assistance to South Vietnam. Most Asians and most American allies in Europe have always had deep reservations about it."

Professor Arthur Larson, Director of Duke University Rule of Law Research Center, following a careful analysis of this alleged U.S. "commitment," has pointed out in a publication of the Center: "The true fact is that the United States has had no obligation to South Vietnam or anyone else under the SEATO treaty to use its own armed forces in the defense of South Vietnam." Moreover, states the journalist commentator Arthur Krock: "Mr. Johnson initially did not rely on the SEATO Treaty as the source of his authority for whatever expansion of our combat force he would deem necessary. That was a later invention of the Department of State. Mr. Johnson found Congressional authority for any military decisions he might make in a resolution passed after an alleged attack by small war-vessels of North Vietnam on two United States destroyers in the Gulf of Tonkin."[11] Senator J. W. Fulbright has since called for a thorough investigation of these Tonkin Gulf incidents so as to test the highly questionable legal validity of the Senate resolution itself. The charade proceeds, while the body count continues and the children burn.

On the other side of the Atlantic, contesting the pretentions of the United States to be in Vietnam at all, the Right Honorable Philip Noel-Baker, Nobel Peace Prize Winner and former Cabinet Minister, addressing the House of Commons on April 21, 1967, said: "President Johnson and Mr. Rusk sometimes say that they were compelled by their SEATO obligations to intervene. But if they were to look at the Treaty, they would see that, by Articles I, IV, and VI, the SEATO Pact specifically and categorically forbids what the United States has done. Every day that the war continues, the whole concept of world order based on law is progressively undermined."

A Legend Evaporates

Thus, we arrive at the following conclusions:
(a) That SEATO was actually conceived and established to nullify the 1954 Geneva Agreements;
(b) That SEATO belied even its title by failing to enlist some of the most important nations of Southeast Asia—such as India, Burma, Nepal, Indonesia and Ceylon—and no other eligible members have since joined;
(c) That SEATO aimed to establish United States military hegemony in Southeast Asia, and that the other participants were either only nominally interested (such as Britain) or defected later (such as France and Pakistan);
(d) That all the parties were already covered by existing security pacts with the United States;
(e) That nations deliberately excluded from SEATO (such as Taiwan and South Korea) were nonetheless pressured to come into the Vietnamese War as "allies";

[11] *New York Times,* August 28, 1966.

(f) That nations inscribed in SEATO's Protocol as being in need of its special "protection" (namely, Cambodia and Laos) consistently rejected such "protection";

(g) That the only other "protected" nation (Vietnam) has since suffered physical and moral dismemberment and destruction at the hands of SEATO's chief partner far greater than any other nation since World War II.

(h) That SEATO affords no legal foundation whatsoever for the Vietnam War and, even if it did, its provisions have been constantly flouted by its own creator, along with its solemn obligations under the U.N. Charter.*

But that is not all. More and more neutral nations of the Third World, which the American public is being told are threatened by Communism, and even some pro-West ones, now fear that U.S. military intervention will be their own fate, unless they receive some guarantee from the World Community. Pending more solid assurances, United Nations publicity is providing them with a partial safeguard. For example, Huot Sambath speaking for Cambodia at the 1967 General Assembly explained: "I have spoken at length about the question of Vietnam because it concerns a neighboring and brother country, but also because the imperialist policy of the United States is preparing other Vietnams in our Third World. Tomorrow the American Government, by virtue of the same theories as those applied in Vietnam, Cambodia, and Laos, will send its marines to Bolivia, Venezuela, or Colombia and its bombers over Cuba. If the United Nations does not oppose with all its force the policy of world hegemony of the United States, there will soon be three or four Vietnams in Asia, Africa and Latin America, with the inevitable prospect of a generalized war."

That this *crie-de-coeur* is not a far-fetched fear has been underlined by such U.S. political analysts as Seymour Melman, Professor of Industrial Engineering at Columbia University. Professor Melman has in many books and speeches long warned against the *self-propelling* nature of the industrial-military complex. He insists that any policy change in the United States "must be as comprehensive as the characteristics and effects of the institutional machine that now propels America in a war-like direction. Stated differently," he says, "a halt in the Vietnam war itself is highly desirable—it would produce substantial benefits for the Vietnamese people and would alter the political atmosphere in the United States. *But the American issue is not the Vietnam war itself, but rather the system of policy and institutions which generate Vietnam wars.*"

Toward the end of 1967, however, with the collapse of President Johnson's personal campaign to disguise the war as an American defense

* The present chapter is confined to the SEATO question; but an authoritative legal case against U.S. military involvement, answering the State Department's own contentions point by point, is presented in *Vietnam and International Law*, prepared by Professor Quincy Wright and a panel of other distinguished American lawyers and political scientists (O'Hare Books, New York, 1967).

of South Vietnam's democracy against North Vietnam's Communist "aggression," a new mood was faintly evident in Washington circles and across the country. At a "Strategy for Peace Conference" of prominent business, professional, and university leaders, with Assistant Secretary of State William F. Bundy as the opening speaker, the Conference broke new ground and recommended that the United States "encourage the Saigon Government to seek a dialogue with the National Liberation Front." Also, Vice-President Humphrey began to notice that there existed *non-Communists* among the Viet Cong, with whom negotiations might be opened.

At last, the SEATO legend of a heroic band of reluctant crusaders coming to the rescue of a beleaguered maiden was being dispelled under the cold light of day. The way to handle an internal rebellion in an Asian country was not to send half a million white soldiers, but to assist the two parties—pro Government and anti Government—toward an acceptably stable political solution. And this was obviously the proper job of the United Nations, not some foreign power in search of grandeur. The United States could at any time—had its military advisers so decided—have kept its bombers and soldiers back in the States, where they would not be imperiled, and, under Articles 51 and 52 of the Charter, handed over its fears and problems to the U.N. where they belong. We know that this gigantic effort to by-pass the United Nations has cost the United States not merely the frequently proclaimed "leadership of the free world," but its confidence in itself. As Arnold Toynbee has pointed out, the United States has already suffered moral defeat. The road back will not be easy; but by pursuing the Charter principles of negotiation and conciliation the United States might eventually recover its own ethical foundations. The reconstruction and reunification of Vietnam, within a neutralized Southeast Asia, following the complete withdrawal of the American forces, becomes a primary concern not merely of the United States but of the whole world community during the 1970's.

Pactomania

SEATO was soon to be "supplemented" by CENTO. "Following the Korean war," reverting to General MacCloskey, "there was a period of pactomania, and Pakistan became the favored anti-Communist recipient of American aid as the key country in the SEATO and CENTO alliances . . . In 1961, the late President Kennedy entertained President Ayub Khan of Pakistan at a glamorous Mount Vernon gala, and the then Vice-President Lyndon Johnson toured Pakistan and struck up the famous friendship with a camel driver."[12]

[12] *op. cit.*

One of the tacit State Department policies at that time was to build a line of defense against "Communist expansion," first across Europe and then Asia, from the Atlantic to the Pacific. Thus, NATO in Europe became linked with SEATO in Asia by means of the Baghdad Pact, of which the U.S. did not even become a member. Dulles attempted in 1955—just a few months after the Manila Pact had failed to win India, Burma, and the major Asian countries—to induce Pakistan to take the initiative. All the usual bribes and arm-twisting were tried, but Pakistan declined to take the bait. So Turkey—already a member of NATO—was persuaded to set the Mid-East ball rolling by joining up with Iraq (capital city, Baghdad).

Each member country was to be appropriately supplied with men, money, and machines to give the Pact brand new American teeth—as both nations had borders with or close to Russia and were comparatively toothless, by Pentagon standards. How did this pretty little scheme proceed? We now can look back on one of the most footling series of diplomatic wangles and miscalculations in post-World War II history. In this brief recital, we need not go far outside the commentaries of one or two authorities whom we shall cite in their respective fields and who have no personal grudges against the alliance system as such.

In short, the 1955 Pact of Mutual Co-operation aimed at ensuring the Middle East "against aggressive and subversive penetration." By Article 5 of the Pact, Iraq and Turkey invited the participation of the Arab League. But this drew an immediate blank. In fact, the Arab League was—and is —more afraid of American infiltration than Soviet, and the cohesion of the League has since been strengthened in consequence. But on April 5, 1955, the United Kingdom announced its accession to the Pact for historic reasons, as the former Guardian of the Middle East. That made three. Pakistan, which already had an alliance with Turkey, became number four on September 23, 1955. And the fifth, Iran, joined on November 3, 1955. But after the revolution in Iraq in July 1958, Iraq took no further part in the Pact and withdrew in March 1959. So that went back to four. A glance at the map will show how few Middle East nations that is. The first Council meeting was convened in Baghdad in November 1955, and the Foreign Ministers of the member nations set up their Secretariat in Baghdad. But in October 1958, for the foregoing reasons, this was transferred to Ankara, Turkey, where it is now located—and the Baghdad Pact became CENTO.

"The cornerstone of any northern tier alignment could only be Turkey, the strongest state in the Middle East," says John C. Campbell in *Defense of the Middle East*. "Already a member of NATO, Turkey had committed its armed forces wholly to the NATO command . . . Turkey happened to be, also, the only firm base from which the Western alliance system and Western power could be extended into the Middle East."[13] Dr. Campbell

[13] J. C. Campbell: *Defense of the Middle East,* Harper & Row, New York, 1960.

139

points out, however, that—as with the Warsaw Pact responding to NATO —"Western initiative to organize the defense of the Middle East had run afoul of Arab nationalism and Arab politics. The American decision to grant arms aid to Iraq and to encourage its participation in regional defense had involved the risk that, in gaining Iraq, the West might have to write off the rest of the Arab world." The West was again helping the Soviet Union to strengthen its own alliances—this time with the Arabs.

The initiative for collective security, Dulles had tactfully told them, had to come from the Middle Eastern nations themselves. Thus, the Pact, having been concluded between Turkey and Iraq, needed to expand laterally. According to Dr. Campbell, "it was Menderes who undertook to sell it to Lebanon and to press it strongly, even threateningly, upon Syria." (Menderes, it should be remarked, was the luckless Turkish Prime Minister who was deposed, tried, and executed in 1961.) But Lebanon stuck to its traditional "middle position" and rejected the invitation; while Syria was so perturbed that it discarded its relatively moderate government (by American standards) for a new one favorable to Egypt and suspicious of the West. Yet Washington had wisely decided against plunging in itself. For Dulles still had his Senate problems. And the result? "Abdel Nasser moved rapidly to form an Egypt-Syria-Saudi Arabia-Yemen alignment," Dr. Campbell records, "that later took the form of a series of bilateral and multilateral pacts under Egypt's leadership and military command." This looks like the familiar story of "X=O" again, or, as Isaac Newton has epitomized it in his third law of motion which pact-makers always forget: "Action and re-action are equal and in opposite direction."

As with SEATO, the role of Britain in CENTO could be said to be minimal. It still revolved round Suez and the various bases held by treaty with Iraq, due to expire in 1957. So the mini-pact between Turkey and Iraq offered an opportunity which Britain needed at that time, since it was open to all states "interested in the peace and security of the region." When Britain joined the Baghdad Pact, Sir Anthony Eden told the House of Commons that "our purpose . . . was a very simple one. I think that by so doing we have strengthened our influence and our voice throughout the Middle East."

The CENTO organization, unlike NATO, is therefore very simple and *ad hoc,* consisting of a Council of Ministers and special committees for military planning, economic co-operation, and communications, as well as for *counter-subversion.* The United States is represented at Council meetings by an observer. It participates in the committees on economics and, of course, specializes on counter-subversion; it has also established permanent liaison with the military committee. It supplied nearly all the "hardware," too. Dr. Campbell makes the cogent remark: "It was in the Pact, but not of it; a participant for practical purposes, but without the legal commitments. To the extent that the formation and growth of the

Baghdad Pact could be considered the results of American diplomacy, the State Department looked upon its handiwork and saw that it was good." In the eyes of its godfather, Dulles, here was a fledgling four nation regional security organization which covered the "open gap," as he saw it, between NATO and SEATO—one more paper barrier against "Soviet imperialism." Yet, as Shakespeare would have put it: "A poor thing, but my own!"

Perhaps we can take Dr. Campbell again as our authority: *"Militarily, the pact offered no prospect of effective defense."* All three who had joined, alongside the United Kingdom, had done so primarily in order to get arms from the United States, rather than out of faith in the Dulles dominos-in-reverse tactics of regional security. Worse, the inability of the United States to join them as a member had left all members with a feeling that they had been deceived by paper promises and let down badly in the event.

United States aid to Iran in 1967 amounted to 190 million dollars, of which 83 million dollars was part of a program of military aid. But to show the illogic of this expensive enterprise, in March 1968, Iran began extensive economic exchanges with the Soviet Union, which United States observers had themselves to admit were "a logical outcome of geography." One important element in the exchanges between the capitalist Iranian monarchy and the Soviet republics is natural gas, and Iran is building a 42-inch pipeline from the oilfields in Khuzistan, in southern Iran, to the Soviet border west of the Caspian Sea. The irony of this is that the line is being built by Western companies.

To bring this essay in futility up to date, with India already an outsider and Pakistan getting out, their long-term dispute over Kashmir had been kept from open warfare by the periodical conciliatory procedures of the U.N. Security Council. When matters flared up again in 1965 the Security Council was able to obtain a cease-fire. On this fragile basis, the Soviet Union persuaded President Ayub Khan of Pakistan and Prime Minister Shastri of India to meet in January 1966 in Tashkent—"neutral ground" in Soviet Asia, conveniently situated to both parties. (This was just across the very frontier to be protected by CENTO; and the hesitant Turks were being pressed at the last CENTO Council meeting in 1967 to place *nuclear* land mines along it.) The unique meeting of minds at Tashkent ended successfully with the signing of a declaration by which both India and Pakistan agreed to withdraw their armed forces to the positions held before fighting broke out in the previous August. Moreover, they agreed to set up joint Indian-Pakistani bodies to consider future steps and to resume normal diplomatic relations, as well as to discourage propaganda against each other within their own countries. "As a result, Russia is enjoying exceptional goodwill on Asia's subcontinent," even General MacCloskey has to confess, in spite of his ardent belief in Western-type pacts. But where is CENTO in all this? Where is CENTO in *anything?*

Attempting to track this same Western virus of pactomania making its tortuous way into the Americas is like penetrating the Amazon jungle itself. In fact, states W. T. R. Fox in *NATO and the Range of American Choice:* "Even for the specialist in Latin American affairs, it is very difficult to describe the Organization of American States, much less the inter-American system, of which it is a part and for which it is often used as a synonym. Ambassador Dreier has called the entire system a juridical and procedural jungle; the O.A.S. is thoroughly entangled in it."[14]

In these circumstances, the best recourse we have is to pinpoint by way of concrete example two recent but quite different case studies—each of which has been the subject of an immense outpouring of contemporary literature—which demonstrate, once again, that arbitrary military intervention cannot hold a candle to the legal processes of the U.N., even if the latter's machinery is not yet developed to cope with every emergency.

The examples here selected are the Cuban missile crisis and the insurrection in the Dominican Republic. Seen in context, these events are really two transient and related episodes. Ever since the 1950's, the O.A.S. has been in an increasing state of crisis. The reasons for this are the relationship of the United States to Latin America, as well as the endemic economic and social problems of Latin America. The tragedy of the O.A.S. is basically a crisis of confidence in leadership.

This is by no means the view taken by pro-alliance enthusiasts such as General MacCloskey, whose *Pacts for Peace* we have already quoted several times as typical of many writers in this field. In his estimate: "On October 22, 1962, the American republics were shocked into a state of unity when they were confronted with proof of the existence of Soviet missile bases in Cuba, with weapons poised to strike the Hemisphere. It was the hour of the Monroe Doctrine and it was enforced as originally intended—against a non-American intervention threatening the peace and security of the continents. . . . For the first time, perhaps, Latin American countries realized that the Monroe Doctrine was multilateral as well as continental, and that action including the use of armed force, or the threat thereof, could be taken as a collective measure of self-defense . . . The American countries faced up to their greatest challenge and met it with a solid front."[15]

The fact that there might be an entirely different interpretation of this ugly episode does not occur to the general—even accepting his romantic picture of "a solid front" as coming within measurable distance of the actual truth. It just happened that in New York there existed the one

[14] W. T. R. Fox: *NATO and the Range of American Choice,* Columbia, New York, 1967.

[15] *op. cit.*

spot on the earth's surface where each of the three contestants—Cuba, Russia, and United States—met each other face to face. The rest of the civilized world was also present, not as onlookers, but as active participants in a drama which touched directly all their lives and fortunes. But the fact that it was again the U.N. which stood between the contenders and secured a last-minute *détente* is completely beyond the general's ken or comprehension.

In those tense never-to-be-forgotten moments in the Security Council chamber in October 1962, the United States and the U.S.S.R. announced in scathing and dogmatic terms their several intentions to risk a world atomic war, rather than give way over the missile build-up in Cuba. It was then that the voice of U Thant of Burma, speaking for "We, the Peoples," uttered the words of wisdom and restraint that won a reprieve from the chain reaction which threatened to turn the Cuban challenge into humanity's Armageddon. It was to the U.N. Secretary-General that every sensible mind turned as U Thant quoted the same phrases which Dag Hammarskjold had used six years before to justify his personal mandate to intervene in the Suez invasion:

The principles of the Charter are, by far, greater than the Organization in which they are embodied, and the aims which they are to safeguard are holier than the policies of any single nation or people . . . A Secretary-General cannot serve on any other assumption than that—within the necessary limits of human frailty and honest differences of opinion—all member nations honor their pledge to observe all articles of the Charter.

Oblivious of the screaming headlines and chauvinistic TV pronouncements which deafened the American public outside, U Thant quietly concluded his historic appeal—*which became the basis of the actions of each of the governments concerned*—thus:

It is after considerable deliberation that I have decided to send the two messages to which I have referred earlier (to Kennedy and Khrushchev) . . . I hope that at this moment, not only in the Council Chamber but in the world outside, good sense and understanding will be placed above the anger of the moment or the pride of nations. The path of negotiation and compromise is the only course by which the peace of the world can be secured at this critical moment.

So, while the rival leaders were striking their defiant postures and the press was squeezing every drop of hate and hysteria out of the latest turn —it could have been the last—of the Cold War, and the unconsulted citizens of the world awaited their fate, Hammarskjold's mantle of "quiet diplomacy" had fallen on the shoulders of U Thant. Adopting Hammarskjold's role—that of go-between—he knew that only by saving the faces of the cold warriors could he save the future of their threatened peoples.

Yet, such is the perversity of man, ever since those unpredictable days, the American public has been consistently retailed the Cold War formula that it was the inflexible resolution of their President to "stand up to Communism" which had saved their skins; whereas the simple recital of the actual events should be sufficient to show that the dreaded missiles were *already in firing position* in Cuba; any aggressive move by their President would have brought down these terrible war-heads upon their cities. All parties accepted U Thant's solution. The invasion of Cuba was called off and the Russian missiles withdrawn. Cuba was saved and the U.S. was saved.

Once again, it was "the path of negotiation and compromise" which proved to be "the only course by which the peace of the world" *was in fact* secured during the Cuban confrontation. The indispensable role of the Secretary-General was modestly summarized by U Thant himself shortly afterwards in a lecture at Johns Hopkins University:

I hope that the spirit of compromise which marked the discussions between the Soviet Union and the United States in the case of Cuba may help the solution of some of the outstanding Cold War issues of the world today . . . issues like Berlin, on which it may become imperative to reach solutions on the basis of compromise and the principle of give-and-take on both sides.

The Great Fear

The contrast between the Cuban crisis and the Dominican intervention is obvious, though both were samples of *outside military interference,* in violation of the U.N. Charter. "The Cuban revolution caused a tremendous stir throughout the Americas, firing the imagination of its friends and arousing the suspicion and concern of its adversaries," states a British authority on Latin America. Professor F. Parkinson continues: "Latin America, it seemed, was shifting rapidly to the center of the world stage, and President Kennedy even remarked that it had become 'the most important area of the world.' " The writer then adds this more realistic note: "The outcome of the Cuban 'missile' crisis of 1962 muffled the enthusiasm of many, while to others the late President's words seemed in retrospect to be exaggerated. But the pendulum then swung too far the other way. Though manifestly lacking the charisma of the Cuban revolution, the Dominican rising was every bit as important in its deeper implications."[16]

Behind both samples of military interference in Central American affairs lies the real problem of South America, as a whole. And that problem can never be solved by guns or marines or measures of quarantine or threats of invasion. The Tenth International Conference of American States which met in Caracas in 1954 was urged on by Secretary of State John Foster Dulles to issue a flamboyant "Declaration of Solidarity for the Preservation of the Political Integrity of the Americas Against the

[16] F. Parkinson in *Yearbook of World Affairs,* London, 1966.

Intervention of International Communism." The aforementioned authority remarks: "The Declaration remained ineffective in practice, as the Cuban case was to demonstrate later. The Conference was characterized by a tenacious United States display of 'unity' asking the Latin Americans for concerted action against Communist subversion, while at the same time showing no great concern for Latin American economic and social difficulties."[17]

John Gerassi, in *The Great Fear in Latin America,* is typical of most independent professional observers of Latin American affairs. He points out bluntly that the present "social and economic structure is decadent, corrupt, immoral, and generally unsalvageable. That change is coming is obvious. That it will come about through revolution is certain." And he poses the enigma: *Who* will lead the revolution? Gerassi's answer is that the actual choice is between Communists "in theory," and Nationalists "in practice." Who will win depends on how the present powers-that-be, including the United States, handle the challenge of change which *both* elements represent.

Gerassi concludes with a salutary warning: "Once in power, the Nationalists will nationalize American corporations—because it will be in their country's interest to do so. They will trade with the Communist bloc —because it will be in their country's interest to do so. And they will even vote, on occasion, against the United States at the U.N.—because it will be in their country's interest to do so. But they will not be our enemies. Nor will they desert 'Western society'—because such desertion will not be in their country's interest."[18]

So much for a general approach to the deeper problem of social change. But how did our cold warriors handle the second episode? One of the best examples of on-the-spot journalism was the reporting of the Dominican Republic crisis in the summer of 1965. Press, radio and television correspondents described things as they *saw* them, not as the U.S. military authorities were announcing in their press releases. The difference was astonishing. As one critic remarked: "These reports helped inform the American people of the full depth of the tragedy in the little Caribbean republic, and helped bring about a partial rectification of Washington policies."[19]

According to *Dominican Diary,* one such on-the-spot day-by-day account, by Tad Szulc, a number of unpleasant facts stand out. The first is the sheer lack of knowledge in Washington as to the nature of the revolt. The U.S. Ambassador, according to Szulc, had virtually no contact with the people leading the uprising and he knew little about their programs or political attitudes. His advice to Washington was worse than useless.

[17] *ibid.*
[18] John Gerassi: *The Great Fear in Latin America,* Macmillan, New York, 1965.
[19] *New York Times,* December 12, 1965.

145

Nevertheless, it was followed. To the myopic vision of the local Embassy officials, a victory by the pro-Bosch forces would have been a routine "victory of Communism." This lack of the basic facts and the purveying of false information by the Embassy, says Szulc, triggered the United States invasion, which followed immediately—tailor-made.[20]

When troops suddenly landed, it was announced that they had come to remove endangered United States citizens; whereas the intervention had been planned behind the scenes in advance as a political move. Washington admitted at later stages that their military forces were there to aid the military junta against the "rebels." As with Vietnam, the U.S. Government constantly shifted ground. Explanations for its imposed presence followed, in familiar pattern, as the objectives which the C.I.A. was attempting to achieve changed. As with Vietnam, no solution was possible without the removal of the reactionary generals (Imbert and Wessin) who had been "created" by the Americans in the first place.

Tad Szulc's brutally frank first impressions were later substantiated by many others. The fourth arm of government had got its own way once more. An outspoken liberal Senator has stated: "U.S. intervention in the Dominican Republic called into question some of the basic precepts of our foreign policy. Yet Administration spokesmen insisted that the landing of United States troops in the Dominican Republic was not intervention because it was a 'response' to the 'intervention' of Communist subversion. Thus, our Government was able to justify our favorable response to the request for support by a military junta in the Dominican Republic a few days later."[21]

Looking back, there can be little doubt that the landing on April 28, 1965 of United States marines and paratroopers was a deliberate violation of the U.N. Charter, as well as of the Charter of the Organization of American States, which laid down in Article 17 that the territory of a State was inviolable and could not be subject, even temporarily, to military occupation. Moreover, the U.S. had acted without consulting O.A.S. members at all, as it was obligated to do, but once again presented them all with a *fait accompli*. The O.A.S. Council was convened only after the landing of U.S. troops.

"Lowest of Crimes"

Thus, in pursuance of the stock formula "to prevent a Communist take-over," the United States illegally airlifted troops to a friendly neighbor. But, this time, military illegality was compounded by an attempt to create

[20] Tad Szulc: *Dominican Diary,* Delacorte Press, New York, 1965.
[21] Eugene J. McCarthy: *The Limits of Power,* Holt, Rinehart & Winston, New York, 1967.

a feudal army under U.S. direction, by providing the O.A.S. with "teeth." Following the initial *fait accompli,* a meeting of O.A.S. met on 1st May, 1965, and a Special Committee was sent to Santo Domingo "to re-establish peace" and normal conditions. But on May 6, the governments of member states present were persuaded to make contingents of their military forces available to form an "Inter-American Peace Force" to support the U.S. invaders. By May 22, approximately 23,000 American marines and paratroopers were operating in the Dominican Republic. But there was so much reluctance on the part of O.A.S. members to co-operate that only one vote served—*that of the Dominican Republic itself*—to create the pretext of an "O.A.S. army."

An alert U Thant at once deprecated this shameless precedent of staging alleged "peace forces" outside the U.N. Other groups of countries —in Asia and Africa, for example—could play the same dangerous game. In the event, it is significant that it was not the U.S.-O.A.S. military men, but the special U.N. mediator sent to the Republic who secured a ceasefire and arranged with the rival leaders the terms of a return to constitutionality. Vidal Zaglio, Uruguayan U.N. delegate, was emphatic: "My country is opposed to the creation of an inter-American force, ostensibly with peaceful goals, but which could some day become a disturbing element, violating the fundamental principles of the Charter. Uruguay is tired of seeing the principles of non-intervention and self-determination flouted and the lowest of crimes committed in the name of freedom."

The first contingents of this *ad hoc* force consisted of 250 soldiers from Honduras, who were flown in by the U.S. air force. Its final composition —however short-lived—consisted of only four out of the twenty-one Latin American republics, as follows:

El Salvador	3
Nicaragua	164
Paraguay	183
Brazil	1,115

Costa Rica has no army, so it contributed 20 policemen. But what of the United States—which, incidentally, does NOT belong to Latin America? Its contingent was 10,900, nearly ten times that of everyone else. By the end of the year, peaceful conditions had not returned. United States and Brazilian troops were still in action in Santo Domingo, attempting to end a battle between the "constitutionalists" and the Dominican armed forces whom the U.S. treated as allies.

In November 1965, another inter-American Conference was held in Rio de Janeiro to lay the groundwork for a stronger Organization of American States. The United States then agreed to extend its Alliance for Progress funds until 1971, as an integral part of O.A.S., thus making Alliance aid a U.S. obligation—no doubt as compensation to reassure

147

some Latin American countries over its illegal intrusion in Dominican Republic affairs. Perhaps the Washington planners suffered their greatest diplomatic set-back, however, when most Latin American nations refused to follow through in the establishment of a permanent "peace-force." Mexico and Chile—most critical of U.S. action—persuaded Colombia not to push through such a resolution.

So that was the end of the world's first regional army. Or was it? On the main issue, Senator Eugene McCarthy has again an apt comment to make on this: "Few states of Central and South America see it as being in their interests to co-operate in the creation of a permanent military force, staffed by Latin American troops, but armed and financed largely by the United States. Latin Americans would assume that the force really would be created to serve United States interests."[22]

Since the débacle over the O.A.S. army the United States has found these countries more and more unresponsive to proposals for collective defense against Communist intervention. They resent U.S. interference more than they fear what the U.S. thinks is "Communism." Sidney Lens takes up this point in *The Futile Crusade:* "It is in our own hemisphere that the final test of anti-Communism is imminent. The irresistible tides of the world revolution threaten to explode throughout Latin America, where our greatest foreign investments lie . . . Can we find ways to aid the aspirations of the great majorities in Latin America, or will our fear of Communism lead to our isolation at last in an embittered Fortress America?"[23]

Perhaps an answer can be found in a view expressed by the indomitable Dr. Spock—a view widely shared by informed and progressive Americans: "The poor in Latin America are becoming so progressively more desperate, that they not only blame their own small owning class, which refuses to share its prosperity with them; they blame American industries which work hand-in-glove with the local industrialists and officials and take large profits out of these countries. Repeatedly *our Government has used its financial and military power to undermine progressive or radical Latin governments* which were favored by the people, but which the United States considered possible threats to its industrial or strategic power. It labels them Communist, whether they are or not . . . The greatest danger to our country is that it will embroil itself in endless civil wars there—always on the unpopular side in the name of anti-Communism."[24] (Italics added.)

Economically, the stumbling Alliance for Progress has not succeeded and, by its very nature, cannot succeed. For one thing, it is quantitatively too trifling, compared with the actual need. Unlike the U.N. Development Program, it is not organized as "seed money," under non-political direc-

[22] *op. cit.*
[23] Sidney Lens: *The Futile Crusade,* Quadrangle Books, Chicago, 1964.
[24] Dr. Benjamin Spock, letter in the *New York Times,* August 10, 1967.

tion. (This contrast between the Alliance and the UNDP techniques is dealt with in Chapter 6.) Senator Eugene McCarthy asserts that this U.S. oriented war-on-want program can barely scratch the surface of the total Latin American problem, so long as the needed substantial investments are being siphoned off into the wrong uses and the wrong places: "At the rate of spending of early 1967, the sum allotted for annual assistance for all of Latin America would not pay for the war in Vietnam for much more than one week."[25]

Meantime, alleged "leftists" in Uruguay are now asking whether democratic reform can be carried out *in spite* of U.S. "assistance," or whether guerrilla actions is their only choice. So far, their reforms have usually brought on military coups—and these have soon put a stop to any reform. For instance, in Guatemala, Jacobo Arbenz Guzman introduced a program of land reform when he became president in 1951—a program similar to the one later recommended by the Alliance for Progress. But it impinged on some unused land owned by the United Fruit Company. Thereupon, the C.I.A. assisted General Castillo Armas in launching a rightist revolution which, in June 1954, overthrew the government and put an end to land reform. Extreme poverty is now as widespread as ever. Yet the call for reform is again being heard. So the so-called leftists are seriously asking: "How *can* the people hope to achieve economic freedom except by guerrilla warfare"?[26]

The frustrated reformists can cite many such cases: *viz.,* Paz Estenssoro in Bolivia, where the socializing effort was quite radical; Juan Bosch in the Dominican Republic; João Goulart in Brazil; even Arturo Illia in Argentina—all deposed by military coups *after initiating social reforms* of the type that all these countries have at some time championed. Worse, the "leftists" are today confronted with yet a new shape of U.S. imperialism—invasion by green berets. They find that, as a part of U.S. military aid, about 1,000 green berets—mostly veterans of service in Vietnam—are currently teaching the tactics of anti-guerrilla warfare in various Latin American countries. Can anyone explain how an importation of green berets from Vietnam will promote trade or increase employment or stabilize the price of coffee?

Commenting on the "bitter battle" to elect a new Secretary-General of O.A.S. in March 1968, an experienced observer said: "One of Mr. Galo Plaza's first jobs will be to live down a feeling in some quarters that he is simply the puppet of the United States. In fact, there is a widespread belief in some Latin American quarters that the O.A.S. is little more than a United States agency." But the same correspondent goes on to state: "In many ways, the crisis over electing a new Secretary-General and the recent administration scandals pale in comparison with the Dominican

[25] *op. cit.*
[26] *The Christian Century,* November 8, 1967.

episode. It is likely that the events of recent months will be forgotten long before the Dominican controversy."[27]

Exclusive Use of Force

The fact that the Santo Domingo intervention was the first time that anyone tried to set up a regional army takes us back to Article 52 of the U.N. Charter, which Washington claimed to have "authorized" this. Article 52 reads:

The Members of the United Nations entering into such arrangements or constituting such agencies shall make every effort to achieve pacific settlement of local disputes through such regional arrangements or by such regional agencies before referring them to the Security Council.

It will be seen that this encouragement of peaceful co-operation gives no shadow of a title of authority to U.N. members to set up regional armed forces. In fact, the next article, Article 53, states in plain language the consistent purpose of the Charter to retain any "enforcement measures," for the exclusive use of the World Organization. It reads (in part): "The Security Council shall, where appropriate, utilize such regional arrangements or agencies for enforcement action *under its authority*. But no enforcement action shall be taken under regional arrangements or by regional agencies without the authorization of the Security Council . . ." (Italics added.)

Many important roles are being played, of course, by the World Organization through regional co-operation, especially in the economic, scientific and technological fields. But the military alliances and other outside self-serving ideological groupings have struck at the very foundations of the World Organization, under the pretext that the Charter provides them with legal standing, in spite of the precisely opposite objectives expressed in the Charter itself. Much is made of the dangers of the Communist challenge. At least we know where we stand in confronting Communist policy and procedures. But this repeated subverting and by-passing of the U.N. by virtually a secret military conspiracy is a knife stuck in the back of the World Organization, while the official delegates are proclaiming respect for the Charter.

"The underlying basis of the Charter was concerted action by the five permanent members," U Thant has stated: "But when nations follow divided loyalties, and when alignments are formed around the super-Powers, the United Nations becomes the forum for propagating rival viewpoints. The United Nations cannot achieve much if the super-Powers do not co-operate. There cannot be true international co-operation if its scope is relegated to the level of satisfying regional or ideological interests."

[27] *Christian Science Monitor,* March 7, 1968.

Rushing In

Happily, we are witnessing today some important Third World developments which carry within them the seeds of effective regional co-operation of a constructive kind, but which owe nothing to the exalted leadership of either the West or the Communists. Although this development is at too early a stage to encourage definitive judgments, various trends in Africa toward co-operation—perhaps "unity" is too pretentious a term—are of high significance for the future.

Alongside the Economic Commission for Africa, established by the U.N. in 1958 to promote action for the economic development directed to raising standards of living throughout Africa and to strengthen trading relations between all the countries of Africa and other countries of the world, a basically political body has emerged from those countries and territories themselves. This is the Organization of African Unity (O.A.U.).

The tireless Secretary-General had these frank words to say when he addressed the Conference of O.A.U. in September 1967:

In between actions at the national and world-wide levels, regional organizations such as the O.A.U. have a most vital role to play . . . In a continent so rich with cultural and ethnic diversity, this slow progress is neither surprising nor discouraging. The O.A.U. is a young Organization. Its goals cannot be expected to be achieved in a few years. Nor can they be achieved by Africans alone. This last point is, in my view, of special importance. *In an increasingly inter-dependent world, regional arrangements must be viewed in their proper context—as a part of the wider international scene.* (Italics added.)

Similarly, on another occasion, when commending the United Nations programs of the regional economic commissions, the Secretary-General warned against the danger of "regionalism turning into provincialism." U Thant urged members of the O.A.U., "whose Charter is based on the same universal principles as the United Nations," to guard against "the dangers of turning inward and not keeping a proper balance between their collective efforts on behalf of Africa and their inescapable duties as members of the World Community of Nations."

As a case in point, Kenya's Minister of Defense recently insisted that the Kenya-Somalia dispute should be kept "entirely within the African family" and be dealt with primarily through the regional conference of eleven East African Heads of State and, secondly, through the Organization of African Unity. Only if they failed to find a peaceful solution would the dispute be referred to the United Nations. This was the honest way of utilizing Article 52. The true function of regional co-operation, as presented in the Charter, is to leave outside parties alone and keep the peace among its own members by methods consistent with the Charter.

Yet there seem to exist no restraints on the activities of self-appointed world-policemen. No one quite knows who is next on the list to be "policed." When the Security Council was discussing the complaint of the Democratic Republic of the Congo on the afternoon of July 10, 1967, one such blatant example was actually in progress. In the final round of debate, a resolution was passed unanimously excluding *all intervention* by outside nations in the Congo. This is how that discussion might be paraphrased:

THEODORE IDZUMBUIR, spokesman of the Democratic Republic of the Congo, complained that the presence of "foreign elements" was a trump in the hands of those behind the plot against his country. On December 10, 1966, 42 "clandestine soldiers" met in Liége, Belgium, ready to leave for the Congo and "were given tickets for Kinshasa and travel formalities were arranged quickly for these men carrying small suitcases and large revolvers. . . . "

JOSE MARIA RUDA of Argentina said that the situation in the Congo had to be followed with great care by the Security Council because . . . the General Assembly had adopted a declaration on the non-admissibility of interference . . . in the civil strife of other countries.

LORD CARADON reaffirmed his Government's policy, and said that the Council had called on all States to refrain from interference in Congolese affairs . . . GOPALASWAMI PARTHASARATHI of India stated that India took a serious view of attempts to interfere in the domestic affairs of States; and AKIRA MATSUI of Japan said that all States had to refrain from interfering in the Congo; while HANS R. TABOR of Denmark stressed that interference in the affairs of the Congo was contrary to the Charter.

And so on around the horseshoe table, leading to a vote in these terms: "Concerned by the threat posed by foreign interference to the independence and territorial integrity of the Democratic Republic of the Congo," the United Nations "condemns any State which persists in permitting or tolerating the recruitment of mercenaries and the provision of facilities to them with the objective of overthrowing the Governments of Member States."

The United States delegate, however, William B. Buffum, had some unexpected last-minute news to convey. He would vote affirmatively for the resolution, but it did not "coincide with our preferences in every respect," he said. On the contrary, "in response to a request from President Mobutu," and "in accordance with United Nations resolutions," his country had just that day sent three C-130 transport planes to assist the President in his efforts against the rebels. (The U.S. delegate did not mention that these planes had carried 150 armed American soldiers into the territory—while the Council's debate was still proceeding.)

Thus, in spite of the "agreement," one member had again presented the Council and the world with a *fait accompli*. U.S. Senators, as did sensible people everywhere, at once condemned this unilateral act of military intervention in the heart of explosive Africa—in the Congo, of all places, where the U.N. had succeeded so narrowly in preserving the integrity of the country. Senator Fulbright asserted that American forces had "no business" in the Congo and the various reasons given for it "don't all hang together"; and another Senator said that "the real danger, if you do this again and again, is that eventually the Russians are going to have to show their strength."

By an extraordinary coincidence, the same afternoon of the Council debate, Chief Justice Earl Warren of the Supreme Court was addressing a Conference on World Law in Geneva, Switzerland. This is what he told the two thousand lawyers present: "Instead of matching each other, soldier for soldier, plane for plane, bomb for bomb, and missile for missile," nations should compete with each other "law for law, treaty for treaty." The Chief Justice contended that "all contacts and relationships in the international community" should be covered by treaties that would either prevent disputes or channel them "into law institutions for peaceful decisions." This, he said, would create "so much law" that disputes grievous enough to cause war "will be guided into courthouses and away from battlefields."

This voice of "the other America" was joined at the Geneva event by Pier P. Spinelli, Director of the United Nations European Office, who told the lawyers that "probably the most serious reverses the United Nations has suffered during the past twenty-two years have occurred when nations abnegated their international codes and conventions and took the law into their own hands." Abdul Rahman Pazhwak of Afghanistan, past U.N. President, pointed out to the Conference that "the ideas of the Charter are very considerably ahead of what international society is prepared to accept today"; therefore, "progress in enforcing the rules of international law has been very slight."

In the final chapter we shall deal more specifically with the development of the rule of law in international affairs. In this chapter we have been mainly concerned with those unconscious or perverted instincts of the opponents of world law who constantly traduce the solemn obligations of the Charter on which the survival of mankind hangs. The growth of the Common Law in past centuries suggests that effective World Law may result not from some cataclysmic revolution in constitution-making, but rather from the day-to-day decisions of statesmen determined to apply the rule of law instead of the law of the jungle in their conduct of state policy.

Part II

BUILDING PEACE
IN THE 1970's

The world's great age begins anew,
The golden years return,
The earth doth like a snake renew
Her winter weeds outworn:
Heaven smiles, and faiths and empires gleam
Like wrecks of a dissolving dream . . .

O cease! must hate and death return?
Cease! must men kill and die?
Cease! drain not to its dregs the urn
Of bitter prophecy!
The world is weary of the past—
O might it die or rest at last!

—Percy Bysshe Shelley
on *Hellas*.

5 SHADOW AND SUBSTANCE

"The shadow of a sailor, of a hangman, and of an ascetic may be quite similar. It is impossible to distinguish them by their shadows, just as it is impossible to find any difference between the wood of a ship and a gallows and of a cross by chemical analysis. But they are different men and different objects—their shadows only are equal and similar."
— P. D. Ouspensky in *Tertium Organum*

The Cold War began as a hot war by British and American soldiers killing Russians—on Russian soil. That was in 1918, when the West made its first, and abortive, attempt to put down the Bolshevik régime. The landing on the Planet Venus of a Soviet space vehicle in 1967, to coincide almost to the day with the 50th Anniversary Celebrations of the Russian Revolution, could never have been foreseen in the chaotic days which ended the First World War.

"The most important achievement in the development of human society over the past half century is the emergence of Socialism beyond the framework of one country, and the formation of a world Socialist system," said Alexei V. Zakharov at the 1967 Session of the U.N. General Assembly: "The Socialist world now comprises over 35 per cent of the population of our planet. But the political map of the world has undergone another very important change. The Great October Revolution struck a tremendous blow at the whole system of imperialist and colonial rule. Whereas half a century ago the population of the colonies and semi-colonies comprised 69 per cent of the world's total, today it accounts for a little over 1 per cent. Over 70 sovereign States have risen from the ruins of the colonial empires."

Even allowing for the exaggeration and exuberance of this claim at the time the Soviet Union was celebrating its 50th Anniversary, and the fact that de-colonialization has owed practically nothing to Russia and most to the U.N., this dramatic change in the map of the earth is basically true. It is equally true that not one of the 70 "new" states (unless Cuba and Mongolia are included) has become a Communist nation.

Yet, until the 1960's, with one or two little-noticed exceptions, no general book seems to have been published in Britain or the United States exhibiting the Cold War as an historical epoch—stretching for half a century—or as a series of escalating events arising directly from the First World War and enfolding a whole generation in its consistent embrace. Such products of one-sided interpretation as the Communist "take-over" of "captive nations" following on the Second World War, and the re-spondent Truman Doctrine of the late 1940's, came quite late in the game. To know why the Cold War cannot be "won"—by anybody—is to know how and why it began. Some of the "new writing" in this field is eloquent of changing attitudes in America.

In *The Futile Crusade,* Sidney Lens sums up the forgotten epoch as follows: "The roots of the crusade lay in the attempts of Churchill and Clemenceau to strangle the Russian Revolution by force of arms from 1918 to 1920. What the West could not destroy, it tried for nearly twenty years to isolate and ostracize. Thus the credo was dormant for two decades, but erupted in full force after World War II, when the old order vanished in China." He brings his charges home to his fellow-countrymen: "Since 1917, Communism has been the 'great fear' in American life; and since 1946, anti-Communism has been the great purpose of our national ex-istence and a basic tenet of U.S. foreign and domestic policy."[1]

Only now, as the Space Age advances, are statesmen and scholars and also ordinary people in the West beginning to understand that the Com-munist regimes of the Soviet Union and China and their border lands—forming together by far the most continuous land block across the earth's surface—are there to stay as a permanent factor in the policies of all nations. The major task now facing Western statesmanship—as well as the expanding Third World—is to know how, first, to accept current reality without loss of freedom and democracy, and, second, to ensure the future peace of the human race by decisions which draw together the divergent political, economic, and ideological systems by which our planet is still divided.

In previous chapters we have sought to show how the West's miscon-ceived policies to "contain" the Communist regimes by means of threats and alliances, bombs and soldiers, have not achieved their proclaimed purposes, and are never likely to. On the contrary, they have led particu-larly the United States up a *cul-de-sac* to a military domination of others which now threatens its own political and economic future, and, if con-tinued, will assuredly lead to the Third World War, beginning in South-

[1] Sidney Lens: *The Futile Crusade,* Quadrangle Books, Chicago, 1964.

east Asia. In this chapter, we attempt to lay down some guidelines for the way back to sanity or, rather, the way forward to an order more in keeping with the requirements of a World Society. For, today, no nation or alliance of nations can gain its security at the expense of another.

In *The Cold War in Retrospect and Prospect,* Frederick L. Schuman similarly reminds us that the legacy of fear and hatred which so bedeviled foreign policy in the 1950's and 1960's had started much earlier:

Within ten months after Russia's October Revolution, Soviet Russia and the West were at war. And the war was not a cold war but a hot war, marked by many casualties and vast destruction. Be it remembered, lest we forget what Russians never forget, that this was war not begun by Communists sending armies against the West, but by the West sending armies against Soviet Russia . . . in another somber chapter of Russia's age-old tragedy of invasion from abroad.[2]

This evil legacy of military intervention, the seed of the Cold War as we have known it since, began immediately after World War I had ended. As Professor Schuman goes on to state: "The outcome of this war was a deadlock or stalemate. The United States and the Allied Powers failed to destroy the Soviet regime and were obliged to abandon their armed intervention and blockade. The Communist rulers of Russia failed to undermine or subvert any of the Capitalist States and were obliged to give up or defer their hopes of World Revolution." So we have continued to live on in this stalemate for half a century. Yet, as we noticed in Chapter 3, hard core nuclear planners now propose to perpetuate that anachronism by switching the direction of their warheads from Russia to China. NATO, we hoped, was to be the last fiasco in this futile crusade. But no! Having failed with NATO, the cold warriors would now overreach Russia and finish the human story where it is alleged to have began, somewhere in the Gobi desert—for the very last time making a desert and calling it peace.

It should be noted that, though *both* sides have failed and will continue to fail to "win," both sides would lose everything in courting an ultimate contest. Some early Revolutionary leaders were convinced that Communism could be extended by war. A Niagara of books, speeches, and sermons have since deluged the West, advertising this belief: Communism wants war, therefore fire must be met by fire. A generation has been conditioned to accept just that. Conversely, anti-Communists have believed that Communism could be destroyed by war. Both sides were wrong; both sides are wrong—and two wrongs will never make a right.

For the first decade and a half Cold War "scholarship" in the U.S. attributed the post-war diplomatic impasse solely to Soviet policy. These one-sided accounts contrast Soviet aggression and expansionism with the sparkling altruism of Washington policy. Only after a series of frustrating

[2] Frederick L. Schuman: *The Cold War in Retrospect and Prospect,* Louisiana University Press, 1962.

attempts at keeping up the good Wartime Fellowship, the legend runs, did the U.S. reluctantly adopt a policy of "containment."

Gar Alperovitz's *Atomic Diplomacy* contradicts this theory in a devastating factual account of the day-by-day diplomacy of President Truman and Secretary of State Byrnes during 1945. He explains the mutual basis for Soviet distrust and aversion to negotiated settlement. He shows that Truman and Byrnes, as early as April 1945, sought to break away from Yalta agreements. Truman tried to undercut the various agreements and understandings made by Franklin D. Roosevelt and deviated from Roosevelt's role as mediator between Churchill and Stalin to accept Churchill's hard-line policy and forge the basis for an "Anglo-Saxon front."[3]

The Cold War was not inevitable, but became so because of the shift in U.S., as well as in British policy. The author also notes the role assumed by hardliners in the State Department after April 1945, a policy rejected earlier by President Roosevelt. This crucial shift did much to cater to Stalin's paranoic view of Western diplomatic objectives.

Like many other recent analysts, Alperovitz also questions the traditional view that Truman used the bomb to terminate the Far Eastern war with a minimal loss of lives. The Truman Administration never seriously considered the Japanese peace feelers; he could have secured the same result without dropping the bomb. Alperovitz concludes that Truman overplayed his hand and succeeded neither in converting the Soviet Union to the U.S. position nor in achieving peace, but rather created a climate of distrust and suspicion that gave way to the Cold War and an atomic arms race. Moreover, it should be remembered that "atomic diplomacy" of this kind prevailed in Washington before the Joe McCarthy blight descended over the land. Once that curse had closed like a dark curtain over the American official mind, there was never hope of reconciliation or understanding.

The end results of this hard-line indoctrination have been illustrated in the first part of this book. Each nuclear scorpion locked in the bottle has been convinced that his survival depends on striking the other scorpion first—for it will be too late afterwards. Much, though belatedly, is now being published to explain the dilemma of the scorpions and how they got locked into a Cold War in the first place. But not anything like enough advice is available on how to get them out. How to get the scorpions out of the bottle is indeed the subject of the second part of this book. But convincing the scorpions is no simple task.

In this chapter we can glance first at some of the arguments, accumulating during the 1960's, for a new look at the Cold War itself. Then we can assess briefly the moral and social damage which it has done, especially to the United States, inflicted with the spate of emotional verbiage

[3] Gar Alperovitz: *Atomic Diplomacy*, Simon & Schuster, New York, 1965.

which streams from the less responsible newspaper offices and radio stations across the country, and also from political leaders who still repeat those time-worn clichés and catchwords that anti-Communism has become for millions of their less-informed constituents. Finally, we might glance at some of those signs of a wider freedom as men try to reach beyond the narrow ideologies which have bound them to an infantile worship of the superman nation-state.

Expectations Denied

Such writings as Martin F. Herz's *Beginnings of the Cold War* attempt to explain the formulative process which characterized America in the early months of 1945, when victory in Europe was in sight. Drawing on current documentary sources, Professor Herz traces the sequence of events leading to mutual distrust arising, for instance, from Russian actions in Poland and, later, the rival occupation policies evolved respectively by the Western allies and by the Russians. Compromises and disagreements at Yalta were followed by tortuous negotiations over the future United Nations. "One of the things that strikes one most forcefully," says Professor Herz, "is that our memories are selective and that, especially, we tend to forget our *expectations.*"

Early in 1945, Americans expected a post-war economic slump—as after the First World War. Business and government were chiefly concerned with measures to mitigate it. Great hopes were entertained for a better post-war world, of course, once the aggressor nations had been defeated—a world in which Russia and her Western allies could work together in a new world organization, toward peace and freedom. But they were disappointed—not because of the special "wickedness" of Russia, but because that was what *war* did to us all. It did not bring peace.

Professor Herz' warning about forgetting our past "expectations" goes uncomfortably close to the root of our military forgetfulness at this time. "Today," he says, recalling America's anxiety in 1945 to induce Russia's participation in the war against Japan, "we have the benefit of hindsight. We know that the atomic bomb became available and we know that even without the atomic bomb Japan would probably have been forced to give up . . . That, however, was emphatically *not* the view of our most qualified military men in the early months of that year." Describing how the expected post-war slump did not come off, he remarks:

It is surprising, then, to recall—even if it requires quite an effort—that the rush of our army to demobilize, the whole sentiment in favor of the speediest possible return of our soldiers, was not unrelated to the quest for jobs. We all wanted to get home quickly because those who would return last were expected to have the hardest times ahead of them.[4]

[4] Martin F. Herz: *Beginnings of the Cold War,* Indiana University Press, Bloomington, 1966.

A frequently repeated Cold War argument has proceeded on the lines that Russia had no moral or legal right to say what should happen in Korea or the North Pacific because she came into the Asian War at the last minute, merely for what she could get. Moreover, while the U.S. disarmed at once, like a peace-loving nation, the Soviet Union retained millions of fighting men in order to take over Eastern Europe. This black-and-white logic—isolated from the inconveniences of economic or geographical reality—has been the stock-in-trade of the anti-Communist crusade for two decades.

There are, of course, many scholars of balance and integrity, like H. Stuart Hughes, who never hesitate to expose the worst of the Communist system, while vigorously opposing Cold War policies:

Our real quarrel is with Communism's tyranny over the mind of man. And I mean this in the widest sense. I mean terror and censorship, arbitrary imprisonment and forced labor, the falsification of history and barefaced lying in international assemblies . . . I am quite ready to agree with the most militant of anti-Communists that in this sense Communism is indeed a "scourge" or a "poison," a dreadful affliction of contemporary humanity.[5]

At the same time, Professor Hughes and other modern historians insist on that degree of intellectual honesty so desperately needed in public life today. As he states: "It goes without saying that the moral condemnation must be even-handed: it implies a similar outspokenness regarding the conduct of our own countrymen or that of our allies. Where Western policy has violated the elementary principles of civilized behavior among peoples—whatever the provocation—the same moral standards apply as in judging the crimes of Communism."

One could wish that D. F. Fleming's monumental two volume survey of five decades, *The Cold War and its Origins,* could become a working textbook of every Secretary of State and Presidential adviser. It brings to the surface historical issues that have been ignored by the usual run of publicists or broadcasters, so that the general public knows little or nothing of them.

Moreover, Professor Fleming seeks to analyze *why* "we are ruled by logic-of-weapon instead of logic-of-peace," and *why* it is that, in spite of our growing danger, "we do nothing effective to escape from the black magic of the fabulous weapons" that are the evil fruit of the Cold War. "Throughout the Cold War years, Western military planning," he states, "has been dictated by the logic of a revolutionary military technology. The new weapons have made us their prisoners. As each new 'ultimate weapon' has been projected—A-bomb, H-bomb, guided-missile—negotiations have been suspended until the latest series of the latest tests could be staged . . . Today the same fantasy-ridden minds are assuring us that over-all

[5] H. Stuart Hughes: *An Approach to Peace,* Atheneum, New York, 1962.

strategy and world policy must be determined by the technology of the latest 'ultimate weapon.' "[6]

Climbing Down

What anti-Communist agitators have done is not to "save" freedom or the "West" or anybody, but to subject freedom and the West and everybody to the inexorable logic of atomic annihilation. While parading in the garb of a savior, the anti-Communist has become a fellow-conspirator in a Game of Death, played by the nuclear strategists behind his back. But slowly the anti-Communist tryanny over men's minds, like its progenitor, is being broken. It is being broken by Americans who see their country's sad predicament and its growing isolation and are rising to defend it from the ordinary crackpots, the super-patriots, the psychotics and the obsessed, and the political climbers who have for too long thrived on it.

When General James Gavin testified before the Senate Foreign Relations Committee in February 1967, he said: "It seems to me that many Americans still think of international affairs in terms of almost a generation ago. They see the world as one in which there are two blocs of power, the Communists and the anti-Communists, a monolithic world in which a Communist conspiracy is out to conquer the world, and the anti-Communists are totally committed to preventing such a conquest. It is a world of bad guys and good guys, with no place for the in-betweens. Actually, the world is no longer like that, for the Communist conspiracy is shattered beyond possibility of recovery."

The full implications of this statement—long accepted by most of the civilized world outside America—have not, however, been *acted* on by the U.S. Establishment. Even in Britain some conservatives, thanks to the NATO fixation, tend to repeat the same Cold War slogans which lost their content at least a decade since. But the change over in public sentiment will not be at all easy in America, however sensibly Britain and Europe have showed the way. For one thing, the Vietnam involvement chains the Administration emotionally—and those who support it—to their past mistakes. For another thing, anti-Communism has paid, and is still paying, rich dividends to those prominent Americans whose enjoyment of national prestige rests on these dubious political stances. Political aspirants like Richard Nixon have built their public careers, as the record shows, on what they have preached about Communism—and they must still go on preaching it. Can these beneficiaries of anti-Communism be expected to climb down from the shabby pedestals which they have erected for them-

[6] D. F. Fleming: *The Cold War and its Origins* (two volumes), Scribner's, New York, 1964.

163

selves on the destroyed reputations and broken careers of their victims?

Dr. Karen Horney's classic, *The Neurotic Personality of Our Time,* contrasts our contemporary political climbers with the attitude of the Pueblo Indians, among whom striving for prestige is definitely discouraged, for there is so little difference in individual possessions between them. It would be meaningless in such a culture to strive for any kind of dominance as a means of self-assurance. That neurotics in our own culture choose this way, Dr. Horney says, results from the fact that in our social structure power, prestige and possession give a feeling of greater security. Perhaps, when a full study of the impact of anti-Communism on American life comes to be made, closer attention will be paid to its cultural roots in a neurotic individualism born of anxiety and feelings of inferiority.

Meanwhile, its poisonous seeds are still fructifying. The United States came out of World War II physically unscathed, far-removed from the wreckage and chaos of post-war Europe and, especially, Russia. Its economic system was not only intact, but running in top gear. Yet the national self-esteem which flowed—and still does in some quarters—from this exceptional state of affairs was really short-lived; a bad conscience and atomic anxiety set in; security escaped through the chinks in the armor of power, prestige, and possession. Now the climb down—especially following the Vietnam War—has had to confront the same hard realities of international life which have long faced the rest of mankind.

This is not the first time that the "arrogance of power" has gone to the head of a self-styled "affluent" nation. Nor do we have to go back to Greece and Rome for examples. Robinson and Beard remind us in their *History of Europe* (1921), used for many years in American schools and colleges:

The World War, which opened in 1914, completely altered the attitude of the rest of the world toward Germany. No one can view the history of that country in the same way that he did before the Prussian military party precipitated that terrible conflict—her government reached a degree of power which tempted it to defy the world and which made her such an international menace that even the great Republic separated from her by the broad Atlantic was forced finally to array its whole strength against her.

This simple parallel may omit many of the international complications which led up to World War I, but the two American historians, who had accorded full praise to Germany's brilliant rise to industrial affluence fifty years ago, correctly assessed the disaster which nonetheless fell upon that country—and the world—when the ambitious military-industrial leaders took over the government and destroyed the prospects of peace for a generation to come.*

* A controversial modern historian, Fritz Fischer, describes in *Griff Nach der Weltmacht* ("The Drive for World Power"), 1961, how a growingly affluent Germany before 1914 was driven into diplomatic isolation by the overbearing self-confidence of its military-industrial hierarchy.

The increasing moral and political isolation of America today is a presage that is not lost on the sensitive minds of her greatest citizens. Unlike the handful of courageous German liberals before World War I who were brutally silenced, they can assert openly with Senator J. William Fulbright:

America is now at that historical point at which a great nation is in danger of losing its perspective on what exactly is within the realm of its power and what is beyond it. Other great nations, reaching this critical juncture, have aspired to too much, and by over-extension of effort have declined and then fallen.[7]

"It has become evident to most of us," writes Marshall D. Shulman in *Beyond the Cold War*, "that the language and ideas of the Cold War are no longer adequate as a guide to international politics today . . . This is not because the conflict of purposes described by the Cold War no longer exists, but because this conflict is no longer the dominating fact of international politics." Professor Shulman, former aide to Secretary of State Dean Acheson, is shocked most of all by the distorted views which the United States and Russia have had of each other's intentions.

"Perhaps the first thing we need to do," he writes, "is to rid ourselves of the 'hard-soft' scale in describing policy choices." He has no use for the "pro-West" and "pro-Communist" labels which, day in and day out, slant and distort news stories and editorials in the bulk of the press and mass media across the country. "Anti-Communism" is no valid policy, he argues. The aim of a new U.S. policy should be "to draw the Soviet Union further toward the acceptance of international processes that make possible adjustments without (general) war."[8]

We arrive, therefore, at the crucial turning-point of our enquiry. Anti-Communism, like anti-anything, cannot be ousted by yet another "anti." To un-fear Communism, to un-hate Russia or China, involves, as Erich Fromm has put it: "The Art of Loving." Destroyers of old dogmas must be men of faith themselves. The genuine anti-Communist comes not to destroy, but to fulfill. The new look at Communism which scholars and writers are now demanding does not mean simply bringing the Soviet Union closer to the U.S. in some sort of rebound alliance—possibly *against* China or somebody else. It does mean that *both* the U.S. and the U.S.S.R. could draw closer to each other politically and ethically by belonging to something bigger than themselves.

"To make possible adjustments without war" is indeed the priority of the 1970's. That is why both the U.S. and the U.S.S.R. signed the U.N. Charter in the first place—now joined by over 120 other nations. This wider union remains the only "guarantee" of planetary survival, if there can be any guarantee for anyone. The U.N. can no longer be treated as the

[7] J. W. Fulbright: *The Arrogance of Power*, Vintage, New York, 1966.
[8] M. D. Shulman: *Beyond the Cold War*, Yale University Press, 1966.

Cinderella of international diplomacy, but as the primary necessity of global integration.

The well-tried techniques of parliamentary democracy do not involve hard-soft policy choices, but a variety of skillful political compromises and diplomatic adjustments. Yet this has been essentially the West's contribution to the political life of the present century. If the same techniques which have been the strength and glory of the West cannot now be expanded to world society as a whole, then nothing can save us from the missile-minds. An anti-Communism which has masqueraded for two decades as the defense of freedom, but which has in fact led the West into the abominations of nuclear suicide, must be exposed as the anti-humanity which it is.

In *An Approach to Peace,* Professor H. Stuart Hughes puts the issue in a nutshell: *"Our chief enemy is not the Soviet Union, but war itself."*[9] If this be so, the trappings and mumbo-jumbo of NATO and the other anti-Communist postures must be scrapped in favor of a thoroughgoing anti-war program. This is the West's problem in essence. And this means a revitalized United Nations in which all nations—most certainly Russia and China—join forces with the rest of the human race against their universal enemy: WAR.

"I think it is time to make a new start," Professor Hughes argues: "It is time to re-think from the beginning the assumption on which American foreign policy and nearly all public discussion of that policy are currently based. We need to establish a new order of priorities and a new hierarchy of values." Because of this, he says: "I believe that most of the problems of the past twelve or fifteen years are irrelevant today . . . I believe that the United States and the Soviet Union *are* very different—but not as different as they are popularly supposed to be. I believe that this difference *is* decisive—but not in the way it is usually expressed. We have more in common with the Russians than either side realizes. Above all, we have a common—and overriding—interest in stopping the drift toward thermonuclear warfare before it is too late."

"We Are Defeating Ourselves!"

The damage that has already been done to the new generation by well-financed anti-Communism crusades and by the vast array of politicos, bureaucrats, newsmen, and publicists, who have been its unwitting agents over the two decades, will take a long time to repair. The less enlightened of these fanatics have even now, as we have seen, merely diverted their attacks from the Russians to the Chinese. *Plus ça change, plus c'est la même chose.*

[9] *op. cit.*

The Vietnam War has served, unfortunately, only to keep Communism more alive by killing more Communists. Day by day, as the butchers' bills have been read out, radio and TV announcers have invariably described enemy dead as "Communists." The label "Communist" is repeated more times than any other political adjective in current use. Yet, how many of those poverty-stricken farmers and peasants—in their teens and twenties, as the same TV screen has revealed—could ever have read a single book on Karl Marx or any other Communist authority, passes belief. It is men, not Communists, who die in war.

Don Luce, an idealistic American agricultural student, yearned to teach the farmers of a poor country how to transplant seedlings, cultivate vegetables and apply fertilizers. In 1958, he went to Vietnam as a member of the International Voluntary Services and ultimately became the chief. But in 1967 he resigned, along with three of the top officials of the I.V.S. These four courageous Americans condemned the war without reservation and urged their country to stop bombing the North, to recognize the National Liberation Front, and to turn over the conflict at once "to an international peace commission and be prepared to accept its recommendations." Don Luce declared: "I could not become part of the destruction of a people I love. . . . What's going on here is changing these people, and it's overwhelming." And he went on: "It's become unbearable to witness the destruction of Vietnamese family life, the home, the agricultural system, the transportation. We're defeating ourselves here."[10]

That is the lesson of Vietnam. By preaching anti-Communism, in season and out of season, to a naïve and impressionable public at home and then ruthlessly practicing it on a small backward country, the United States has plunged to its own moral defeat—whatever military victory it might have been seeking over its "Communist enemies."

The irony is that this defeat of American ideals has owed nothing to the tiny group of card-carrying Communists whose weight and importance are usually magnified out of all reason, despite the fact that they have no adequate spokesman in public life or, for that matter, in the arts, sciences or professions to propound their hopeless cause, while their economic power is nil. "To suppose," writes Alan Barth, editorial writer of the *Washington Post,* "that in peace-time 54,000 or 540,000 Communists, however disciplined, however enthusiastic, could overthrow the United States government and make the American people accept them as masters is as rational as a belief in sea serpents or dragons." It is the anti-Communists who have transformed the American "way of life" into a way of danger and death, and brought contempt and derision on their country from across the world.

One of the most gratifying reactions to the United States invasion of

[10] *New York Times,* September 24, 1967.

Vietnam, however, has been an upsurge of movements, books, and journals in defense of its traditional democratic ideals and of world peace. Such a stirring of the public conscience has never happened before in United States history. Toward the end of the 1960's more and more commercial publishers—usually so timid of unorthodox positions—have been willing to produce for an expanding market, as the present narrative has shown, works repudiating the Cold War and condemning United States militarism, as a threat to the American future. Book club and paperback editions have reached an enormous public, especially the young. The warfare state is itself under siege.

Among this swelling side of dissent and disgust, *The Military Establishment* by John M. Swomley throws needed light on the dark powers of the Pentagon over U.S. economic life, and on its vast publicity machine, and especially on how modern militarism works hand in glove with right-wing extremism. The subtle influence of the military on religion and education is carefully documented. Professor Swomley claims that, so deep has the rot eaten into public and economic life, "nothing short of total world disarmament can restore the United States to thoroughgoing civilian control and to government by the people."

He points out that "one of the most dangerous results of the alliance between the military and industry is the growth of a large right-wing extremist movement. Most of the groups that make it up receive heavy financial support from industry and substantial organizational support from professional military officers." Swomley devotes many pages simply to listing the names and relationship of well-subsidized organizations whose irresponsible excesses occasionally break through a tacit press censorship which normally protects them from public exposure.

"Among the key leaders of the John Birch Society," he states, "are a score of retired colonels, generals and admirals and one former Marine sergeant, Matthew McKeon, who was court-martialed for taking his trainees on a training march that resulted in death for many. Still others not listed as leaders are members. Among these is General Edwin Walker, who distributed John Birch Society literature in his division and who was reprimanded by the Army only after unfavorable publicity about his efforts to influence the voting of his troops forced the Army's hand."

Another right-wing group with military ties, records Swomley, "is the Manion Forum, founded by a former dean of Notre Dame's College of Law. The Manion Forum includes a weekly radio program of a network of over 200 stations in 41 states as well as a monthly newsletter. Manion, who is on the John Birch Society Council, features interviews and talks by leading right-wing people, including military and retired military men."[11]

Nor should it be forgotten—though it is an embarrassing memory which

[11] J. M. Swomley: *The Military Establishment*, Beacon Press, Boston, 1964.

many political leaders are now trying to forget—that the "mass base" of Dulles' disastrous foreign policy was McCarthyism at home. American casualties in Vietnam are part of the high price which a new generation has been forced to pay for this discreditable epoch.

"McCarthy's movement is made up of frustrated, insecure and frenzied elements of the middle class who are prey to the demagogic offerings of a scapegoat for all their difficulties and worries." Thus reasoned M. Weiss in a contemporary account, *McCarthyism: American Fascism on the March:* "Communism is that scapegoat. The mass base of McCarthy's support includes every fascist and would-be-fascist group gnawing at the vitals of America. The rags and remnants of the Coughlin movement, the Silver Shirts, Christian Frontiers, America Firsters, G.L.K. Smith's supporters, Legionnaires, Catholic War Veterans, scabs, F.B.I. stool-pigeons, professional red-baiters and strike-breakers, Ku Klux Klanners, lynchers, vigilantes, hooligans, and gangsters are in McCarthy's movement."[12]

Not unnaturally, there has been a carry-over of McCarthyism (now a standard dictionary term) into military affairs—sometimes of an unexpected naïveté. Washington religious circles were disturbed when it was found that one of the Air Force training manuals alleged that Communism had infiltrated the churches. (Other Air Force manuals gave instructions on how to operate social clubs and how to entice customers to order alcoholic drinks.) The authorities identified the writer of the Air Reserve Training Center manual that contained the propaganda on Communism in the churches and explained that his superior had approved the manual only after "a cursory review." Doubtless, the Prince of Peace would get a poor rating in such hands.

"It" and Mr. Nutter

There are two basic appeals—one emotional and the other pragmatic—that proponents of anti-Communism rely on. The emotional line is well exemplified in ex-Senator Barry Goldwater's *Why Not Victory?* when he attacks Senator J. W. Fulbright's innocence and says: "The Senator from Arkansas says he does not know what victory would mean—as he puts it—'in this age of ideological conflict and nuclear weapons' . . . If Senator Fulbright finds difficulty in understanding what victory would mean, perhaps he should spend a little thought on the question of what defeat—*the only alternative to victory*—would mean. This is a frightening thought—what would defeat mean?" Goldwater then insists that "total victory" is the *only* way to "survival."

The level of abstraction which Goldwater reaches in this typical piece of sophistry is evidence of the "blagh-blagh" language which Stuart Chase

12 M. Weiss, *McCarthyism: American Fascism on the March,* Pioneer Publishers, New York, 1953.

169

in his *The Tyranny of Words* designated as the verbal escapism of the uncultivated mind. Cold warriors constantly take refuge in something termed "it." Citing Charles Nutter of International House, New Orleans, Barry Goldwater develops the "it" formula like this:

Communism is an international conspiracy which has restored slavery to the world. . . .

It has captured, enslaved, and exploited a billion people against their will, and plans to capture the remaining two billion people on earth.

It has destroyed freedom, liberty, independence, human rights and dignity wherever possible.

It has interfered and intervened times without number in the domestic affairs of free nations.

It has established deceit, dishonor, destruction, death and disaster as recognized, accepted, and necessary instruments of an international policy. . . .

It has made man the "producing animal" which Karl Marx labeled him.[13]

We need only take the point about "freedom" by way of example, for it brings up the moral decadence that has become the price of the Goldwater type of philosophy in America. Professor Thomas Parkinson of Berkeley University, California, states in a college journal: "It is extremely difficult to find clean money in this country, and the general taint of the Cold War obscures most human energy in some way or other . . . Speaking in the narrowest professional terms, the Cold War in general and the Vietnam War in particular have destroyed the freedom of an entire generation of college students and the will to resist bigotry and lies of their professors. There are honorable exceptions to the general tone of indifference, neglect, greed, and opportunism that afflicts the academy as it does the entire country."

Yet this Good versus Evil dichotomy presented on countless public platforms and at businessmen's luncheons by the Goldwaters and Nixons and Reagans and Wallaces—as though nuclear strategy could somehow defend the Good against the Evil—is not shared by the strategists themselves. For them Good and Evil are irrelevant. The Game is all. Victory is what matters, for itself. Anatol Rapaport thus describes the nuclear Neanderthals in *Strategy and Conscience:*

Being specialists concerned with the intricacies of the Game, they play it for its own sake. But the ordinary person, who is not an addict of the Game, would be horrified by it, if "to lose the game" did not mean for him the worst possible outcome, worse than all the obscene horrors of the nuclear holocaust. It appears, then, that the military with its technical and intellectual cohorts retains its grip on the popular mind in somewhat the same way that the medieval church did, namely, as a protector against the Devil.[14]

According to Rapaport, "the central core of one's ethos must be defended. It is most easily defended if it is seen as an absolute Good threatened by an absolute Evil. The Good-Evil dichotomy nourishes the

[13] Barry M. Goldwater: *Why Not Victory?* New York, 1962.
[14] A. Rapaport: *Strategy and Conscience,* Harper, New York, 1964.

Devil image. The Devil image justifies the model of current history as an apocalyptic struggle." Unfortunately, by making the Devil the crux of foreign policy decisions, the United States and her "allies" have suffered defeat after defeat. This is very bad for morale, for, in the Calvinistic tradition, the Good is supposed to triumph.

As long ago as 1958, U Thant warned against these foreign policy crudities when, as Burmese U.N. delegate, he addressed the annual meeting of the American Academy of Political and Social Sciences in Philadelphia, and said:

Let me be candid. When American foreign policy did concern itself with what was happening in the rest of the world, it did so out of fear and suspicion—fear of Communism and suspicion of Communist motives. Fear and suspicion are both undesirable states of mind. They breed hatred, and hatred in turn breeds cruelty and intolerance. Fear of Soviet Communism led the United States, and those who follow her lead, to take a distorted view of the world situation. . . . The U.S. policy toward China is unreal. It needs a thorough re-examination and reappraisal.

Since that date, this same psychosis has produced episodes like the Lebanon and Santo Domingo interventions, and, worst of all, the Vietnam involvement itself. Each one of them can now be seen as an instalment of a systematically organized holy war—as U Thant precisely phrased it—against Communism. It was disingenuous for the chief U.N. delegate from the U.S., Arthur Goldberg, to contest this description, as he did on March 28, 1966, by falling back on the false analogies of "police" action:

This war is *not* a holy war against Communism as an ideology. It does *not* seek unconditional surrender—from North Vietnam or anyone else. . . . It is, I suggest, another step in a limited operation of a policing type—an operation designed to check violence as a means to settle international disputes.

A far more perceptive explanation of what was actually happening was given by Professor Seymour Melman, when he insisted that "the Department of Defense is not oriented to the Vietnam War as an *ad hoc* situation. Rather, that particular war must be understood as part of a system of military-political intervention in many places in the world for which the U.S. Government has been making technical and other preparations. If the Vietnam War were halted tomorrow, there would remain a host of places in the world where the American military establishment, governed by its managerial machine, has already established a major foothold in the form of armed forces in use, or in preparation, for participation in the suppression of internal civil wars."

Anti-People's Wars

While the Good-Evil appearance is maintained for home consumption, the suppression of people's wars has moved up on the list of the Penta-

171

gon's priorities. As we noted in the last chapter, in some parts of this expanding anti-Communist campaign, permanent base-camps are preparing thousands of guerrilla fighters to put down social revolutions in developing countries struggling to free themselves of obsolete or oppressive systems. *Some* Communists, near-Communists, pro-Communists, or even "leftists," are most likely to be found among the revolutionaries, but that fact does not call for the landing of U.S. marines.

"Today, while the Communists successfully tie their kite to nationalism," says Sidney Lens, "we find ourselves defending the status quo in a critical period of world revolution. Anti-Communism has burdened us with the questionable role of preventing further revolutions, lest they be Communist led. Thus we have turned our backs on the heritage of our own Revolution, and we continue hysterically to ignore the realities of the world situation."[15]

On the Japanese island of Okinawa, still under military occupation, in spite of two decades of vigorous protest for the Japanese population's freedom, A. M. Rosenthal of the *New York Times* wrote: "The bow and arrow is just about the only type of weapon that is not part of the chilling inventory of Okinawa, which has become a sort of huge department store of the techniques of warfare. On this steamy island, part of the Ryukyu chain that is flung like a rope between Japan and Taiwan, United States troops train in every kind of warfare known to man. . . . The island is really one huge base, sixty-seven miles long. Each of about 45,000 military men on the island has his own skill and job. But the mission of the base is to prepare men for every kind of warfare—from retaliation to nuclear attack, through conventional battle of army against army, to unconventional or guerrilla battle in the jungle . . . It is also an island where 800,000 Okinawan civilians and about 10,000 American women and children try, as best as they can, to live separate from the constant reminder of Okinawa's chief industry—warfare."

In ancient fable, on such an island another Circe transformed men into beasts; but this was done by mythical magic, not modern science. The explosion of the Chinese bomb on the mainland, however, has shaken the security of Okinawa—two hours' air journey away. The appeals of Tokyo to have their island back may still receive more generous consideration in Washington—thanks to mainland China!

Anti-Communism is most irrelevant of all, both as a program and as a technique, to the problems of the developing countries. It provides no answer to that other "ism"—*nationalism*—which is feeding the violent changes proceeding throughout the non-Communist world. The rational counterpoise to the varied forms of nationalism springing up around us today is to be found, of course, in the flexible institutions of *inter*-nationalism growing alongside them. The American brand of anti-Communism

[15] *op. cit.*

172

has not only strengthened Communist initiative in the "new" nations; it has also obstructed the healthy spread of democratic nationalism.

"The United States," says Sidney Lens, "sidetracked and repressed by a negative anti-Communism, is rapidly approaching the most critical moment in its history. It is being called on to respond to the most dire challenge it has ever faced. It can follow the principles of the past, toward futility and eclipse, or it can chart a new, positive course that will renew its vigor."[16]

Cuba is a case in point where a nationalistic revolution, which owed nothing or little to outside Communism, could have been assisted by its powerful neighbor in creating the structure of a democratic socialist state. In place of boycotts and blockades and quarantine measures, everything should be done by the economically advanced nations to further international co-operation across the fragile frontiers of these fledgling states, so as to bring them into the world community.

Some Americans have seen this and tried to convince their fellow-countrymen to act on it. Adlai Stevenson, returning from a tour of Asia in 1953, told his compatriots that India and some other Asian countries "do not accept the thesis that everyone has to choose sides, that they have to be for or against us. Nor do I believe that we should press alliances on unwilling allies. After all, we had a long record of neutrality and non-involvement ourselves, and the important thing is that such nations keep their independence and don't join hostile coalitions."

The gravest danger of turning every insurrection in every small backward country into an anti-Communist war to protect the temporary gains of private enterprise, or what not, is that a reverse action may well transform every "people's war" into a war against United States imperialism. "The Administration's decision to send large numbers of troops to Santo Domingo," says Professor Fleming, "to protect and evacuate American citizens and to prevent 'another Cuba' has aroused Latin American anger and fear of us. If the United States continues to intervene in every small revolution which seems capable of turning Communist, it will find itself encircled by a hostile world. The Fortress America which would perforce result would lower our living standards, endanger nuclear war, and usher in a new era of McCarthyism, none of which would be conducive to individual freedom."[17]

Moreover, the stalemate in both Korea and Vietnam has shown, to the chagrin of the mathematical missile-men, that nuclear weapons have no power whatsoever over "wars of liberation." This is a startling new discovery. Nuclear strategy is impotent against the Che Guevaras, who have their stalking grounds in mountains and jungles, and who revolutionize

[16] Sidney Lens: *op. cit.*
[17] D. F. Fleming: *The Annals of the American Academy of Political and Social Science,* July 1965.

the villages scattered over wide rural areas. Military planners of the old school are beginning to wonder whether "modern" wars can ever be "won" at all! Thanks to SEATO, CENTO, and the rest of the status quo alliances, National Liberation Fronts will automatically take on tomorrow the role of "people's wars" diverted outward against American imperialism. Actual Communists will not be lacking in turning every nationalist movement into an anti-American one to suit their own purposes. So it has come about that the anti-Communists are now being hoisted on their own petard.

In the terminology of Clausewitz, a "people's war" meant a *national struggle expressing the will of the whole people*. Today, such struggles are challenging oppressive social and obsolete economic systems of half the Afro-Asian and South American continents. By sending anti-Communist soldiers into these recurrent danger zones under the pretext of "a limited operation of the policing type," America's self-proclaimed "holiness" crusades will soon assume such a diabolic quality that other Western leaders will be compelled for their own protection to protest.*

Even conservative and normally "pro-American" voices in Europe can be heard in frequent protest at this growing interference and lawlessness. "We are accustomed to subversion in British territories, but the last nation we would have expected to find subverting the Constitutional Government of a British territory is the United States," the *Sheffield Telegraph* recently pointed out: "This was, however, undoubtedly what happened in our colony of British Guiana, now independent Guyana." Similarly, *The Sunday Times* documented this disreputable story of the overthrow of Prime Minister Jagan in a subversive operation that cost 170 dead, hundreds of wounded, and ten million pounds' worth of economic damage. "Nor do the Monroe Doctrine, the proximity of Guyana to the United States and the fear, exaggerated no doubt, of a mainland Cuba to disturb the political balance of the hemisphere, do anything to excuse the methods employed by Washington," insists the sedate voice of independent conservatism in Britain.

The C.I.A. has become a byword in the United States for political assassination, bribery, deceit and international mischief-making; revelation after revelation of its nefarious comic-opera techniques in subverting the regimes of other countries suddenly filled the columns of the world's press during 1967. Responsible U.S. leaders have since been calling for an end to these Mafia-like illegalities in the name of anti-Communism. "Renewed emphasis is needed on international law and moral constraint, and termination of the immoral and lawless policies of interventionalism," again urges Professor Melman: "This is required for reasons of basic military security and the quality of our lives . . . the American example of

* L.B. Miller's *World Order and Local Disorder* (Princeton, 1967) explains the vital role of the U.N. in easing the growing pains of the "new" countries.

lawlessness and immorality feeds back to the development of military competence, even in many smaller states, that can become a significant military security threat to the United States itself."[18]

In today's complex world, there are profoundly different views about the nature of freedom and the meaning of justice, say the authors of *After 20 Years: Alternatives to the Cold War in Europe:* "But to turn such feelings into a Holy War for or against a set of beliefs is self-destructive." Insisting that anti-Communism is both irrelevant to the new nations' problems and also an obstacle to the growth of an effective international order, the authors state:

It is only the naïve who believe that the eradication of the last traces of Communism from the world will open the way to a world community, or a Pax Americana. The obstacle to a rational world society is not the Soviet Union nor China nor the United States. It is man—his greed, his will to power, his destructive impulses. Yet man's ingenuity, courage and rationality have devised institutions to restrain these impulses in order to build civilizations.[19]

De-Polarizing the Bi-Polarizers

To restrain the destructive impulses which motivate these anti-Communist crusades involves a double educational process: first, to *understand* the character of present day nationalism, whether it be in China or the tiniest South American republic; and, second, to *assist* these nationalistic movements to relate to the advanced nations in terms of a co-operative world order.

U Thant put his finger on the first of these elements in July 1967 when he said of the war in Southeast Asia: "I am convinced that the war cannot be brought to an end until the United States and her allies recognize that it is being fought by the Vietnamese not as a war of Communist aggression, but as a war of national independence." He compared it with America's own war of independence against Britain. It was anti-Communism which accounted for America being bogged down militarily and morally in Vietnam—not freedom or democracy. For this reason this "totally unnecessary war," U Thant said, "cannot be won by either side."

Since the aspirations of the developing countries, as they are called, are so dependent for their fulfillment on the new institutions and the operative techniques being fashioned by the World Organization, the second phase of this educational process can best be pursued in the chapters which follow. But the dangers of the split mind are all too evident as the present debate proceeds.

For example, a glance through the scholarly pages of *The Atlantic*

[18] Seymour Melman in *Sane World,* September 1967.
[19] Richard Barnet and Marcus Raskin: *After 20 Years: Alternatives to the Cold War in Europe,* Random House, New York, 1967.

Community Quarterly, and similar quasi-academic journals on both sides of the Atlantic, reveals an almost consistent Cold War dialectical pattern. With rare exceptions, the strategists and diplomatists, generals and professors who habitually contribute to this highly selective literature start from the assumption of a bi-polarized world: i.e., of two nuclear powers frozen in homicidal opposition. British policy has somehow to be grafted onto one side and the Eastern "satellites" to the other—with minor adjustments to accommodate Britain's shifting role in Europe, or (say) Rumania's propensity to slip away from earlier partners.

More awkward adjustments of the international landscape have had to be made in recent issues of these Atlantic dialogues. The Third World is usually portrayed as a common hunting ground for each of the bi-polarized giants in turn—not as a reality in itself. More difficult still to accommodate has been the revised position to be assigned to the Chinese in this post-Copernican NATO universe. Pundits of the Atlantic Dream depict the new China in varying postures between being Russia's biggest headache and becoming America's major nuclear antagonist. The conundrum is *how* to fit these bothersome untidy elements of reality into the neatly bi-polarized assumptions on which half a lifetime of trans-Atlantic scholasticism has been postulated in vain.

How to keep the Cold War intact has, in fact, become an over-anxious concern of the Nixons and Rusks, of the Tellers and Kahns, who know full well that the Ptolemaic system is obsolete. The dilemma faces them equally in Africa, Asia, and Latin America.

By way of token examples, we can refer briefly at this point to Africa and Southeast Asia. For instance, in his opening essay in *African Diplomacy,* Vernon McKay states quite simply:

It should be emphasized, however, that the Cold War is not the key issue to Africans. They remain preoccupied with the domestic imperatives of nation-building and economic development, while striving simultaneously to build African unity and to free the rest of Africa from white supremacy and foreign rule.[20]

Nearly a decade of mounting witness of African spokesmen at the United Nations has documented that simple thesis beyond question. And when the heads of twenty-two African States met in Monrovia in 1961 to discuss a wide range of African problems, this author (who was present) never heard the words "Communism" or "Cold War" mentioned once. "I am convinced," writes one of the best known opposition leaders in Kenya, Oginga Odinga, in *Not Yet Uhuru,* "that the external vested interests at play in Kenya are not Communist forces, but the result of involvement of an increasing number of politicians in British, American and West German commerce and big business."[21] How like the Latin American dilemma this sounds!

[20] Vernon McKay (editor): *African Diplomacy,* Praeger, New York, 1966.
[21] Odinga: *Not Yet Uhuru,* Hill and Wang, New York, 1967.

Similarly, a recent high-level study published by the British Institute for Strategic Studies points out that Southeast Asia does not "require" any American "presence" on the mainland. A so-called Asian power balance does not depend on any Soviet-United States understanding, nor an attempted settlement between Communist China and non-Asian powers. Such a balance could be established only "as numerous *local* political arrangements are worked out and consolidated, and as the non-Communist states in the area acquire strength and confidence and live together." This very point was made in Chapter 4: namely, that if and when the foreign military forces can be evicted from their unlawful occupation of Southeast Asia, the people who live there can and will create their own institutions of public order and area stability for their own good.

According to *The Economist,* there may now be taking shape a decisive shift of attitude toward China in the Third World. This could lead, in time, to a clear-eyed effort by its principal neighbors—including, some day, Indonesia—to join in "a system of purely Asian solidarity that would really provide a balance for China's great weight in terms of manpower—specifically, military manpower. That time is not yet. . . . It may not arrive until there is one final 'discovery' of China—by the Chinese themselves."[22] And, according to Edwin O. Reischauer, U.S. Ambassador in Japan from 1961 to 1966, who was himself born and bred in Tokyo, the United States can never impose "peace" on Asian countries. He states that "the waves of change in Asia have been stirred up not by Communism, but by nationalism in many political forms. . . . We should encourage legitimate and constructive Asian nationalism, *whatever its form.*" (Italics added.)[23]

Chasing After Fables

The transposition of the Devil into an Angel of Light calls for a complete reversal of U.S. policy. That reverse process will not be easy for reasons we have already noted. It would seem that St. Paul's phophecy in his letter to Timothy has come to fruition in modern times: "For a time will come when they will not endure wholesome teaching; but according to their whims, they will gather to themselves teachers who will tickle their ears. They will indeed turn away from hearing the truth and chase after fables."

This shift of emphasis has to begin with the recognition that a Cold War foreign policy does not provide a workable framework for solving any of the problems that confront the Western world today. What lies "beyond" the Cold War, asks Marshall D. Shulman in his *Beyond the Cold War.* He has two sensible answers. First, he says: "We should address ourselves to the necessity of providing a democratic alternative to

[22] *The Economist,* October 23, 1965.
[23] E. O. Reischauer: *Beyond Vietnam,* Knopf, New York, 1967.

the totalitarian model of development in Asia, Africa, and Latin America, and of encouraging the forces of nationalism in these areas to find their expression, not in identification with Communism and not in demagogic violence, but in the tradition of a constructive and integrative nationalism." Shulman wants us to assist the new states and the new movements to find their own feet in *their own way*. Nationalism is the most potent source of political energy in the world today, he says, and it should be channeled into the drive to discover what modernization should mean for each people on its own terms. (The Czechs have since proved that.)

But he goes further and insists that the West has a fundamental interest "in encouraging the growth and acceptance of an international system among the nation-states—'system' here not necessarily meaning a particular institutional form, but more broadly referring to the deepening of habits of co-operation and restraint, the strengthening of accepted procedures for managing change and limiting conflict." Rejecting the notion that we should "fight fire with fire," and thus contribute to the degradation of international conduct, Shulman concludes his plea on a pragmatic note:

The United Nations now has the possibility of becoming a universal institution, but it is in a phase of growth in which it is absorbing a greatly enlarged constituency. As with any living political organism, it must rediscover in experience how it must function under changed circumstances, and this will take time, and faith.[24]

Since the World Organization is such a "living organism"—one that requires faith, as well as time and experience, for its full development— harsh judgment of its known inadequacies must be withheld until faith can be translated into works. Meanwhile, the major obstacles in its path must be seen for what they are, so that they may be removed or reduced.

Transforming our top-heavy military hierarchy into a socially useful instrument of international civilian development will indeed be formidable. But there are partial answers even to this problem. Perhaps public reaction of horror and disillusionment to the failures and futilities of the Vietnam War as it moves toward a negotiated settlement will assist in the process of de-escalating the generals during the 1970's. Edward Bernard Glick's *Peaceful Conflict* details a realistic plan for using the armies of the world to meet social-economic development needs. Dr. Glick suggests how the discipline, training, and technical skills of the armed forces can be re-deployed, not only in preventive counter-insurgency of a *civic* nature, but for all-round national economic and social development. He recalls the often forgotten *civic* role of armies—from Biblical times to today—as colonizers, organizers, civilizers, and nation-builders. So why must the army only do "military" things?

He reviews how armies in Latin America, the Middle East, Africa, and the Far East have been and are involved in social and economic develop-

[24] Marshall D. Shulman: *Beyond the Cold War,* Yale University Press, 1966.

ment. Accepted that his proposals may require stringent safeguards to check unilateral military intervention, Dr. Glick does not neglect to deal with the dangers in expanded civic action programs carried out by the military; but he concludes that the long term benefits accruing to the developing countries, as well as to developed countries, would be worthwhile, and at the same time provide the United States with an opportunity to utilize present reality toward international good.[25]

Dr. Glick's interesting proposals represent at least a step toward the wider non-national peacekeeping programs which form the subject of Chapter 7. Professor Melman of Columbia University also has long been urging attention to this question of transfer of highly qualified manpower from warfare to welfare. In calling for a drastic change in U.S. foreign policy, he says that, as growing numbers of Americans of all occupations and political allegiances are moved to oppose present Administration foreign policies, "that is precisely the strategic moment for efficient operation of the Policy Change strategy." He goes on to suggest, therefore, that a "process of moving the federal government toward policy change for peace will surely involve retraining and relocating the people that are now servicing the military establishment." But he admits that, while such reorientation can be done with individuals, "it is rather doubtful that the institutions of the state machine (the Defense Department, C.I.A., etc.) can be transformed into civilian organizations."[26]

Undoubtedly, such a switch from chasing insurgencies wherever they may occur across the globe to devising a transfer of personnel and funds to aid world development might have a most salutary effect on the United States itself. The Administration is, in fact, now being forced to deal with "insurgents" much nearer home.

"The Fire Is Here"

"The fire is here," warns the writer James Baldwin: "In spite of thousands of prayers, pleas and predictions, the treatment of Black People in the United States has been allowed to continue basically unchanged. The educational opportunities of Black People continue to be inferior. The housing of Black People continues to be inferior. The right of Black People to full equality continues to be challenged. The fire is *here*."

Education, jobs, houses—here is the gist of New America's own social revolution. Long delayed non-discrimination legislation, dragged through Congress against the opposition of implacable filibusterers, has barely touched on the basic economics and financing of this Twentieth Century Revolution. It needed, alas! the brutal assassination of Dr. Martin Luther

[25] E. B. Glick: *Peaceful Conflict,* Stackpole, Harrisburg, 1967.
[26] *Op. cit.*

179

King in April 1968 to break the log-jam; but, even so, the new laws have not measured up at all to the national challenge. And the result? The following staccato paragraphs, actually appearing on the front page of the press of the "thriving" industrial city of Detroit, reflected what was happening in a score of other United States cities in 1967:

This haggard city is a mirror of a civilization going backward. Its smoke, blood and gunfire are the most tragic testaments to date that urban America cannot keep up with the accumulating problems of the modern age.

Federal troops on street corners. Tanks firing at night in streets where the lights have been shot out. Wretched, bleeding men in hospital emergency rooms.

Jails so teeming with miserable prisoners that it is a question whether legal processes really mean much. Buildings gutted by fire. Weapons everywhere.

Take all these ingredients and mix them with fear, alarm, bewilderment, hatred, despair and hopelessness—that is *our city!*

Is this a journalistic exaggeration? Displayed as a full-page official advertisement in leading New York newspapers, commending the important role of the National Guard at this time, appeared such items as the following:

THE TRAGIC AND VIOLENT UPRISINGS OF THE SUMMER HAVE NO PARALLEL IN THE HISTORY OF OUR COUNTRY.

SHOTS ARE FIRED FROM ROOFTOPS AND HOUSES.

STORES ARE LOOTED.

THE LAW IS IGNORED.

CITIES ARE AFLAME.

Yet, about the same time of the riots, an article appeared in the *New Center News,* a business journal of Detroit, written by C. Allen Harlen, "a commercial property owner" in the area, describing his visits to four defense bases and installations. His experiences aboard an aircraft carrier contained the following enthusiastic pen picture:

The U.S.S. Ranger, as ships go, is one of the largest in the Fleet . . . it has a complement of 80 airplanes, some of which were seeing action for the first time while we were aboard. It has a complement of 5,000 people, of every conceivable skill and all run by the clock. Everything is scheduled, and everything follows schedule within the ship . . . All the planes were put into the air in 20 minutes, sometimes from the 4 catapults, no more than a few seconds apart. The men and their uniforms and the colors could just as well be men from Mars. . . .

A little calculation (plus some imagination) would indicate that this vast displacement of capital and equipment and human robots of "every conceivable skill," if applied instead to the rehabilitation of the ghetto in downtown Detroit, might help transform the rebellion spreading across

U.S. cities into a program of social evolution which could become the hallmark of a modern democracy.

But outright revolt is not the only form of crime plaguing the self-proclaimed "leader of the free world." Says another commentator on the present collapse of the American Dream: "Director J. Edgar Hoover's annual crime report makes chilly reading. In 1966, a trifle under 3.25 million serious crimes were committed in the United States. This was an increase of 11 per cent over 1965. Since 1960, serious crimes have increased by 62 per cent over-all, with violent crimes jumping 49 per cent and property offenses 64 per cent. In the 1966 crime report there were 10,920 murders, 231,800 aggravated assaults, 153,420 robberies. Director Hoover blames these gruesome statistics chiefly on an 'increasing tendency toward public disregard for law and order.' "

Then, according to a Senate study, four and a half million American children need psychiatric treatment at varying levels of intensity. One Senator was reported as saying that "we reap our annual harvest of close to 600,000 delinquents" from this group of disturbed young people.[27] But America surely cannot export its crime problem to Southeast Asia? Are the three billions of dollars spent each month in destroying Vietnam not needed to save America from America—not Communism?*

The revolution which the United States truly awaits today is at base a moral one. Some *nineteen million* children are living in poverty and near-poverty in the country, according to a report issued by a non-profit organization, the Citizens' Committee for Children of New York. The president of this group asserts that "there is an urgent need of some form of family or children's allowance program in this country to help combat poverty." And this is only a beginning.

Yet a generation of young idealists are being destroyed while these appeals to save America's youth ring out. In a published interview emanating from Saigon, a young man of twenty-six has this to say about himself: "I am not a warmonger, but flying over the beach is a great thrill, like playing Russian roulette, taking LSD, or having sex." By flying over the beach this junior lieutenant meant flying into North Vietnam from one of the carriers in the Gulf of Tonkin. "When you press the pickle and see the bombs drop," he went on, "you suddenly think, my God, what am I doing here? . . . Then, when you land and it's all over, you're just utterly washed out."

He told his interviewer that he thought that there was too little respect for military men in the United States: "But we do live a gentleman's war out here. This is one of the reasons the naval officer corps is still respected. We sit down to dinner attended by stewards and we go to bed between

[27] *New York Times,* October 18, 1966.

* A New York judge, in sentencing a youth for murderous assault, added: "People like you should be in Vietnam killing the Viet Cong, instead of your fellow citizens."

sheets." His chief worry was whether his professional skills were being properly used in this war. "I know why I'm fighting. We are committed to fighting Communism *everywhere*. We're going to have to fight China some time. But I don't think I'm fighting in the most effective way." Then this twenty-six-year-old all too accurately described the real nature of this anti-people's war: "There aren't such things as civilians over there. I've seen kids with rifles shooting at us. If that kid hits my engine or fuel line I'm finished." A final infantile confession: "I happen to be rather hawkish. I have to be. In Washington people talk about the greater risks of escalation, but there can't be any greater risks for me. . . . My attitude's one of self-defense."[28]

From the ground level in North Vietnam, however, James Cameron published his graphically illustrated report entitled: *Here is Your Enemy.* He dedicated the book "to an old lady who lives in the village of Nanh Nganh, which is unfortunately near to a strategically important bridge. The bridge, as far as I know, still stands; but the old lady had her left arm blown off by one of the bombs that went somewhat astray. She was more fortunate than her daughter, who was killed. She said: 'I suppose there is a reason for all this, but I do not understand what it is. I think I am too old now ever to find out.' "[29]

Describing why the Vietnamese were determined to continue their fight to uphold the Geneva Agreements against the American invaders, Cameron queries: "Is it possible that those who control the policies of the United States now think of 'international Communism' as a veterinary doctor thinks of rabies: as something not susceptible to treatment, but as a disease that as a social duty must be put down by elimination? If that is the case, then there is logic in the belief that it is possible to cure Communists of Communism by blowing it out of their heads with high explosive, and to woo people into the ways of democracy and freedom by burning them up with phosphorus and napalm."

Someone has likened the effect on the American democracy which practices such philosophies to that unexpected tragedy on the ocean seas when the *Titanic* was struck by a submerged ice-floe. After the collision, which was hardly felt by the steamer at the time, the great liner at first seemed to be intact and unhurt and continued to move. But a death wound had been inflicted under the surface of the water. It was merely a question of time.

Who Leads for Peace?

If the advance impact of coming peril is not being registered so acutely in the United States as it is in some other Western countries, it is for

[28] The London *Observer,* September 24, 1967.
[29] James Cameron: *Here is Your Enemy,* Holt, Rinehart & Winston, New York, 1966.

four special reasons. Firstly, because of—as analyzed in the previous chapter—the all-persuasive influence of the military on national life. The contrast between Britain and the U.S. in this respect is quite unarguable with any British citizen who has lived for long in the United States. The same sense of astonishment at this omnipresent militarism is likewise experienced by Swiss, Danes, Canadians, and other Westerners working in the U.S. whose outlook back home is not dominated by this systematically inculcated fear of Communists or by the excessive demands of the generals.

Secondly, Big Business has a vested interest in keeping the Cold War a continuing source of revenue. Professor Ralph E. Lapp says in *The Weapons Culture:* "Even with this brief survey we can sense the spread of the weapons culture through our society, extending to almost every phase of our life. Because this impact is not felt as a flash flood but more like the gradual rise of a swollen river, the American people are as yet only imperfectly aware of how far the infection has spread in our society." Then he goes on to show how the forces of military, industrial, political, and scientific interests are conspiring to plunge the nation into a new phase of the arms race: "In July 1967, L. Mendel Rivers, Chairman of the House Armed Services Committee, released a report titled: 'The Changing Strategic Military Balance—U.S.A. vs. U.S.S.R.' It turns out that this is not a committee report at all, but rather a private paper which is given the Committee's imprimatur. The report is actually the work of a Cold War institution called the American Security Council whose chairman, Robert W. Galvin, is chief executive officer and chairman of the board of Motorola, Inc. The American Security Council describes one of its major functions as 'the mobilization of U.S. business in the continuing Cold War.' "[30]

Thirdly, the general press across the country, with few exceptions, exercises a quasi-censorship over foreign affairs. This limited news coverage—seeing that the great bulk of daily newsprint goes into commercial advertisements—pre-empts a balanced all-round view of what really goes on outside America. Such foreign news as is analyzed by the syndicated columnists is for the most part slanted in favor of the current Washington line on anti-Communism, and the U.N. is dealt with in terms of conflicts.

Fourthly, and for the same reasons, the mass media which occupy an inordinate amount of the leisure time of most families across the land are even more selective than the mass-circulation press, when it comes to acutely controversial topics. T.V. and radio networks naturally support the Establishment, so a blanket of popular prejudice, with its built-in texture of self-approval, has served to perpetuate the very policies which are destroying the American way of life.

If the foregoing emphasis appears to be placed unfairly on the respon-

[30] R. E. Lapp: *The Weapons Culture,* Norton, New York, 1968.

183

sibility of the United States, there are several special reasons why we should expect much more from the present national leadership:

(1) The concept of "world leadership" has been dinned into every high school child's head for so long, that "world leadership" in peace, if once the right formula can be found, should by this time have an easy head-start.

(2) The reserves of wealth—especially when a genuine switch is made from military to civilian needs—could sustain an immense contribution to peacemaking operations, both through the World Organization and bilaterally, which no other nation could at present match.

(3) The pent-up idealism of the American people—which never fails to obtain adequate coverage in the mass media—need no longer be directed into abortive and discredited military adventures abroad.

(4) The domestic effect of an all-out peacemaking gesture through the World Organization or otherwise—whatever its response abroad—would be a godsend to the American people themselves; for example, the Peace Corps, which was initiated as an outward-looking act of goodwill to foreigners, has become one of the most successful inward-looking programs for training young Americans to become good citizens of the world.

Nevertheless, in view of the impediments outlined earlier, the *actual* leadership toward a new peace initiative and for a revived World Organization must surely come from the European side of the Atlantic. Before the century is over, a genuine "Atlantic Community" could well emerge—using the word "community" in its spiritual sense—through open debate by parliament, press, and people in the Western world on how to lift Western civilization—at least politically—to the world level. This would, indeed, form a new peace initiative. It is example that matters, and example begins with those who have such confidence in their way of life that they are willing to test it out as a working model for the human race.

For that reason, we have already argued that this positive sort of peace initiative would belong primarily to Britain and the Commonwealth. Britain is blessed with close partners who have stood the test of time and whose relationship is not basically military, or even military at all, such as Canada, next door to the United States, and India, the biggest democracy in Asia. Behind a Commonwealth lead, fresh influence might be expected from some of the African countries of the Third World, who, like India, have rejected both the Cold War and the alliance system. Such peace initiative was evident, and was unanimously followed, when Britain's chief U.N. delegate, Lord Caradon—dubbed by U.S. journalists as "miracle man"!—took up the Middle East turmoil late in 1967 at the Security Council and mapped out, point by point, the long and difficult path that lay ahead, but along which the involved countries have since slowly moved.

Certainly, British political leaders have an advantage when it comes to extending democratic procedures to global issues, as when the Prime Minister declared in the House of Commons on April 26, 1966: "Britain has got to play her part in trying to get the world further out of that chapter in its history where it has to think so much in terms of alliances, defenses and balances of power. *The instrument for that is the United Nations,* probably as well-equipped or as ill-equipped for that job as the English Parliament was for governing the country when it was first assembled. It found it then an extremely difficult job because of the great centers of independent military power that there were in various parts of the country. And it had to learn and develop a great deal *the process of making power subject to common interest and the rule of law."* (Italics added.)

Nor, in Europe, are the three Scandinavian countries to be underestimated. Small nations are contributing their big men to the World Organization. A new view of a world order based on co-operation instead of coercion is coming into focus at the U.N. from the type and quality of the exceptionally qualified persons who speak for the smaller democracies and have no military cliques blocking their endeavors: Dr. J. G. deBeus of the Netherlands; Edward Hambro of Norway; Per Haekkerup, ex-Foreign Minister of Denmark; Frank Aiken of Ireland; Hanson of Finland; Franz Matsch of Austria; Amintore Fanfani of Italy (former General Assembly President). Such examples can easily be multiplied. In Chapter 8 we shall return to look at some of the international personalities who are redeeming the national politics of despair. Here we are beginning to listen to the language of the New Man.

Crisis Means Opportunity

Frequent break-throughs from the old anarchy to the new order are bypassing the veterans of the Cold War at a dozen points. From Latin America to the south and from Canada to the north comes an increasing insistence on nuclear-free zones; while steady co-operation through the Economic Commission for Latin America and the other world-based agencies forms part of a U.N. initiative which makes all talk of Communist "infiltration" from tiny Cuba look foolishly trivial by comparison.

The time is soon coming when the quick-draw silo men will have served their turn and must emerge from their Kafkaesque underground. A dynamic civilization has been moving over their heads. The untapped spiritual riches of Western culture and the priceless experience of its political and social institutions over the centuries have barely been applied to the needs of a divided world; yet these constitute the one positive gift the West can offer to the human race. No other form of international security could take its place, if the U.N. were to fail to develop into a supranational democratic organism.

"Human welfare is the same in general character for all human beings;

and this, being the democratic objective, it is limited by no national frontiers . . ." says Professor Errol E. Harris in *Annihilation and Utopia:* "The principles of democracy cannot apply to Britishers, or to Americans, or to Western Europeans only. Of their very nature they apply to everybody, and genuine democrats have a duty to extend them to all the nations of the earth."[31]

Frederick L. Schuman explains that, in Mandarin, the ideographic sign for "crisis" consists of two symbols; one means "danger" and the other means "opportunity," and he goes on to remark:

The danger is not Communism *per se,* although many among us quite honestly and sincerely believe that Communism is our greatest danger. Our greatest danger . . . is a continuation and extension of international anarchy, of power politics, of war—all of which are age-old habits of mankind—into the thermo-nuclear age, when persistence in such habits may well spell the end of the human species.[32]

If we do not at once negotiate an end of the arms race and their concomitant alliances, as a step toward negotiating an end of the Cold War, he asserts, the effective control of our destinies, East and West alike, *will pass out of the hands of our political leaders into the hands of professional militarists and of the munition-makers.* As amply illustrated in Chapter 3 of this book, policy-making already is moving from the hands of the policy-makers into the hands of the button-pushers. "This danger is greater in America than in Russia," states Professor Schuman, "for in Russia the army is fully controlled by the Party."

If we believe, however, that the real strength of the United States—in fact of the whole Anglo-Saxon world—lies in its responsiveness to the claims of the democratic process, then the remedy for international anarchy, power politics, and war itself must surely lie in extending the democratic process on a world scale at all costs. Can this be left to the Communists—the Russians or the Chinese, or even the Third World? If the Anglo-Saxon world cannot match danger with opportunity, who can? It is to that challenge that we must attempt an answer in our remaining chapters.

Apart, then, from defusing the obsolete military alliances, which was the starting point of this book, the vital opportunity which beckons the West today is to win the peoples of China into a full working relationship with the rest of the human race. Such an act of creative statesmanship cannot wait for Communism to evaporate overnight. Even now a new generation is being conditioned by the old in the West to replace an iron-curtain by a bamboo one, yet neither is visible from Outer Space.

Given that basic shift in foreign policy, three major organizational tasks

[31] E. E. Harris: *Annihilation and Utopia,* Allen & Unwin, London, 1966.
[32] F. L. Schuman: *The Cold War: Retrospect and Prospect,* Louisiana State University Press, 1962.

186

confront the 1970's which above all else demand Anglo-American initiative and responsibility, namely:

(1) Reducing the "gap" between the rich and poor countries, so that modern technology and "know-how" can be put at the service of the developing peoples;

(2) Establishing standing U.N. peacekeeping forces on a financially sound basis, so as to cope with emergency situations wherever they may arise;

(3) Building the United Nations central structure into a permanent parliamentary body, with appropriate world law-making functions.

There is nothing "unrealistic" about any of these specific programs of international action, which make up the last three chapters of this book. They are inherent both in the written text of the Charter and in the common aspirations of millions of people across the globe.

The immense program of public persuasion which is necessary to realize them is already discernible in the numerous governmental and nongovernmental bodies concerned with world peace and United Nations affairs. A growing spate of literature, both technical and informational, is reaching into the fresh minds of that half of the world's population who are younger in years than the U.N. itself. For this is no "one shot" program. Every existing channel of peaceful development and international co-operation needs to be utilized to the utmost; and many others added as our speeding technology proliferates its recurrent surprises.

Abdul Rahman Pazhwak of Afghanistan, President of the 1966 General Assembly, ended his brilliant term of office with these words:

"Ours is a world of seething change, revolutionary change, but these mutations themselves are not always evident. In such a dynamic world all elements, political, and economic, are in a perpetual state of transition, and only one factor remains fixed: our goal for world peace; our steadfast determination to attain that goal."

6 BALANCE OF HOPE

"To the age-old task of maintaining the balance of
power must now be added the task of maintaining the
balance of hope—hope in the proposition that the
under-developed societies of the world can take
science and technology into their lives without deny-
ing the values of freedom and tolerance."

—Eugene R. Black in *The Diplomacy
of Economic Development*

The story of the Sikh who, returning to India after many years,
sat down among his suitcases on the Bombay docks and wept is by no
means unique. During the years abroad he had forgotten what Indian
poverty was like. In London it was easy for a Sikh student to forget the
misery of Bombay.

The stench and the squalor of the Bombay dockland has to be seen to
be believed. The nauseating sight of malformations, the pathetic beggars
riddled with leprosy, with stumps of arms and withered legs—had nothing
changed? The shore itself is used as an open-air lavatory and when the
wind blows the wrong way, as it usually does, the city smells of excrement.
Any evening one stumbles upon the pavement dwellers, who do not even
have a hut in a shanty-town to call their own. They were probably born
on the streets; and it is likely they will die there. They number half a million
—one tenth of the city's population.[1]

An English political observer returning from Calcutta recently said:
"Calcutta looked a hell for anyone without money and was a torture to
behold . . . I left the city early because I simply could not bear to witness
the naked miseries and degradation of the people who live in and on the
streets. The situation is getting visibly worse. The city, always over-

[1] Summarized from V. S. Naipaul's *An Area of Darkness,* Andrew Deutsch, London,
1967.

188

crowded, has rent its seams. The sewers are overladen, the water is dangerous. The ancient killers—smallpox, tuberculosis, and cholera—enjoy a new life. And you can see hungry, dust-smeared, naked children lying hopelessly on the dirty pavements of the busiest shopping streets . . ."[2]

This author can personally testify to this stark picture of the overcrowding, squalor and despair in both Bombay and Calcutta—though it must in fairness be added that the latter city, in particular, has never been able to accommodate the influx of an extra million or more Hindu refugees and their offspring who came in from Moslem Bengal as a result of the partition.

Yet the physical contrasts in the world's newly independent countries are no less overwhelming. This author can recall both the elegance and the impressiveness of a Republic Day celebration in the out-of-this-world gardens of the Presidential Palace in New Delhi, and—not less impressive in its way—on the outskirts of the Indian capital, a Low-Cost Housing Exhibition, which was itself a miracle of mammoth planning, drawing thousands of town-planners and housing authorities from all over Asia.

How can this be? This disparity? Is there just a thin veneer of government-inspired prosperity and showcase publicity beneath which millions of "We, the Peoples" rot and grovel without hope of a better life? Is the "balance of hope" all one way—toward the indigenous "upper class" families and the government officials?

Following independence, the Congress Party of India performed remarkable achievements in both foreign affairs and domestic policy. This was the era of dynamic neutrality and of Afro-Asian solidarity, with most of Africa still under colonial rule. Under the Nehru Government the still ruling princes were stripped of all but their titles and privy purses. At the same time, under the first and second plans, huge steel plants and dams were built with collaboration from any country willing to help. The average Indian's chance of living was increased by twenty years. The number of primary schools more than doubled and more universities and technical colleges were established. But, somehow, the balance of development went askew and, in reshaping agriculture, the Government failed most resoundingly.

The landlords formed the largest pressure group within Congress, and no real land reform was possible unless Congress was prepared to lose the support of the village Establishments, which it was not. The result is that Indian agriculture today is not essentially different from what it has been through the ages. While irrigation and fertilizers have been introduced in some places, methods of cultivation and ownership have remained the same. The country is consequently unable to feed more than two-thirds of its population. An Indian authority, Bhaichand Patel, states that forty million acres of land that could be cultivated are still lying unexploited and

[2] Clive Jenkins in the London *Tribune,* August 18, 1967.

more than three-quarters of the farmed land has no irrigation facilities. So today India is more dependent on foreign food to feed the people than ever before. And no one gives food without strings anymore! India's stand on Vietnam is less clear-cut than it might be, thanks to its present dependence on American wheat.

Nor does India, still the world's biggest democracy, stand alone in seeking the balance of hope. When this author worked for a time at a magnificent mahogany desk in an air-conditioned office in a certain West African capital, he looked down from his windows through the palm trees and over gorgeous garden blossoms to the miserable hovels on the edge of the town, where it seemed obvious that the most elementary utility and sewage devices were still in the blueprint stage. The developing world is just this. This proximity; this ridiculous, unbelievable contrast; this confrontation across a thousand years' gap—it has really happened. It is a fact of modern life.

"The Ivory Coast did not disguise its pride and pleasure," reports the bulletin of the world's leading organization of writers, "in being host to 150 delegates from eastern and western Europe, from South and North America, from Asia, and from Australia and New Zealand; the Soviet Union also sent a delegation of three writers as observers. Official delegates were housed in a new deluxe hotel—with air-conditioning, swimming pool, cocktail bars, and exotic restaurants (a roof-top Italian *ristorante* and an American hamburger counter and bowling alley). When the opening ceremony was celebrated in the Congressional Hall, the red carpet was rolled out, literally and figuratively. Delegates walked up the steps through a double row of scarlet-uniformed, gold-helmeted guards with raised sabers. Inside, on the high dais, sat the President of the Republic, and below him Cabinet Ministers and the diplomatic corps."[3]

The Dark Face of Poverty

There is a double problem here. The East-West confrontation lingers still in the disordered minds that we have studied in the previous chapter; but, as Adlai Stevenson once put the matter before the Economic and Social Council of the U.N.: "By the chances of history and geography, the developed nations are largely to be found to the north of the Tropic of Cancer. . . . Ideology makes no difference here. Soviet Russia belongs by income and growth to the developed 'north,' Ghana to the developing 'south.' " Stevenson thus echoed the credo of U Thant who for a long time has been downgrading the East-West conflict, in face of the far more serious North-South challenge.

Yet the major confrontation of our time also runs down the middle of

[3] *P.E.N. News,* September 1967.

the developing countries themselves. Development has begun—it began with independence, hardly a decade ago—but it has in many cases not gotten beyond the front gate of the government house. It is only the superficial Western observer, however, who thinks in terms of looking for culprits among the fledgling bureaucracies of Africa or Asia, though the sharpening of knives against the new Afro-Asian leadership is proceeding apace among the political backwoods men of the West.

All the vast problems of change have swept down on the doorsteps of the new nations at the same moment. Their countries are speeding from feudalism into the jet age with hardly an interval between. Yet, in the midst of all this, "population growth has swallowed up their margins, and their per capita growth hovers around zero," Adlai Stevenson told the U.N. body; and, pausing only a moment on the wretched statistics of their frustrated economies, he reminded the Council: "We are talking about pain and grief and hunger and despair, and we are talking about the lot of half of the human race."

"We shall conquer, no doubt, the dark face of the moon," Stevenson continued in the last speech he made, "but I would hope we can with equal confidence conquer the dark face of poverty and give men and women new life, new hope, new space on this planet." But on what is this new hope based? Not on theory or on U.N. resolutions, indeed, but on solid achievements:

Out of the research that is connected with weaponry, with space and with the whole wide range of needs of our civilian economy, we are constantly making new breakthroughs—new methods, new products, new sources of food or energy or medical relief that increase our capacity to reproduce wealth still further. We have harnessed energy to take us into outer space and to convert saline waters into drink for the thirsty. The isotopes which grow from nuclear experiments can revolutionize medical and agricultural research. And we know not what new still undiscovered sources of abundance lie ahead.[4]

Stevenson recognized the indispensable part that the World Organization must play from now on in the scientific and technological revolution of our time: "We stand here in the presence of exciting breakthroughs in nutrition, in farming, in water use, in meteorology, in energy. All these are vital, and it is particularly gratifying that the United Nations Advisory Group of Scientists have put the development of water resources and the evolution of new high-protein diets at the top of their list of points needing special attack."

Since he spoke, the U.N. Development Program has raised "seed money" and set its experts to work on just these priorities in over three score countries. Nobody can yet predict whether the balance of hope will lie in mankind's favor. Neither can anyone doubt that that outcome depends on what the leaders of the advanced countries decide to do with

[4] *ECOSOC Records,* July 9, 1965.

their much-proclaimed "affluence." We cannot escape the necessity of choice.

According to one American biologist, Paul Ehrlich, on the one hand, mankind has already lost the battle to feed itself; hundreds of millions of people will starve to death sometime between 1970 and 1985. Professor Ehrlich of the Biological Sciences Department at Stanford University, California, has asserted that many people will die of famine in spite of any crash programs which might be started now. He added that plans to tap marine food, synthesize food from petroleum, and use desalination plants to make deserts fertile—in which programs the whole U.N. family is now engaged, with 80 per cent of its combined staff working in the field —were impractical in the short run and would not save mankind from the crisis. Instead, the biologist has urged that a massive propaganda campaign should be launched to convince people that a reduced and stabilized population alone could give them "a long-range chance of health, happiness and prosperity."[5]

According to Dr. Harrison Brown, overseas secretary of the U.S. National Academy of Sciences, on the other hand, a world population of *nine billion* could probably be supported at the United States standard of living with nuclear-generated electricity. The population of the world now stands at 3.5 billion, and could double by the end of the century. Dr. Brown maintained that nuclear power could make it possible to place cities in arid coastal regions and supply them with desalinated water. "Such a development," he said, "would open up vast areas of India, Pakistan, the Middle East, and North Africa, Brazil, Chile and Peru for human habitation."[6]

Once again, it is a question of choice; what the old-fashioned strategist calls "available options"—except that he is playing with death, whereas our concern is with more abundant life. How, then, do we propose to dispose of our nuclear productive capacity? "There is now stockpiled in the earthman's arsenals the equivalent of 28,000 pounds of destructive force for every possessor of the gift of life on earth," states Norman Cousins, writing in the *Saturday Review;* and he noted: "Some of the nations have been energetically brewing virulent disease germs and other organic substances that can invade the vital organs of humans, producing convulsions or other forms of intense suffering beyond the reach of the constructive sciences to cure or allay . . . These activities have diverted useful energies that might otherwise go into the making of what could be a rather splendid existence."

The choice is there. The facts are known. The decision is our own.

In spite of the criminal waste behind our alliances and their vast arsenals of oblivion, the problems facing the developing countries, and the world

[5] *The New Scientist,* London, December 15, 1967.
[6] *New York Times,* December 28, 1967.

community as a whole, can hardly be exaggerated. Of the 3.5 billion persons now inhabiting the earth more than two-thirds are living in countries with an annual per capita income of less than a few hundred dollars in terms of goods and services. On a global basis, more than 63 million mouths to feed are being *added yearly*. World food production is clearly failing to keep pace, particularly in those countries where the majority of the people are already undernourished. Over half of the world's adult population—some 700 million persons—are still illiterate, and of the world's school-age children, only about half attend school. All this has a direct bearing on future development. In some of these underprivileged countries there is still only one doctor for more than 50,000 persons.

Beneath the social level lie, of course, the economic requirements of modern living. The present demand for electric-power expansion alone in the developing countries requires at least two billion dollars in annual investment—a topic to which we return below. Yet, although the problem of alleviating world poverty seems as formidable as ever, there is room for encouragement because we are living in an age blessed with immeasurable resources and technical knowledge. There is, above all, a growing awareness of the fact that the condition of all mankind is amenable to improvement. Everything depends on converting the balance of terror into a balance of hope.

"Growth Depends on Growers"

One of the new men, Robert K. A. Gardiner, the dynamic secretary of the United Nations Economic Commission for Africa (E.C.A.), described recently how the U.N. Commission was dealing with the Awash River in East Africa, a lazy stream flowing through virgin land, with a few nomads shepherding their cattle among cacti and elephant grass. "Now, fields had sprung forth. Cotton was pushing off the herds of camels. Ostriches and zebras were retreating to the edge of the plain at the foot of the mountains," and he continued: "In less than a year, a tract of East African bush was being propelled into a Twentieth-Century economy. Over the continent, the 'lost world' is disappearing. Railroads slice the equatorial forest. Through overloaded buses, a glimpse of the city world is reaching into the bush."

This is but a beginning, says Gardiner. In many countries, the lot of the average African is hardly better than in the first year of his country's independence. Yet the great process of transition has started. The African farmer is discovering both his needs and his strength. Through radio and even newspapers, he is turning the big city's message to his advantage, and becoming a political force in his own right. The United Nations can be credited with the initial push for the Awash River project and three hundred others like it on the Continent. With only four million dollars a year, E.C.A. is no Marshall Plan, but Africa was never like post-war Europe and demands its own techniques under African leadership.

When the colonial period ended, African countries were strangers even to one another. The only links between them went most often through Europe. There was virtually no African transport, whether by air, rail or road. So the Commission's first duty was to establish a general inventory of resources on which the new governments could build methodical development plans. Africa had only a few dozen statisticians. (In 1963, after its first population census, Nigeria learned that it was a country of 55 million inhabitants, instead of the 35 million formerly listed.) The United Nations has bridged this sort of gap by opening an Institute of Statistics in Morocco, and training centers in Tanzania, Ghana, Ethiopia and Cameroon. By 1970, the Continent will have 3,000 statisticians. As economic information began to pour in, the Commission has been able to establish industrialization programs. For development has to start with *facts*.

Not the least of the new problems, as we noted above, lies in the imbalance between town and country. There is a saying in Abidjan that runs: "How're you gonna keep them down on the farm once they've seen Abidjan?" The question is one that Ivory Coast officials are beginning to answer with a number of imaginative approaches. Shantytowns are growing around the edges of the lagoons as fast as skyscrapers rise in the commercial heart and residential neighborhoods of this West African capital. Hence, "to seek a harmonious balance between city and country," declares the new Plan Law, the law puts its present size at about 425,000, but projects that "according to the most moderate estimates" half a million inhabitants will be accommodated by 1970 and a million ten years later.

For one thing, President Felix Houphouet-Boigny works in shirtsleeves on his own farm. For another thing, movie theatres have been set up by the Government in the villages and 4.5 million people are provided with entertainment they would otherwise only find in the cities. Youth clubs have also been established with as much energy as open-air cinemas to keep youngsters from being bored in their villages.[7]

This human approach may seem naïve to the sophisticated West, but it is typical of many developing countries today. George Ivan Smith, former United Nations representative in East and Central Africa, has stressed: "We have collided with the obvious truth that growth depends on growers, upon human beings, on their outlook, their will to achieve some objective, their capacity to achieve it measured not only in terms of their skills, but in their health and strength and indeed *in their spirit*."

In this same spirit, an African farmer in the new Kenya that is so swiftly arising remarked: "It's difficult to say whether we are doing better than the white man." Gilbert Thuo Watoro went on: "We are doing as well. We

[7] *New York Times*, December 19, 1967.

194

have increased the size of the herd. Give us enough time and we will do two or three times as well." Mr. Watoro is one of the 30,000 black African farmers the Kenyan Government has helped to settle on a million acres in the highlands that had been farmed by white settlers from the days when Kenya was a British colony. Moreover, Mr. Watoro and his partners have been paying back their land bank loan on schedule, every six months.[8]

Growth depends on growers. But development also needs money, especially long-term investment money, when it comes to sustained industrial growth. These young and ambitious governments will get their investments —which means materials and mechanics, equipment and skills, know-how and organization—from whatever quarter they can. This obviously raises some difficulties, internal and external. Especially since the "rich" countries are, for various reasons, tapering off the rate of some of their earlier investments. All the African countries are planning their future; but how can they plan effectively unless they have reasonable assurance of continuing external assistance and trade possibilities?

For example, Uganda, to judge from its new Five-Year Plan, is growing increasingly disillusioned with orthodox foreign aid. The Plan assumes, in fact, that Uganda is not going to receive much outside help; it aims instead to squeeze more investment money out of local resources. The Plan frankly states: "In recent years the growth in the flow of financial resources from the developed countries to the poorer parts of the world has been checked." Yet the Plan envisions a total investment of over 600 million dollars between now and the middle of 1971. Uganda expects to raise 140 million dollars of this in foreign loans and grants, and 56 million dollars through the regional and semi-public planning and financing bodies which are springing up in both Africa and Asia.

It may surprise some people, who still think of Africa and Asia as objects of Western charity, dependent on Lady Bountiful of the Victorian Age, to discover how rapidly financial and other sophisticated development institutions, both continental and regional in scope, are springing up under the United Nations initiative. But these are not mere offshoots of Western capitalism. These burgeoning regional and governmental bodies are forging self-help together with loan and investment opportunities which fall outside the dwindling foreign aid devices belonging to a defunct colonial era. Unfortunately, however, the Cold War still imports its economic overtones, though the new leaders of Africa and Asia are, for the most part, trying to "balance" West against East, when necessary, in securing the outside aid that they all need so badly.

Such a case arose in 1967 when Mainland China agreed to construct one of the most costly projects ever undertaken on the continent of Africa. This involves construction of a 1,000-mile railway from the East African port of Dar-es-Salaam, Tanzania, to land-locked Zambia (formerly North-

[8] *New York Times,* August 6, 1967.

195

ern Rhodesia). A number of Western construction firms had rejected the project as incapable of development. The Peking Government thereupon pledged the equivalent of 300 million dollars for the railway. This would make it the third biggest "foreign aid" scheme in Africa—after the Aswan Dam in Egypt and the Volta River Project in Ghana. The Tanzam railway agreement was actually signed in Peking by the Tanzanian Finance Minister and the Zambian Financial Secretary. President Julius Nyerere of Tanzania, however, scoffed at criticism that the construction "would bring thousands of Chinese to Africa." He took what is increasingly becoming a confirmed African point of view: "Our political system is strong enough to withstand any foreign ideology!"

In fact, so sensitive are some Afro-Asian governments becoming of this Western propensity to look at their pressing needs in terms of Cold War rivalry, that the Nigerian Government sent in August 1967 a formal protest to the United Nations, resenting "prejudiced and unbalanced reports appearing in certain sections of American and European Press" concerning its arms purchases. Asserting that Britain and the United States had been "Nigeria's traditional suppliers of arms and still remain Nigeria's first choice for arms purchase for many reasons," they asserted their right to turn to the Soviet Union for arms "strictly for cash on a commercial basis," because "American and other Western Governments had failed to prevent the intolerable and scandalous situation in which private Western arms dealers had organized massive supplies of all types of arms to Nigerian rebels." Nigeria still maintained its "traditional foreign policy of non-alignment," the Government stated, and therefore "hopes that all friendly governments will avoid bringing in any Cold War complications which are irrelevant."

By an unexpected coincidence U.S. Vice-President Humphrey happened to be visiting Zambia a few weeks after the Tanzam project was accepted, and he expressly told Kenneth D. Kaunda, President of Zambia, that the United States was prepared to co-operate with the International Bank for Reconstruction and Development (the World Bank), the Export-Import Bank and Zambia herself in the hard-surfacing of the 300 mile stretch of road which paralleled the aforementioned railroad; in fact, the U.S. might even assume ten million dollars of an estimated twenty million dollar cost of this road. The road in question, like the railway, has strong political significance, since it has become a symbol of Zambian—indeed, of Pan-African—economic independence. As Zambia need no longer rely on supply lines running through white-ruled areas south of the Zambezi River, its leaders need not fear that their vital imports could be suddenly cut off, if any of the three white regimes to the south chose to do so. Mr. Humphrey's visit apparently came at a psychological moment; the race between the railway and the road will be fascinating to watch—but the Zambians will benefit from both.

The Good War

It affords some relief, therefore, to turn once again from the Cold War to what has well been described as the Good War. Although it must be admitted that bilateral forms of foreign aid, with their conflictual overtones, still account in over-all figures for about ten times the amount of multilateral assistance at present being provided through the U.N. Family, the latter is steadily winning a *qualitative* popularity, dollar for dollar. More important, it has ushered in a new order of *international* responsibility for the developing lands.

"The Good War," says Marion Maury, who has long worked in the field, "is being waged on the many fronts of poverty—on dry desert sands and in thick tropical forests, in teeming new shantytowns and in rural communities static in their ancient ways, in the urban centers of emerging nations and on the wastelands of forgotten peoples. It is being fought wherever hopelessness holds in bondage the untold potential of man and the earth on which he lives. It is a war not against men or nations, but against the sinister impersonal pull of economic disaster and social disintegration to which any group or region can fall victim."[9]

Describing what he calls "the new concept" of foreign aid, Senator J. William Fulbright states: "I propose its conversion from an instrument of national foreign policy to an international program for the limited transfer of wealth from rich countries to poor countries in accordance with the same principle of community responsibility that in our own country underlies progressive taxation, social-welfare programs, and the effective transfer of wealth from the rich states to the poor states." And he concludes:

Instead of being a weapon in the ancient and discredited game of power politics, aid could become, like educational exchange, a means for changing the nature of the game, for civilizing it and for adapting it to the requirements of survival in the nuclear age.[10]

That "the nature of the game" is, in fact, changing becomes more apparent from year to year. For example, about two-thirds of the total lending of the U.N.'s World Bank exceeded a billion dollars for the first time during 1966-67 fiscal year, and covered eighty-two nations in 527 separate loans. These low cost loans have provided high-priority projects for electric power and transportation, followed by agriculture, education, and industry. Loans made in 1967, for example, made possible basic power projects in Peru and Tanzania, a new road project in El Salvador, and telecommunications in the Republic of China (Taiwan) and Singapore.

The International Finance Corporation (an affiliate of the Bank) has

9 M. Maury: *The Good War,* Bartlett-Macfadden, New York, 1965.
10 J. W. Fulbright: *The Arrogance of Power,* Vintage, New York, 1966.

been taking the lead in one of the most critical development problems, as we have seen, namely, the lag in agriculture. Investments aimed at increasing fertilizer output in low-income countries come to over 25 million dollars in Brazil, India and Senegal.

To fill out further details of this new concept of financial and economic aid to the developing countries would indeed fill many volumes of what can properly be called vital statistics.* But this new concept goes far beyond the mere mechanics of broad non-political investment. As Marion Maury points out in *The Good War:* "The United Nations with its related bodies is a world storehouse of political, economic and social experience, and a center to which all nations can turn for the exchange and implementation of ideas." This means, in practice, that the World Organization provides a continuous flow of basic information necessary for the dovetailing of efforts, both to avoid duplication and waste and also to discover where the most important needs of nations lie and how they can most effectively be met.

"With each passing year new re-organizations take place within the United Nations," states Mrs. Maury, "to avoid overlapping and to facilitate the means by which countries can ask for and obtain the help they need. When a new set of circumstances demands the creation of a new arm or agency, the United Nations seeks the advice and suggestions of all its member states and agencies in deciding upon the best way to meet the changing situation. As a living organism the United Nations is subject to growth, adaptation and restructuring."

Out of the confluence of the "new" countries themselves have come many changes in the structure of the U.N., as we have already noted. For example, in 1966 UNCTAD was set up—the United Nations Conference on Trade and Development. Meeting in the "Vigyan Bhavan," which the Government of India placed at the disposal of the United Nations, about 1,400 representatives of the 132 states, members of UNCTAD, participated in early 1968 in the biggest world trade assembly ever held. If results were not spectacular and few concessions were wrung from the affluent countries, at least the "77," as they are termed—i.e. the less-advanced countries—by numbers alone exerted a new force in shaping a fairer pattern of world trade from that of the Nineteenth Century. In New Delhi economic and finance ministers from over a hundred states committed their countries to expand trade relations among states "having different economic and social systems" and thus to improve East-West trade. Measures to increase food production were initiated, as well as for the transfer of technology, know-how, and patents to the developing world. Would the Western trading community have seriously looked at any of these problems *from the have-nots' point of view,* but for UNCTAD?

* *See,* for an elementary survey of the whole field, the author's *World of Promise,* Oceana, New York, 1965, and *Decade of Development,* Coward-McCann, New York, 1966.

198

The cynic who asserts that multiplication of meetings between impoverished countries can never produce riches like rabbits from a conjurer's hat overlooks that, in the new global economics, *organization* counts as a primary factor of production. To support this, we can instance, first, a "low-level" national project, like tourism, and then proceed to a multination enterprise like the Mekong Delta Scheme.

As an illustration of the former, a mile-long runway has been constructed close to the world's largest Buddha, high up in the remote Hindu Kush mountains. Until recently, these Giant Buddhas, carved out of the mountainside sixteen centuries ago, were virtually inaccessible to the foreign visitor. The air field arose from a survey under an International Civil Aviation Organization (ICAO) expert and was financed by the U.N. Development Program (UNDP). Afghanistan is one of many low-income countries whose governments have asked for such technical aid from the UNDP. Returns can be quick from this sort of action. In 1966, Afghanistan earned 1.5 million dollars in hard currency from tourism; eight years ago its income from this source was nil.

Another UNDP tourism project involves capital investment of over one million dollars in a Yugoslav plan for the South Adriatic region, where tourist development has been hampered by lack of modern facilities. New hotels, roads, and airports are emerging, as well as master plans for the old towns of Dubrovnik, Budva, and Ulcinj. The Project Manager is the same Polish architect who was in charge of the rebuilding of Warsaw after the war. Such U.N. stimulus to national self-help is by no means negligible. Revenue from international tourism represents more than 24 per cent of the national income in Barbados, more than 6 per cent in Mexico, more than 5 per cent in Jamaica; Austria covers a large trade deficit by income from foreign tourism amounting to 500 million dollars a year.

"Co-Production" Is the Word

To equip the United Nations to play the leading world role (as it will eventually play) in the global war on want, the General Assembly created in November 1965 a streamlined Development Program through a merger of the Expanded Program of Technical Assistance (begun in 1950) and the U.N. Special Fund (set up in 1959). This was a key decision which, in the words of Secretary-General U Thant, "firmly established the United Nations' position in the front lines of one of the most critical struggles of our times."

The United Nations Development Program (UNDP) is, therefore, the outgrowth of fifteen years' experience by the U.N. Family in raising the standards of life for the people of low-income countries. The Program helps them to make full and effective use of their own natural and human resources. The Program works closely with their governments to *attract the capital* and train the manpower needed to improve agriculture, industry, transport, and their educational and social services. The way it does this is to make available experts and consultants, as well as to provide basic equipment and award fellowships for advanced training abroad.

How is all this paid for? Voluntary contributions from some 120 Governments have been financing the Program so far, and nearly 200 million dollars was raised in 1967. The 3,500 large and smaller-scale projects currently supported by UNDP in 150 countries call for a total expenditure of 1.5 billion dollars. Over half of this sum is being contributed by the developing countries themselves. This means a free and continuing partnership between the World Organization and the aided countries— a very different concept from "foreign aid" (always with some strings attached) or private investment operations aimed at the profits of the home investor.*

Under the Program's auspices, 36,000 technicians and advisers from more than one hundred countries have been sent into the field, 35,000 fellowships have been provided to men and women of the developing countries for advanced training abroad, and 140 million dollars' worth of specialized equipment and services have been furnished for project operations. The results to date have been quite astonishing; the whole human race has become the richer. Over one and a half billion dollars in development investment has flowed in for the first thirty studies of natural resources and nearly three hundred thousand men and women have been trained in their own countries for productive occupations. Moreover, millions of dollars have been saved or earned, following the introduction of more productive methods in farms, factories and public utilities, and hundreds of millions of people protected from malaria, tuberculosis and other crippling diseases.

The inner secret of the organization of this experiment in One World living lies in the network of over eighty U.N. field offices, staffed by highly qualified international and national personnel, of all nationalities and races, especially selected for their specific tasks. They work closely with local governments and with the whole family of U.N. agencies in identifying needs for assistance and facilitating the planning and execution of the projects. With the successful first two years' working of UNDP and a long waiting list of new projects ahead, the world has begun at last to balance hope with solid achievement.

"Progress in international co-operation since the last War," says Philippe de Seynes, U.N. Under-Secretary for Economic and Social Affairs,

---

* "Resolving today's most serious long-term crisis, the crisis of global poverty, could open the way to a more peaceful and prosperous era than any in human experience" —opening words of the impressive and illustrated UNDP report for 1968, obtainable gratis from United Nations Headquarters, New York.

"has been rapid and impressive. New horizons have opened up . . . Positive answers have been found to questions posed by the emergence of the Third World, *which is certainly the most complex phenomenon which the world has had to face in the last 150 years* . . . The technology of the Second Industrial Revolution is quickly leading to the internationalization of production."

In fact, this development of international production is being called by the U.N. planners "co-production," since it involves so high a degree of co-operation at all levels. Barely two years old, UNDP has already made world economic history. "The United Nations Development Program with which I am associated," explains its Administrator, Paul G. Hoffman, "has three principal responsibilities: First, to assist the developing countries in identifying the *physical resources* within their country which can be exploited profitably. Second, to assist in the *training* of nationals so that effective use can be made of those resources. (The day has gone when developing countries are willing to have their resources exploited by outsiders.) And third, to assist in the establishment of *applied research* laboratories, so that the benefits of modern science and technology can be brought to bear upon their development problems."

This declaration by one of the pioneer businessmen of America means that the Victorian Age is dead. Orthodox "investment," involving the exploitation of the natural resources of the "poor" world in favor of the affluent nations, is on the way out. The Capitalism-versus-Communism syndrome will soon become a museum piece.

Moreover, the *human* resources of the Third World nations are being developed, under the U.N. Family system, in a manner which would have been inconceivable in the heyday of colonial empires. Paul G. Hoffman again has this interesting comment:

I would like to say that the UNDP and the U.N. family of agencies have also made a small but significant contribution in the battle against ignorance. More than 300,000 nationals of the developing lands have been equipped *in their own countries* with technical knowledge, working skills, and professional experience essential for increasing economic output and improving social conditions. Among them are over thirty thousand managers, supervisors, marketing specialists, entrepreneurs and skilled workers; over eleven thousand specialists in public utilities and services; nearly seven thousand secondary school teachers; and nearly forty thousand engineers and technicians.

One result of the educational activities promoted by UNDP has been to prove beyond all doubt that men and women in the developing countries can learn as well and as quickly as those in the industrial nations. They have, even more, an almost insatiable thirst for knowledge and achievement. This is perhaps the real answer to the problem of the time-gap posed at the beginning of this chapter.

The increasing demands being made today on UNDP by the needy countries are largely due to the fact that, in contrast to spasmodic outside private investments of the old variety, even of otherwise acceptable "foreign aid" programs, UNDP is equipped in its policy and personnel to deal with the *whole* economic and social complex of problems facing an applicant government. The fundamental difference between the two methods is that UNDP is *solely* concerned with the welfare and interests of the country in need of help, whereas methods which have earned the derogatory name of "neo-colonialism" have a dubious past and a still more doubtful future.

We have in Chapter 4, for example, criticized Alliance for Progress projects as being not only inadequate in quantity, but basically wrong in approach. Why is this? Adolf A. Berle, former Assistant Secretary of State and a specialist on Latin American affairs, makes an important observation which aptly enforces this view:

These governments were to be provided with funds for capital development on a scale unknown in their history. *They did not have adequate local instruments and expertise* capable of putting more than a fraction of these funds to work. Still less, save in rare instances like Venezuela and Costa Rica, did they have political doctrine and administrative machinery calculated to bring the results of capital application and development to the direct benefit of the less-favored sectors of their own peoples. And how far could—or should—an instrument like the Alliance for Progress, conceived and financed in the United States, *undertake the task in other countries of reorganizing politics,* reforming taxation, accomplishing land reform, developing systems of national planning? (Italics added.) [11]

Money is still desperately short. Paul G. Hoffman urged at a recent UNDP Board meeting of thirty-seven member countries the doubling of economic assistance from the developed to the less-developed countries. Warning that without adequate financing "the developing drive is bound to falter and fail," Hoffman calculated that a doubling of the flow of development aid was well within the capacity of the advanced industrial states. The gross flow of assistance, he said, was 12 billion dollars in 1966 (the last year for reliable figures). But when repayments on loans, interest payments and dividends were deducted, the actual burden of development assistance on the world's taxpayers was only about three billion dollars. To the UNDP administrator this sum was "quite disproportionate" to the estimated gross national product of the major donor countries in 1966 of 1,500 billion dollars and the *150 billion dollars spent by these countries for military purposes.*

We are back again with the problem of choice, with the price the underfed and underhoused and underemployed millions of the human race are paying to keep going the war games of the NATO generals and their rivals. We have in the first part of this book cited the contentions of the

[11] *New York Times Book Review,* November 19, 1967.

nuclear strategists who feared peace at any price. We now know that what they are really offering us is *war at any price,* for it is in the impoverished regions of the earth that the seeds of war are being sown.

River of Life

It is when we come, however, to U.N. enterprises like the Lower Mekong River project that the basic difference is so startlingly revealed between war and peace methodology in dealing with the impoverished peoples.

A remark of George Woods, former Chairman of the World Bank, can be specifically applied to this Southeast Asian enterprise: "There is," he said, "a hard core of men and women from all countries who are dedicated to getting on with the job of development. I just wish these men and women could be heard more in their own lands and throughout the world. I just wish they were accorded the prestige which politicians and military men in all countries still reserve too often for activities which impede economic development and at times make progress virtually impossible." The international banker continued:

When is it that men and Governments will come to attach the same priority, the same prestige, to providing jobs and to producing things society wants, which is now attached to preparing for war or to waving the flags of nationalism?

The Mekong is the third largest river in Asia. It flows for 2,600 miles through hills and mountains, forest lands and delta, out into the South China Sea. The part of the river under U.N. development is the Lower Mekong and begins at the Burmese and Chinese borders. With its tributaries, it waters most of Cambodia and Laos, half of South Vietnam, and a third of Thailand. The seventeen million who live in the actual basin are mostly farmers and fishermen, whose horizons do not extend far beyond their villages—except those hundreds of thousands of desperate victims caught between the two sides of the U.S.-Vietnam war.

In 1958, an international task force initiated by the U.N. Economic Commission for Asia and the Far East began surveying the Mekong's potential. This world team was composed of Canadian, United States and Philippine cartographers and aerial photographers; Australian civil engineers; and British and New Zealand navigation experts and hydrographers. Another team of Japanese, French and U.S. engineers carried out surveys aimed at irrigation and power developments. By 1963 this planning stage was completed. Several hydrologic stations had also been established and the work of "leveling" the main river and aerial-mapping the mainstream and tributaries had been carried out.

In March 1966, a concrete dam on the Nam Pong River in north-eastern Thailand was put into operation. The opening of Nam Pong marked the completion of the second unit in the vast Mekong Project, envisioning the eventual use of this mighty river by over twenty-five million people in Thailand, Laos, Cambodia and Vietnam. The dam at Nam Pong already has two turbines in operation and a third ready for installation. Its reservoir will offer irrigation water to the arid area of the northeast, opening 55,000 acres to more intensive rice growing, with the possibility of growing two crops a year instead of one.

While work on tributary dams is under way, engineering studies have been completed on the gigantic Pa Mong project on the main stream of the Mekong, sixteen miles west of Vientiane. The Pa Mong Dam will create a reservoir as large as Lake Erie and offer irrigation water for 2.5 million acres. This dam acoss the Mekong will have added significance because no bridge at present crosses the river anywhere along its 1,500 mile length from the Burmese border to the China sea.

All this ground work had been accomplished in spite of formidable natural obstacles of mountains and jungle, and even the violent political relations prevailing among the four countries. Cambodia and Thailand had more than once broken off diplomatic relations, while Laos and Vietnam were increasingly disrupted by the civil war, which was the pretext for the massive invasion of the Americans from 1965 onwards. Yet the building of bridges, physical and moral, and of "co-production" under the U.N. has gone steadily on. Peace has snatched her victories from the jaws of calculated violence.

In the next chapter we shall turn to the U.N.'s fundamental task of peacekeeping, so some words from U Thant may help to keep these relationships in proportion: "At times when political crises test to the utmost the capacity of the United Nations system to carry out its primary function of keeping the peace, it is heartening to turn to its activities in the field of economic and social development through international co-operation and to see that these activities have a solidity, a continuity, and a momentum of evolution that are too strong to have been, so far, seriously or lastingly disturbed by disputes between States."

Meanwhile, alas! the manpower, the machines, and the money which could have brought Western civilization so speedily to Southeast Asia and have transformed it into a much-vaunted "showpiece of democracy" have instead defoliated and poisoned this tiny developing land with the barbaric practices of the modern military complex and the arrogance of power. The damning contrast between the two ways of life that present themselves to the earth's leaders and peoples today could hardly be more plainly revealed than in the World Organization's life-bringing project quietly arising along this mighty river among the smoke and ashes, the fears and hatreds of the Vietnam War.

7 THE BLUE HELMETS

"The convictions of peace must pull abreast and then
ahead of the inventions of war. The United Nations,
building on its successes and learning from its failures,
must be developed into a genuine world security
system."

—John F. Kennedy, September 20, 1963.

In the struggle of the 1970's between the United States and the
United Nations for the "mastery" of the world (in the pragmatic sense of
that term), the Soviet Union today—and, presumably, China tomorrow—
will probably not play the major role, except, perhaps, to perform a
function never really expected of Communist countries, and that is to
speed the development of the U.N. as a truly *world* institution.*

This is not so paradoxical as it may seem, because the increasing military involvement of the United States in the 1960's in various parts of the
world, culminating in the disastrous Vietnam War—but by no means stopping there—has had the effect, on the one hand, of bringing the Communist countries closer to U.N. ideology and policies, as we have already
noted. On the other hand, the withdrawal of France from NATO, as well
as the collapse of the U.S.-based alliances in Southeast Asia and the
Middle East, and the rejection by the Organization of American States
of a regional army under U.S. control in South America, has brought the

* In February 1968 the Department of Defense refused a request of Senator J. W.
Fulbright to de-classify and make public a secret study (originally entitled "Pax
Americana") on how the United States could "maintain world hegemony in the
future." (*New York Times,* February 16, 1968). The Assistant Secretary of Defense
wrote to Mr. Fulbright: "If the hypotheses, suggestions or conclusions contained in
the study were construed as future policy of the United States, the study would be
susceptible to misinterpretations and could produce serious repercussions abroad."
Subsequent enquiry brought to light the existence of other classified studies supporting U.S. "world hegemony." U.S. military spokemen express no doubts about their
assumed world role.

Washington military establishment for the first time up against the harsh realities of an absolute choice. It has to be either security through the U.N. system or else—what?

The virtual isolation of the United States intervention in Vietnam— able neither to move forward nor move back, and losing face either way before an increasingly hostile world opinion—brings us a long way from the Korean type of U.N.-sponsored operation, under United States direction and control. Genuine peacekeeping belongs to neither one nor the other type of war; it is the purpose of this chapter to explain why.

Because of the exorable logic-of-weaponry described in earlier chapters, the most powerful military system in the world has been confronted with the biggest single policy decision of this century: namely, to turn for national survival to the World Peace Organization, which the U.S. itself did so much to found for this very purpose, or escalate its lethal "commitments" until the literal crack of doom.

Shortly before his retirement as Secretary of Defense, Robert McNamara made this remarkable statement: "A nation can reach the point at which it does not buy more security for itself simply by buying more military hardware—we are at that point. The decisive factor for a powerful nation—already adequately armed—is the character of its relationships with the world."

That is the central issue of this chapter—to know when to stop "buying more military hardware" and what to do instead about "relationships with the world." For, according to a recent study on U.N. peacekeeping issued by the Brookings Institution, "compared with all other nations, the United States is more than adequately armed; but this vast arsenal, never even approximated in history, does not guarantee the peace—neither do military alliances such as NATO, SEATO, CENTO, and ANZUS, nor forty-two defense treaties with individual governments."[1]

That is plain language. But, as we have noticed again and again in the foregoing pages, the very momentum of the U.S. military alliances and the Iron Mountain mentality that inspires them is dragging its otherwise peaceloving people into sterile anti-Communist adventures all over the globe, which all end in futility and disappointment. This is indeed a perilous journey, unless the goal is changed.

The number of international outbreaks of violence has increased each year, said former Secretary of Defense McNamara, from thirty-four in 1958 to fifty-eight in 1965; and most of these have occurred in the Third World states of Asia, Africa, Latin America, and the Middle East. But Arthur M. Cox, the author of *Prospects for Peacekeeping,* follows up this point: "Undoubtedly there will continue to be brushfires each year, ignited by struggles for power within governments, insurgencies and counter-insurgencies, external subversion, racial tension, religious con-

[1] Arthur M. Cox: *Prospects for Peacekeeping,* Brookings Institution, Washington, D.C., 1967.

206

flict, and border disputes. As in the past, most of these will be resolved by the action of individual governments. . . . But some of them will get out of control and will require an international fire brigade. The United States alone cannot take this responsibility throughout the world, and the alternatives to U.S. power are very slim."

It is because the United Nations is the principal depository of peacekeeping experience and authority in the world today—despite its obvious imperfections—that it stands as the only effective alternative to the much greater imperfections of U.S. power. "The U.N. has demonstrated on several occasions," Arthur M. Cox states, "a capacity to conduct effective peacekeeping operations with military personnel in disputes where U.S. forces would not have been welcome, and where their unilateral interposition would probably have had disastrous consequences for the United States."

That this view is by no means shared by all Americans in high office was expressed by Senator Henry M. Jackson, Chairman of the Subcommittee on National Security and International Operations, speaking to the National Press Club in 1962: "The United Nations is not, and was never intended to be, a substitute for our own leaders as makers and movers of American policy. The shoulders of the Secretary-General were never expected to carry the burdens of the President or the Secretary of State. But do we not sometimes act as though we could somehow subcontract to the United Nations the responsibility for national decision-making?"

A complete response cannot be attempted in these brief pages to Senator Jackson and to those who, like him, have never taken the full measure of the U.N.'s capacity to grow to the stature of those who believe in it and are willing to learn from their own sad experience. But we can attempt to explain why an "international fire brigade" is worth more to life on this planet than the type of unilateral decision-making on which he appears to rely, with the U.N. as a mere subcontractor.

Since so much has been said and written about the peacekeeping role of the U.N. in recent years—and can be explored in detail in some of the works cited in these pages—this chapter can confine its argument more specifically to answering these simple questions:

(1) What does U.N. "peacekeeping" mean?
(2) Who is involved in it?
(3) What are its prospects?

Peacekeeping Means Truth

"I had been a serving soldier," says General E. L. M. Burns of Canada, one-time Chief of Staff of the U.N. Truce Supervision Organization: "I was happy in the service, and felt I was pursuing an honorable profession, and was sustained by the philosophy that war, however regrettable many of its features, was inevitable in the then state of development of the human race; and that peoples who refused to contemplate the possibility of war, and, indeed, to prepare for it, would be likely to be pushed off the world's stage." But he proceeds:

The atom bombs on Hiroshima and Nagasaki changed all that thinking . . . It did not need pages of labored scientific and humanitarian explanation to convince me that there could be no quarrel between the so-called civilized nations whose settlement would be worth paying the price of the destruction that would be caused by an atom war.

Once convinced, as he says, that war was "something to be avoided at almost any cost, the alternative way to settle international differences had to be some supranational machinery for the purpose." Hence, "whatever the imperfections of the Organization, and whatever faults might develop in its functioning," declared this first of the Generals of Peace, "the ideal of the prevention of a war which would destroy countless million man-years of thought and labor was *there,* in the United Nations Charter." Accordingly, concludes General Burns: "The idea of working for the United Nations appeared to me as an extension of my way of life as a servant, first military, then civil, of Canada . . . I was to get my pay and my orders from the United Nations, and to this Organization and the Secretary-General at its head, I should owe my loyalty."[2]

Thus, after four years of arduous duty, combining the new roles of Guardian of the Peace with those of skilled negotiator and impartial conciliator, Burns describes how the United Nations Truce Supervision Organization (UNTSO) and later the United Nations Emergency Force (UNEF) succeeded in large measure in keeping the bitter conflict between Israel and her Arab neighbors under U.N. control. According to the General, the first key to peacekeeping is to get the *facts*. He states:

When an armed conflict is in progress it is difficult to tell what is actually happening. Both sides put out their own versions of events, usually censored and sophisticated. . . . What is really going on? That is the question which the United Nations first of all wants answered when it sends military observers to Palestine, or anywhere else. Later, if either of the U.N. organs have made decisions or recommendations, it will want observers to tell it whether the parties are complying with them. Observers and observation groups are therefore an essential part of any peacekeeping machinery which the United Nations is likely to set up.

Truth, as the Secretary-General once remarked, when deploring the Vietnam conflict, is still the first casualty in any war. That conflict in particular has revealed a "credibility gap" between the facts and the official presentation of the facts that has become notorious, for the U.N. has been excluded from that battlefield. So Burns has put his finger on

[2] E. L. M. Burns: *Between Arab and Israeli,* Clarke, Irwin & Co., Toronto, 1962.

the fundamental difference between the *soi-disant* "police action of a limited kind" (a term with which Arthur Goldberg once graced the Vietnam War) and peacekeeping under the United Nations. The first requirement of peace is *truth*. "What is really going on?" What are the facts? That is where genuine police action to protect the world community begins.

Second, peacekeeping means impartiality. In the next chapter, more will be said about "the neutral man." Those who downgrade the role of the go-between in world affairs are apt to find strange bedfellows, as when Khrushchev declared that there were no "neutral men"; while Dulles, in opposing the 1954 Geneva Accords, spoke of "neutralism" as immoral. Happily, the U.N.'s experience of peacekeeping, under the severest conditions, has brought to public attention a realistic application of Charter principles, as this chapter seeks to show, which was hardly conceivable two decades ago.

Paradoxical though it may seem, the very mixed character of the U.N., with the strongly one-sided attitudes shown by many of its members, makes eventually for a high degree of impartiality when it comes to collective action, within the limits set by the Charter. Apart from the adage "there is safety in numbers," there are many reasons for this. One of the chief is the proved stability and long experience of the Secretariat, which the press tends to overlook when reporting international crises. Arthur M. Cox points out:

At the heart of the controversy over the future of the United Nations lies the question of the willingness of the super-powers to support and contribute to a genuinely impartial Secretariat led by a Secretary-General who strives to represent the Charter and the consensus of 122 disparate, sovereign nations. The Secretariat is the only organ of the U.N. transcending national interests and national boundaries. It is here that trust and respect must be built if the U.N. is to act successfully as a world organization.[3]

It should not be thought, however, that the constant striving for impartiality within the Secretariat springs from a computerized mechanism of faceless men. We are not dealing with a War Office, but a Peace Office. Another Peace General, with a crystalline mind, writes a very lively and not uncritical account, at times, of his career as a servant of the World Organization in *Soldiering for Peace*. The author, Major-General Carl von Horn's reaction to the simple humanity of his superiors in the Secretariat can be gauged from the following early passages in a behind-the-scenes autobiography concerned with protecting the Charter's principles in Palestine, the Congo, and Yemen:

Although hard experience had taught me to be skeptical of high-faluting words such as "ideals," and I was already familiar with unrewarding service, I was confident that in becoming an "international soldier" I was entering a

[3] *op. cit.*

209

new and very worthwhile period of my life. . . . As Ralph Bunche rose from behind his desk with outstretched hand, I was aware that never in my life had I met a man with such kind eyes. No one could have made me more welcome or done more to reinforce the feeling already implanted by Cordier, that I had come into an organization dedicated to preserving world peace and the service of mankind.[4]

Third comes speed. In spite of the fact that unilateral military interventions are usually carried out suddenly and with great secrecy, the World Organization has in most cases acted with remarkable speed. Sometimes, the U.N. personnel are there first—as in the case of Lebanon. In the Suez operation, the blue helmets began to arrive nine days after the invaders landed. Even more important is the manner in which the whole organization acts as an advance warning system. Arthur M. Cox looks optimistically ahead of present experience when he suggests that: "if the threat to the peace, or the requirement for help, can be ascertained while it is still small, the possibility for effective control increases. There is a need for a more efficient system of information sharing, especially some arrangement to bring warning intelligence to the attention of the Secretary-General. It is not inconceivable that some day the U.N. will be given access to information obtained from space satellite systems, to electronic intelligence, and to other 'black box' information obtained from the gadgets of modern technology."

Peacekeeping in Action

The foregoing principles will be borne out in the short summary that follows of what, in barely a decade, the U.N. has already done as peacekeeper. In this respect, however, we do not include the war in Korea under this head. As a major Cold War episode, it falls, in this author's view, outside responsible U.N. peacekeeping. General Romulo, former General Assembly president, put it bluntly when the Russians could not exercise their veto because they were absent: "The Security Council was saved from total impotence only by the narrowest of accidents." But one point should never be forgotten: the Vietnam War is sometimes wrongly presented as of the same type as Korea—i.e. "to stop Communist aggression"; but the fact that the U.N. has given no support whatsoever to U.S. intervention in Vietnam (quite the reverse) remains sufficient proof of that gross error, for the U.S. action is without moral or legal validity and can never bring about peace until it stops.

"What is U.N. peacekeeping?" asks the author of the Brookings study; and he replies: "It is an extraordinary military art because it calls for the use of soldiers not to fight and win, but to prevent fighting, to maintain

[4] Carl von Horn: *Soldiering for Peace,* David McKay, New York, 1967.

210

cease-fires, and to provide order while negotiations are being conducted. . . . The soldiers who wear the blue insignia of the U.N. are politically neutral and not authorized to fire unless fired upon. They are given their mandate by the United Nations—a clear modification of national sovereignty. U.N. peacekeepers do not intervene in a dispute unless the host government or one of the parties to the dispute calls for assistance or at least consents to the will of the U.N. majority that a peace force should be sent."

We have quoted this capsule description because it amplifies what we noted in the Introduction as essentially police duties, in distinct contrast to war-making actions by sovereign states, even if the latter proclaim them as police action. Let us note, too, how varied are the functions of the U.N. policemen.

The U.N. presence, as it has come to be called, ranges from the dispatch of a few hundred officers in jeeps as observers or fact-finders in a dispute in Greece or Lebanon or Kashmir in order to check the spread of conflict, to larger peacekeeping operations which have used organized military units. The United Nations Emergency Force (UNEF) maintained the cease-fire in the Suez area from December 1956 until June 1967. During these ten years upwards of 6,000 men served in UNEF, with contingents from Brazil, Canada, Colombia, Denmark, Finland, Sweden, Norway, Indonesia, India and Yugoslavia. Next came the Congo operation from 1960 to 1964, the most complex of them all. Thirty-four states sent a total of 93,000 soldiers to keep order in the Congo, at a total cost of 402 million dollars, which precipitated a major political and financial crisis at the U.N. Finally, the U.N. has been in Cyprus since March 1964, where 6,000 men from the United Kingdom, Canada, Finland, Ireland, Denmark and Sweden have helped to maintain the local peace and prevented, as noted in Chapter 1, a possible war between Greece and Turkey at the end of 1967. This is no mean record.

"The Cyprus action serves as a cardinal example of the possibility for all member states—irrespective of their power, influence or size—to promote the cause of peace," declared Per Haekkerup, Danish Foreign Minister, at the Twentieth General Assembly. He opened an important development in the history of peacekeeping by announcing that all the Nordic countries had begun to formulate a stand-by force and that the Danish Parliament had established a force of about 950 Danish soldiers. The Danish Foreign Minister then brought up a very crucial point which we shall consider below. He continued:

When we speak of U.N. peacekeeping forces, we mean forces used in operations such as those undertaken in the Congo, in Yemen, in Gaza, in Cyprus and in other parts of the world. They are *not* the forces envisaged in Chapter VII of the Charter, which deals with measures that may be taken by the Security Council against the will of a government to maintain or restore international peace and security. The actions for which the Danish stand-by force is contemplated are actions taken under Chapter VI of the Charter, which deals with the pacific settlement of disputes.

In Ottawa that summer the representatives of twenty-three countries from all parts of the globe had, in fact, met to discuss military and technical experience gained in previous U.N. operations. The purpose of this meeting of peacekeepers was to enable those who had actually been on active U.N. service to exchange experience on their technical work *in the field* for the benefit of the individual countries in their future build-up of stand-by forces. Canada's External Affairs Minister, Paul Martin, extended the Danish minister's argument as follows: "We regard the evolution of this concept, as distinct from the concepts envisaged in Chapter VII of the Charter, as affording the most significant example of the vitality of this Organization and its capacity for change in response to changing circumstances." Peacekeeping has evolved steadily, he noted, from the "designation of an observer group to assist India and Pakistan in avoiding further conflict in Kashmir, to the dispatch of a United Nations force to the island of Cyprus early this year, where Canadian soldiers have been helping to keep the peace." The U.N. presence had been used increasingly to prevent unstable situations from erupting into open conflict. Hence, Martin added, "We have over the past years maintained a stand-by force which is available on short notice should it be requested by the U.N. for participation in duly authorized peacekeeping operations."

"Enforcement" Ruled Out

Thus, the ball has been set rolling by the small and middle powers to equip the U.N. with a permanent police force. But, note, this does *not* mean enforcement. As this is the central issue of the current debate, we must spend a few moments on it. Chapter VII of the Charter is headed: "Action with Respect to Threats to the Peace, Breaches of the Peace, and Acts of Aggression." This chapter, calling for "combined international enforcement action," begins with Article 39, which reads:

The Security Council shall determine the existence of any threat to the peace, breach of the peace, or act of aggression and shall make recommendations, or decide what measures shall be taken in accordance with Articles 41 and 42, to maintain or restore international peace and security.

Under Article 41 the Security Council may call on U.N. members to apply such measures as interruption of economic relations or of rail, sea, air, postal, radio or other communication services and the severance of diplomatic relations. Article 42 declares further: "Should the Security Council consider that measures provided for in Article 41 would be inadequate . . . it may take such action by air, sea, or land forces as may be necessary to maintain or restore international peace and security."

Thus we arrive at the type of "collective security" carried over from League of Nations days and employed by the U.N. throughout the frustrating and inconclusive Korean War. But this is not peace-*keeping* action. The crux of all such enforcement procedures is *outside* military action against states that must first be designated as "aggressor" or "peace-breaking" by the Council. But, in fact, Chapter VII has become moribund and its "military staff committee" a polite fiction. Outside military alliances—NATO, SEATO, CENTO—have come to dominate the scene instead. This is not primarily because of the veto in the Security Council, as some authorities allege, but because of the fact that military action taken by some states against other states, under whatever auspices, are acts of war, not policing. Sooner or later, the old shibboleths of "collective security" must be scrutinized afresh.

The role of the U.N. by its very nature is peacekeeping, not war-making. To this end many U.N. delegates have been asking the General Assembly to insert a new chapter between VI and VII—even if the myths of Chapter VII must be retained for the sake of form. Such a revised Charter would then follow the sequence: "Pacific Settlement of Disputes," "Peace-Keeping Operations" and "Action with Respect to Threats to the Peace. . . ." What hope is there of that? Fortunately, as we have seen, the "new chapter" has been operating in practice, even if no change has been made in the text. This is how needful human institutions grow— by action, not words.

Since the Security Council has failed to exercise the powers conferred on it in 1945 under Chapter VII, enforcement action has not worked, with the minor exception in 1966 of authorizing the British to stop by military (naval) means an oil-tanker bound for Beira, running the U.N.-sanctioned blockade of Rhodesia. So Chapter VII of the Charter has been all but a dead letter. Instead, troops in the blue helmets from a score of different nations have been serving, as we have noted, in dangerous situations all around the world. They are not "enforcing" the peace, but "keeping" it. The distinction is basic.

Barriers Against War

Among the major interventions was the United Nations Emergency Force sent into the Suez in 1956. This operation was undoubtedly a success within the strict limits imposed by the political conflict. It provided a face-saving justification by which British and French forces were successfully and speedily evacuated from Egypt. It also ended the long period of raiding across the border of the Gaza Strip and most, but not all, of the

Arab-Israeli guerrilla activity. It was because there was little improvement in the *political* situation that war broke out again in June 1967.

It should not be forgotten that for eighteen of the twenty years the State of Israel has existed, the sole barriers against continuous war were the four armistice agreements, concluded by means of United Nations mediation in 1949, and also the U.N. peacekeeping machinery in the area, namely, the Truce Supervision Organization in Palestine and, later, UNEF.

In fact, it is part of the irony of peacekeeping that the main criticism leveled at UNEF from certain quarters came when the units were *withdrawn* by the Secretary-General at the demand of Egypt in May 1967. This criticism—though unjustified in terms of the facts and legalities—revealed both the strength and the weakness of U.N. policing, based on mutual consent and not on any sort of enforcement. Both sides in the dispute had to play fair with the U.N., however much they detested each other—but neither did.

From the outset, UNEF, though placed as a peacekeeping force between Egypt and Israel, was located only on territory of the United Arab Republic. The Israelis never would agree to permit the Force on their side of the armistice lines. Thus the United Nations presence, though vital to both parties, depended exclusively on U.A.R. accommodation and consent. When this was precipitously ended, the old conflict was resumed. When President Nasser insisted that U Thant withdraw the Force, two contributors to it, India and Yugoslavia, announced that they would withdraw their contingents unilaterally. U Thant's renewed appeal to Israel to have UNEF units on their territory was again denied. U Thant could not, therefore, delay the decision by taking the issue to the General Assembly, as some badly informed critics said he should have done. Moreover, as he closely documented in his report, Egyptian armed forces had already moved into the UNEF positions. Even if there could have been some delay, due to consideration by the General Assembly, the results could have been no different.

Happily, the United Nations retained an important double role in the area. An expanded Truce Observer Mission was at once approved by the Security Council, and cease-fire observers were stationed on both the Israeli and U.A.R. sides of the Suez Canal, which had now become the cease-fire line. And the Secretary-General's special representative went immediately to the area to mediate. But the June 1967 events have only pressed home the need for making improvements in the authority and organization of United Nations peacekeeping machinery for the future.

In his 1967 Annual Report, the Secretary-General pointed out that "There is a profound lesson to be derived by this Organization from recent developments in the Middle East. United Nations peacekeeping and peacemaking activities had their genesis in Palestine. They have been more prolonged, more intensive and more varied in that area than in any conflict-situations elsewhere . . . The United Nations has had considerable success over these twenty years in stopping fighting in the area by means of mediation, cease-fire, truce and armistice agreements, in restoring quiet along acutely troubled lines and generally in containing explosive situations." Nevertheless, the Secretary-General went on to assert: "The basic issues which provoke the explosions remain unsolved . . . The failure of the United Nations over these years to come to grips with the deep-seated and angrily festering problems in that area has to be considered as a major contributing factor to the war of last June, although, naturally, primary responsibility inescapably rests with the parties involved. I am bound to express fear that, if again no effort is exerted and no progress is made toward removing the root causes of conflict, within a few years at the most there will be ineluctably a new eruption of war." *Both* parties were now bound to apply the collective judgment of the U.N., especially the all-round settlement proposed by Britain and agreed unanimously by the Security Council, which alone is competent to serve their best and mutual interests.

The experience of the Congo raised, on the other hand, enormous problems of finance, of command, of organization, and of discipline. But, by it, the World Organization established certain basic principles about how it should go into action of this kind. The then Secretary-General of the United Nations, Dag Hammarskjold, handled the complex political and logistical issues with astonishing dexterity under the authority of his own office. There were no precedents to go on and every sort of complication seemed to arise at the same moment.

The Congo story has been told too often to be repeated here. But one result of the Congo operation has been strong pressure for the development of a higher level of training and efficiency among U.N. forces. It has been realized that the Organization cannot recruit its own forces at present, as the cost would be beyond its budget. Moreover, a standing force would hardly be appropriate to the kind of situations into which the United Nations has so far been drawn. Meanwhile, as noted above, a number of countries have responded, including Canada, the Scandinavians, Brazil and the Netherlands, and set aside volunteer units to be trained in the techniques which experience has suggested will be needed for U.N. duties.

Since the Congo operation was concluded, prolonged study and debate has been devoted to peacekeeping functions, to which only passing reference can be made here. A highly competent "Committee of Thirty-three," composed of chief U.N. delegates, has been in almost constant session for almost three years. Many governments have set their own experts to work on what has become the world's major problem: How to *keep* the peace through the U.N. This is, indeed, a decisive turning point in human affairs—away from war.*

It is sufficient to stress that *advance planning* to meet emergency operations—which naturally involves all the technical questions of recruitment and training the units to be contributed—has already received wide approval by the experts. One of the most competent of these, General Carl C. von Horn, states from his own intensive experience in the Middle East and elsewhere:

Pre-planning is the key to the success of any future U.N. emergency forces. Without advance planning, any eventual operation is prejudiced from its beginning . . . [We need] to have in being, now, a planning staff or Military Advisory Group to study the organization, command elements and logistical back-up for a future force. Needless to say, the composition of the force would vary according to the geographical or political conditions in the theater involved, but certain standardization of methods and procedure could be studied and set down, now, by such a staff.[5]

Is Financing the Obstacle?

Much of the time of the Committee of Thirty-three has been spent on finding the money: first, in clearing the debts arising from the past Palestine and Congo operations; and, second, in devising means for sharing future costs of peacekeeping as they arise. As regards the first, the position can be boldly stated that, by early 1968, after many millions of dollars had been contributed voluntarily by certain countries to meet the deficit, about 35 million dollars or slightly more (depending on alternative methods of calculation) remained outstanding to put the U.N.'s past peace-keeping accounts in credit. Britain and some Commonwealth countries, the Scandinavian and other small and middle countries had kept their promises of two years earlier and made their voluntary contributions to put the U.N. back on its financial feet.

But neither the United States nor the Soviet Union, nor France and some of the smaller countries, had fulfilled their promises to make voluntary payments to cover the rest of the deficit. Either one of the superpowers could undoubtedly break this deadlock at any time, since none of the voluntary payments was intended or announced as being reciprocal. But the lingering curse of the Cold War still lies heavy on the U.N., since the fiasco imposed on the Twentieth Assembly by the ill-judged threat to deprive the Soviet Union and France of their votes led to nothing but confusion and acrimony. (The voluntary contribution still awaited from the

* A thorough analysis for the serious student will be found in D. W. Bowett: *United Nations Forces, A Legal Study of U.N. Practice,* Stevens, London, 1967.
[5] *The Functioning of Ad Hoc U.N. Emergency Forces,* A Study of the World Veterans Federation, Helsinki, 1963.

United States would be insufficient, it is estimated, to keep the Vietnam War running for a single day.)

Meanwhile, existing peacekeeping proceeds on an *ad hoc* basis. As is the case of the Cyprus operation, the Secretary-General has to come cap in hand to the Security Council every few months to ask for the current costs. There is little fear, however, that these will not be covered; never has the world received so much for so little, and the Big Powers know this.

"In reality, however, this is not a financial problem, but a political one," stated the U.N. correspondent of the London *Economist:* "The United Nations needs only about 3.5 million dollars a month to maintain both of these forces [UNEF and UNIFCYP]. This is a very small amount of money, in relation to the wealth of the world as a whole—and also in relation to the enormous costs and enormous damage that a relapse into large-scale conflict in one of the areas concerned would involve. The real question is, how many nations are willing to give even a modest amount to support these peace-keeping operations? . . . The whole future of the U.N. peace-keeping operations now depends on whether a fairly large number of states which are not major powers, but which have quite adequate financial resources, are now willing to say to the major powers something like this: 'We shall not wait for you any longer. If necessary we shall provide all the money for these operations ourselves. We can do so very easily. The cost is so small that, if most of it is shared among perhaps twenty quite wealthy nations, their taxpayers will barely notice it.' . . . Something like this is, I believe, the only practical way now open to us to ensure that the existing U.N. capacity for peace-keeping work can be maintained and gradually enlarged."[6]

There are, however, longer term problems concerned with the financing of peacekeeping which are still a long way from solution. The recommendations of the important Committee of Thirty-three are still awaited. As the Canadian representative, Mr. Tremblay, summarized the basic issue very clearly in May 1966: "On authorization of peacekeeping operations, there is a clear disagreement in principle regarding the respective roles of the Security Council and the General Assembly. While believing that their roles are complementary, and thus not contradictory or conflicting, my delegation sees no point in further argument on this matter . . . In practice, it will be noted, *this disagreement in principle has, fortunately, not prevented the United Nations from continuing to function in this field.*"

The Canadian representative then introduced the following proposal which has since received increasing support as the planning of future peacekeeping proceeds:

There is one aspect of authorization on which members should be able to agree: that is the importance of associating peacekeeping with peaceful settlement. No peacekeeping operation should be authorized unless recommenda-

6 Andrew Boyd: "Peacekeeping in Danger," *The World Federalist,* July 1967.

tions are made regarding peaceful settlement as well, although we recognize in practice that there are bound to be occasions when peacekeeping action cannot be delayed . . . Peacekeeping operations are only a means to an end, and not an end in themselves. The end, or goal, is of course the *peaceful settlement of the dispute* which made the peacekeeping operation necessary. (Italics added.)

Playing Games With Crisis

In approaching the complicated topic of peaceful settlement as an alternative to war, however, one primary difference is so obvious that it is generally overlooked. That is the assumption—bred in the minds of peoples and leaders alike—that war is "inevitable." One proof of this—for which ample evidence was provided in Chapter 3—is that military strategists advising governments on specific lines of action believe in the war system as the be-all and end-all of their faith. That the human race has reached the point where it is technically possible to get rid of war never crosses their paleolithic minds.

To quote, again, General Maxwell D. Taylor: "We must have faith in deterrence and live by that faith if we are to have power which assures the peace." It is this fundamental theological error which stamps the ridiculous games which the strategists play in their think-tanks—and with the lives and fortunes of the earth's millions outside. Hence, the observation of Professor Rapaport that to talk to pyrotechnocrats in the language of peacemaking is like talking to the morally deaf.

But what are their games worth? General Sidney F. Giffin, a research associate of the Institute for Defense Analysis (of which General Maxwell D. Taylor is President), is described as a participant and analyst of various kinds of Cold War games sponsored by Washington. In his book, *The Crisis Game, Simulating International Conflict,* he explains the art of "crisis gaming" and presents two sample "scenarios" to illustrate its value "as a major tool of the higher levels of government" and as a depository of "the assumption of Cold War strategy."[7]

His reconstruction of the actual Cuban crisis of 1962 is one of these sample scenarios, but can be passed over as a supreme example of special pleading, in so far as it ignores what this author regarded as the crucial feature of the Cuban confrontation (see Chapter 4): namely, that the United Nations was the one spot on the globe where the three parties involved in decision-making *met face to face,* not only with each other, but, even more important, with the rest of the human race. It was at this physical confrontation that the actual decision was made to keep the

[7] S. F. Giffin: *The Crisis Game, Simulating International Conflict,* Doubleday, New York, 1965.

218

peace on the basis of the military compromise and mutual withdrawal put forward by the Secretary-General.

But General Giffin's other sample is indicative of what really goes wrong with the war gamesters. He projects the Kashmir dispute from the date he is actually writing (March 1965) into the year 1966. It should be enough to test the sense and the validity of this type of play-acting by comparing General Giffin's imagined scenario with the two major developments, sketched earlier in the present book, as they actually occurred. We recall, first, the prompt and firm handling of the issue by the Security Council and, after thorough discussion of all the relevant facts, the arranging of the cease-fire, and, second, and most important of all, the comprehensive give-and-take compromise arrived at—of all places—in Tashkent, through the good offices of the Soviet Union, with the later approval of the U.N.*

In a contemporary account written at the scene under the title "Miracle Without Precedent in the East," Cyril Dunn, a British commentator in New Delhi at this time, wrote as follows: "By midnight last night the armies of India and Pakistan had completely withdrawn behind their own frontiers on a 700 mile front stretching from the Pir Panjal mountains that enclose the Kashmir Valley to the sand dunes of the Great Indian Desert of Rajasthan and Sind. The whole difficult operation has been carried out in less than five weeks, with only 'inadvertent' shots from either side, and the first vital obligation of the Soviet-sponsored Tashkent peace agreement has been discharged . . . This morning thousands of villagers on both sides of the frontier stand poised to return to their shattered villages and neglected fields in the battle area."[8]

To study the Giffin speculation, however, contrasted with the historic facts in 1966, one realizes that Kashmir is dealt with, not for the dispute that it is, and has been ever since 1948, but as a segment of U.S. foreign policy—a minor pawn in the Cold War game played between Peking and the Pentagon. In fact, Giffin's two opposing "teams" are lined up under the labels Sino-Pakistan *versus* U.S.A.-India! No one would suggest that the Kashmir problem has been solved by the U.N.-Tashkent settlement—or will be in the foreseeable future—but, at least, it has been removed as one explosive factor from the hideous and selfish game being played by two nuclear bigots, whose concern is not with the peace of the people of Kashmir but their own strategic advantage one over the other.

In these simulated Cold War games the imaginary "pieces" are unconsciously invented and manipulated so that the U.S. must always win, or,

* H. S. Gururaj Rao's *The Legal Aspects of the Kashmir Problem* (Asia Pub. House, Bombay, 1967) is one of the many "background" works on this topic—as far removed from the Americanized military games books as is Newton's *Principia* from a science-fiction story.

[8] The London *Observer,* February 27, 1966.

at least, the enemy side loses. One wonders what classified games the RAND strategists are now preparing in secret for the millions of innocent bystanders who have everything to lose, whichever side "wins."*

The truth is that there is no dispute between sovereign states which cannot be resolved through today's advanced international political and juridical machinery and peaceful communication technology, without resort to violence and bloodshed and war. But the games are not devised to come out that way. Nor can any dispute be resolved by peaceful means if the sterile faith and the political assumptions of the Taylors and Kahns and Giffins guide the super-powers. The fate of our multi-cultural civilization was surely never meant to be risked on the atomic chess-boards of either Communists or their anti-Communist partners in mutual genocide.

It doesn't make sense. Many other skills and minds and procedures are at work today on the resolution or lessening of conflict between the sovereign states, large and small, which still divide the Planet between them. Although a *final* answer to war is not in sight, men of good sense and goodwill are everywhere learning that deterrence is obsolete and a revolution in the spirit of man is taking its place. It is always a question of choice.

A World-Wide Alliance

It is not that the U.N. has a ready-made answer to every crisis; it is a question of *choice of method* when each crisis arises. "It is surprising," says Professor Arthur N. Holcombe, "that practical statesmen should consider NATO a more promising instrument of action in the public interest than the U.N. Organization . . . Confronted by the challenge of the dispute over the control of the Suez Canal, NATO was manifestly more ineffectual than the U.N. The latter organization ascertained which parties were the aggressors and then censured them. This action certainly contributed something to the cessation of active hostilities. But NATO did nothing."[9]

Appealing to the nuclear powers on behalf of one of the smaller states that has already contributed many dedicated men to world peacekeeping in Cyprus, in the Congo (where quite a number of them were killed) and elsewhere, the Deputy-Prime Minister of Ireland, Frank Aiken, told the Twenty-second General Assembly that the super-powers had grossly underestimated "the political change necessitated by ever-advancing science and technology," and that they still clung foolishly to "the out-

---

* General Giffin states: "At RAND and more recently at the Hudson Institute, Herman Kahn and his colleagues have set about the writing of fictional world futures. Like the scenarios used in politico-military games . . . the Kahn future worlds describe possible situations without pretending that they are probable situations."

[9] Arthur N. Holcombe: *A Strategy of Peace*, Harvard U.P., 1967.

moded belief that great nuclear Powers, unlike small States, have no need of strengthening the peacekeeping capacity of the United Nations—the belief that they can still guarantee instead their own national security and prestige by increasing their military power and by extending their alliances and political and economic influence." On the contrary, he said:

The best guarantee against attack now and in the future, for both great Powers and small States, is to counter the ever-growing destructive power and range of modern weapons, not by organizing ever-stronger group alliances against group alliances, but by organizing effective collective measures against aggression as envisaged in Article 1 of the Charter—*a world-wide alliance which is inherently stable and in which every heart and hand can be united against an aggressor.* (Italics added.)

In thus bringing the world's leaders back to the first principles of the Charter, we recognize the gulf that exists between the obsolescence of military alliances and the growing authority of the World Organization. Happily, Britain has perceptibly, since its mistaken and costly defiance of the Charter in the Suez dispute of 1956, moved forward in support of war-prevention programs under the dynamic initiative of Lord Caradon, its chief U.N. spokesman. Backing Ireland's appeal for more specific peacekeeping machinery, the British delegate stated in November 1967 that "the British Government—and, we believe, the vast majority of the membership of the United Nations—regard the United Nations as the forerunner of a world authority. . . . Meanwhile our aim must be to make the United Nations as efficient an instrument as possible for its present more limited role. In our view, a vital part of that role is peacekeeping action with the co-operation of the parties to help contain disputes, to halt violence, to create conditions and time in which the parties may search for peaceful solutions."

In the next, and final, chapter some of the pre-conditions of this emerging "world authority" will be considered. We may still be a long way from some form of World Government, but it is already clear, as the search for peacekeeping remedies proceeds on the basis of actual trial and experiment, that a new factor has appeared which was never so evident when the U.N. began nearly a quarter of a century ago. It is that the World Organization has become something tangible in its own right.

States at war against each other can no longer act bilaterally—as though their conflict were a private matter between themselves. War anywhere threatens peace everywhere. We saw this with regard to the Arab-Israeli war, the Vietnam conflict, the Cyprus question, the Kashmir dispute, the Congo collapse, and the rest. When a state goes to war with another state, it goes to war *against the whole U.N.*—unless, that is, it were to receive authorization from the U.N. But, conversely, it can no longer ensure its own survival without the help or mediation, or other peacekeeping services of the U.N., applied to its particular predicament.

This is, perhaps, the most significant factor that has emerged from the lengthy and arduous peacekeeping debate over the last few years, and it is of paramount importance for the human future. The Secretary-General must have had this long-term development in mind when he stated with his usual cautious foresight in an address at the University of Denver, in April 1964, on "Strengthening the United Nations":

It is often suggested that the time has come for a permanent international peacekeeping force to be established under the United Nations. Obviously this would be a great step forward, but I do not believe that the time has yet come for such a radical advance . . . To provide the United Nations with its own permanent international force would give it some of the trappings of a World Government, which at present it definitely is not. The very existence of such a force would imply, if the force is to be used effectively, a very considerable surrender of the sovereignty by nations, which in its turn would require the acceptance by public opinion of new and radical political principles.

8 TOWARD WORLD LAW

"We are here not merely to reflect the conscience of
the world and make speeches that echo those feelings;
we are here to unite, to co-operate, to organize economic existence, and above and beyond economic
well-being and as a basis for such well-being, to
establish peace."
— Victor Andrés Belaúnde of Peru,
on the day of his death (1966)

Half the population of the globe is younger than the United
Nations. It is that half of the people now living on this earth who will
enter the Twenty-first Century and take along the United Nations with
them. So our final question is: What sort of World Organization shall it be?

"We are now moving into a chapter of human history in which our
choice is going to be, not between a whole world and shredded-up world,
but between one world and no world. I believe that the human race is
going to choose life and good, not death and evil." This was Arnold Toynbee's way of introducing the Twenty-first Century. For he goes on to say
with assurance: "I therefore believe in the imminence of one world, and I
believe that, in the Twenty-first Century, human life is going to be a unity
again in all its aspects and activities." Above all, he says: "In the field of
politics, nationalism is going to be subordinated to world government."[1]

Addressing a youth audience at Toronto in September 1967, Paul G.
Hoffman, Administrator of the United Nations Development Program,
said: "You have every right to be heard, for our world of today is literally
a young world, the youngest, in fact, in all human history, and unlike
everything else I know of it is getting younger all the time. Already in the
developing countries of Asia, Africa and Latin America some 65 per cent
of the inhabitants are under twenty-five." And he added: "Every gener-

[1] Arnold Toynbee: "One World or No World," *New York Times Magazine,* April
5, 1964.

ation, of course, inhabits a world it did not make. But your generation, to a greater degree than any I can think of, has shown that it is dissatisfied with the state of the world that is being handed down to it."

The earlier chapters of this book have dealt with some of the grounds for that dissatisfaction; the later ones have sought to stress the dynamic impulses, which like seedlings in a frozen soil are attempting to force their way to the new sunlight. As these pages have shown, a distinct break-away has occurred in man's global concepts and age-long habits which makes a return to the anarchy of sovereign states too perilous to entertain. This final chapter could, therefore, best touch on some of the basic re-quirements of a world order which would serve, at least, as an advance token of the New Century.

"Man has gained command of entirely new means of influencing minds on a planet-wide scale," writes a modern novelist: "Already, now, we are faced with the question of how this rostrum can be utilized for communica-tion with a world-wide audience in the name of our ideas—and the ques-tion grows increasingly more urgent." Danill Granin, Soviet novelist, thus presented his One-World view in the November 1967 issue of *Inostrannaya Literatura*.

His surprisingly fresh essay ignores Communist orthodoxy and employs an almost Western historical determinism to sustain his argument for the One-World solutions he proposes. "It is precisely the anxieties, disasters and concerns for the future," Granin explains, "that further the unification of humanity." To his mind, such problems as feeding the earth's popula-tion cannot be solved within the framework of a single country. The urgent problem of fresh water supply is itself a planet-wide problem. "The same has become true," he asserts, "of the problem of combating the 'flu, of weather forecasting and weather control, of radio-communications and astronomy; while more and more problems emerge which can be solved only by international effort on an earthwide scale." In fact, he says, under the pressures of change, "the earth is gradually coming to be regarded as a unified organism and the word 'cosmopolite' has acquired a new mean-ing."

This doesn't sound a bit like what Communism is supposed to be! And perhaps the skeptic will not want to take the word of an isolated novelist. He may want further proof that the plain facts of modern communication and proximity have not been passed unnoticed by Russian leaders. Let the skeptic listen, then, to Premier Aleksei N. Kosygin's comments on the same theme in an interview on French radio-television recently: "It is an error," he said, "to believe that all international problems can be resolved by the two great powers. We believe in the United Nations, where all countries, large and small, are represented." . . . "The international situ-ation is now very grave," the Soviet Premier continued: "Leaders of all countries are obliged to take all necessary measures to maintain peace."[2]

2 *New York Times,* July 10, 1967.

Allowing for the interpretation of these sentiments in traditional Communist terms, this admission is not really surprising—nor should it be surprising that hard-headed Communists have caught up with the global requirement of an inter-related planet, whatever Karl Marx or John Birch has said the the contrary. It simply means that leaders of all countries are *obliged*—not because of pacts or charters, ideologies or "ways of life"—to take "all necessary measures" to establish the sort of world order which conserves the totality of mankind's achievement for future generations. As Takeo Miki, the Foreign Minister of Japan, reminded the Twenty-second U.N. General Assembly:

We are now entering the last third of the Twentieth Century. Both the first and second one-thirds of this Century were marred by disastrous world wars. . . . The great and solemn responsibility that we, the living, bear to future generations is to save the last third of the Twentieth Century from nuclear tragedy and to ensure that the doors of the Twenty-first Century, holding out unlimited possibilities for the well-being of mankind, will open to an era of true world peace.

Opening New Dimensions

We might consider, first, some of the human investment which has already been applied to establishing such a world order; second, some of the new forms which international co-operation has assumed; and, finally, some of the roles individuals are playing and might be expected to play toward these ends. These are general guidelines only and will not be dealt with in rigid compartments in what follows.

First, the investment which has already been made toward a world of law has not had anything like its due publicity or recognition. There are millions across the earth who at present know nothing of it or think little about it, although the evidence is all around them. The public response has been stimulated for so long by war propaganda and actual war-making that relatively few people realize that—apart from the localized Korean or Vietnam type of conflict in which the U.S. has been involved—world peace *has* been maintained for over two decades. The reason for this is not the loudly proclaimed balance-of-terror, but simply that the overwhelming majority of peoples and their governments want it that way and need it that way.

Equally important, and in spite of warring factions within and between some states, the very functions of the nation-state have for two decades been expanded into a fast-growing network of worldwide communication and proximity in economics, technology, and many other areas of vital human discourse, as we noticed particularly in Chapter 6.

As one example, the International Civil Aviation Organization, which is one of the U.N. Family farthest removed from power politics and therefore the least publicized, recorded for 1967 the highest volume of traffic for the world's airlines ever known in one year: 236 million passengers for a total of 171,000 million passenger-miles on scheduled services, representing increases of 18 per cent and 20 per cent over 1966. Without the regulatory and co-ordination functions of I.C.A.O., air navigation would become a man-made aerial jungle.

This was the main point that David Mitrany was attempting to make in *A Working Peace System*. First published in London during World War II, amid a spate of peace plans and falling bombs, Dr. Mitrany's pioneer classic, stressing the essential nature of a durable world order, became a milestone in the political thinking of our century. Mitrany put forward the concept of "functionalism" as the logical reply to the dangers that overlapping nationalisms presented to the world community. In short, international anarchy would be superseded by the co-operation of independent sovereign nations with common interests so as to create the *supranational* institutions which all of them needed. This bold concept seemed at first too good to be true. It immediately came under attack by those who asserted that it ignored questions of "power" and dodged the alleged necessity of military force. But the functionalist simply replied: "But it *works!*"

In his introduction to a recent U.S. edition, Professor Hans J. Morgenthau has summed up Mitrany's thesis as follows:

According to Professor Mitrany, an international community must grow from the satisfaction of common needs shared by members of different nations. International agencies, serving peoples all over the world regardless of national boundaries, could create by the very fact of their existence and performance a community of interests, valuations, and actions.[3]

Mitrany believed that when such international agencies were numerous enough and served the wants of most peoples of the earth, loyalty to these institutions and to the world community would become as strong as or stronger than the loyalties now shown to the separate national societies. "The weakness of the League of Nations," he said, "lay in the fact that it was limited to the task of organizing stability. In this respect, the United Nations Charter shows a great advance, and it is significant that the changes which at San Francisco were made in the original draft all tended to add weight to the economic and social functions of the new international organization." Nevertheless, he admitted that, "in a field which is so vast and complex and in which the participants are so different in outlook and levels of organization, common ways of thinking and of doing things will not be easy to achieve."[*]

[3] David Mitrany: *A Working Peace System* (Revised edition), Quadrangle Books, Chicago, 1966.
[*] A contemporary analysis of Dr. Mitrany's original case by a number of British political scientists was edited and published by the present author and entitled: *World Organization, Federal or Functional*, C.A. Watts, London, 1944.

U Thant developed this same theme in a recent address:

In this century political ideology has taken the place formerly occupied by religion as a main source of strife in the world. . . . The world is, mercifully, an infinitely varied place. If we could start pragmatically by working together on the problems which urgently concern all peoples, differences of ideology and other apparently insoluble conflicts might be seen in a new light as wasteful and unnecessary, and may thus work themselves out over a period of time.

What is, however, so striking about Mitrany's approach is that, since he developed his thesis, the functional growth of a working world order has far outstripped his prophecies, as well as the mental and moral grasp of most contemporary leaders—and certainly their capacity to apply the new approach to major policy decisions. The contrast between the militaristic obscurantism portrayed in the first part of this book, based on "our-country-right-or-wrong" absolutes, and the concrete evidence of world co-operation featured in the second half—as *real* by any rational standard and far more realistic in practice than the speculative nonsense of nuclear strategy—is some indication of Mitrany's pragmatic foresight.

Hence, our still-to-be solved problem is how to bridge the gap, not between Communist and non-Communist worlds—that has already been largely done—but between the coercive minds of the last century, who still hold political power, and the co-operative minds of the New Century, who still lack that power. And this is, intrinsically, not primarily a question of governmental machinery, but of men.

"It is the war system that must be identified with stability, the peace system with social speculation," is the conclusion of *Report from Iron Mountain*. It is this fallacious conclusion which vitiates the whole mountain of syllogisms which underlies it. The vicious circle runs: War is necessary to stabilize the nation-state; peace can never stabilize the nation-state; therefore, peace can never become a substitute for war; so war must continue in order to stabilize the nation-state.[4]

But Dr. Mitrany exposed this fallacy a quarter of a century ago. To begin with, "War as a stabilizer" is itself a contradiction in terms, as any history book will show. And the search for an "accepted external menace" —i.e. "substitute enemies"—to give the nation social cohesion within may satisfy a Treitschke or a Hegel, but not a Nehru or a U Thant or a Toynbee or the growing millions of the earth's citizens whose "interests, valuations, and actions" are spilling over the borders of the fictitious Iron Mountain games-board into the world community beyond. There are no human beings in Iron Mountain, only gamesmen robots.

"Organizing stability" was, according to Mitrany, just where the League of Nations began. But the working *peace* system that has since evolved, as opposed to a substitute-for-war system, presents not merely a difference

[4] L. C. Lewin: *Report from Iron Mountain*, The Dial Press, New York, 1967.

in degree, but a difference in kind. The area of "organized stability" on which the author of the alleged Report bases his case can no longer remain the nation-state—not even for Americans. In fact, unless the area of stability becomes co-terminous with the area of humanity, the nation-state is itself doomed. Its continued existence depends on "organizing stability" for the earth. The Iron Mountaineers, like the searchers for the Blue Bird of Happiness, have stumbled on the goal of their search, while looking for something else. War *is* their "external menace," peace *is* their "substitute for war." As A. J. Muste said: "There is no way *to* peace; peace *is* the way."

So this chapter will deal especially with the men who are organizing global stability. It is always the way men *think* that counts. Two of these new men of action and vision met recently at the United Nations Headquarters, when the following exchange took place between Nobel Peace Prize Winner Ralph Bunche and American Astronaut John Glenn:

DR. BUNCHE: I wish on this unprecedented occasion to introduce a pioneer in the truest sense of the word, leading the world into an epoch of greatness, of unknown potentiality. . . .

COLONEL GLENN: To be here at the United Nations . . . is a salute to this World Organization by all of us in the United States who are connected with the great team effort to explore the new frontiers of outer space . . . The flights in which we have been taking part are not only a national team effort but international as well. The tracking arrangements themselves for our flight required the co-operation of many nations.

In a little broader sense of course the entire effort to explore outer space rests on many scientific disciplines whose growth over the years has been entirely international. As space science and space technology grow still further and our projects become more and more ambitious, we will be relying more and more on international team work. And the natural center for that team work is the United Nations . . . We have an infinite amount to learn both from nature and from each other. We devoutly hope that we will be able to learn together and work together in peace.

To complete this episode, it should be added that shorty after Glenn's visit, Major Gherman E. Titov, second of the Russian Cosmonauts who had made seventeen orbits of the earth some six months before Glenn, also visited the United Nations. Titov spoke in almost the same terms as Glenn had done, stressing that space science ought to be developed internationally and that space exploration should be used solely to advance world peace. These are the new men who are fashioning the world of tomorrow.

The Peace Scientists

As we follow the astronauts into space, two objectives come into view: first, co-operation must replace competition in space exploration; and, second, outer space must be developed as an area of peace, not war. The

World Organization has made steady progress in translating both these principles into binding legal agreements. But the *application* of the U.N.'s resolutions and draft treaties remains, unfortunately, with those politicians who still assume that peace grows out of the muzzle of a gun—or the shaft of a silo. The space issue is basically, therefore, not a scientific but a moral choice between two ways of living on this planetary spacecraft of ours.

Consider this poignant summing-up of Adlai Stevenson, which came at the end of his last speech at the summer session of the Economic and Social Council at Geneva in 1965, a few days before his death:

> We travel together, passengers on a little space ship, dependent on its vulnerable reserves of air and soil; all committed for our safety to its security and peace; preserved from annihilation only by the care, the work, and I will say the love we give our fragile craft. We cannot maintain it half fortunate, half miserable; half confident, half despairing; half slave—to the ancient enemies of man—half free in this day. No craft, no crew can travel safely with such vast contradictions.

In 1961 the General Assembly began work on the Outer Space Treaty, thus to shape the first laws for Outer Space. They agreed unanimously that international law, including the United Nations Charter, should henceforth govern the use and development of Outer Space. The Assembly has since called on all states never to place "weapons of mass-destruction" in Outer Space; both the U.S.S.R. and the United States have undertaken "not to station in outer space any objects carrying nuclear weapons, or other kinds of weapons of mass destruction." By 1966, this new World Law bound *all* states not to orbit weapons or station them in Outer Space or to encourage anybody else to engage in such actions. Thus, as Mitrany prophesied, supranational technologies are beginning to bind state governments from the start.

We have evidently moved a long way from the stereotyped either/or views of the Chairman of the Policy Planning Council of the State Department, Walt W. Rostow, who could write in these doctrinaire terms:

> We are engaged in an historic test of strength . . . The ultimate question at issue is whether this small planet is to be organized on the principles of the Communist Bloc or on the principles of voluntary co-operation among independent nation states, dedicated to human freedom.[5]

It seems astonishing that *World Law* should have begun its codification in Outer Space through voluntary agreement of all the members of the U.N. Under World Law, astronauts are given the status of "envoys of mankind." They shall receive from all nations all possible assistance in case of distress. Spacecraft and their personnel must be returned to the country of origin, if they fall on other territory. In 1968, a detailed code fixing liability for loss or damage was being worked out by the U.N. Space Committee. Most important, "celestial bodies" shall be "free from use by all States on a basis of equality and in accordance with international law."

[5] Department of State Newsletter, April 1962.

No celestial body is to be the subject of national *ownership;* for national flags belong to earth—not heaven. Furthermore, if a State has reason to believe "that one of its space activities is harmful to other States, it will undertake international consultations before proceeding with it."

Yet we cannot take for granted that the sensible principles evolving stage by stage under U.N. auspices will convince all the pre-Copernican minds who are endeavoring to fit space sciences into national orbits. We can cite one typical example from the academic world: "U.S. initiative in formulating space laws," states Robert D. Crane, "can serve not only to promote scientific research and economic progress and to facilitate the growth of a free and peaceful world order, but to implement on a higher moral level our military and political strategies." But how can the abominations of nuclear war on earth be thought of as serving a "higher moral level" in space?

"United States initiative in the development of international space law can provide a better political atmosphere for our deterrence strategies and also add another order of magnitude to our deterrence mix," continues the same writer, for "one of the most efficacious steps in building ideological deterrence and achieving ultimate victory in the ideological conflict would be to embark on a carefully prepared and politically integrated campaign to develop international law."[6]

Into the Ocean Depths

Undaunted by such Outer Space skeptics, World Law is also about to descend into the depths of the oceans. The High Seas are already governed by traditional International Law—at least, in time of peace. They cover six-sevenths of the globe and no nation has the legal right to "control" them. Beneath them large areas of the planet exist which have not yet been appropriated by any single nation, or even investigated. But this may not last long, unless mankind's rights are asserted openly and United Nations jurisdiction is proclaimed over, under, and within the High Seas.

The sea-bed becomes more important to science and industry and especially as a resource for feeding the planet, as modern apparatus plunges deeper. We now come to some specific proposals. The ocean floor outside the limits of present national jurisdiction, declared Gopalaswami Parthasarathi of India at the Twenty-second General Assembly, must be used exclusively for peaceful purposes, in terms of the same principle already embodied in the Outer Space Treaty. Unfortunately, the "advanced" countries might use the sea-bed for setting military bases or to test nuclear weapons unless restrained by international law. "To enter into a power struggle in a scramble for areas in the deep sea would be to repeat the tragic errors of history," he stated during a debate, when over

[6] "Law and Strategy in Space," *ORBIS,* University of Pennsylvania, July 1962.

forty governments supported a plan proposed by the mini-state of Malta.

The small island of Malta had urged four principles: (a) the sea-bed and ocean floor beyond the continental shelf should not come under the sovereignty of any nation; (b) the underwater resources should be regarded as the common heritage of mankind; (c) this new environment should be reserved for peaceful purposes; and (d) future exploitation should be aimed especially at raising the economic levels of the developing countries. The delegations agreed that the United Nations was the appropriate agency which could co-ordinate and direct the development of such valuable untapped resources. This was the beginning.

It may be recalled here that, in 1958, the Conference on the Law of the Sea held in Geneva adopted four partial conventions dealing with what could be described as the surface and the edges of the seas. But technological progress has taken place since then and the time has come for the world community to take the next step and to decide on what additions to international law are required to regulate deep sea resources in the interests of mankind.

A spokesman of another small island state, Cyprus, went further and proposed that title to the sea-bed and ocean floor beyond the accepted limits of national jurisdiction should be legally vested in the World Organization *in trust for all nations*. Zenon Rossides of Cyprus contended that bringing legal order to "a part of the earth's inner space" would mark a breakthrough in international co-operation and could prove "a turning-point in United Nations development and in the future of mankind." Moreover, Rossides recalled, the need for *independent* sources of U.N. income was apparent to everyone; here was an untapped store of permanent revenue. The international character of such new resources would facilitate their distribution among all needy countries, whether coastal or landlocked.

Another urgent element came strongly into the 1967 discussions: the dumping of radioactive waste into the open sea. All nations bore mutual responsibility as to what went into and came out of the oceans. None of the legal problems involved are simple ones, however. For example, it was accepted in 1958 that control over the "continental shelf" was vested in the coastal State, as an extension of its own land mass. But whether States would agree to limit their claims in favor of some international arrangement, curtailing their jurisdiction to some agreed distance from their shores, is still undecided. Opinions also differ on the legal status of the sea-bed and the ocean floor. National sovereignty could doubtless be acquired over the surface of the sea-bed, some experts say, provided that this did not interfere with freedom of navigation; but others have urged quite differently that this area rightly belongs to the international community and should pass under the legal control of the World Organization.

"To begin removing plants or animals from the sea at the rates needed to supply the world population of 1980 or 1990 may upset a very large, yet delicate, system," explains a scientist, J. F. Wehmiller: "Thermal pollution and radioactive waste from nuclear reactors can have equally uncomprehendable effects. So we are confronted with a world-wide conservation problem. The only organization with a hope of handling the problem is the United Nations. . . . How long will it take for the powers-that-be," he asks, "to realize this same responsibility to the world environment, in the protection and conservation of a resource which knows no national boundaries?"[7]

Happily, a general answer to such anxieties as the foregoing has already been provided by actual experience. Following up the success of the International Geophysical Year of 1957-58, when the U.N. Family carried out specific tasks on weather research in common, the Antarctic program was launched. During the I.G.Y., Antarctica had become a continent-sized laboratory for scientific experiment. As a result, the Antarctica Treaty was signed by twelve nations in 1960 and this vast expanse of scientific and strategic resources came directly under international jurisdiction—backed by *all* the U.N. membership. Scientists and observers are now working together at one end of the globe as international experts, not as representatives of governments.

The preamble of this pioneer treaty declares "that it is in the interest of all mankind that Antarctica shall continue forever to be used exclusively for peaceful purposes and shall not become the scene or object of international discord." The twelve member-nations have agreed to shelve, for at least thirty-four years, any new territorial claims to the Antarctic continent, and not to allow political or military factors to interfere with expeditions. The Treaty bans nuclear explosions, provides for unlimited inspection to see that this rule is carried out, and prohibits the deposit of atomic waste.

One of the new peace scientists, Georges Laclavère, president of the Scientific Committee for Antarctic Research, has made this comment: "This is the first treaty ever drafted to protect scientific research and to entrust a non-governmental organization with full power to determine the programs. Here is a pattern for harmonizing relations between science and governments. Is it not a paradox that the continent most hostile to man should be the one to have done the most for the cause of peace?"

Sovereignty as Defiance

The stumbling-block of state sovereignty is, however, still too much with us. It seems to get in the way every time that most nations, acting cooperatively within the World Organization, combine their faith in a

7 *New York Times,* November 26, 1967.

232

long-term decision which will eventually benefit them all. The odd-man-out can sometimes be a small nation whose geographical or strategic position or its support by one or more of the great powers gives it a temporary ascendancy in the play of power politics. Before passing to some of the more hopeful aspects of the merging of national sovereignties, therefore, we can review briefly two areas of present-day conflict where small countries have thwarted the united endeavors of the World Organization to solve their own problems for them, while giving lip-service to the rule of law for everybody else.

By way of two contrasting current examples, we can mention *from the standpoint of U.N. authority,* the quite different cases of South Africa and Israel. In the first case, following years of bitter debate and two advisory opinions by the World Court, South Africa still refused to acknowledge its accountability to the U.N. over South-West Africa. The South African government was prepared, it said, to negotiate a "new" trusteeship agreement on its own terms, with the three remaining parties of World War I (France, Britain and U.S.A.), but only provided that such an agreement exempted South Africa from becoming accountable (through the making of annual reports and so on) to the U.N. This recalcitrance was made in the face of almost unanimous and repeated insistence by the whole U.N. membership. State sovereignty, already adequately safeguarded under Article 2 (7) of the Charter, could thus be turned into an instrument of defiance against the world community.

Similarly, when the Israeli government was under consistent pressure from practically the whole membership of the U.N. in 1967 and a unanimous Security Council resolution to evacuate the occupied territory of the Arab States, including the Old City of Jerusalem and other holy places which were held by force of arms and in contravention of international law and the U.N. Charter, the Tel Aviv government persisted throughout lengthy debates in both the Assembly and Security Council in attempting to shift its own accountability to the U.N.—which had provided Israel with its legal status—to the neighboring Arab nations. But the U.N. has held firm and, in March of 1968, another unanimous Security Council resolution strengthened its stand.

No doubt future cases will arise where small nations in a strong bargaining position, because of prior belligerent acts, or small nations supported by powerful ones, will obstruct the collective judgment of the world community, acting through the U.N. Yet the time may well come when both South Africa and Israel and other small states, facing the implacable hostility of their neighbors, will need the support or protection of the world community—in the same way that the social deviant needs the safeguards of the society against which he transgresses.

It is most important, therefore, that the United Nations, when acting as an entity representing the world conscience, does not waver or derogate from its intrinsic authority, when confronted, as it so frequently is, with deviations from its Charter's laws and obligations. If it holds resolutely to its collective responsibility as a *world authority*, that authority will grow. No nation, however self-righteous, can be judge and executioner in its own cause. Sooner or later, "rebel" governments must come to heel, for the long-term interests of their own peoples lie with the establishment of a stable world legal order, not with international anarchy.

Power Grows With Action

Furthermore, the U.N. should be invested with yet wider responsibilities than it now has; and each crisis can be consciously used to strengthen the Organization. At first, the obstacles in the way of implementation of some of its decisions may seem insurmountable. But power will grow with function, when that function can be seen to be increasingly in the long-term national as well as international interest.

Undeterred by past reverses, the Special General Assembly had the courage, in August 1967, actually to set up an Administrative Council for South-West Africa and formally transferred its legal power to it. At the Council's first meeting, the Secretary-General presided and made this significant observation: "The coming into operation of this Council constitutes an important step towards the assumption by the United Nations of its responsibilities under the General Assembly resolution of October 27, 1966, which terminated South Africa's mandate in South-West Africa and made that Territory a direct responsibility of this Organization. By that decision the General Assembly, after twenty years of fruitless negotiations, reaffirmed that . . . . the people of the Territory 'have the unalienable right to self-determination, freedom, and independence in accordance with the Charter' . . . . Having taken that almost unanimous decision, the United Nations has now to arrange for the transfer of the administration of the Territory and the setting up of the necessary governmental machinery, and negotiating that transfer with the least possible upheaval and of administering South-West Africa until independence with the assistance of a United Nations Commissioner."

U Thant further indicated that, however obstructive the government of South Africa might be for the time being, the best interests of South Africa were involved, "since the world community is confronted in southern Africa with an explosive situation which, if unresolved, could undermine the very basis of co-operation between the races in Africa for many years to come."

As with all political institutions, occasions arise when an essentially *moral* choice has to be made, come what may. And the Secretary-General concluded this historic assertion of U.N. authority with these words:

The work of the Council offers a fresh point of departure, a new possibility of reconciliation, a chance to stem the growing racial hostility in that part of the world. All member States should heed the General Assembly appeal and co-operate to the full in making effective the U.N. decision which they so overwhelmingly endorsed.

With regard to the Israeli government's continued occupation of its neighbors' territories, a similar challenge has to be met head on. An ingenious argument is put forward by a British political scientist, H. G. Nicholas, who remarked that, although the role of the U.N. in the Middle East crisis may be marginal, it is nonetheless crucial. At this stage of its development, the Organization is being *used* by nations to suit their own convenience and to advance their own interests. But the fact that they are doing so is also advancing the United Nations.[8]

Professor Nicholas concedes that the capacity of the U.N., while involved in this type of crisis, is indeed limited. Its ability to act, he says, depends on three factors: (a) the shock of the crisis to those involved; (b) the consensus of the voting (the Assembly vote condemning the attempt to "unify" Jerusalem was carried without a negative vote); and (c) the ability of the Secretary-General and his staff to get plans off the ground, when once decided on. On this last point, the Secretary-General's able negotiator, Gunnar Jarring, backed with what has been termed the "miraculous" unanimity of the Security Council on November 22, 1967, left at once for the troubled Middle East and by April 1968 he had made reasonable progress. The warring parties all need him, while pretending not to.

In spite of the hard positions taken by both Israelis and Arabs, U.N. solutions were the only solutions within the bounds of logic or human possibility. Neither side was capable of acting *by itself*. To break the deadlock, action could come only from outside the area of mutual recrimination and continuing conflict; and the U.N. is the only institution equipped to give that help. The fact that the Secretary-General had had his observers already on the spot had been a beginning; and they are being steadily augmented. The sensible thing was tactfully to widen this role. Even if the obstacles are enormous, the U.N.—limited though it now is— has again been found to be indispensable. There are no private wars any more; peace is indivisible.

These two seemingly intractable examples enforce the functionalist argument. Peace can be built only on what *exists*. As regards the former example, it rests on the authority of the U.N. to safeguard the rights of

[8] H. G. Nicholas: *Has Israel Really Won?* Fabian Tract, No. 367, London, October 1967.

dependent peoples as a "sacred trust"; and, as regards the latter, it rests on the continuing work of the refugee and specialized organizations, UNWRA, UNICEF, FAO, WHO, UNTSO—all the U.N. agencies are actually working in the Middle East. Every step will help and be a step forward to the next.

Professor E. B. Haas makes this comment in his important book, *Beyond the Nation State:* "Step-by-step schemes of material co-operation, evolving in an unplanned fashion, will eventually work themselves out in the direction of a world-wide system of co-operation, for which a constitution will merely be a symbolic crown, recognizing officially what has been true in fact for some time." This approach, insists Haas, is based on the supposition that man will seek his own rational advantage by increasing his physical welfare in co-operating with other men when necessary.

Mitrany's view was just this, too, that service rather than social conflict is the *natural* condition of man, and will win in the end. "Like the modern group therapist," says Professor Haas, "the Functionalist rejects the notion that group conflict is inevitable. Conflicts can be creatively transcended without self-conscious sacrifice. Politics need not be envisaged as the crude clash of interests, each rationally conceived and defended, but may yield to problem-solving. Interests need not be 'reconciled' if they can be 'integrated' at a higher level of perception by engaging the actor in a 'working effort.' "[9]

We have deliberately taken the seemingly impossible deadlock of the 1967 Arab-Israeli War, however, to stress that no miracles can be looked for; but, at the same time, the U.N.'s personnel and institutions are actually there to be used. If the will and patience to use them can be developed, there is nothing impracticable *in itself* for a "package deal," covering effectively policed frontiers (with U.N. policing agents on both sides); free navigation through the Suez Canal and other international waterways; an independent, non-denominational and neutralized status for Jerusalem; sovereign recognition of the State of Israel and equal recognition of the rights of the Palestinians; comprehensive refugee resettlement; and an internationally supported Middle East development plan. All this is technically and legally practicable, seeing that an all-round adjustment along these lines is in the common interests of each one of the Middle East countries, and of the world at large. We now have a working blueprint in front of us of planned peacemaking. Authority has been transferred from both the warring and the onlooker governments to the only organization which can function for them all. The U.N. has received from its diversified membership the overwhelming majority vote needed to set this process of "integration" in operation. It will succeed when governments and peoples honestly back its endeavors and refuse to aid and abet the belligerents.

[9] E. B. Haas: *Beyond the Nation State,* Stanford University Press, 1964.

Neutral Man

In this book we have rejected the logic-of-weapons ethos of the RAND strategists as amoral and anti-human, and reiterated that it is not a military or political solution which matters, but a moral one. This is because, in the end, no less than the beginning, solutions to war and violence and annihilation rest with *men*—not with their machines or self-projecting systems. "The only salvation from the tragic *dénouement* lies in the characters of men. Their deliverance depends upon their own moral attitudes, not simply upon policies or on theories" . . . , says Professor Harris: "If the race of men is too blind to read the signs of the times and too selfish and too complacent to take proper measures for their own safety, perhaps they are not worth saving."[10]

That men *are* worth saving is the *raison d'être* of the World Organization. The opening words of the Charter are: "To *save* succeeding generations from the scourge of war . . . ." But no one can at this stage give the final answer to the many problems of peaceful settlement which confront the World Organization. Yet one factor is constant. The world community needs a special quality of man to see this kind of program through. Behind the new international machinery must be the man of vision, acumen, courage, and integrity.

A surprising number of such men, as we have seen, have already arrived and are working on all levels of functioning world service. Others are being trained. They will form a new generation of international civil servants and also, we trust, national leaders morally different from the nuclear strategists and the spiritually deformed generals of World War I and II who have unhappily never found their place in the United Nations world.

Some of these new men will never achieve their goals in their own lifetimes, but will lay foundations for others to succeed them. We can revert once more to our South African and Israeli examples, to keep the discussion on a severely pragmatic basis.

Michael Scott grew up in the London slum which was his father's parish and has spent most of his years since then living among the poor—in England, in India, and most notably, in southern Africa. A career of devoted work began when he went to South Africa for his health but spent his time working in a leper colony. When, in 1948, the Herero tribe of South-West Africa asked him to help prevent the annexation of their small country by the Union of South Africa, he came to New York to plead South-West Africa's case personally before the United Nations General Assembly, and has done so every year since then. The Assembly has resolved in his favor each time; but South Africa ignores the resolutions, as we have seen. He has not given up. He has given a voice and, indirectly, a vote and a

[10] E. E. Harris: *The Survival of Political Man,* Johannesburg, 1950.

status before the World Community to a small people who had no other hope. He set up a precedent in the right of petition, which has since been steadily enlarged. In his autobiography, *A Time to Speak,* Michael Scott speaks for the underprivileged of the human race. There is a time to sow, and a time to reap. The reaping in South Africa has still to come. It will assuredly come, through either the blood of vengeance or the tears of repentance.[11]

Today, it is no longer the lonely white man who champions the black man's cause. Africa and Asia, as we noted in Chapter 6, are sending in their best sons to the U.N. partnership. These men are a brake on the Western concept of Cold War, even though they bring their own big problems with them. "We have a new breed of professional diplomat now," says Hermod Lannung of Denmark, one of the senior and most experienced of old-world diplomats: "It may be true that some cherished customs have vanished. In the old days, the chairman of a committee would have felt obligated to maintain strict neutrality—now they make political speeches. Yet, the newer, younger diplomats from Asia and Africa are doing well," he avers, "and in the last few years have shown a new maturity."[12]

Speaking of two African colleagues who had succeeded him as president of the Security Council, Ambassador Arthur J. Goldberg said: "The role of the Council president is sometimes misunderstood by the public because a Council president must be the servant of the Council and must also represent his own country. Ambassador Kante of Mali in acting as the servant of the Council was able with great objectivity to make clear the important distinction between these two roles. . . . As for Ambassador Adebo (of Nigeria), many of us call him Mr. United Nations."

It must not be thought, however, that this rapidly growing functional machinery, though infinitely preferable to the secret politicking of militaristic governments, can escape the sickness of national rivalries. When Count Bernadotte, conciliator between the Jews and the Arabs, was assassinated in 1948, Ralph Bunche was appointed in his place. The ability, energy, and, above all, the personal integrity of this one man, so the records show, came within an ace of securing a give-and-take compromise between the contestants, which might well have become the basis of a permanent peace treaty, as envisaged by the General Armistice Agreement. Dr. Bunche had all the facts at his command; he went directly to the leaders of the governments and armies involved; he quieted some and bullied others; he enjoyed the confidence of all.

But certain governments with a strategic "interest" in the Middle East prevailed on the General Assembly to set up a so-called Conciliation Commission, consisting of representatives of three member-states— France, Turkey and the United States—which went to work early in 1949

11 Michael Scott: *A Time to Speak,* Doubleday, New York, 1958.
12 *New York Times,* October 12, 1967.

and continued through the abortive Beirut and Lausanne Conferences of that year. Earl Berger points out in *The Covenant and the Sword* that this was "the fundamental reason for the failure of the conciliation effort. The Commission was composed of men chosen by and responsible to their respective governments, not the United Nations. Each acted as an agent of his government while he was carrying out his duties as a member of a United Nations commission." These states agreed on one thing only, says Professor Berger: "that an Arab-Israeli settlement must not harm these interests. . . . Even assuming that all the members were anxious for a settlement—something that is by no means certain—they could not devise a policy agreeable to themselves which would meet the needs of the Arabs and the Israelis."[13]

This example could be multiplied a thousand-fold in the annals of the U.N. It points to the unique role which the "neutral man" can play. Earl Berger concludes his account as follows:

It was only the United States which had the influence and power necessary to weld the Commission into an effective organ of conciliation. But, like the French and the Turks, the Americans appear to have rated peace as secondary to the protection of their own interest.

"Holiness" in Action

The neutral man, par excellence, is of course the Secretary-General. It would be invidious to add to the many references given earlier in this book to his mediating and conciliating function amidst today's towering military rivalries. Yet it is symptomatic of how, imperceptibly and almost unnoticed, the *assumption* is growing, in high and low places that, whatever the problem, however involved the conflict, the Secretary-General can somehow—merely because he *is* the neutral man—get national statesmen out of the hole they have dug for themselves.

When Greece and Turkey were on the edge of war at the end of 1967 over Cyprus and—naturally—their common NATO membership counted for little or nothing in the imminent encounter, it was the U.N. Secretary-General who stepped into the breach and gave the assurance that the Cypriot leaders needed and that all three parties ultimately accepted as the conditions of peaceful settlement.

The British conservative opposition leader (Sir Alec Douglas-Home), speaking at that time in the House of Commons, found himself in essential agreement with the Government when he stated that, while he did not think the British Foreign Secretary could do much to hasten the end of the Vietnam War, he nevertheless himself believed that "the Secretary-

[13] Earl Berger: *The Covenant and the Sword: Arab-Israeli Relations, 1948-56,* Routledge, London, 1965.

General of the United Nations could, with great advantage, put up a plan, using all the organs of publicity at his command, for the future of Southeast Asia, Laos, Vietnam and Cambodia, a plan based on non-alignment and a co-operative economy assisted from outside. To begin with, it would of course have to be internationally policed," Sir Alec continued: "The appeal of this would be that it held out a prospect, which was not there now, of an honorable alternative to the policy of vendetta and revenge." In other words, while all else had failed and even the Joint-Chairman of the Geneva Conference (the Foreign Secretary) could no longer re-convene it, the Secretary-General could himself help to put this distraught corner of the human race back on its feet.

It was Dag Hammarskjold who first introduced the "neutral man" con-cept into the public arena when he replied emphatically to Nikita Khrush-chev's assertion that "there are no neutral men," only neutral nations. But Hammarskjold's neutrality was of the positive kind. Did he not record in his private memoirs?—

In our era, the road to holiness necessarily passes through the world of action.

Typical of the essentially pioneer character of the Organization he headed, Hammarskjold always matched responsibility with courage. When he was asked whether the Secretary-General should do nothing when his adherence to the principles of the Charter ran into the opposition of cer-tain governments, he replied in his Oxford speech in 1961: "Would such refuge be compatible with the responsibility placed upon the Secretary-General by the Charter? Is he entitled to refuse to carry out the decision properly reached by the organs, on the ground that the specific imple-mentation would be opposed to positions some Member States might wish to take? . . . . Of course the political organs may always instruct him to discontinue the implementation of a resolution; but when they do not instruct him and the resolution remains in effect, is the Secretary-General legally and morally free to take no action, particularly in a matter considered to affect international peace and security?"

Since the leader was himself the servant of the peoples of the world as a whole, so Hammarskjold expected the World Organization always to put truth—that is integrity—first:

I am not neutral as regards the Charter. . . . I am not neutral as regards facts. . . . But what I do claim is that even a man who is in that sense not neutral can very well undertake and carry through neutral actions, because that is an act of integrity.

There is no weakness here—no shilly-shallying between two rival camps of the Cold War. This meant fixing one's goal on more lasting objectives than the next general election or the paper promises of a callous military junta. The neutral man exhibits a quality that Hammar-skjold once passed on to a U.N. staff meeting and which he called: "Loyalty to the Future."

In a similar sense, Prime Minister Nehru, though a national statesman, responding to the shallow recriminations of John Foster Dulles, introduced the term "non-alignment." Nehru practiced a *positive* neutrality which took no part in promoting the militarist ambitions on either side of the Cold War, but stood between them—as India did in negotiating the frustrating prisoners-of-war exchange to end the bloody Korean conflict and in sending Indian units into the Congo or Palestine under the U.N. banner.

The Federalist Solution

Emphasis has so far been on how "functionalist" principles have been applied in terms of action programs over the past two decades. Another approach to world order has also been claiming the approval of men of goodwill, however, which looks more to political or constitutional change in the U.N. framework.

"One of the prime difficulties of the United Nations to date, as the recent Middle East crisis demonstrated," declared Norman Cousins at the Oslo Congress of the World Federalist Movement in July 1967, "is that it lacks authority to deal with fundamental causes of conflict or to create a basis for workable relationships among nations; but it is expected to rush into action when the relationships become explosive. The central need, therefore, as world federalists see it, is to give the United Nations the *peacemaking* authority it does not now have, and to enlarge its *peacekeeping* functions, which it has now only to a limited degree."

By way of comparison, Cousins pointed out that the Constitutional Convention in Philadelphia from 1787 to 1789 established certain basic principles pertaining to the allocation of authority between the individual states and the entity then being created to protect their citizens and their common interests. World federalists recognized that the American experience and the world situation today are not fully analogous; but, even so, they believed that world peace required "a clear-cut, authoritative definition both of the limits of national power and of the area of effective jurisdiction of the world body. The nations should retain the right to maintain their own cultures and political institutions, but the United Nations should have authority in matters related to world security and world development." The issue could not have been more clearly presented.[14]

Similarly, Cousins said, world federalists believed that the present highly inflammable arms race cannot be fully eliminated until something takes the place of the arms. "This 'something' must be a U.N. with a capacity to create and maintain the general conditions of safety." This is the very principle discussed in Chapter 7. But we have exposed earlier

[14] Norman Cousins: *The World Federalist,* September 1967.

in this book an obstacle which Norman Cousins seems to overlook, namely, the influence of a powerful and vicious alliance system which throttles every peace, as well as every federalist, idea in its cradle. Every world federalist should recognize that the NATO-SEATO complex is Federalist Enemy No. 1 and a direct challenge to his concept of a world authority.

But we would do well to keep in mind, also, the emphasis which a well-known international lawyer, Ernest A. Gross, former U.S. delegate to the U.N., has brought to his long study of the Rule of Law in world affairs:

It is erroneously assumed that the disordered condition of the world results from the absence of codes, courts, and constabulary. A clearer perspective might be gained by approaching the matter just the other way round. The lack of rules and the inadequacy of machinery for co-operation are surely symptoms, rather than causes. They reflect almost total absence of the prime prerequisites of any legal system: an organized will and a moral purpose.[15]

World Federalists insist, however, on a stricter view of law-making than that given earlier, when World Law was envisaged as emerging gradually from the functional operations of the present World Organization. Norman Cousins carried that view further when he stated:

The proper enactment and enforcement of statutes, fixing the rights and obligations of the individual nations and establishing the jurisdiction of the United Nations—this is what is meant by World Law.

But since World Federalists have not managed to devise a procedure to bridge the gap between the present U.N.'s admitted deficiency and its future effectiveness as a truly federal World Organization, the problem of *how* is still with us. For that reason, no single step that enhances the growth of its authority can be dispensed with. The functional and federal approaches need each other.

Peace Through World Law by Grenville Clarke and Louis Sohn is undoubtedly the most detailed handbook in this field.[16] Unfortunately, the questions it raises are too complex for simple treatment here, though the thoroughgoing Clarke-Sohn proposals have been preceded and followed, as we have noticed, by an ever-growing stream of prophetic writings on ways and means to a governed world, going back to *The Anatomy of Peace* by Emery Reves, shortly after World War II, and the "Draft Constitution," prepared by a group of scholars under Dr. Robert M. Hutchins and Professor Cesare Borgese of the University of Chicago two decades ago. On both sides of the Atlantic, in fact, this body of non-governmental discussion and research has been directed to the simple proposition: *How* to transform the present United Nations from a con-

[15] Ernest A. Gross: *U.N., Structure for Peace,* Harper & Row, New York, 1962.
[16] G. Clarke and L. Sohn: *Peace Through World Law,* Harper & Row, New York, 1963.

federation of nation-states into a federation of peoples, endowed with the powers and functions to prevent war and organize world peace."*

"Of the two possible forms of World Sovereignty, only one can solve the main problem before us," says Professor Errol E. Harris (now of Kansas University) in his earlier thought-provoking work *The Survival of Political Man:* "Conquest and world dominion by one power, the dream of all dictators since Alexander the Great, means, today, the destruction of empire by the very process of subduing it." He goes on to assert that there remains the federal form of organization as "the only one which can preserve national freedoms and is suited to so vast and complicated a process as world government."

The two main features of the world federal system, according to Professor Harris, are that it permits, first, the maximum of freedom in the administration of national *domestic* affairs; and, secondly, the decentralization of the functions of government, "without which the sheer weight of legislative and administrative business of world organization would be intolerable." In other words, the working functions of government have to be decentralized or federalized. The proximity of these two terms brings us back to this important consideration: federalizing *down* from a world authority—as stressed in an earlier chapter—is not the same thing as federalizing *up* from the nation-state. The grouping of existing States into sub-federations would probably be necessary, Harris asserts, so immense are the tasks confronting World Government. But not as a *preliminary* step to world federation, because the formation of regional federal bodies, *each with its own sovereign power* (for that is what "federation" means), "would merely reduce the number of rival Sovereigns whose relations would still remain unregulated."

Thus, Professor Harris underlines the argument already advanced that military alliances which become federations would still remain military rivals—and this "would not diminish the menace of war nor solve the contemporary problem." Professor Harris also lends support to the view expressed in Chapter 2 when he states that "the formation of a United States of Europe, for instance, or of other new federations in the New World, Africa or Asia would, if brought about *without reference to an all-inclusive union,* only exacerbate the present crisis. A European union would certainly arouse suspicion and opposition from Russia . . . ."[17]

The possible exception to this particular thesis, however, would be the emergence of an indigenous African organization that—unlike the Cold War regional groupings deprecated in Chapter 4—repudiates the traditional concept of Western-type military alliances and their Communist rivals, and which also excludes from African soil the universal

---

* A general background to this development was given in this author's *Revolution on East River,* Abelard-Schuman, New York & London, 1956.
[17] *op. cit.*

abomination of nuclear weapons. The same principle would apply, for instance, to a *neutralized* Southeast Asia Federation.

Among pioneer scholars contributing to this new view of functional-federal world order, we can instance an administrator whose life experience has been in developing one fruitful branch of World Law, which since the beginning of this Century has borne the significant name of International Labor Legislation and which covers, directly or indirectly, the daily working conditions of the great mass of the earth's citizens. Dr. C. Wilfred Jenks has summarized his own positive contribution to World Law, both as a senior official in the International Labor Office and as a jurist, in his comprehensive *Common Law of Mankind*. This might fittingly be described as the lawyer's underwriting of Mitrany's economic and social gospel of human unity.

According to Dr. Jenks, the functional and the federal approaches have a common field of operation:

Internationally, we are working our way towards a new form of functional federalism, rather than towards central executive authority under a central, quasi-parliamentary control. . . . It is impossible to transpose government institutions, originally evolved for small national States, to a world of 3,000 million people, which may shortly be one of 6,000 million. If the law is to be an effective instrument of freedom and welfare, we must devise new institutional forms, which are not simply a transposition of national government, but represent a new epoch in political thinking.[18]

This new epoch in global political thinking is, in fact, finding support in many quarters today. Thanks to the U.N.'s campaign to spread and improve the teaching of international law, especially in the developing countries, a fresh generation of law students is being prepared to apply these concepts in their later careers. The director of international law studies for the University of Columbia, Professor Wolfgang Friedman, states: "The development of the law of nations cannot be found solely on the horizontal plane. There have also been far-reaching vertical changes in the law of nations which still lack comprehensive analysis. . . . Both in volume and scope, the area of international institutions and agreements has greatly widened. International law is today actively and continuously concerned with such divergent and vital matters as human rights and crimes against peace and humanity, the international control of nuclear energy, trade organizations, labor conventions, transport control, or health regulation. This is not to say that in all or any of these fields international law prevails. But there is no doubt today that they are its legitimate concern."[19]

[18] C. Wilfred Jenks in a Symposium: *International Law in a Changing World*, Oceana, New York, 1963.
[19] W. Friedman: *Law in a Changing Society*, Columbia, New York, 1959.

But, continues Friedman, to this traditional sphere of *negative co-existence,* "modern needs and developments have added many new areas expressing the need for *positive co-operation."* This "positive co-operation" has in many cases set up permanent international bodies, and, he adds: "this move of international society, from an essentially negative code of rules of abstention to positive rules of co-operation, however fragmentary in the present state of world politics, is an evolution of immense significance for the principles and structure of international law."[20]

A World Parliament?

At this early stage in its evolution, it would be unwise to claim too much, but we can at least draw courage from the fact that more and more responsible statesmen in more and more countries are beginning to think of the U.N. as a parliamentary body. (In the case of some countries it is seen to be a more efficient and credit-worthy body than their own national institutions.) Even if the World Organization at present lacks so many of the attributes of a sovereign parliament, a General Assembly which has trebled its membership to over one hundred and a quarter nations and has been called to order for its (say) one-thousand-six-hundred-and-fifty-sixth meeting cannot possibly be regarded as the same primitive body that held its first session in London in 1946, with most of Africa and Asia absent. Not less significant, the Security Council held forty-six meetings in 1967 alone (thirty-three were on the Middle East crisis); while seventy Council meetings were held in 1966, thus sitting practically every week.

Prime Minister Wilson's comparison with the early fumblings and failings of the English parliament may still assume too much, if we attempt to use an ancient yardstick to measure a global organization of this size and complexity in the Space Age. The last chapters of this book have surely given an indication of the organic—that is to say, functional—growth of world law *around* its parliament, rather than within it. Perhaps a formal parliament will be a mainly deliberative organ of the world community and be formed last, instead of as its primary law-making body, as some world federalists have been assuming?

The way its leaders feel is as important as how they think. "No political system is workable," says Professor E. E. Harris, "unless the members of the society in which it is embodied believe in its efficacy and are willing to work it in sincerity. World government, therefore, remains utopian as long as men fail to understand fully the predicament in which

[20] W. Friedman: *The Changing Structure of International Law,* Columbia, New York, 1966.

they find themselves today and so refuse to believe in the necessity for the one adequate remedy."[21]

This *feeling* for a parliamentary body, with its technical committees and voting procedures, its impartial handling of controversial debate, its careful protocol and personal courtesies—even the insults that are frequently traded across the floor in high House of Commons style—is being accepted by more and more discerning participants, representing all cultures, languages, and political systems. Sometimes procedural disputes within the U.N. take a long time to resolve; but precedents are thereby established which are creating a substantial code of internal or regulatory law.

Former Supreme Court Justice Arthur J. Goldberg, making his first appearance at the General Assembly in September 1965 as the chief U.S. delegate, remarked: "It is not appropriate for me to record my profound feeling of high privilege to participate in the work and deliberations of this great world parliament." He added a few minutes later: "Every parliamentary body must somehow resolve the issues before it or cease to have any useful existence."

Abdul Rahman Pazhwak of Afghanistan, presiding at the 1560th meeting on September 19, 1967, pointed out that: "During the past twelve months, the General Assembly has met in three separate sessions and has been in a state of nearly continuous deliberation. This development, if continued, might well mark the evolution of this world body into a virtual year-round parliament of nations." When that same Assembly did adjourn in late December, it fixed its reconvening for the following March. And so it goes on almost through the year.

Perhaps the supreme value of the World Organization is that it substitutes the counting of heads for the breaking of heads. This means that Khrushchev's vote counted the same as Adlai Stevenson's when it happened one day that the chief delegates of the U.S.S.R. and the U.S.A. walked down the aisle almost side by side in response to the General Assembly roll-call to deposit their respective voting slips in the ballot-box. It is ironical that the mass media at that time did not tire of describing Khrushchev pounding his shoe; but singularly failed to notice his voting in the democratic manner. How else *can* the world community regulate its affairs?*

Admitted that the parliamentary character of the World Organization has a long way yet to go and also that World Law as it develops will be bound to acquire different characteristics from municipal law, it is still

---

21 E. E. Harris: *Annihilation and Utopia,* Allen & Unwin, London, 1967.

* It should be stressed that the foregoing generalizations leave untouched the considerable body of legal research which has been devoted to the resolutions of the General Assembly and other U.N. organizations as a *source* of international law, much of which material is admirably summarized for the serious student in Obed Y. Asamoah: *The Legal Significance of the Declarations of the General Assembly of the United Nations,* Nijhoff, The Hague, 1966.

a fact that in imperceptible degrees the forum on New York's East River is offering mankind options which are indispensable to man's universal government and common peace.

Many of its unique services are becoming accepted almost unconsciously by the world at large. It has already rendered war less likely, by reason of its "advance warning" devices, as Abdul Rahman Pazhwak aptly phrased it when General Assembly President.

Not the least important among the many uses of the perennial debate covering (in the words of the Charter) "any questions or any matters within the scope of the present Charter" is that it lifts the underground maneuvers of the power struggle between the big nations into the open. *U.N. Headquarters is a glass house by function as well as architecture.* The whole miserable rivalry of the Cold War conspiracies, in which the Big Powers have invested so much energy, money and personnel, is constantly dragged into the glare of debate and cross-examination. No one can hide anything for long at the U.N. Secrecy may still have a traditional role at the edges of diplomacy; but, in spite of some painful risks, the lying and the plotting of the Cold War have to defend themselves before the court of world opinion. Some of these unhappy intrigues are described without fear or favor to any particular side in Paul W. Blackstock's *The Strategy of Subversion*. Pieces of this distressing record came to the surface in the world's press in 1967 when various journals uncovered the ramifications of the C.I.A. among student and cultural organizations and in interfering in government policies abroad.[22]

This is not the place to enlarge on the corruptness and the gross immorality of a James Bond technique pursued in Cold War politics. Sufficient to know that this network of spying and deceit, which seeks to embroil neighboring nations in endless wars and rumors of wars, is now subject to exposure to the light of day in the glass house on East River. Some political reputations may be lost, but mankind can breathe a little more freely in consequence.

A True University

Finally, the World Organization's *teaching* function has never been fully assessed or understood. "The United Nations is an international school," says Marion Maury, "a university in the true sense of the word. But it is more than that, for it is the agency through which international plans are translated into action programs that affect daily life in all parts of the globe. It is not just an idea maker—it is also a doer." Governments, no less than individuals—promoters of political theories, en-

[22] Paul W. Blackstock: *The Strategy of Subversion, Manipulating the Politics of Other Nations,* Quadrangle Books, Chicago, 1964.

thusiasts for world order or social progress or criminal reform or artificial languages—all have received from the Organization's collective wisdom something far more valuable than any contribution any one of them could possibly bring to it. There are many would-be reformers of the U.N.—including the People's Republic of China—but the fact is that the U.N. is constantly reforming the reformers.

No single nation is bigger than the United Nations—either geographically or ideologically. Yet the U.N. is bigger than the sum of its parts. There is a universal sovereignty enshrined in it which reduces its component territorial sovereignties to their relative size. It is this *plus* factor which matters supremely for everybody. Referring to his own Buddhist faith, the Secretary-General recently deplored the egoism which prevailed among the leaders of nations—"blind to the needs and the reality of others." All nations and ideologies, U Thant said, were guilty of an egoism which was bad for all, "because it does not exist for long by itself. It becomes, in course of time, the parent of the twin sins of pride and prestige. If there is one lesson that history teaches us, it is that wealth and power, pride and prestige, are not only transitory, but even illusory."[23]

U Thant has constantly called for a moral renaissance based on a conscious search for truth and a repudiation of violence. "So many of the problems that we face today," he points out, "are due to, or the result of, false attitudes—some of them have been adopted almost unconsciously. Amongst these is the concept of narrow nationalism—'my country, right or wrong.' It is the lack of truth in international relations that leads to the conscious or unconscious adoption of double standards."

In this book we have challenged, therefore, both the scheme of values and the moral capacity of the nuclear strategists and their military masters —along with their anti-human computers and ghoulish war games and shattered alliances—to solve the very problems that they have done so much to create or, at least, to perpetuate. Yet, as Professor Errol E. Harris stresses in *Annihilation and Utopia:* "The enormity of the threat of the nuclear holocaust facing mankind at the present time tends to paralyze our capacity for practical thinking and to produce a numb indifference to the unimaginable horrors that may at any time result from the present policies of the nations."[24]

So we have set against the nuclear nihilists and the spiritual numbness that their mechanistic doctrines have induced in the public mind that quality of integrity toward the human community which Hammarskjold set as his personal standard, and by which he died in the line of duty as a man of peace.

No less a servant of truth and examplar of that new breed of men for which we pleaded in our first chapter, U Thant tells us that "history

[23] U Thant: "Faith and Peace," an address at Toronto, October 20, 1967.
[24] *op. cit.*

teaches us that no durable solution can be found for any human problem except by persuasion and by common consent. . . . We have therefore to go back," he says, "to the first principles and to observe the Charter commitment regarding the non-use of violence or the threat of violence in international relations." But the Charter without "We, the People" is as faith without works; hence he affirms:

The United Nations must be accepted in the hearts and minds of the peoples of the world as *their* Organization and as a useful and necessary part of their lives.

——— : ———

APPENDICES

1. Relevant U.N. Charter Provisions

2. Text of NATO and SEATO Treaties

3. Further Reading List

RELEVANT U.N. CHARTER PROVISIONS

CHARTER of the UNITED NATIONS

(Articles 1, 2, 51, and 52)

Chapter I
PURPOSES AND PRINCIPLES

Article 1

The Purposes of the United Nations are:

1. To maintain international peace and security, and to that end: to take effective collective measures for the prevention and removal of threats to the peace, and for the suppression of acts of aggression or other breaches of the peace, and to bring about by peaceful means, and in conformity with the principles of justice and international law, adjustment or settlement of international disputes or situations which might lead to a breach of the peace;

2. To develop friendly relations among nations based on respect for the principle of equal rights and self-determination of peoples, and to take other appropriate measures to strengthen universal peace;

3. To achieve international co-operation in solving international problems of an economic, social, cultural, or humanitarian character, and in promoting and encouraging respect for human rights and for fundamental freedoms for all without distinction as to race, sex, language, or religion; and

4. To be a center for harmonizing the actions of nations in the attainment of these common ends.

Article 2

The Organization and its Members, in pursuit of the purposes stated in Article 1, shall act in accordance with the following Principles.

1. The Organization is based on the principle of the sovereign equality of all its Members.

2. All Members, in order to ensure to all of them the rights and benefits resulting from membership, shall fulfill in good faith the obligations assumed by them in accordance with the present Charter.

3. All Members shall settle their international disputes by peaceful means in such a manner that international peace and security, and justice, are not endangered.

4. All Members shall refrain in their international relations from the threat or use of force against the territorial integrity or political independence of any state, or in any other manner inconsistent with the Purposes of the United Nations.

5. All Members shall give the United Nations every assistance in any action it takes in accordance with the present Charter, and shall refrain from giving assistance to any state against which the United Nations is taking preventive or enforcement action.

6. The Organization shall ensure that states which are not Members of the United Nations act in accordance with these Principles so far as may be necessary for the maintenance of international peace and security.

7. Nothing contained in the present Charter shall authorize the United Nations to intervene in matters which are essentially with the domestic jurisdiction of any state or shall require the Members to submit such matters to settlement under the present Charter; but this principle shall not prejudice the application of enforcement measures under Chapter VII.

. . . . . .

Article 51

Nothing in the present Charter shall impair the inherent right of individual or collective self-defense if an armed attack occurs against a Member of the United Nations, until the Security Council has taken measures necessary to maintain international peace and security. Measures taken by Members in the exercise of this right of self-defense shall be immediately reported to the Security Council and shall not in any way affect the authority and responsibility of the Security Council under the present Charter to take at any time such action as it deems necessary in order to maintain or restore international peace and security.

CHAPTER VIII
REGIONAL ARRANGEMENTS

Article 52

1. Nothing in the present Charter precludes the existence of regional arrangements or agencies for dealing with such matters relating to the maintenance of international peace and security as are appropriate for regional action, provided that such arrangements or agencies and their activities are consistent with the Purposes and Principles of the United Nations.

2. The Members of the United Nations entering into such arrangements or constituting such agencies shall make every effort to achieve pacific settlement of local disputes through such regional arrangements or by such regional agencies before referring them to the Security Council.

3. The Security Council shall encourage the development of pacific settlement of local disputes through such regional arrangements or by such regional agencies either on the initiative of the states concerned or by reference from the Security Council.

4. This Article in no way impairs the application of Articles 34 and 35.

TEXT OF NATO AND SEATO TREATIES

NORTH ATLANTIC TREATY
(Done at Washington, D.C., April 1949*)

The Parties to this Treaty reaffirm their faith in the purposes and principles of the Charter of the United Nations and their desire to live in peace with all peoples and all Governments.

They are determined to safeguard the freedom, common heritage and civilization of their peoples, founded on the principles of democracy, individual liberty and the rule of law.

They seek to promote stability and well-being in the North Atlantic area.

They are resolved to unite their efforts for collective defense and for the preservation of peace and security.

They therefore agree to this North Atlantic Treaty:

Article 1

The Parties undertake, as set forth in the Charter of the United Nations, to settle any international dispute in which they may be involved by peaceful means in such a manner that international peace and security and justice are not endangered, and to refrain in their international relations from the threat or use of force in any manner inconsistent with the purposes of the United Nations.

Article 2

The Parties will contribute toward the further development of peaceful and friendly international relations by strengthening their free institutions, by bringing about a better understanding of the principles upon which these institutions are founded, and by promoting conditions of stability and well-being. They will seek to eliminate conflict in their international economic policies and will encourage economic collaboration between any or all of them.

Article 3

In order more effectively to achieve the objectives of this Treaty, the Parties, separately and jointly, by means of continuous and effective self-help and mutual aid, will maintain and develop their individual and collective capacity to resist armed attack.

Article 4

The Parties will consult together whenever, in the opinion of any of them, the territorial integrity, political independence or security of any of the Parties is threatened.

Article 5

The Parties agree that an armed attack against one or more of them in Europe or North America shall be considered an attack against them all, and

* The Treaty came into force on August 24, 1949, after the deposition of the necessary ratifications.

consequently they agree that, if such an armed attack occurs, each of them, in exercise of the right of individual or collective self-defense recognized by Article 51 of the Charter of the United Nations, will assist the Party or Parties so attacked by taking forthwith, individually and in concert with the other Parties, such action as it deems necessary, including the use of armed force, to restore and maintain the security of the North Atlantic area.

Any such armed attack and all measures taken as a result thereof shall immediately be reported to the Security Council. Such measures shall be terminated when the Security Council has taken the measures necessary to restore and maintain international peace and security.

Article 6**

For the purpose of Article 5, an armed attack on one or more of the Parties is deemed to include an armed attack
—on the territory of any of the Parties in Europe or North America, on the Algerian Departments of France,*** on the territory of Turkey or on the islands under the jurisdiction of any of the Parties in the North Atlantic area north of the Tropic of Cancer;
—on the forces, vessels, or aircraft of any of the Parties, when in or over these territories or any other area in Europe in which occupation forces of any of the Parties were stationed on the date when the Treaty entered into force or the Mediterranean Sea or the North Atlantic area north of the Tropic of Cancer.

Article 7

This Treaty does not affect, and shall not be interpreted as affecting, in any way the rights and obligations under the Charter of the Parties which are members of the United Nations, or the primary responsibility of the Security Council for the maintenance of international peace and security.

Article 8

Each Party declares that none of the international engagements now in force between it and any other of the Parties or any third State is in conflict with the provisions of this Treaty, and undertakes not to enter into any international engagement in conflict with this Treaty.

Article 9

The Parties hereby establish a Council, on which each of them shall be represented, to consider matters concerning the implementation of this Treaty. The Council shall be so organized as to be able to meet promptly at any time. The Council shall set up such subsidiary bodies as may be necessary; in particular it shall establish immediately a defense committee which shall recommend measures for the implementation of Articles 3 and 5.

** As amended by Article 2 of the Protocol to the North Atlantic Treaty on the accession of Greece and Turkey.
*** On January 16, 1963 the French Representative made a statement to the North Atlantic Council on the effects of the independence of Algeria on certain aspects of the North Atlantic Treaty. The Council noted that, insofar as the former Algerian Departments of France were concerned, the relevant causes of this Treaty had become inapplicable as from July 3, 1962.

Article 10

The Parties may, by unanimous agreement, invite any other European State in a position to further the principles of this Treaty and to contribute to the security of the North Atlantic area to accede to this Treaty. Any State so invited may become a party to the Treaty by depositing its instrument of accession with the Government of the United States of America. The Government of the United States of America will inform each of the Parties of the deposit of each such instrument of accession.

Article 11

This Treaty shall be ratified and its provisions carried out by the Parties in accordance with their respective constitutional processes. The instruments of ratification shall be deposited as soon as possible with the Government of the United States of America, which will notify all the other signatories of each deposit. The Treaty shall enter into force between the States which have ratified it as soon as the majority of the signatories, including the ratifications of Belgium, Canada, France, Luxembourg, the Netherlands, the United Kingdom and the United States, have been deposited and shall come into effect with respect to other States on the date of the deposit of their ratifications.

Article 12

After the Treaty has been in force for ten years, or at any time thereafter, the Parties shall, if any of them so requests, consult together for the purpose of reviewing the Treaty, having regard for the factors then affecting peace and security in the North Atlantic area, including the development of universal as well as regional arrangements under the Charter of the United Nations for the maintenance of international peace and security.

Article 13

After the Treaty has been in force for twenty years, any Party may cease to be a Party one year after its notice of denunciation has been given to the Government of the United States of America, which will inform the Governments of the other Parties of the deposit of each notice of denunciation.

Article 14

This Treaty, of which the English and French texts are equally authentic, shall be deposited in the archives of the Government of the United States of America. Duly certified copies will be transmitted by that Government to the Governments of the other signatories.

SOUTHEAST ASIA COLLECTIVE DEFENSE TREATY
(MANILA PACT)

The Parties of this Treaty,

Recognizing the sovereign equality of all the Parties,

Reiterating their faith in the purposes and principles set forth in the Charter of the United Nations and their desire to live in peace with all peoples and all governments,

Reaffirming that, in accordance with the Charter of the United Nations, they uphold the principle of equal rights and self-determination of peoples, and declaring that they will earnestly strive by every peaceful means to promote self-government and to secure the independence of all countries whose peoples desire it and are able to undertake its responsibilities,

Desiring to strengthen the fabric of peace and freedom and to uphold the principles of democracy, individual liberty and the rule of law, and to promote the economic well-being and development of all peoples in the Treaty Area,

Intending to declare publicly and formally their sense of unity, so that any potential aggressor will appreciate that the Parties stand together in the area, and

Desiring further to co-ordinate their efforts for collective defense for the preservation of peace and security,

Therefore agree as follows:

Article I

The Parties undertake, as set forth in the Charter of the United Nations, to settle any international dispute in which they may be involved by peaceful means in such manner that international peace and security and justice are not endangered, and to refrain in their international relations from the threat or use of force in any manner inconsistent with the purposes of the United Nations.

Article II

In order more effectively to achieve the objectives of this Treaty, the Parties, separately and jointly, by means of continuous and effective self-help and mutual aid will maintain and develop their individual and collective capacity to resist armed attack and to prevent and counter subversive activities directed from without against their territorial integrity and political stability.

Article III

The Parties undertake to strengthen their free institutions and to co-operate with one another in the further development of economic measures, including technical assistance, designed both to promote economic progress and social well-being and to further the individual and collective efforts of governments toward these ends.

Article IV

1. Each Party recognizes that aggression by means of armed attack in the Treaty Area against any of the parties or against any State or territory which the Parties by unanimous agreement may hereafter designate, would endanger its own peace and safety, and agrees that it will in that event act to meet the

common danger in accordance with its constitutional processes. Measures taken under this paragraph shall be immediately reported to the Security Council of the United Nations.

2. If, in the opinion of any of the Parties, the inviolability or the integrity of the territory or the sovereignty or political independence of any Party in the Treaty Area or of any other State or territory to which the provisions of paragraph 1 of this Article from time to time apply is threatened in any way other than by armed attack or is affected or threatened by any fact or situation which might endanger the peace of the area, the Parties shall consult immediately in order to agree on the measures which should be taken for the common defense.

3. It is understood that no action on the territory of any State designated by unanimous agreement under paragraph 1 of this Article or on any territory so designated shall be taken except at the invitation or with the consent of the government concerned.

Article V

The Parties hereby establish a Council, on which each of them shall be represented, to consider matters concerning the implementation of this Treaty. The Council shall provide for consultation with regard to military and any other planning as the situation obtaining in the Treaty Area may from time to time require. The Council shall be so organized as to be able to meet at any time.

Article VI

This Treaty does not affect and shall not be interpreted as affecting in any way the rights and obligations of any of the Parties under the Charter of the United Nations or the responsibility of the United Nations for the maintenance of international peace and security. Each Party declares that none of the international engagements now in force between it and any other of the Parties or any third party is in conflict with the provisions of this Treaty, and undertakes not to enter into any international engagement in conflict with this Treaty.

Article VII

Any other State in a position to further the objectives of the Treaty and to contribute to the security of the area may, by unanimous agreement of the Parties, be invited to accede to this Treaty. Any State so invited may become a Party to the Treaty by depositing its instrument of accession with the Government of the Republic of the Philippines. The Government of the Republic of the Philippines shall inform each of the Parties of the deposit of each such instrument of accession.

Article VIII

As used in this Treaty, the "Treaty Area" is the general area of Southeast Asia, including also the entire territories of the Asian Parties, and the general area of the South-West Pacific not including the Pacific area north of 21 degrees 30 minutes north latitude. The Parties may, by unanimous agreement, amend this Article to include within the Treaty Area the territory of any State acceding to this Treaty in accordance with Article VII or otherwise to change the Treaty Area.

Article IX

1. This Treaty shall be deposited in the archives of the Government of the Republic of the Philippines. Duly certified copies thereof shall be transmitted by that Government to the other signatories.

258

2. The Treaty shall be ratified and its provisions carried out by the Parties in accordance with their respective constitutional processes. The instruments of ratification shall be deposited as soon as possible with the Government of the Republic of the Philippines, which shall notify all of the other signatories of such deposit.

3. The Treaty shall enter into force between the States which have ratified it as soon as the instruments of ratification of a majority of the signatories shall have been deposited, and shall come into effect with respect to each other State on the date of the deposit of its instrument of ratification.

Article X

This Treaty shall remain in force indefinitely, but any Party may cease to be a Party one year after its notice of denunciation has been given to the Government of the Republic of the Philippines, which shall inform the Governments of the other Parties of the deposit of each notice of denunciation.

Article XI

The English text of this Treaty is binding on the Parties, but when the Parties have agreed to the French text thereof and have so notified the Government of the Republic of the Philippines, the French text shall be equally authentic and binding on the Parties.

Understanding of the United States of America

The United States of America in executing the present Treaty does so with the understanding that its recognition of the effect of aggression and armed attack and its agreement with reference thereto in Article IV, paragraph 1, apply only to Communist aggression but affirms that in the event of other aggression or armed attack it will consult under the provisions of Article IV, paragraph 2.

In witness whereof the undersigned Plenipotentiaries have signed this Treaty.

Done at Manila, this eighth day of September, 1954.

Protocol to the Southeast Asia Collective Defense Treaty

Designation of states and territory as to which provisions of Article IV and III are to be applicable:

The Parties to the Southeast Asia Collective Defense Treaty unanimously designate for the purposes of Article IV of the Treaty the States of Cambodia and Laos and the free territory under the jurisdiction of the State of Vietnam.

The Parties further agree that the above mentioned states and territory shall be eligible in respect of the economic measures contemplated by Article III.

This Protocol shall enter into force simultaneously with the coming into force of the Treaty.

In witness whereof, the undersigned Plenipotentiaries have signed this Protocol to the Southeast Asia Collective Defense Treaty.

Done at Manila, this eighth day of September, 1954.

FURTHER READING LIST

The following books have been consulted, among others, in preparing this work and are suggested for further reading.

Alperovitz, G., *Atomic Diplomacy*, Simon & Schuster, New York, 1965
Aron, R., *The Great Debate*, Doubleday, New York, 1965

Barnet & Raskin, *After 20 Years*, Random House, New York, 1967
Beaton, L., *The Struggle for Peace*, Institute for Strategic Studies, London, 1966
Beaufre, A., *NATO and Europe*, Knopf, New York, 1966
Beaufre, A., *Deterrence and Strategy*, Praeger, New York, 1966
Berger, E., *The Covenant and the Sword*, Routledge, London, 1965
Bowett, D. W., *Self-Defense in International Law*, Manchester University Press, 1958
Bowett, D. W., *United Nations Forces*, Stevens, London, 1967
Brodie, B., *Escalation and the Nuclear Option*, Princeton, 1966
Brown, J. P., *New Eastern Europe*, Praeger, New York, 1966
Burns, E. L. M., *Between Arab and Israeli*, Clarke, Irwin, Toronto, 1962
Buchan, A., *The Future of NATO*, International Conciliation, New York, 1967
Buchan, A., *NATO in the 1960s*, Praeger, New York, 1963

Cameron, J., *Here is Your Enemy*, Holt, Rinehart, New York, 1966
Campbell, J. C., *Defense of the Middle East*, Harper & Row, New York, 1960
Coffin, T., *The Armed Society*, Penguin, London, 1966
Coffin, T., *Passion of the Hawks*, Macmillan, New York, 1964
Chowdhury, S. R., *Military Alliances and Neutrality*, Longmans, Calcutta, 1966
Clarke & Sohn, *Peace Through World Law*, Harper & Row, New York, 1963
Cottrell, A. and Dougherty, J., *Politics of the Atlantic*, Praeger, New York, 1964
Cox, A. M., *Prospects for Peacekeeping*, Brookings, Washington, 1967

Drummond, R., *Duel at the Brink*, Doubleday, New York, 1960
Dulles, E. L., *Berlin, The Wall Is Not Forever*, Chapel Hill, 1967

Farran, C. O., *Atlantic Democracy*, Praeger, New York, 1957
Fleming, D. F., *The Cold War and Its Origins*, Scribner's, New York, 1961
Fox, W. T. R., *NATO and the Range of American Choice*, Columbia, New York, 1967
Friedman, W., *The Changing Structure of International Law*, Columbia, New York, 1966
Friedman, W., *Law in a Changing Society*, Columbia, New York, 1959
Fulbright, J. W., *Arrogance of Power*, Random House, New York, 1966
Fulbright, J. W., *Old Myths and New Realities*, Random House, New York, 1964

GERASSI, J., *The Great Fear in Latin America*, Macmillan, New York, 1965
GLICK, E. B., *Peaceful Conflict*, Stackpole, Harrisburg, 1967
GIFFIN, S. F., *The Crisis Game*, Doubleday, New York, 1965
GOLOVINE, M. N., *Conflict in Space*, St. Martin's, New York, 1962
GOOLD-ADAMS, R., *John Foster Dulles: A Reappraisal*, Appleton-Century, New York, 1962
GROSS, E. A., *U.N.: Structure for Peace*, Harper & Row, New York, 1962

HAAS, E. B., *Beyond the Nation State*, Stanford University Press, 1964
HAMMARSKJOLD, D., *Markings*, Allen & Unwin, London, 1966
HARRIS, E. E., *Annihilation and Utopia*, Allen & Unwin, London, 1967
HARRIS, E. E., *The Survival of Political Man*, Johannesburg, 1950
HERZ, M. F., *Beginnings of the Cold War*, Indiana University Press, 1966
HODSON, H. V., *The Atlantic Future*, Longmans, London, 1964
HORN, C. VON, *Soldiering for Peace*, McKay, New York, 1967
HOROWITZ, D., *The Free World Colossus*, Hill and Wang, New York, 1965
HUGHES, H. S., *An Approach to Peace*, Atheneum, New York, 1962
HUNTLEY, J. R., *The NATO Story*, Manhattan Co., New York, 1965

JENKS, C. W., *Common Law of Mankind*, Stevens, London, 1961
JENKS, C. W. (& others), *International Law in a Changing World*, Oceana, New York, 1963
JOYCE, J. AVERY, *Revolution on East River*, Abelard-Schuman, New York, 1956
JOYCE, J. AVERY, *The Story of International Co-operation*, Franklin Watts, New York, 1965
JOYCE, J. AVERY, *World of Promise*, Oceana, New York, 1964

KAHN, H., *On Escalation*, Praeger, New York, 1966
KASER, M., *Comecon*, Oxford University Press, 1967
KELSEN, H., *Law of the United Nations*, Praeger, New York, 1950
KIELMAN, R., *Atlantic Crisis*, Norton, New York, 1964
KNORR, K., *Uses of Military Power*, Princeton, 1966

LAPP, R. E., *Kill and Overkill*, Basic Books, New York, 1962
LAPP, R. E., *The Weapons Culture*, Norton, New York, 1968
LENS, S., *The Futile Crusade*, Quadrangle, Chicago, 1964
LEWIN, L. C., *Report from Iron Mountain*, Dial Press, New York, 1967

MACCLOSKEY, M., *North Atlantic Treaty Organization*, Richard Rosen Press, 1966
MACCLOSKEY, M., *Pacts for Peace*, Richard Rosen Press, 1966
MCCARTHY, E. J., *The Limits of Power*, Holt, Rinehart & Winston, New York, 1967
MCNAIR, A., *Law of Treaties*, Oxford University Press, 1961
MARTIN, L. W., *Neutralism & Nonalignment*, Praeger, New York, 1962
MAURY, M., *The Good War*, Bartlett-Macfadden, 1965
MIDDLETON, D., *The Defense of Western Europe*, Appleton-Century, New York, 1952
MITRANY, D., *A Working Peace System*, Quadrangle, Chicago, 1966
MUNK, F., *Atlantic Dilemma*, Oceana, New York, 1965

NEBLETT, W. H., *No Peace with the Regulars*, Pageant, New York, 1957

PADELFORD & GOODRICH, *U.N. in the Balance,* Praeger, New York, 1965
POUNDS, N. J. G., *Divided Germany and Berlin,* Von Nostrand, New York, 1962

RAPAPORT, A., *Strategy and Conscience,* Harper & Row, New York, 1964
RAYMOND, J., *Power at the Pentagon,* Harper & Row, New York, 1964
REISCHAUER, E. O., *Beyond Vietnam,* Knopf, New York, 1967
REISMAN, D., *Abundance for What?,* Doubleday, New York, 1966
ROGOW, A. A., *James Forrestal, A Study,* Macmillan, New York, 1964
RYAN, C., *The Last Battle,* Simon & Schuster, New York, 1966

SALVADORI, M., *NATO, 20th Century Community,* Von Nostrand, New York, 1957
SCHUMAN, F. L., *The Cold War: Retrospect and Prospect,* Louisiana University Press, 1962
SHOTWELL, J. T., *The United States in History,* Simon & Schuster, New York, 1956
SHULMAN, M. D., *Beyond the Cold War,* Yale University Press, 1966
SLYCK, P. V., *Peace: The Control of National Power,* Beacon, Boston, 1963
STANLEY, T. W., *NATO in Transition,* Praeger, New York, 1965
STEEL, RONALD, *The End of the Alliance,* Viking, New York, 1964
SWOMLEY, J. M., *The Military Establishment,* Beacon Press, Boston, 1964
SZULC, T., *The Bombs of Palomares,* Viking, New York, 1967
SZULC, T., *Dominican Diary,* Delacorte Press, New York, 1965

TINKER, H., *Ballot Box and Bayonet,* Chatham House, London, 1964

WEISS, M., *McCarthyism,* Pioneer Publishers, New York, 1953
WORLD VETERANS FEDN., *Ad Hoc U.N. Emergency Forces,* Helsinki, 1963
WRIGHT, QUINCY, *Role of International Law,* Oceana, New York, 1962
WRIGHT, QUINCY, *A Study of War,* University of Chicago, 1965

NOTE: The considerable range of United Nations documents consulted in the preparation of this work are not listed above, but their sources are usually indicated in the main text.

INDEX*

Acheson, Dean, 46(q)

Adebo, S.O., 238

Afghanistan, 199

Africa: and China, 195, 196; and Cold War, 195, 196; economic conditions, 193-196; military in, 94; objectives, 176; nuclear-free zone, 45, 68, 243, 244; regional groupings, 151, 193, 194, 243, 244

Africa, North, 50

Aggression, 29, 44, 54, 71, 113, 119, 122-125

Aiken, Frank, 185, 220(q), 221(q)

Alaska, 104

Albania, 55-57

Albee, Edward, 6(q)

Aldabra Island, 85

Alfange, Dean, 9(q)

Algeria, 20

Alliance for Progress, 147-149, 202

Alliluyeva, Svetlana, 23

Alperovitz, Gar, 160(q)

American Association for the Advancement of Science, 84, 85

American Security Council, 183

Antarctica Treaty, 232

Anti-communism: *See* Communism

Arab League: and CENTO, 139

Armas, Castillo, 149

Arms control, 92, 98, 101

Arms race, 63, 64, 106, 107, 160, 186, 241

Aron, Raymond, xv(q), 38(q)

Asamoah, Obed Y., 246n

Asia, Southeast, xvi, 69, 79, 117-128, 132-138, 158, 159, 177, 203, 204, 240, 243; neutral confederation of states, 128n, 240, 243

Australia: and SEATO, 122, 126, 135; and Vietnam (South), 134, 135

ANZUS Treaty (Australia-New Zealand-U.S.), 127, 135

Austria, 33, 34, 44

Averoff, Evangelos, 5

Baghdad Pact: *See* Central Treaty Organization (CENTO)

Baldwin, Hanson W., 104(q), 107(q), 108

Baldwin, James, 179(q)

Bao Dai, 120

Barnet, Richard, 175(q)

Barth, Alan, 167(q)

Beard, Charles, 164(q)

Beaton, Leonard, 100(q), 101(q)

*(q) indicates reference to quotation by person listed.
 n indicates reference to footnote.

263